BRICS MEDIA

Bringing together distinguished scholars from BRICS nations and those with deep interest and knowledge of these emerging powers, this collection makes a significant intervention in the ongoing debates about comparative communication research and thus contributes to the further internationalization of media and communication studies.

The unprecedented expansion of online media in the world's major non-Western nations, exemplified by BRICS (Brazil, Russia, India, China and South Africa), is transforming global communication. Despite their differences and divergences on key policy issues, what unites these five nations, representing more than 20 per cent of the global GDP, is the scale and scope of change in their communication environment, triggered by a multilingual, mobile Internet. The resulting networked and digitized communication ecology has reoriented international media and communication flows. Evaluating the implications of globalization of BRICS media on the reshaping of international communication, the book frames this within the contexts of theory-building on media and communication systems, soft power discourses, and communication practices, including in cyberspace. Adopting a critical approach in analysing BRICS communication strategies and their effectiveness, the book assesses the role of the BRICS nations in reframing a global communication order for a 'post-American world'.

This critical volume of essays is ideal for students, teachers and researchers in journalism, media, politics, sociology, international relations, area studies and cultural studies.

Daya Kishan Thussu is Professor of International Communication at Hong Kong Baptist University. For many years he was Professor of International Communication at the University of Westminster in London. Author or editor of 19 books, he is Managing Editor of the Sage journal, *Global Media and Communication*.

Kaarle Nordenstreng is Professor Emeritus of Journalism and Mass Communication at Tampere University in Finland. A former Vice-President of the International Association for Media and Communication Research and President of the International Organization of Journalists, he has written or edited more than 60 books.

Internationalizing Media Studies

Series Editor: Daya Kishan Thussu

For a full list of titles in this series, please visit https://www.routledge.com/Internationalizing-Media-Studies/book-series/IMS

BRICS MEDIA

Reshaping the Global Communication Order?

*Edited by Daya Kishan Thussu
and Kaarle Nordenstreng*

Routledge
Taylor & Francis Group

LONDON AND NEW YORK

First published 2021
by Routledge
2 Park Square, Milton Park, Abingdon, Oxon OX14 4RN

and by Routledge
52 Vanderbilt Avenue, New York, NY 10017

Routledge is an imprint of the Taylor & Francis Group, an informa business

British Library Cataloguing-in-Publication Data
A catalogue record for this book is available from the British Library

Library of Congress Cataloging-in-Publication Data
Names: Thussu, Daya Kishan, editor. | Nordenstreng, Kaarle, editor.
Title: BRICS media: reshaping the global communication
order? / edited by Daya Kishan Thussu and Kaarle Nordenstreng.
Description: New York: Routledge, 2020. |
Series: Internationalizing media studies |
Includes bibliographical references and index.
Identifiers: LCCN 2020028327 (print) | LCCN 2020028328 (ebook) |
ISBN 9781138604025 (hardback) | ISBN 9781138604032 (paperback) |
ISBN 9780429468759 (ebook)
Subjects: LCSH: Intercultural communication–Developing countries. |
Communication–Political aspects–Developing countries. | Mass media–Political aspects–Developing countries. | Developing countries–Foreign relations. | BRICS.
Classification: LCC HM1211.B745 2020 (print) |
LCC HM1211 (ebook) | DDC 303.48/209724–dc23
LC record available at https://lccn.loc.gov/2020028327
LC ebook record available at https://lccn.loc.gov/2020028328

ISBN: 978-1-138-60402-5 (hbk)
ISBN: 978-1-138-60403-2 (pbk)
ISBN: 978-0-429-46875-9 (ebk)

Typeset in Bembo
by Newgen Publishing UK

CONTENTS

PART IV
BRICS and changing communication practices

CONTRIBUTORS

Kriti Bhuju is completing her PhD at the Communication University of China. A former journalist and a development communicator in Nepal, her research interests include international and development communication, new media and technology and media literacy.

Elena Bykova, PhD, is Professor at the Higher School of Journalism and Mass Communications, St. Petersburg State University. She received a PhD in Philological Sciences in 2012 and her research interests include journalism and mass communication, advertising, theory of speech activity and semantics. Author of more than 80 academic books and articles, among her publications is *Speech Structure of a Modular Text* (2011).

Leonardo Custódio, PhD, is a postdoctoral researcher in Minority Studies at Åbo Akademi University, Finland. His research focuses on how people who suffer from social and racial inequalities engage in media activism for justice and change. He is the author of *Favela Media Activism: Counter-publics for Rights in Brazil* (Lexington Books, 2017). He is also one of the coordinators of the Anti-Racism Media Activist Alliance, a three-year activist-research initiative (2018–2020) that promotes knowledge exchange and international networking among anti-racist scholars and activists in Finland, Brazil and other countries.

Dmitry Gavra is Professor and Chair of Business communication and Public Relations at School of Journalism and Mass Communications of St-Petersburg State University, where he was Director of the Sociological Research Center (1996–2000). He was Deputy Director of the St-Petersburg Center for Public Opinion Studies at the Russian Academy of Sciences (1989–1996) and since 2017 he has been President of the Russian National Public Relations Education Association.

Author of eight books as well as more than 120 articles, his current research relates to the sociology of journalism, political consulting, business communications and public relations.

Barry Gills is Professor of Global Development Studies, Department of Political and Economic Studies, University of Helsinki, Finland. He is the Editor-in-Chief of the *Globalizations* journal and a book series editor for the *Rethinking Globalizations* series (Routledge). He has written widely on world system theory, globalization, the political economy of development, global crises, democratization, the politics of resistance and social transformations in the global South. He is a fellow of the World Academy of Art and Science.

Liziane Soares Guazina is Professor and Vice Dean at the Faculty of Communication, University of Brasilia, where she is also leader of the Culture, Media and Politics Research Group and coordinator of the Study Center on Media and Politics. She was visiting scholar at Università Degli Studi di Milano (2019–2020). Her current research includes political communication, political journalism, public communication and the relationship between populism and the media.

Zhengrong Hu, PhD, is Editor-in-Chief of China Education Television and also Vice Chairman of Chinese TV Artists Association and Chairperson of Journalism and Communication Discipline Evaluation Group, the National Degree Committee of the State Council. He was President of the Communication University of China (2016–2018), Chair of the National Journalism and Communication Discipline Supervisory Committee (2013–2017) and President of the China Communication Association (2006–2010). He has published widely both in English and Chinese, including the *Annual Report of China's International Communication* (2014–2018), *Global Media Industries* (2011–2018), *Thirty Years of Chinese Media: 1978–2008* (2008), and a number of refereed journal articles. He was a research fellow at Kennedy School of Government at Harvard University (2005) and Leverhulme Visiting Professor (2006) at University of Westminster in London.

Savyasaachi Jain, PhD, is a Senior Lecturer at Cardiff University. He teaches journalism and documentary, drawing upon his vast experience as a journalist, documentary filmmaker and international media trainer. His research interests lie in international journalism, Indian media, global media systems and the development of journalistic practices and standards.

Deqiang Ji, PhD, is Associate Professor of International Communication and Vice Dean of the 'Institute for A Community with Shared Future' at the Communication University of China. He serves as Vice Chair of the International Communication Section of the International Association for Media and Communication Research and Member of the Program Committee of Dialogue of Civilizations Research Institute (Berlin). His research covers several interrelated fields, including media and digitization, the political economy of communication and international communication. He is published widely both in Chinese and in English in such journals as *Chinese Journal of Communication, Media, Culture & Society, Javnost-the Public, Global Media and China*, etc.

Marko Juutinen, PhD in Political Science from Tampere University (2020), where he has worked as project researcher. He has published articles in *Third World Thematics: A TWQ Journal, Journal of the Indian Ocean Region,* the Finnish language journals *Kosmopolis* and *Poliittinen talous*, book chapters in edited volumes by the Tampere University Press and by Barbara Budrich as well as two co-authored monographs with Jyrki Käkönen by the Finnish publishing house Into Kustannus and the Indian think tank Observer Research Foundation. Juutinen is the winner of BISA Working Group's Contemporary Research on International Political Theory Essay Prize of 2019.

Jyrki Käkönen, PhD from the University of Turku (1986), is Professor Emeritus of International Relations at Tampere University (1998–2007) and Tallinn University (2007–2015). In 1988–1998 he was director of Tampere Peace Research Institute. His current research interest is in the changing international order. Among his recent publications are *Battle for Globalisations? BRICS and US Mega-Regional Trade Agreements in a Changing World Order* (with Marko Juutinen, 2016); *Revisiting Regionalism and the Contemporary World Order* (edited with Elise Féron and Gabriel Rached, 2019); *Shedding Light on a Changing International Order* (edited with Elise Féron, Marko Juutinen and Karim Maiche, 2020).

Michael Keane is Professor of Chinese Media and Communications at Curtin University in Perth, Australia. His key research interests are digital transformation in China; East Asian cultural and media policy; television in China, and creative industries and cultural export strategies in China and East Asia. Author or editor of 18 books on Chinese media, his latest book (with Haiqing Yu, Susan Leong and Elaine Zhao) is *Culture, Technology and Platforms: Chinese Digital Presence in the Asia-Pacific* (Anthem, 2020)

Tatu Laukkanen is a film scholar and industry professional, affiliated with the Department of Communications at the University of Tampere and also a member of Tampere Research Centre for Russian and Chinese Media. He received his PhD in 2017 from the Department of Comparative Literature at the University of Hong Kong and undertakes research on BRICS cinema. Recent publications include the article 'Sino-Brazilian Cinematic Connections: Yu Lik-wai's Plastic City' Ideias, UNICAMP, Brazil, 2019.

Winston Mano is a Reader and the Director of the Africa Media Centre at the University of Westminster in London. Author or editor of several books on media and communication in Africa, he is the Founder/Editor-in-Chief of the *Journal of African Media Studies*. He studied in Zimbabwe, Norway and Britain. He is a Senior Research Fellow at the University of Johannesburg.

viola candice milton is a professor in the Department of Communication Science at the University of South Africa. She is editor-in-chief of *Communicatio: South African Journal for Communication Theory and Research*. Her research focuses on the negotiation of media policy in South Africa, as well as issues of media, citizenship and identity. She most recently co-authored, with P. Eric Louw, *New Voices Over the Air: The Transformation of the South African Broadcasting Corporation in a Changing South Africa*.

Musawenkosi Ndlovu is an Associate Professor in Media Studies at the University of Cape Town and a Mandela Mellon Fellow in the W. E. B. Du Bois Institute at Harvard University. He holds a PhD in Cultural and Media Studies from the University of KwaZulu-Natal. His teaching and research interests are on international communication and on youth and news media.

Kaarle Nordenstreng, PhD from the University of Helsinki (1969), is Professor Emeritus of Journalism and Mass Communication at Tampere University (Finland). His research has focused on communication theory, international communication and media policies. He has written or edited over 60 books, including *Normative Theories of the Media: Journalism in Democratic Societies* (with Christians *et al.*, 2009) and *A History of the International Movement of Journalists: Professionalism Versus Politics* (with Björk *et al.*, 2016). He has been Vice-President of the International Association for Media and Communication Research (1972–1988) and President of the International Organization of Journalists (1976–1990).

Raquel Paiva is Professor at the Communication School (Federal University of Rio de Janeiro), a research fellow at CNPq (Brazilian National Research Council) and the author of ten books on communitarian communication, as well as being a journalist and writer. She is the Head of the Laboratory for Studies in Communitarian Communication and Head of the National Institute for Studies in Communitarian Communication, founded in 2013.

Svetlana Pasti, PhD, is Docent and teacher at the University of Tampere in Finland. Her research is in journalism studies in Russia and BRICS countries. She is the author of two monographs: *A Russian Journalist in Context of Change: Media of St. Petersburg* (2004) and *The Changing Profession of a Journalist in Russia* (2007) as well as more than 30 peer-reviewed chapters and articles including in such journals as the *European Journal of Communication* and *Nordicom Review*. She is co-editor (with Jyotika Ramaprasad) of *Contemporary BRICS Journalism* (Routledge, 2017) and a 2015 special issue of *African Journalism Studies* entitled *The BRICS journalist: Profession and practice in the age of digital media*.

Fernando Oliveira Paulino is Professor and Dean at the Faculty of Communication, University of Brasília and Director of International Affairs of the Latin American Communication Researchers Association (ALAIC) and former Associate Ombudsman of Public Radio in Brazil. He is also one of the founders of the Summer School of Communication Research in Latin America. His research and teaching activities focus on media, citizenship, the right to communicate, social change, accountability and public policies.

Peixi Xu is Professor at the Communication University of China, Beijing where he is also Director of the Global Internet Governance Project. He obtained his PhD from the University of Tampere, Finland. His research interests include Internet policy and international communication. Among his recent publications are *Global Governance: From Traditional Media to the Internet* (Tsinghua University Press) and *The Shaping of Cyber Norms: Origins, Disputes, and Trends* (China Social Sciences Academic Press).

Jyotika Ramaprasad is Professor in the School of Communication at the University of Miami. Her research interests include journalism studies and communication for social change and are particularly focused on Africa and Asia. She is the co-editor of *BRICS Journalism: Non-Western Media in Transition* (Routledge, 2017). Her work in these areas is published in the *Gazette, The Harvard International Journal of Press/Politics, Asian Journal of Communication, Social Marketing Quarterly* and *Journal of Health and Mass Communication.* She is on the editorial board of *Journalism and Mass Communication Quarterly.*

Iiris Ruoho, PhD, is Head of the Communication Sciences Unit at Tampere University in Finland. A specialist in drama studies and gender criticism, her latest research interests are in digital culture, gender and leadership, and the Chinese media. Author of numerous research papers, she has been a visiting scholar at the University of Texas in Austin (1995, 1997), the University of Oregon in Eugene (2006) and Fudan University in Shanghai (2011). She has been a board member of the Nordic Institute of Asian Studies and Kone Foundation (Fudan Sino-Finnish Scholarships). Her latest publications dealt with the journalism and gender (2018) and the political power of Twitter (2019).

B. P. Sanjay is Professor at the Department of Communication, University of Hyderabad and adjunct professor at the Manipal Academy of Higher Education, Manipal, in India. He was Vice Chancellor of Central University of Tamil Nadu and Director, Indian Institute of Mass Communication, New Delhi. With a teaching and research career spanning over four decades his interests are media studies, political economy and development communication. His participation in the Satellite Instructional Television Experiment during 1975–1976 led to his subsequent focus on studies of technology transfer that formed part of his doctoral studies at Simon

Fraser University, Canada. He was a UNESCO consultant to the University of Nairobi.

Muniz Sodré is Professor Emeritus at the Federal University of Rio de Janeiro, research fellow at CNPq, journalist, writer and the author of over 30 books in the fields of communication, Brazilian culture and fiction. He is a visiting professor at several universities in Brazil and abroad. He was a member of the Economic and Social Council for the Presidency of the Republic (2003–2005) and was also the President of the Brazilian National Library (2005–2010). He is a member of LECC and INPECC.

Joseph Straubhaar is the Amon G. Carter Sr. Centennial Professor of Communication in the Radio-Television-Film Department and Director of the Latino and Latin American Media Studies Program at the University of Texas at Austin. His current research concerns global television, the BRICs, television in Brazil and Latin America, and the digital divide in Brazil and Texas. He is co-author of *Television in Latin America* (2013) and the author of *World Television: From Global to Local* (2007).

Daya Kishan Thussu is Professor of International Communication at Hong Kong Baptist University. He was Distinguished Visiting Professor and Inaugural Disney Chair in Global Media at Schwarzman College, Tsinghua University in Beijing in 2018–2019. For many years he was Professor of International Communication at the University of Westminster in London. Author or editor of 19 books, his latest publication is *International Communication – Continuity and Change*, third edition (2019). He is the Founder and Managing Editor of the Sage journal *Global Media and Communication* and series editor for two Routledge book series: *Internationalizing Media Studies* and *Routledge Advances in Internationalizing Media Studies*.

Elena Vartanova is Professor, Dean and Chair in Media Theory and Media Economics at the Faculty of Journalism, Lomonosov Moscow State University. A member of the Russian Academy of Education and of the Presidential Council on the Russian Language, as well as Board member of the Higher Attestation Commission, she is author or editor of numerous publications, and her research focuses on Russian and foreign media systems, media economics, digital transformation and digital divides. She is President of the Russian National Association of Media Researchers and editor-in-chief of two Russian academic journals, *Media Almanac* and *Mediascope*.

Herman Wasserman is Professor of Media Studies at the University of Cape Town. He has published widely on media ethics, media in Africa and media in new democracies. His latest book is *The Ethics of Engagement: Media, Conflict and*

Democracy in Africa (Oxford University Press, 2020). He is Editor of *The Annals of the International Communication Association* and Editor-in-Chief of the journal *African Journalism Studies*. He is a Fellow of the International Communication Association and a member of the Academy of Science of South Africa.

Ying Zhu is a Professor of Cinema Studies at the City University of New York and Director of the Centre for Film and Moving Image Research at the Academy of Film, Hong Kong Baptist University. She has published nine books, including *Soft Power with Chinese Characteristics: China's Campaign for Hearts and Minds* (co-edited with Kingsley Edney and Stanley Rosen, 2020) and *Two Billion Eyes: The Story of China Central Television* (2013). Zhu is the recipient of a US National Endowment for the Humanities Fellowship (2006), an American Council of Learned Societies Fellowship (2008) and a Fulbright Senior Research Fellowship (2017). She is working on a manuscript on Sino-Hollywood relations.

FOREWORD

Understanding global communication in a polycentric world

Barry K. Gills

PROFESSOR OF GLOBAL DEVELOPMENT STUDIES, UNIVERSITY OF HELSINKI

The world order established in the aftermath of the Second World War is now undergoing profound transformations. After decades of accelerating globalization processes, there is no longer any doubt that we are witnessing a transition towards a more pluralistic and polycentric world. While some commentators and academics lament the perceived decline of the 'liberal world order', others see a promising opportunity for positive change as the dominance of the former hegemonic powers recedes. A 'hegemonic transition' in world order entails far more than only a change in the configuration of economic and military power. Rather, such historical periods entail far reaching changes in 'international society' as a whole, including its main institutions, international norms, ideologies, interests, mentalities and cultural forms.

We are in a period not only of contending geopolitical and strategic interests but of contending paradigms of economic, social and political order and organization. The 'rise of the BRICS' within the structures and practices of world order points to the emergence of a post-Western centric world order, one that challenges the traditional communication hegemony of the West (and especially of the US). As one of the editors of this volume has asserted, 'BRICS communication has the potential to pluralize and democratize global information and communication agendas and thus set the stage for a new global communication order...' (Thussu, 2015, from the Introduction).

An emergent counter-narrative is visible, one pressing for the need for more inclusive and cosmopolitan epistemological perspectives and research culture, including the recognition of multiple non-Western modernities in a world increasingly characterized by digitalization and mediatization, a multi-lingual internet and global social mediascape. The rising cultural influence and technological capacity of the BRICS and, indeed, many other so-called 'developing economies' carries with it a profound wave of wider global cultural change.

The challenge to inherited Eurocentric epistemology and framing of global communication extends to the realm of the academic study of communication. The challenge to Eurocentric framing of global communication studies is in motion in both practice and theory. The hybridization of communication systems and models, where 'national', 'regional' and 'transnational' systems blend and overlap, is one of the key structural tendencies shaping this emergent new global communication order. Each of the BRICS nations has not only expanding domestic or national communications but also regional and global reach and influence. This new global mediascape is as yet under researched but will become increasingly prominent in the years to come.

Divergence and plurality has always characterized the BRICS as a group, and the category itself is, of course, problematic analytically. That being said, the BRICS as a group of countries certainly constitutes a recognizable and valid subject of academic study. This excellent collection of essays brings together an outstanding set of experts and encompasses analysis of cases from each of the BRICS countries, as well as comparative and global analyses. It constitutes an important and pioneering study in the field of global communication studies, challenging inherited dominant framings and discourses in the field. The editors and contributors do not shy away from critical analysis of the internal and external contradictions, nor the competition and rivalry amongst the BRICS countries themselves. The authors address the controversies surrounding the expanding global power and practices of BRICS communications, and the nuances and ambiguities of their increasingly significant impact upon national, regional and world order. The readers of this volume will discover a wealth of empirical and analytical material helping us to understand the emergent paradigms of communications in the twenty-first century, in the transition to a post-Western-centric world order.

INTRODUCTION

Daya Kishan Thussu and Kaarle Nordenstreng

In the 1842 poem, *Morte d'Arthur* by the celebrated British poet Alfred Lord Tennyson, the dying King Arthur says, 'The old order changeth, yielding place to new'. Although this was referring to a mythical time, it can stand in for the rapidly modernizing transformations of the nineteenth century and the challenge this posed to traditional values. In his international bestseller, *World Order*, the former United States Secretary of State, Henry Kissinger defined world order as 'the concept held by a region or civilization about the nature of just arrangements and the distribution of power thought to be applicable to the entire world' (Kissinger, 2014: 9). The seventeenth century saw the birth of what is said to be the first modern 'world order' at the Peace of Westphalia in 1648 after 30 years of war in Europe, 'without the involvement or even the awareness of most other continents or civilizations', as Kissinger has noted. In modern times, however, the term 'New World Order' is associated with US President Woodrow Wilson, who used the phrase in connection with the formation of the League of Nations following the First World War and it has still become a short-hand for identifying major global shifts and restructurings, real or desired.

In 1974, during the Cold War, the Non-Aligned nations led by India managed to convince the UN General Assembly to pass a resolution to establish a New International Economic Order to create a more equitable global economic system (Bhagwati, 1977), followed in 1978 by the endorsement by the UN of a New World Information and Communications Order (NWICO), sponsored by UNESCO to reduce the imbalances in the 'one-way flow of information' from the West to the rest of the world (MacBride *et al.*, 1980; Nordenstreng, 2012; Vincent and Nordenstreng, 2016).

The end of the Cold War, too, was celebrated as the dawn of a 'new world order', attributed to President George W. Bush addressing the UN General Assembly in September 1990. The RIC troika (Russia, India, China), set up in 1999 as a

Russian initiative to promote multi-polarity in a US-imposed, unipolar, post-Cold War world, also spoke of a 'new world order'. Despite Russian reservations, in the new liberal, free-market and globalized world order, the rules were set largely by the victors of the Cold War, the US and its Western allies. Three decades on, this Western model of a liberal world order has been increasingly questioned (Layne, 2018; Mearsheimer, 2018; Porter, 2020), as the West has weakened arguably due to the rise of large non-Western countries, exemplified by the BRICS nations – Brazil, Russia, India, China and South Africa. 'The idea that liberal global governance is the only or even the most important thing that stands between order and anarchy is deeply misleading', writes one commentator (Hurrel, 2018: 97). Others argue that the 'mentalities and power structures of the leaders of the liberal international order … [are] constructed by hierarchical, imperial and racial–civilizational ways of thinking' (Parmar, 2018: 172).

This order, led by the US government and the Bretton Woods institutions (the World Bank, the International Monetary Fund and the World Trade Organization) is increasingly being challenged at a time when the role of the US and Western Europe as the main engine of global growth appears to be diminishing (Mishra, 2012; Kiely, 2015; Thies and Nieman, 2017; Khanna, 2019; Stuenkel, 2020). The US withdrawal from the Trans-Pacific Partnership (TPP) trading agreement, as well as the uncertain future of the Transatlantic Trade and Investment Partnership (TTIP), which linked the European Union with the US, are two recent developments that indicate the relative retreat of the West, especially the US. President Donald Trump's 'America First' agenda and the US withdrawal from UNESCO and the 2016 Paris Climate Accord, as well as Britain's exit from the EU are other key indications that spaces have been created, within which, it is argued, the BRICS countries could articulate a very different view of a 'new world order' (Kiely, 2015; Mearsheimer, 2018).

The liberal hegemonic order is being eroded, in particular, by powers such as China and Russia, which have provided 'exit options' from US hegemony to many developing countries (Cooley and Nexon, 2020). As Zakaria notes: 'On every dimension other than military power – industrial, financial, social, cultural – the distribution of power is shifting, moving away from US dominance. That does not mean we are entering an anti-American world. But we are moving into a post-American world, one defined and directed from many places and by many people' (Zakaria, 2008: 4–5).

BRICS as a grouping has the potential for promoting major changes in the global order (Stuenkel, 2020), while some see possibilities of a 'post-Western', 'sustainable modernity', based on Asian histories and cultures (Duara, 2014). As the old order begins to fray at the seams, there is also alarmist talk of 'deepening disorder', with the implicit suggestion that disorder will rule in a post-Western world led by the authoritarian governments that dominate BRICS and this will erode democracy (Tharoor and Saran, 2020). Already, the BRICS countries have evolved strategies of coexistence to develop a future global order (de Coning, Mandrup and Odgaard, 2015) and, although they may not have fully challenged 'Western ideational control of global governance', they have 'transformed the image of the international liberal order' (Salzman, 2019: 140, 144), especially among the developing countries. The demand of a pluralistic world order has 'purchase in the policies, traditions, and practices of many countries in the global South. Emerging powers have long stressed the need for pluralism and for recognition of difference and diversity' (Hurrel, 2018: 100).

BRICS building a new global order?

As we approach two decades since Jim O'Neill, a Goldman Sachs executive and later a minister in the UK government coined the BRIC acronym in 2001 to refer to the four fast-growing emerging markets – Brazil, Russia, India and China (O'Neill, 2001; reassessed a decade later in O'Neill, 2011), it is high-time to evaluate how far, if at all, these major non-Western powers are re-shaping the global order in a 'post-American' or even a 'post-Western' world (Zakaria, 2008; Stuenkel, 2016; Acharya, 2018; Khanna, 2019; Stuenkel, 2020).

Although 'BRIC' was a catchy corporate phrase, popularized by the mainstream Western media and enthusiastically adopted around the world, the countries which were thus described in this neoliberal discourse used the acronym to create an international informal political alliance, linking major countries in Asia, Europe and Latin America (South Africa was added in 2011 on China's request to expand BRIC to BRICS). Set up as a formal group in 2006 and holding annual summits since 2009, BRICS has been perceived in the West as challenging the 'Washington consensus' (Ban and Blyth, 2013; Xing, 2014; Roberts, Armijo and Katada, 2018). The BRIC alliance was actually first floated by Russia but it gained salience in the wake of the 2008–2009 global financial crisis, when China began to dominate the discourse, given its growing economic power and global ambitions. From the Chinese perspective, BRICS was a convenient forum to reassure the world that it was not the only 'rising' power – as there were other major countries 'on the rise'.

BRICS is much less institutionalized and coherent than other groupings in which BRICS members exchange views, for example, the China-sponsored Shanghai Cooperation Organization (in operation since 2003, which includes Russia, and since 2017, India) and IBSA (a forum between India, Brazil and South Africa, also in operation since 2003). However, unlike these organizations, the BRICS as a group has been demanding a greater say in global affairs, particularly in global governance (Kirton and Larionova, 2018). As the US has withdrawn from UNESCO and from the UN Human Rights Council, as well as ending all funding to the UN agency for Palestinian refugees, the BRICS nations, particularly China, may try to fill the gap. China has surpassed Japan as second-largest contributor to the UN and it also provides the biggest contingent of troops for UN peacekeeping missions among the five permanent members of the Security Council.

China, Brazil and India have, for example, coordinated their negotiating efforts within the WTO to champion trading rights for developing countries (Lesage and de Graaf, 2015; Stuenkel, 2016; Hopewell, 2016). Russia and China – both permanent members of the UN Security Council – have also often cooperated within international institutions but the alternatives they have promoted may not always be acceptable to their BRICS partners. Russia, a former 'superpower' and a major military and energy power in the contemporary world, has also rallied support from other BRICS nations to resist the Euro-Atlantic world order and current system of global governance (Salzman, 2019).

While the West is looking inwards, BRICS countries, and China in particular, are globalizing. When the country opened up to global businesses in the late 1980s, its presence in the international corporate world was negligible but, by 2019, China had 119 companies in the *Fortune Global 500*, just behind the US (121), while three of the top ten global corporations, in terms of revenue, were Chinese. In comparison, the other BRICS nations had a modest presence, Brazil (8), India (7) and Russia (4), while South Africa was absent from the list (*Fortune*, 2019). On the basis of purchasing power parity (PPP), China's Gross Domestic Product (GDP) surpassed that of the US in 2014, making it the world's largest economy. In actual GDP terms, China's economy is second only to the US – but larger than all the other BRICS combined. While other BRICS nations are often clustered under 'rising powers', China is seen as a 'risen' power and therefore a serious challenger to the US-defined world order (Zeng and Breslin, 2016; Allison, 2017; Frankopan, 2018; Mearsheimer, 2018; Khanna, 2019).

However, as Chinese investments have further globalized, BRICS seems to have been overshadowed by China's 'Belt and Road Initiative' (BRI – formerly known as the 'One Belt, One Road'), which will become the world's largest infrastructural intervention, encompassing 900 projects (valued at about $1.3 trillion) and involving more than 100 countries and 29 per cent of global GDP (Frankopan, 2018). Creating information and communication networks is part of the BRI projects, backed by a $40 billion Silk Road Infrastructure Fund, capitalized mainly by China's foreign exchange reserves, estimated in 2019 to be more than $3 trillion. The China-initiated Asian Infrastructure Investment Bank (AIIB) – set up in 2016 – together with the Shanghai-based New Development Bank (NDB), established in 2014 by the BRICS nations, are also involved in financing these projects (Xing, 2019). As China's focus has moved from BRICS to BRI, it has floated the idea of 'BRICS Plus', introduced at the 2017 BRICS summit in Xiamen, which would entail inviting other large economies to join, especially those linked with the BRI.

BRICS: managing divergent interests

BRICS as an analytical category is not unproblematic, partly because of the different political and communication systems, and the disparities in power relations and levels of development within this group of large and diverse nations. The BRICS states comprise approximately three billion people (40 per cent of the global population) and, in terms of GDP, they account for nearly $17 trillion (22 per cent of the world's economy). Yet, intra-BRICS trade is merely 15 per cent of world trade. For many commentators, the differing geopolitical and economic interests of the individual BRICS countries inhibit cooperation towards a common objective (Pant, 2013; Sparks, 2015).

The most significant threat to BRICS solidarity is perhaps the shift in China's focus to its Belt and Road Initiative mentioned above, which has been identified, not only by the West, as the infrastructure for a new Chinese global empire. China's new 'empire', writes one observer, 'will be an informal and largely economic one, posited on cash and held together by hard infrastructure' (Miller, 2017: 17). The BRI raises geopolitical concerns among two BRICS members, Russia and India. Many of its projects in central Asia impinge on what Russia has traditionally considered its 'near abroad', while some projects may also interfere with the Russia-led Eurasian Economic Union, in operation since 2014 and aimed at promoting free movement of goods, labour, services and capital between Russia, Belarus, Kazakhstan, Kyrgyzstan and Armenia. Given the close economic and political ties between Moscow and Beijing, Russia has not openly expressed its reservations. Instead, it has been promoting the idea of 'Greater Eurasia', a project of Eurasian integration that would link China, Russia and Central Asia in a new economic and political bloc: Russian President Vladimir Putin has called it 'a civilisational project for the future'.

India, which has 'enduring rivalries' with China (Paul, 2018: 15), was one of the few major economies not to attend the first Belt and Road Forum in 2015. New Delhi has been vocally opposed to the China-Pakistan Economic Corridor, part of the BRI, since some of its projects operate in territory claimed by India. The China-India dynamic is particularly significant for the future of the BRICS grouping and indeed globally (Bajpai, Huang and Mahbubani, 2016; Sen, 2017; Duara and Perry, 2019). Under Narendra Modi's nationalist government, India is progressively moving closer to the US in geo-strategic and economic terms. Although India does not fully share the US government's view of China as an ideological opponent to the liberal world order, it seems to have generally followed the US rhetoric about the so-called 'China threat', if not in official pronouncements, but certainly in media narratives and in regular reports from US-financed or -oriented think tanks based in India.

US-India relations have been strengthened in recent decades, particularly in defence and security. Modi has endorsed India's participation in the US-sponsored coalition of democracies in Asia-Pacific region, grouping the US with Australia and Japan (the so-called Quad) to check the military expansion of China in the South China Sea, now being termed the 'Indo-Pacific' (Hall, 2019). Independent of global geopolitical shifts, the long-standing and still unresolved border disputes between China and India, which have their roots in colonial times, continue to bedevil their relationship, though remarkably no fire has yet been exchanged in anger along the 3,500-km-long border since the 1962 war between the two nations. However, forums such as BRICS can also 'open up avenues for discussion and engagement' and NDB and AIIB have 'helped manage the rivalry' (Paul, 2018: 15).

Unlike Russia and India, both of which share a long border with China and even longer histories, Brazil and South Africa have a different kind of relationship with the Asian giant – more economic than cultural. There is a Western perception that the conventional democracies in BRICS – India, Brazil and South Africa – given their closer ties to the West, could act as a counterweight to the emerging 'axis of authoritarianism' between the economic power of China and military strength of Russia (Ellings and Sutter, 2019). All BRICS countries have some concept of democracy at the centre of their existential definitions, as shown in the first articles of their respective constitutions: Brazil is 'a legal democratic state', Russia 'a democratic federal law-bound state', India 'a sovereign democratic republic', China 'a socialist state under the people's democratic dictatorship' and South Africa 'a democratic and open society'. China's coupling of democracy and dictatorship calls to mind the former Soviet-type 'people's democracy' but it also reflects the classic Chinese model of good governance.

Indeed, the democracy represented by contemporary China and Russia is quite different from that prevailing in the other BRICS countries. The annual Democracy Index produced by the Economist Intelligence Unit, places Brazil, India and South Africa in the category of 'flawed democracies'; Russia and China in the 'authoritarian regimes' category (EIU, 2019), while the Freedom House classification of countries into 'free', 'partly free' and 'not free', shows Brazil, India and South Africa as 'free', but Russia and China as 'not free' (Freedom House, 2019). Admittedly, these are Western typologies, which should be seen as partly ideological. Russia and China are not apologetic about their notions of democracy, which differ drastically from the Western tradition. Putin claims that 'liberalism has become obsolete' and Russia's official doctrine is a variant of the old idea of Kremlin-sponsored 'guided democracy' (Putin, 2019), while China's President Xi Jinping defines its system as 'consultative democracy' (Huang, 2014).

On a global scale, the Western version of liberal democracy has become tarnished since the election of leaders such as Trump – a property tycoon who had never held a public office and whose claim to fame was a reality TV show – and many other right-wing populist leaders across Europe. The BRICS countries have also contributed to exposing the instability of this 'Western' model of democratic governance. The right-wing shift in India with the election of Modi as Prime Minister in 2014 and again in 2019, and the election of the far-right, former army captain, Jair Bolsonaro as President of Brazil in 2018 – both admirers of the US President and his policies – have also weakened BRICS solidarity.

Mention of backsliding from and even the 'death of democracy' (Levitsky and Ziblatt, 2018), with formulations such as 'democracies don't die, they are killed' (Jones, 2018) in an age of populism, defined as 'new despotism' by a leading scholar of democracy (Keane, 2020), is increasingly made in academic and policy literature. An echo of such sentiments reverberated in the 2020 Munich Security Conference report which noted: 'Far-reaching power shifts in the world and rapid technological change contribute to a sense of anxiety and restlessness. The world is becoming less Western. But more importantly, the West itself may become less Western, too. This is what we call "Westlessness"' (Munich Security Report,

2020: 6). The BRICS nations, and particularly China, are keen to benefit from such political and cultural ennui.

Reframing a new global communication order?

Although the US imprint on the global communication space – both hardware and software – remains profound (Thussu, 2019; Boyd-Barrett and Mirrlees, 2019), it is also the case that, as a result of a mobile, globally networked and digitized communication infrastructure, circulation of content from the BRICS nations has increased: television news in English and other international languages from Russia (RT) and China (China Global Television Network – CGTN), as well as entertainment from India (Bollywood), Brazil (telenovelas) and South Africa (infotainment and entertainment). With the convergence of mobile communications technologies and content via a multi-lingual Internet, such flows are growing and increasingly being noticed in Western capitals as challenging their traditional communication hegemony. As more people connect, content from BRICS countries is likely to become more visible globally and this may have the potential to contribute to a new global communication order, in which US communication and media is less predominant. In terms of volume if not value, the already enormous and steadily growing communication emanating from two large BRICS nations, China and India, is likely to grow further as digitization becomes entrenched in everyday life, in the age of the Internet of Things. In such a communication ecology, it has been argued, 'it no longer makes sense to view online and offline spaces as distinct spheres, either technically or politically, with the virtual would somehow separate from the real world. They are entangled' (DeNardis, 2020: 11).

In 2019, more than 850 million Chinese citizens were online, making it home to the world's largest number of Internet users. In the same year, four of the top ten Internet companies in the world ranked by market capitalization were Chinese, including search engine Baidu, e-commerce giant Alibaba and social-media company Tencent – the so called 'BAT'. By 2019, China's e-commerce sales were the largest in the world, double those of the US, and China also leads the world in mobile payments with their value in 2019 totalling more than $13 trillion, according to Chinese government data (CNNIC, 2019). AliExpress, Alibaba's payment system, is already being used in many countries including Russia, France, Spain and Poland; with BRI its geographical spread is likely to expand, especially in the rest of the global South, challenging the US position in this lucrative field of e-commerce (CNNIC, 2019; *China Internet Report*, 2019). Other BRICS nations have also demonstrated extraordinary growth in digital communication. In the last two decades, India has seen exceptional expansion in Internet take-up: in 2000, only 5.5 million Indians (with a penetration rate of 0.5 per cent of the population) were online; by 2019 that figure had climbed to 600 million (and the penetration rate had crossed 45 per cent of the population) (KPMG Report, 2019). Russia, Brazil and South Africa, too, have witnessed a major expansion of online communication.

As the world becomes increasingly mobile, networked and digitized, BRICS countries have the potential to pluralize and democratize global information and communication agendas and thus set the stage for a new global communication order – a NWICO 2.0 for the digital age (Thussu, 2015). Such a communication order will contribute to reforming global governance structures and to loosening Western control of the institutions, ideologies and practices that maintain the US at the helm of the international hierarchy (Kirton and Larionova, 2018). Narratives legitimizing such power structures are embedded in the Western intellectual and policy arena and distributed across the world through their formidable media and communication networks. The BRICS nations pose a challenge by providing a complementary, if not a counter narrative, especially in the context of international development. Four out of the five BRICS nations remain in the category of developing countries, despite an impressive record of poverty reduction in recent decades especially in China, which has become a major global aid donor (Soares, Scerri and Maharajh, 2014; Gu, Shankland and Chenoy, 2016; Neuwirth, 2020).

The framing of a new global communication order would also entail reconfiguring discourses on communication and media systems in relation to international political and economic structures and dynamics. Flew and Waisbord have criticized the concept of the media system itself as a 'conceptual leftover of mid-century functionalist sociology'. Despite this, they argue that such a conceptual construction 'enables an aggregation of structures and dynamics in ways that allow for the systematic study of media, politics, and policies. It assumes that important structures and dynamics "thicken" around "media systems" that are bounded by the politics of nation-states, without denying the significance of globalization' (Flew and Waisbord, 2015: 622, 623).

The primacy of the nation state in providing the infrastructure, legal framework and ownership and regulatory rules and regulations remains in place, despite exceptional growth of online communication in the digital age. Comparative models of media and communication systems have ignored the extraordinary expansion of the media among the BRICS nations, which can provide empirical evidence in the context of digital globalization. Hallin and Mancini's 2012 edited collection *Comparing Media Systems Beyond the Western World*, for example, excludes any discussion of India (one of the largest and most complex media and communication systems 'beyond the Western world'). There is need to widen the range of variables and to create a more comprehensive typology based on empirical research to measure a media or communication system. Some scholars have cautioned against nation-centrism and methodological nationalism, arguing for a globalization model that recognizes 'a shift from analysis of the vertical relationship between media institutions and political structures towards horizontal dimensions of media cultures and cultural flows across national borders' (Hardy, 2012: 197). The hybridization of communication models – when the national, the regional and the transnational overlap – is another field which remains largely under-researched.

Another marker for a reframed global communication is likely to be the transformation of media and communication policies and practices. Driven by the exponential growth of communication in BRICS countries, particularly in China and India (which account for more than a third of the planet's population, its two largest global diasporas and the two biggest Internet populations), communication practices are set to change (Graham, 2019). One of the key issues in the age of the Internet of Things will be governing the 'cyberspace, with its core, the Internet, and its rapidly growing users and participants, and the formal and informal institutions that seek to provide forms of order in the cyber arena' (Choucri and Clark, 2019: 5). BRICS nations will increasingly play a significant role in this, given that China has the world's largest Internet whose hardware and software is controlled, unlike elsewhere, apart from the US, by the national companies or government, challenging the US-defined 'open internet' (Segal, 2018).

Framing a new global communication order would also entail reconfiguring discourses on strategic communication, including soft power (Cull, 2019). As Joseph Nye, who coined the term, has noted 'in behavioural terms, simply put, soft power is attractive power' (Nye, 2004: 6). To make countries attractive, there is growing recognition of the importance of communicative processes in global communication. Monroe Price uses the framework of neoliberalism to analyse 'strategic communication' in a globalized era, where the 'capacity of the state to exercise authority in a world in which large-scale strategic communication of others (including other states) becomes a defining factor in establishing a state's legitimacy including the stress of the continuing burst of trans-border information flows' (Price, 2015: 19).

Comparative and international studies of soft power tend to be dominated by American formulations, although in the case of BRICS each country appears to be applying its own version of strategic communication to promote their geo-political interests (Chatin and Gallarotti, 2018). In US policy, academic and media circles, China and Russia are increasingly described in terms of 'sharp power', which 'pierces, penetrates, or perforates the political and information environments in the targeted countries' (Walker and Ludwig, 2017: 13). Despite such criticism, China is most active in promoting its soft power, integral to its 'going out' strategy, which entails globalizing China's vision and countering negative portrayals of the country in the US-dominated international media. To this end, an estimated $7 billion are earmarked for external communication, including the expansion of Chinese broadcasting networks notably CGTN (China Global Television Network), which, apart from English, operates Spanish, French, Arabic, German and Russian channels, as well as special editions for the US and for Africa. Yet, according to the London-based *Portland Soft Power Index 2019*, China was 27 out of the 'Soft Power 30' list, a ranking dominated by European nations. Other BRICS nations fared equally badly: Brazil was at number 26 and Russia was last on the list, while India and South Africa were not included (Portland, 2019).

Reframing global communication studies

The transformation of the global media and communication landscape, including the rise of the BRICS countries, challenges the analytical frameworks of communication theories, which remain deeply embedded within a Eurocentric discourse. During the ideologically driven Cold War years, such formulations as the 'authoritarian' versus 'liberal' theory debate shaped the academic discourse, failing to notice that large civilizational powers such as China (the Sino–Soviet rift had taken place in the 1950s) and India (a founding member of the Non-Aligned Movement) did not fit into such a neat bipolar division of the world.

The BRICS nations could contribute significantly towards building a more inclusive theory of global communication that takes on board the extraordinary changes in large countries with long histories and rising economic and cultural power (Thussu, 2009; Hobson, 2012). Ignoring non-European modernities, philosophies, history and culture is a blind-spot in mainstream communication research and in other fields, including International Relations, as two leading scholars note: 'IR has been largely built on the assumptions that Western history or Western political theory *are* world history and world political theory' (Acharya and Buzan, 2019: 3, emphasis in the original).

One key reason for such absences in the field of communication studies stems from the fact that the intellectual markers in terms of research agendas, publications, grants and projects, are hugely influenced by Western, or more specifically, US elite universities, as well as US-based professional organizations such as the International Communication Association (Wiedemann and Meyen, 2016). As post-modern, identity-inspired discourses and data-driven scholarship have been globalized, a Western-centric epistemology has received a new lease of life, evoking debates among many scholars (Thussu, 2009; Christians and Nordenstreng, 2014; Lee, 2015; Wasserman, 2018).

At the same time, expanding and internationalizing media and communication studies has been necessitated by the transformation of media and communication in Asia (Gunaratne, 2010; Chen, 2010; Wang, 2011; Chan and Lee, 2017). In Brazil, scholars see 'BRICS an appropriate standpoint for discussing the problem of multipolarity' and 'challenging Western centrism in international media studies' (de Albuquerque and Lycarião, 2018: 2884). In South Africa, the need for the 'decolonization' of media and communication studies has been pointed out (Nyamnjoh, 2011; Wasserman, 2018). However, legitimate and much-needed critiques of the supposed universalization of Western theories should not lead scholars into the parochialism of the local and the national. Lee recommends that they adopt 'epistemological autonomy' to make their mark on global or cosmopolitan theory (Lee, 2015).

While sensitivity to cultural specificity and a firm grasp of historical continuities are important, a keen sense of understanding global trends and cultural interactions are even more critical in order to comprehend the emerging world order. Calls have also been made for 'a higher degree of self-reflexivity among media and communication scholars' in the West about their 'own potential complicity in the marginalization of knowledge from elsewhere' (Willems, 2014: 428). However, within the BRICS countries there is very limited intercultural communication or media exchange: all five are largely dependent for their international-oriented content on US-supplied media, as well as for the main theoretical approaches to the study of media and communication. Comparative studies among BRICS nations – for example, India and China (Jeffrey and Sen, 2015); China and Russia (Meng and Rantanen, 2015) and South Africa and India (Rao and Wasserman, 2015) – remain few and far between. Nevertheless, BRICS nations have the potential to reframe global communication research and thus contribute to the democratization of global media in a polycentric world. This collection is a modest contribution to fill the gap.

Outlining the chapters

The book is divided into four parts: Part I – Challenging dominant discourses in a new world order – frames the discussion about the contribution the BRICS nations have made in helping to shape a new world order. In Part II – Media and communication structures and systems – the focus is on the media and communication systems of the five BRICS countries, which are essential to an understanding of how media function in a given nation and indeed internationally. The chapters in Part III of the book – BRICS and global strategic communication – evaluate the role of communication in the soft power promotion of the five nations. Part IV of the book – BRICS and changing communication practices – examines three key aspects of BRICS communication – journalism, entertainment and the Internet. Rather than looking at individual countries, as in the previous two parts of the book, this part takes a pan-BRICS perspective to analyze key media and communication trends.

Challenging dominant discourses in a new world order

The three chapters in the opening section of the book reflect upon the emerging contours of a new global order in which BRICS can play a vital part. Chapters in this part demonstrate that counter-narratives are emerging, based on different readings of global geopolitics, communication paradigms and media structures and systems. The chapters thus contribute to encouraging researchers to recognize the pressing need for an innovative, inclusive and cosmopolitan research dialogue, one that cuts across disciplinary and intellectual boundaries to address the emerging landscape of global communication in a polycentric world.

In the opening chapter of this section, Marko Juutinen and Jyrki Käkönen, Finnish scholars in International Relations at Tampere University, set the geopolitical stage for the role of BRICS nations in framing a different kind of world order. They point out that, while many commentators view BRICS as an indication of the emergence of a new world order, others do not consider the grouping to be a viable and coherent international organization, as they have little collective diplomatic or political strength. This 'BRICS paradox' is at the heart of their analysis, based on a review of BRICS summit documents and other material. They investigate the potential of using alternative concepts arising from BRICS' own cultures, including *tianxia* theory, with its roots in ancient China, as well as *mandala* theory, originally formulated in India in the third century BC.

The second chapter that challenges dominant communication discourses is by Muniz Sodré and Raquel Paiva, two of Brazil's leading scholars, based at the Federal University of Rio de Janeiro, along with Kaarle Nordenstreng and Leonardo Custodio, who closely worked with them on the BRICS project. The chapter reminds us about the ongoing shifts in the current paradigms of media and communications studies and provides an example of a distinctive approach articulated in Sodré's new book *The Science of the Commons* (2019).

In his chapter Savyasaachi Jain from Cardiff University in the UK and a former award-winning documentary-maker in India, critiques media system theories and their conceptual and empirical limitations. He argues that the currently-dominant framework developed by Hallin and Mancini, while providing the basis for some illuminating studies, suffers from many limitations: the existing typologies of media systems are not very applicable to the BRICS countries, as the underlying assumptions, approaches, reference points and analytical variables draw upon experience of a restricted geographical spread of media systems. Jain, currently finishing a book on media systems, suggests three broad approaches to study BRICS media systems: to move beyond the focus on political and economic systems; to deepen the inquiry past the normative and structural levels and, to undertake grounded studies of media systems.

Media and communication structures and systems

Chapters in this part of the book provide an overview of media and communication systems in the five BRICS nations. Following on our initial investigation of media systems in the BRICS nations (Nordenstreng and Thussu, 2015), in this volume the attempt is to provide a more comprehensive overview of communication structures. Though each chapter is distinct and covers a particular BRICS country, one underlining theme that emerges from these chapters is the need to broaden the variables to include indigenous cultures, local histories and experiences to understand media and communication structures and systems.

In their chapter on Brazil, Fernando Paulino and Liziane Guazina, both based at the University of Brasilia in the Brazilian capital, focus on the impact of the turbulent political environment since 2013 on the media system and on how information is disseminated to and shared by the public, with increasing use of social media and the Internet. Identifying the complexities of a communication system in a vast and diverse country, Elena Vartanova, Dean of School of Journalism at Lomonosov Moscow State University, writes in her chapter that the unprecedented growth of digital communication has transformed the Russian media system, traditionally dominated by state-run media institutions and structures. The trend towards centralization of media and communication power and its impact on policy making is also highlighted, as is the primacy of television, despite the huge uptake of digital media.

A more historical approach is adopted by B. P. Sanjay in his contribution on the Indian media and communication system. Sanjay, a veteran of communication studies in India, delineates the development of media industries in one of the largest communication spaces on the planet, tracing it from colonial times to the era of print and broadcast media and the challenges it faces in the age of digital communication. Questions of media ownership and the trend towards entertainment-driven content are also raised in the chapter, arguing that they contribute to the shrinking of the public sphere in the world's largest democracy.

A different approach is adopted by Zhengrong Hu, Deqiang Ji, Peixi Xu and Kriti Bhuju – based at the Communication University of China in Beijing, where Professor Hu was formerly the President – in their chapter on the Chinese media. The chapter argues that it is important to avoid 'static and one-dimensional assumptions that may detract from understanding the ongoing dynamic processes by which the media in China have been re-defined, re-invented, re-organized, and re-located in an increasingly connected, massively digitized, datafied and globalized Chinese society'. Given the globalization of Chinese media and communication, such a formulation is an important antidote to the conventional framing of China's media and communication system purely within a censorship/state control model.

The main theme of the chapter on South African media by viola milton and Winston Mano is the role of public-service broadcasting in post-Apartheid society and how it has been challenged in recent years. Milton, based at the University of South Africa in Pretoria, and Mano, Director of the Africa Media Centre at the University of Westminster in London, have both written extensively on the need to develop African communication paradigms to decolonize the discourse and encourage democratic participation within 'local histories, practices and contexts', thus helping to create an 'Afrokology' of communication.

BRICS and global strategic communication

The chapters in the third part of the book largely focus on the soft-power communication aspects of the five nations. Contributors explore various dimensions and manifestations of the soft power of the BRICS nations. The chapters analyse the different and distinct approaches adopted by BRICS governments and corporations, to promote their respective strategic communication in a media globe which continues to be dominated by the US-version of what constitutes soft power.

Joseph Straubhaar, who has spent a lifetime studying Brazil while based at the University of Texas in Austin, argues in his chapter that the commercial cultural industries in television and music have been crucial in promoting Brazil globally. Particularly important, he points out, are the telenovelas, watched around the world. The role of successive Brazilian governments in promoting entertainment is highlighted as an example of embedded synergies between private media and communication interests and foreign policy.

Russian soft power is discussed by Dmitry Gavra and Elena Bykova –from St. Petersburg State University – examining it within a historical context and exploring the roles of art, literature and music, as well as education in Russian soft-power discourses. The primacy of culture is also central to the chapter on the Indian soft power by Daya Kishan Thussu. Taking a historical perspective, he argues that the soft power of ancient civilizations such as India needs to be historicized. Emphasizing the importance of traditional cultures and faiths, the chapter relates India's culture to its large diaspora and popular entertainment.

Cinema and entertainment are also the focus of the chapter on Chinese soft power by Ying Zhu, currently based at Hong Kong Baptist University, and Michael Keane, a prolific writer on Chinese media-related issues, based at Curtin University in Australia. Their chapter provides a new perspective on Chinese cultural power (manifest in cinema, diaspora and digital communication) and, in the process, help balance the news and current affairs aspects of most academic and policy studies of Chinese soft power. The last chapter in this part, by Herman Wasserman and Musawenkosi Ndlovu from the University of Cape Town evaluates the rise and decline of the soft power of South Africa within the continent. South Africa has been a major media power in Africa, for decades but, they argue, with the availability of competing material from across the world and the growth of local media content, the influence of South African transnational media, and the country's soft power, has diminished.

BRICS and changing communication practices

While the previous two parts of the book look at media in individual BRICS countries, the final part of the book takes a pan-BRICS perspective to analyse journalism, entertainment and the key issues surrounding cyber communication. The chapter by Jyotika Ramaprasad from the University of Miami and Svetlana Pasti from Tampere University, is based on extensive empirical research they undertook while editing a volume on journalism in BRICS countries, a pioneering project in itself (Pasti and Ramaprasad, 2017). The authors argue for a 'localization' approach to the historical legacies and current dynamics of journalism, looking specifically at journalists' beliefs about their roles and professionalism, as well as the functions of journalism in their respective countries. The contribution by Tatu Laukkanen and Iiris Ruoho, also both based at Tampere University, examines how screen entertainment – films and television drama – has been transformed in the post-liberalization era in Brazil, Russia, India and China. The study of popular media in a comparative manner, for example, the 'nationalist blockbuster', particularly popular in China and Russia, provides valuable inputs to internationalizing communication studies in an approach they call 'BRICS as method' – an interpretive framework for thinking through the heterogeneous, multi-platform entity of entertainment of the BRICS countries.

The book ends with a future-oriented chapter by Daya Kishan Thussu, which aims to contextualize the framing of a new communication order within a global cyberspace being consistently contested among the major powers. The chapter argues that although in terms of its infrastructure, economics and governance, the

Internet continues to be dominated by the US, this domination is being increasingly challenged by the BRICS countries. The chapter discusses this within five domains: infrastructure, commerce, regulation, weaponization and surveillance of cyber space, and the developmental dimensions of the Internet. In all five domains, the contributions of the BRICS nations are delineated. This is done with the thematic of 'de-Americanizing' the Internet, a process in which the BRICS nations are playing a crucial role, a reflection of their growing presence and assertiveness related to global cyber-issues, despite strong divergences and some convergences within the group.

This edited collection, following the publication of two other related books – *Mapping BRICS Media* (Nordenstreng and Thussu, 2015) and *BRICS Journalism: Non-Western Media in Transition* (Pasti and Ramaprasad, 2017) – both brought out in Routledge's Internationalizing Media Studies series – is the culmination of a four-year pioneering research project (2012–2016) to study media in the BRICS nations funded by the Finnish Academy (see https://research.uta.fi/brics). It is hoped that this collection will be a significant addition to ongoing debates about comparative communication research and thus contribute to the further internationalization of media and communication studies.

We want to express our profound gratitude to all academic and support staff involved in the project, and especially the contributors to this volume, which brings together distinguished scholars from BRICS nations and those with intellectual expertise about the countries discussed in the book. Our thanks are also due to Barry Gills, Head of Development Studies at Helsinki University, for writing the foreword for this volume, and we are extremely grateful to Liz Thussu for her professional input in the editing process. Finally, a special thanks to the senior editor at Routledge, Natalie Foster, who commissioned the series and patiently saw it through to publication with support from her excellent team, particularly Jennifer Vennall.

References

Acharya, Amitav (2018) *The End of American World Order.* Second edition. Cambridge: Polity.

Acharya, Amitav and Buzan, Barry (2019) *The Making of Global International Relations.* Cambridge: Cambridge University Press.

Allison, Graham (2017) *Destined for War: Can America and China Escape the Thucydides Trap?* New York: Houghton Mifflin.

Bajpai, Kanti, Huang, Jing and Mahbubani, Kishore (eds.) (2016) *China-India Relations: Cooperation and Conflict.* London: Routledge.

Ban, Cornel and Blyth, Mark (2013) The BRICs and the Washington Consensus: An introduction. *Review of International Political Economy,* 20(2): 241–255.

Bhagwati, Jagdish (ed.) (1977) *The New International Economic Order: The North-South Debate.* Cambridge, MA: MIT Press.

Boyd-Barrett, Oliver and Mirrlees, Tanner (eds.) (2019) *Media Imperialism: Continuity and Change.* Cambridge: Polity.

Chan, Joseph and Lee, Francis (eds.) (2017) *Advancing Comparative Media and Communication Research.* New York: Routledge.

Chatin, Mathilde and Gallarotti, Giulio (eds.) (2018) *Emerging Powers in International Politics: The BRICS and Soft Power*. London: Routledge.

Chen, Kuan-Hsing (2010) *Asia as Method: Toward Deimperialization*. Durham, NC: Duke University Press.

China Internet Report (2019) *China Internet Report 2019*. Hong Kong: *South China Morning Post*. Available at www.scmp.com/china-Internet-report.

Choucri, Nazli and Clark, David (2019) *International Relations in the Cyber Age: The Co-Evolution Dilemma*. Cambridge, MA: MIT Press.

Christians, Clifford and Nordenstreng, Kaarle (eds.) (2014) *Communication Theories in a Multicultural World*. New York: Peter Lang.

CNNIC (2019) *Statistical Report on Internet Development in China*. Beijing: China Internet Network Information Center (CNNIC). Available at https://cnnic.com.cn/IDR/ ReportDownloads/201911/P020191112539794960687.pdf

Cooley, Alexander and Nexon, Daniel (2020) *Exit from Hegemony: The Unraveling of the American Global Order*. Oxford University Press.

Cull, Nicholas (2019) *Public Diplomacy: Foundations for Global Engagement in the Digital Age*. Cambridge: Polity.

de Albuquerque, Afonso and Lycarião, Diógenes (2018) Winds of change? BRICS as a perspective in international media research. *International Journal of Communication*, 12: 2873–2892.

de Coning, Cedric, Mandrup, Thomas and Odgaard, Liselotte (eds.) (2015) *The BRICS and Coexistence: An Alternative Vision of World Order*. London: Routledge.

DeNardis, Laura (2020) *The Internet in Everything: Freedom and Security in a World with No Off Switch*. New Haven: Yale University Press.

Duara, Prasenjit (2014) *The Crisis of Global Modernity: Asian Traditions and a Sustainable Future*. Cambridge: Cambridge University Press.

Duara, Prasenjit and Perry, Elizabeth (2019) *Beyond Regimes: China and India Compared*. Cambridge, MA: Harvard University Press.

EIU (2019) *Democracy Index 2019*. London: The Economist Intelligence Unit. Available at www.eiu.com/topic/democracy-index

Ellings, Richard and Sutter, Robert (eds.) (2019) *Axis of Authoritarians: Implications of China-Russia Cooperation*. Washington: National Bureau of Asian Research.

Flew, Terry and Waisbord, Silvio (2015) The ongoing significance of national media systems in the context of media globalization. *Media, Culture & Society*, 37(4): 620–636.

Fortune (2019) Fortune Global 500. *Fortune*, August.

Frankopan, Peter (2018) *The New Silk Roads: The Present and Future of the World*. London: Bloomsbury.

Freedom House (2019) *Freedom in the World 2019: Democracy in Retreat*. Washington: Freedom House. Available at https://freedomhouse.org/countries/freedom-world/scores

Graham, Mark (ed.) (2019) *Digital Economies at Global Margins*. Cambridge, MA: MIT Press.

Gu, Jing, Shankland, Alex and Chenoy, Anuradha (eds.) (2016) *The BRICS in International Development*. London: Palgrave Macmillan.

Gunaratne, Shelton (2010) De-Westernizing communication/social science research: Opportunities and limitations. *Media Culture & Society*, 32(3): 473–500.

Hall, Ian (2019) *Modi and the Reinvention of Indian Foreign Policy*. Bristol: Bristol University Press.

Hallin, Daniel and Mancini, Paolo (eds.) (2012) *Comparing Media Systems Beyond the Western World*. Cambridge: Cambridge University Press.

Hardy, Jonathan (2012) Comparative media systems, pp. 195–206 in F. Esser and T. Hanitzsch (eds.) *Handbook of Comparative Communication Research*. London: Routledge.

Hobson, John (2012) *The Eurocentric Conception of World Politics*. Cambridge: Cambridge University Press.

Hopewell, Kristen (2016) *Breaking the WTO: How Emerging Powers Disrupted the Neoliberal Project*. Stanford: Stanford University Press.

Huang, Cary (2014) China's Xi Jinping supports 'democracy'… but not in the Western sense. *South China Morning Post*, September 24. Available at www.scmp.com/news/china/article/1599068/xi-supports-democracy-not-western-sense

Hurrell, Andrew (2018) Beyond the BRICS: Power, pluralism, and the future of global order. *Ethics & International Affairs*, 32(1): 89–101.

Jeffrey, Robin and Sen, Ronojoy (eds.) (2015) *Media at Work in China and India: Discovering and Dissecting*. New Delhi: Sage.

Jones, Erik (2018) Democracies don't die, they are killed. Review essay. *Survival*, 60(2): 201–210.

Keane, John (2020) *The New Despotism*. Cambridge, MA: Harvard University Press.

Khanna, Parag (2019) *The Future is Asian: Commerce, Conflict, and Culture in the 21st Century*. New York: Simon & Schuster.

Kiely, Ray (2015) *The BRICs, US 'Decline' and Global Transformations*. London: Palgrave Macmillan.

Kirton, John and Larionova, Marina (eds.) (2018) *BRICS and Global Governance*. London: Routledge.

Kissinger, Henry (2014) *World Order*. New York: Penguin Press.

KPMG Report (2019) *India's Digital Future: Mass of Niches- KPMG in India's Media and Entertainment Report 2019*. Mumbai: KPMG India, August.

Layne, Christopher (2018) The US-Chinese power shift and the end of pax Americana. *International Affairs*, 94 (1): 89–111.

Lee, Chin-Chuan (ed.) (2015) *Internationalizing 'International Communications': A Critical Intervention*. Ann Arbor: University of Michigan Press.

Lesage, Dries and de Graaf, Thijs Van (eds.) (2015) *Rising Powers and Multilateral Institutions*. Basingstoke: Palgrave Macmillan.

Levitsky, Steven and Ziblatt, Daniel (2018) *How Democracies Die*. New York: Crown.

MacBride, Seán *et al*. (1980) *Many Voices, One World: Communication and Society Today and Tomorrow*. International Commission for the Study of Communication Problems. Paris: UNESCO.

Mearsheimer, John (2018) *The Great Delusion: Liberal Dreams and International Realities*. New Haven: Yale University Press.

Meng, Bingchun and Rantanen, Terhi (2015) A change of lens: A call to compare the media in China and Russia. *Critical Studies in Media Communication*, 32(1): 1–15.

Miller, Tom (2017) *China's Asian Dream: Quiet Empire Building along the New Silk Road*. London: Zed Books.

Mishra, Pankaj (2012) *From the Ruins of Empire: The Revolt against the West and the Remaking of Asia*. London: Penguin.

Munich Security Report (2020) *Munich Security Report 2020 -Westlessness*. Munich: Available at https://securityconference.org/assets/user_upload/MunichSecurityReport2020.pdf

Neuwirth, Rostam (2020) The end of 'development assistance' and the BRICS, pp. 15–33 in J. de Oliveira and Y. Jing (eds.) *International Development Assistance and the BRICS*. Singapore: Palgrave Macmillan.

Nordenstreng, Kaarle (2012) The New World Information and Communication Order: An idea that refuses to die, pp. 477–499 in J. Nerone (ed.) *Media History and the Foundations of Media Studies*, Volume 1 of A. N. Valdivia (ed.) *The International Encyclopedia of Media Studies*. Chichester: Wiley-Blackwell.

Nordenstreng, Kaarle and Thussu, Daya Kishan (eds.) (2015) *Mapping BRICS Media*. London: Routledge.

Nye, Joseph (2004) *Soft Power: The Means to Success in World Politics*. New York: PublicAffairs.

Nyamnjoh, Francis (2011) De-Westernizing media theory to make room for African experience, pp. 19–31 in H. Wasserman (ed.) *Popular Media, Democracy and Development in Africa*. London: Routledge.

O'Neill, Jim (2001) *Building Better Global Economic BRICs*. Global Economics Paper No: 66, November 30, Available at www.goldmansachs.com/ourthinking/archive/archive-pdfs/build-better-brics.pdf

O'Neill, Jim (2011) *The Growth Map: Economic Opportunity in the BRICs and Beyond*. London: Penguin.

Pant, Harsh (2013) The BRICS fallacy. *The Washington Quarterly*, 36(3): 91–105.

Parmar, Inderjeet (2018) The US-led liberal order: Imperialism by another name. *International Affairs*, 94(1): 151–172.

Pasti, Svetlana and Ramaprasad, Jyotika (eds.) (2017) *BRICS Journalism: Non-Western Media in Transition*. London: Routledge.

Paul, Thazha Varkey (2018) Explaining conflict and cooperation in India–China rivalry, pp. 3–23 in T. V. Paul (ed.) *The China-India Rivalry in the Globalization Era*. Washington: Georgetown University Press.

Porter, Patrick (2020) *The False Promise of Liberal Order*. Cambridge: Polity.

Portland (2019) *The Soft Power 30: A Global Ranking of Soft Power 2019*. London: Portland. Available at https://softpower30.com/wp-content/uploads/2019/10/The-Soft-Power-30-Report-2019-1.pdf

Price, Monroe (2015) *Free Expression, Globalism and the New Strategic Communication*. Cambridge: Cambridge University Press.

Putin, Vladimir (2019) Interview with *Financial Times*, June 28. Available at www.ft.com/video/d62ed062-0d6a-4818-86ff-4b8120125583

Rao, Shakuntala and Wasserman, Herman (2015) A media not for all. A comparative analysis of journalism, democracy and exclusion in Indian and South African media. *Journalism Studies*, 16(5): 651–662.

Roberts, Cynthia, Armijo, Leslie and Katada, Saori (2018) *The BRICS and Collective Financial Statecraft*. Oxford: Oxford University Press.

Salzman, Rachel (2019) *Russia, BRICS and the Disruption of Global Order*. Washington: Georgetown University Press.

Segal, Adam (2018) When China rules the web: Technology in service of the state. *Foreign Affairs*, 97(5): 10–18.

Sen, Tansen (2017) *India, China, and the World: A Connected History*. Lanham: Rowman and Littlefield.

Soares, Maria, Scerri, Mario and Maharajh, Rasigan (eds.) (2014) *BRICS: Inequality and Development Challenges*. New Delhi: Routledge.

Sodré, Muniz (2019) *The Science of the Commons. A Note on Communication Methodology*. London: Palgrave Macmillan.

Sparks, Colin (2015) How coherent is the BRICS grouping? pp. 42–65 in K. Nordenstreng and D. K. Thussu (eds.) *Mapping BRICS Media*. London: Routledge.

Stuenkel, Oliver (2016) *Post-Western World*. Cambridge: Polity.

Stuenkel, Oliver (2020) *The BRICS and the Future of Global Order*, Second edition. New York: Lexington Books.

Tharoor, Shashi and Saran, Samir (2020) *The New World Disorder and the Indian Imperative*. New Delhi: Aleph.

Thies, Cameron and Nieman, Mark (2017) *Rising Powers and Foreign Policy Revisionism: Understanding BRICS Identity and Behaviour Through Time.* Ann Arbor: University of Michigan Press.

Thussu, Daya Kishan (2009) Why internationalize media studies and how, pp. 13–31 in D. K. Thussu (ed.) *Internationalizing Media Studies.* London: Routledge.

Thussu, Daya Kishan (2015) Digital BRICS: Building a NWICO 2.0? pp. 242–263 in K. Nordenstreng and D. K. Thussu (eds.) *Mapping BRICS Media.* London: Routledge.

Thussu, Daya Kishan (2019) *International Communication: Continuity and Change.* Third edition. New York: Bloomsbury Academic.

Vincent, Richard and Nordenstreng, Kaarle (eds.) (2016) *Towards Equity in Global Communication?* Second edition. New York: Hampton Press.

Walker, Christopher and Ludwig, Jessica (2017) From 'soft power' to 'sharp power': rising authoritarian influence in the democratic world, pp. 8–25 in *Sharp Power: Rising Authoritarian Influence.* Washington: National Endowment for Democracy. Available at www.ned.org/wp-content/uploads/2017/12/Sharp-Power-Rising-Authoritarian-Influence-Full-Report.pdf

Wang, Georgette (ed.) (2011) *De-Westernizing Communication Research: Altering Questions and Changing Frameworks.* London: Routledge.

Wasserman, Herman (2018) *Media, Geopolitics and Power: A View from the Global South.* Chicago: University of Illinois Press.

Wiedemann, Thomas and Meyen, Michael (2016) Internationalization through Americanization: The expansion of the International Communication Association's leadership to the world. *International Journal of Communication,* 10: 1489–1509.

Willems, Wendy (2014) Provincializing hegemonic histories of media and communication studies: Toward a genealogy of epistemic resistance in Africa. *Communication Theory,* 24: 415–434.

Xing, Li (2014) *The BRICS and Beyond: The International Political Economy of the Emergence of a New World Order.* London: Ashgate.

Xing, Li (2019) China's pursuit for the 'One Belt One Road' Initiative: A new world order with Chinese characteristics? pp. 1–27, in L. Xing (ed.) *Mapping China's 'One Belt One Road' Initiative.* London: Palgrave Macmillan.

Zakaria, Fareed (2008) *The Post-American World.* London: Allen Lane.

Zeng, Jinghan and Breslin, Shaun (2016) China's 'new type of Great Power relations': a G2 with Chinese characteristics? *International Affairs,* 92(4): 773–794.

PART I

Challenging dominant discourses in a new world order

1

THE BRICS PARADOX[1]

Marko Juutinen and Jyrki Käkönen

Since its inception in 2009, the BRICS group of countries (Brazil, Russia, India and China – joined in 2011 by South Africa) has sought to represent itself as an institution of change and reform, and as a voice of the developing world (Thakur, 2014). One potential interpretation of BRICS is that it is a new initiative of transnational politics, reflecting global power transitions, the possible end of US dominance, as well as the final countdown of the liberal international order. Other institutions of such a new world order would be, for example, the Shanghai Cooperation Organization (SCO) and the Asian Infrastructure Investment Bank (AIIB). This interpretation, however, is contested by scholars who argue that there is little if any evidence to support the view that BRICS is an institution of a different kind of globalization (Bond, 2016).

These different and conflicting interpretations of BRICS represent what we would like to call the BRICS paradox. The concept of paradox refers to a claim that is apparently based on sound reasoning from true premises, but which leads to logically unacceptable conclusions. In this chapter, we identify three paradoxes. First, that because BRICS members are so different, they cannot form a functioning alliance. Second, that because BRICS have demanded changes in international organizations, they constitute a challenge to the current international order. Third, because BRICS has formed new financial institutions, it is functioning as a model or promoter of alternative financial governance. The idea that BRICS represents change or the voice of the global South, at the same time as seeming to be well integrated into the international system as a loose grouping of neoliberal countries, pertains to this paradox.

By presenting and reviewing the three paradoxes, this chapter interprets current debates on BRICS, showing that it appears to be a little bit of everything. As a result, the contribution of this chapter to the ongoing BRICS debates is not a presentation of new data, but interpreting old data and previous debates in new manner. Moreover, using this work as a stepping stone, this chapter seeks to propose ways to better understand BRICS. This it does by proposing structural imperialism and non-Western perspectives as potential ways to understand BRICS without a paradox.

Thus, this chapter argues that perhaps the BRICS paradox is not as much about BRICS as it is about the conflict between different theoretical conceptualizations of BRICS. The classic *mandala* ('circle' in Sanskrit) from the Indian indigenous tradition of foreign policy analysis or *tianxia* ('All under heaven' in Mandarin) system from the Chinese, one may provide more suitable perspectives in which to understand and evaluate its role and nature. These two perspectives would at least fit the context of a post-hegemonic world order and what appears to be the return of the past (Juutinen, 2018; Käkönen, 2020).

Paradox of an unlikely alliance

The first ten years of BRICS' existence have not made it easy to define what BRICS is about. It is hardly a political organization, although it is more than just a forum for talks. Certainly, it is not a security organization, although at the 2015 BRICS summit in Ufa in Russia, Russia tried to bring BRICS and SCO closer to each other. Neither is it an economic cooperation organization or a free trade area. In internal BRICS trade China is an important partner to everyone else but, otherwise, mutual trade within BRICS is still insignificant. BRICS' 11th Summit was held in 2019 in Brasília, the capital city of Brazil. While the association has entered its second decade, it is still questionable whether it has come to stay, or whether its diversity will cause it to disintegrate. It is hardly ever mentioned in Western reports on the state of the world (see for instance, *Global Trends*, 2017; *Global Trends to 2035*, 2017).

What we have learned from the first BRICS decade is that the five members have their own reasons to cooperate and that, as a group, BRICS is able to act in international fora. Many scholars argue that these reasons are not enough for a strong and viable political alliance and might drive the countries apart. For example, Katzenstein (1996) has argued that a strong alliance necessitates common culture, geographical proximity and a similar type of institution: BRICS can boast none of these.

For Russia, BRICS is an important element to balance the encroachment of the transatlantic world on its Western borders. It has brought Russia closer to China. In Russian world politics, BRICS is understood as an alliance by the major non-Western powers against Western hegemony. Therefore, in the Russian imagination the goal of BRICS is to reorganize if not revolutionize the current international order (Novikov and Skriba, 2019: 587, 591).

For China, BRICS is a valuable tool to increase its own political weight to match its economic strength. This is not the only reason why BRICS matters for China. In the classical Chinese imagination, BRICS can be seen as one of the means to return China to the centre of world politics. At the same time, in Chinese foreign policy,

BRICS is hardly the top priority in transforming the international order. It is one element among others, like China-financed AIIB (Asian Infrastructure Investment Bank). According to some scholars, China's main instrument in transforming the world is the Belt and Road Initiative (BRI) (Xi, 2017). Others argue that for China's foreign policy, BRICS is a mechanism to unite all major non-Western powers (Lukin and Xuesong, 2019: 622).

Russia and China are the strongest military powers in BRICS: of these two, only Russia is capable of confronting the United States. According to the traditional Chinese worldview, China's own development is dependent on a stable and peaceful international order. Brazil and South Africa have an interest in BRICS for regional reasons. For both, cooperation with Russia, China and India can support their role as a potential regional leader. At the same time, membership in BRICS gives them a chance to participate in the construction of possible Asia-centric world order.

India is in a more complicated situation: it simply cannot stay outside and leave the gate open for a Chinese hegemony in Asia and maybe even in the future global order. For India, membership in BRICS allows it to keep an eye on China. For BRICS, India's membership makes it hard to become an anti-Western coalition. This is because of India's current close economic, political and cultural relations with the US, its participation in Quad (the Quadrilateral Security Dialogue, which links it with Japan, Australia and the US) and strong commitment to the liberal international order (e.g., Pant, 2016; Juutinen, 2018).

Moreover, while BRICS political economies differ, for example, from the US economy and none are great fans of the Washington Consensus, this does not validate the hypothesis of systemic change or an alternative economic model (e.g., Muhr, 2016; Juutinen, 2019). Indeed, internally the BRICS are very different in terms of their economic structures. Russia is heavily dependent on its oil and gas exports and has a poorly diversified economy. India has a booming services sector but about half of its population survive on small-scale agriculture. There are as many poor Indians as there are Europeans all together, but there are also as many rich Indians as Germans. China, on the other hand, is the most important trading partner of all the major powers of the world and, while many are dependent on China, China is dependent only on a few. Interestingly, China's economic ties are much closer to the European Union and US than to India, for example, or other BRICS countries. Indeed, China's economic and military clout in South Asia intensifies the tension between the two (Pant, 2016).

In the context of integration theories, it is the diversity of BRICS members that makes the group a weak political actor. The diverse interests of its members make it complicated, if not impossible, for BRICS to define a coherent agenda and policy for changing the international order. However, BRICS has survived its childhood and is entering its teenage years. It has been argued that events in Eurasia have always defined world history (Frankopan, 2015; Cunliffe, 2017), and BRICS brings together huge parts of Eurasia. However, Islamic Central Asia, as well as the Islamic world in general, is outside the association. This may be changing, as China's BRI brings Central Asia into close contact with BRICS. Russia's interest in connecting

BRICS and the Eurasian Economic Union (the 2015 treaty which links Belarus, Kazakhstan and Russia) has the same function.

BRICS diversity and the diverse interests of its members are not necessarily symptoms of weakness. The Xiamen summit in 2017 demonstrated how working together was important for BRICS members. Just a few days before the Xiamen summit, the potential conflict between India and China in Doklam on the border with Bhutan threatened the opening of the summit. To ensure the summit could go ahead, India and China found a solution, at least temporarily (Woody, 2018). BRICS and SCO are two of the few institutions where India and China are inclined to work together.

In forcing two of its members to settle their bilateral problems, the Xiamen summit demonstrated that BRICS still had a role. The interest shown by other countries in BRICS tells the same story. The Xiamen summit was organized in the form of BRICS+. China invited Egypt, Guinea, Tajikistan, Thailand and Mexico to participate in the summit. In addition to Egypt and Mexico, Argentina, Indonesia, Iran, Turkey and Nigeria are on the potential new members' list. The next step could be to invite some of them as permanent observers.

In terms of China-India cooperation, another important achievement in Xiamen was the adoption of a mutual stance against terrorism. For the first time, the summit condemned Pakistan-supported terrorist organisations active in Kashmir (BRICS, 2017: Article 48). Here China took a stand against its all-weather friend Pakistan. China did this most likely to construct a peaceful context for advancing the China-Pakistan Economic Corridor (part of BRI), which India sees with a great degree of suspicion, as it passes through the disputed area of Pakistan-administered Kashmir and ends up in the port of Gwadar, suitable not only for cargo but also for military purposes (Pant, 2016: 368, 369). Since then, India's rapprochement with the US and China's deepening ties with Pakistan may have disrupted this Sino-Indian understanding about terrorism, because neither one of the two summits after Xiamen mentioned Pakistan-supported or any other terrorist organization (BRICS, 2018; 2019).

The paradox of BRICS Challenge Theory

BRICS Challenge Theory divides into two main lines of hypothesis: that BRICS poses, first, a challenge to the hierarchy between states in the current system, and, second, that it seeks to challenge the whole liberal international order. Challenging the hierarchy between states is relevant in a state-centric analysis of foreign policies, and particularly for the US and its allies (e.g. Tammen *et al.*, 2000). From an institutionalist perspective, on the other hand, the question of state order is irrelevant, as long as global relations are mostly about rules and norms, and as long as decision making takes place in international organizations between many instead of by one (e.g. Ikenberry, 2001; Acharya, 2016). From an institutionalist perspective, it is relevant to study BRICS in relation to current institutions or norms, rules and international organizations.

Despite diverse national interests, BRICS members have common interests, rendering support for the idea that BRICS is indeed a functioning institution of global politics and a viable alliance between rising powers. BRICS countries share the view that the Western powers and values have an immoderate influence in global governance. This makes BRICS an institution that at least challenges the Western hegemony. Rejecting Western universalism, a common goal for all BRICS members is a multipolar world order, reflecting the diversity of interests. The Xiamen and Johannesburg BRICS summit declarations are clearly in support of the institutions of global governance. It is in BRICS' interests to strengthen the role of the UN, the Security Council, the World Trade Organization (WTO), as well as the G20 in global governance but with a more decisive role for India, Brazil and South Africa in the UN context. BRICS gives support for further globalization, the realization of the Paris Agreement on climate change and is strongly against protectionism (BRICS, 2017; 2018). However, current members China and Russia are not ready to see any other BRICS country as permanent UNSC members (BRICS, 2017; 2018).

Despite such disagreements among BRICS members, it has been able not only to survive the first ten years but also to create new functioning financial institutions. In 2014, BRICS launched the New Development Bank (NDB) and the Contingent Reserve Arrangement (CRA) in response to the US failure to yield its dominance in the global financial institutions. NDB – also referred to as the 'BRICS bank' – is an institution led by developing countries. In practice it endorses the developing world's independence from the still Western-led Bretton Woods system. With the New Development Bank, BRICS has established, in addition to the World Bank and the IMF, its own model for the rest of the developing world, though the aim is not to replace those Western-led institutions. However, it is still open to question how much the NDB represents a new kind of system of global financial governance. In the WTO, on the other hand, three of its members, Brazil, India and China, played a crucial role in upsetting the former balance of power by increasing the influence of the developing world (Hopewell, 2016).

Some scholars maintain that BRICS political economy represents simultaneously rising South-South cooperation as well as a rupture from the Western-centric economic imperialism. Niall Duggan (2015), for example, has argued that BRICS are changing the rules and norms of globalization, with a new agenda of global economic governance. His conclusion was based partly on the BRICS stance towards the Washington Consensus, and partly on the discourse of development in BRICS summit declarations. However, Duggan does not show the existence of an actual agenda. Instead, he just demonstrates existence of a discourse that deviates from the Washington Consensus and, as Mielniczuk (2013) has argued, this could have long-standing effects on the social construction of global governance.

Research into the political economies of the BRICS countries shows that they have not fully absorbed the values and policy prescriptions of the global institutions of economic and financial governance. Specifically, most scholars agree that the BRICS members have a critical approach towards the dominant political-economy paradigms of the Washington Consensus, including a market-oriented regulatory system, fiscal austerity and comprehensive liberalization of trade (Schmalz and Ebenau, 2012; Babb, 2013; Fourcade, 2013). Simultaneously, the BRICS have retained varying measures of direct or indirect state control over markets (Stephen, 2014; Nölke *et al.*, 2015), most notably in China (McNally, 2012; van der Pijl, 2012; Jiang, 2014). Moreover, at the UN, China and Russia have used their veto in the Security Council to support their strategic interests and the fundamental values of national integrity, or both at the same time, for example in the case of Russia's military intervention in Syria (Stuenkel, 2014).

The current US government views the existence of BRICS as a challenge to its hegemony, particularly from two key members, Russia and China, who appear to threaten the Western liberal democratic order. The US National Security Strategy (2017: 25) and National Defense Strategy (2018: 2) declare that great power competition has returned and that the challenger states seek 'to shape a world consistent with their authoritarian model—gaining veto authority over other nations' economic, diplomatic, and security decisions'. BRICS has no common agenda for change. Seeking greater influence in the international organization can be an objective in its own right. It does not necessarily imply an agenda to change the system. Indeed, Sarah Babb (2013) has shown that there is no 'BRICS Consensus' to oppose the Washington Consensus.

In consequence, the scholarly BRICS debate does not render support for the BRICS Challenge Theory in the sense that BRICS is actively promoting a systemic change. It is true that BRICS members have used their position to challenge US agendas in the UN and the WTO but that does not mean that they would not have played by the rules. Disagreeing is fully acceptable. Governance in the UN and WTO today is much less about hierarchy than it was during the unipolar moment after the Cold War. It is more about democratic decision-making among peers, which is much more difficult than managing a hierarchical system. Governance is bound to be more prone to disagreements, shifting alliances and timely negotiations, but that is something that comes with pluralism and evidences the viability of cooperation instead of its demise. The BRICS group underlines its support for global institutions and multilateralism: 'We emphasize the importance of an open and inclusive world economy enabling all countries and peoples to share in the benefits of globalization. We remain firmly committed to a rules-based, transparent, non-discriminatory, open and inclusive multilateral trading system as embodied in the WTO' (BRICS, 2017: Article 32). 'Upholding development and multilateralism', the group notes, 'we are working together for a more just, equitable, fair, democratic and representative international political and economic order' (BRICS, 2017: Article 2).

Therefore, there is, so far, insufficient evidence to agree with the BRICS Challenge Theory that BRICS poses either a challenge to the hierarchy between states in the current system, or that it seeks to challenge the whole system. Hierarchy between states is constantly evolving and, of course, from the perspective of a dominant power wishing to retain its dominance, the rise of new powers is a challenge.

The paradox of alternative institutions

The BRICS policy of development finance is embodied by its two institutions, the New Development Bank (NDB) and the Contingent Reserve Arrangement (CRA) launched in 2016. NDB was set up to mobilize resources for infrastructure and sustainable development projects in BRICS and other emerging and developing countries. CRA, on the other hand, provides a financial safety net for BRICS through the establishment of a currency reserve. These tasks overlap with the work of the World Bank and the IMF.

Since its first summit in 2009, BRICS has demanded reforms in the IMF, especially about voting quotas rather than the organization's development policies. In their demands, moreover, BRICS did not act alone. In fact, BRICS absorbed its reforms agenda from a previous agreement among major global powers that had already been reached in 2008 (under the auspices of the G20 summit). The US Congress, however, did not agree with the reforms, which would have ended US dominance in the institution. Thus, at the Ufa summit in 2015, BRICS leaders declared, '[w]e remain deeply disappointed with the prolonged failure by the United States to ratify the IMF 2010 reform package, which continues to undermine the credibility, legitimacy and effectiveness of the IMF' (BRICS, 2015: Article 19).

Democratization of the international institutions is one of the fundamental values of BRICS. While global institutions of development finance are run arguably on the basis of 'dollar and vote', BRICS institutions are run on 'country and vote' basis. In the NDB, decision-making power is equally divided between the five BRICS member states. Yet, while the NDB is open for all UN members, the country and vote principle is reserved only for BRICS members. According to the founding agreement of the NDB, the voting power of the five original members shall not fall below 55 per cent of total votes, whereas the maximum voting power for any new member state shall not exceed 7 per cent. Thus, the NDB will remain dominated by the BRICS, even if its membership expands. In this regard, it is similar to the IMF and the World Bank, in which the developed countries still retain a disproportionate influence compared to their role in the global economy (NDB, 2014: Articles 5, 6, 8, 11; IMF, 2018).

With an initial authorized capital of $100 billion, the NDB and the CRA (also set at $100 billion) have the financial means to make an impact. For comparison, the capital of the International Bank for Reconstruction and Development (part of the World Bank group) is $230 billion. In the IMF the total amount of special drawing rights in 2015 was about $240 billion, which converts to about $340 billion. Two additional factors contribute to the financial relevance of the NDB and CRA. First, as they are open to new members – for example, Turkey, Indonesia and Mexico have already shown interest in joining – the NDB and CRA have the potential to increase their financial power. Moreover, BRICS countries are better positioned to invest in development finance, as their share of global savings is larger than the combined share of the US, EU and Japan (ORF, 2015). How can BRICS use that financial leverage?

The purpose of the NDB is to channel funding for development and infrastructure projects in emerging and developing countries 'complementing the existing efforts of multilateral and regional financial institutions' (NDB, 2014: Article 1). Rather than a challenger, the NDB is thus complementary to the World Bank and the IMF. The key difference is that BRICS financing is delinked from the policy reforms and conditions that the traditional institutions are known to require. In the Bank's strategy this is clearly stated in the following manner: 'National sovereignty is of paramount importance to NDB in its interactions with member countries. NDB's mandate does not include prescribing policy, regulatory and institutional reforms to borrowing countries' (NDB, 2017: 11).

Moreover, instead of embracing the existing Western ideology of development, the NDB would seem to invite discussions and debates on the nature of development. This is an important inference, because it implies that the NDB may seek to distance itself from the paradigms of development that still prevail in the predominant international financial institutions. The NDB's General Strategy states: 'The bank will constructively engage the international community as an independent voice on development trends and practices. As a new institution, NDB has much to learn from the wealth of experience of multilateral and bilateral development institutions, as well as civil society and academic organizations' (NDB, 2017: 11).

The NDB could in this manner be represented as an alternative institution to the Washington-based institutions and to the neoliberal globalization policy promoted by them. However, some recent NDB lending suggests that this might actually not be the case. In 2018 the NDB granted a $200 million loan to Durban port in South Africa to increase its container capacity. Critics argued that the port was subject to broad public opposition, as well as being mismanaged and that its expansion would only increase these problems, while adding to South Africa's already high debt burden. The Durban loan, it has been suggested, 'makes a mockery' of claims that 'BRICS bloc acts differently from arrogant Washington bankers' (D'Sa and Bond, 2018).

The Contingent Reserve Arrangement (CRA), on the other hand, is organically linked to the IMF and its reform policies. The objective of the CRA is to provide a safety net against potential shocks in global financial markets and the possible resulting balance of payment problem. But if and when any BRICS country or other (future) member of the CRA has to rely on its lending, and when it needs more money than 30 per cent of its borrowing quota, it must first seek structural adjustment loans from the IMF before it can receive more support from the CRA. Apparently, the CRA recognizes the political reforms of Washington Consensus as well as the supremacy of IMF.

It is thus possible to think that the CRA demonstrates BRICS' approval of the Washington-based ideology of economic development, which led the 'lost decade' in Latin America in 1980s – denoting loss of economic and social development caused by privatization, dismantling of social infrastructure and soaring unemployment (see Stiglitz, 2002; Bond, 2016, among others) – and is currently causing the same kind of distress in some countries in southern Europe.

From the perspective of BRICS as a challenger to the Washington Consensus, CRA linkage to IMF policy reforms would pose an analytical dilemma: the apparent contradiction between rejecting conditional development finance on one hand and committing themselves to structural adjustments on the other. A possible solution to this dilemma comes from the understanding of BRICS' role in development finance as an additional provider instead of a challenger. Their rejection of conditionality does not emanate from the conviction that the Washington Consensus is wrong but from a conviction that it is not the only truth or a comprehensive perspective on development. BRICS may thus be willing to continue to cooperate with the IMF, even by subjecting themselves to structural adjustments, while simultaneously constructing development without the same conditions.

BRICS finance initiatives do not appear to provide an alternative to the imperialist or liberal international order, neither are they a striking example of South–South cooperation in the Bandung spirit by connecting the South against international structures benefitting the North. In the next section we seek an alternative theoretical perspective to challenge these interpretations.

BRICS without a paradox

As discussed above, the different representations and understandings of BRICS are debatable or even paradoxical. In this final section we consider the possibility of BRICS without a paradox. To estimate whether and how BRICS possibly change the international order and system we rely first on the theory of structural imperialism proposed by Johan Galtung (1971) and then on perspectives drawn from ancient traditions of international relations from the two ancient BRICS nations: China and India.

According to Galtung's theory, the international system consists of centres and peripheries, but there can also be semi-peripheries in between. The system is vertically organised and hierarchical, as well as unequal. The centres have the power over their peripheries and peripheries are dependent on their centres. This is a feudal system, where the centres are connected to and interacting with each other as well as vertically with their peripheries, but the peripheries are horizontally fragmented, and the structure of the system prevents them cooperating (Figure 1.1).

Peripheries basically relate vertically with the centre or via the semi-periphery. Horizontal interaction is mostly missing, or it is prevented even between the peripheries of the same centre. Also, the roles and activities of the peripheries are marginalized within multilateral international institutions, which are dominated by the centres. In addition to the basic structure of the system, Galtung identifies five different forms of imperialism: economic, political, military, communication and cultural. Domination of the centres can be just one-dimensional, or two or more forms can overlap.

Resisting or changing the system requires horizontal cooperation within the periphery. For Galtung, horizontal interaction is the strategy for 'de-feudalization' of the international system. However, the reduction of vertical interaction is also

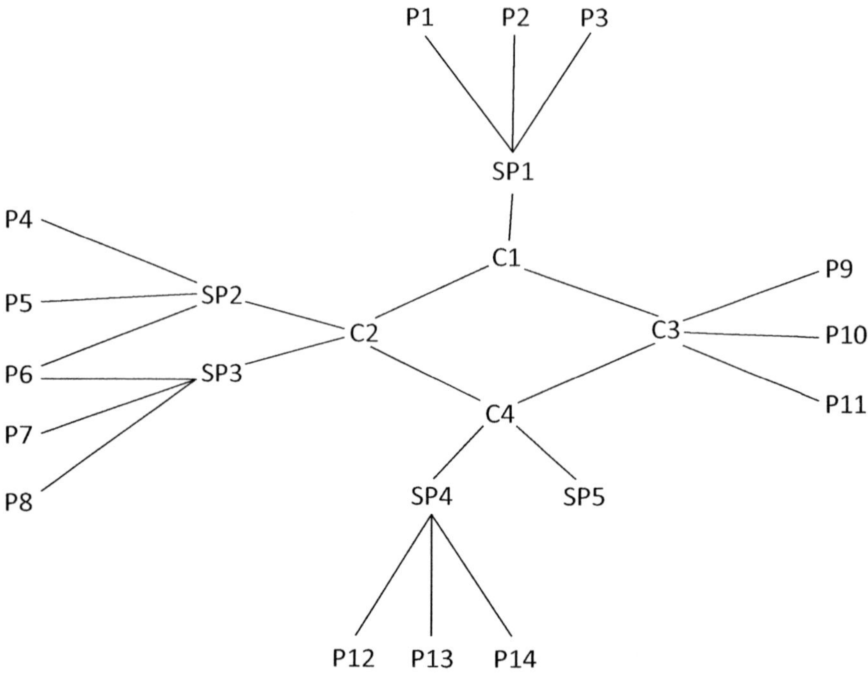

FIGURE 1.1 A hypothetical feudal international system

needed. Peripheral countries should also establish viable international organizations of their own for global governance. Increasing horizontal interaction should further lead to increasing self-reliance in the periphery, to make the periphery less dependent on the centre. Finally, the system will only change when the power of the periphery is brought closer to that of the centre (Galtung, 1971).

While understanding BRICS in this context as a counter strategy to structural imperialism and its role in changing the international order, it is possible to draw a few conclusions. BRICS connects one former centre state and four semi-peripheries, if not peripheral states. As a grouping it reduces fragmentation within the system and provides possibilities for some non-centre states to have a voice in the system. BRICS as such is an institution of the periphery for global governance and it has created two more institutions of the periphery: the NDB and the CRA. Already this has given more options or created new centres for peripheries to cooperate with.

It could be argued that, to some extent, BRICS has already changed the feudal system to make it a little more equal and democratic. However, the interaction of the periphery with the BRICS members and its institutions creates new relations of dependence, although that might reduce the dependence on traditional centres. BRICS cooperation has also increased the role of some peripheral or semi-peripheral states in the multilateral institutions of global governance, e.g. G20, but this has not changed the fundamental orientation of the institutions. Some of the BRICS countries have also come closer to the traditional centres. And it is difficult to argue that China, India or Russia function as a semi-periphery for either the US or the EU.

In the BRICS context it is also possible to say that China and India have largely resisted the Western colonization of mind and culture, and that indigenous ideas could form the basis of a new theorization of social and international systems. While BRICS may seem to present a paradox for Western-centric theories of International Relations, it may appear to be a viable and rational international institution and actor in a non-Western theoretical context. Therefore, we argue that the role of BRICS can be analysed in the context of two indigenous theories of *tianxia* and *mandala*.

The roots of *tianxia* go back more than 2,000 years in Chinese history and Confucian social philosophy. There are several interpretations of *tianxia* and our intention is not to discuss these or to present a coherent version of it. For us it is enough to pick up some characteristics from the theory and for the discussion around it to demonstrate how this theory might explain why membership of BRICS is a rational choice for China, and it is a viable international organization.

The *tianxia* concept refers to a China-centric international system and helps to explain how China interacts with the world around it. It can be visualized as a series of concentric circles in which China forms the centre of the system. Next is the circle of tributary states that could adapt to Chinese civilization. The outer circle is the barbaric world that threatens the Chinese civilization (Ren, 2010: 103, 106–7; Callahan, 2008: 755). This system aimed to establish peace with China's immediate neighbourhood and opened the gates for China's peaceful expansion. *Tianxia* is also a system that can transform an enemy into a friend (Callahan, 2008: 752, 756). Chinese economic prosperity formed the base of the system, which would be the incentive for other countries to interact with China. In Chinese understanding, China's moral and cultural superiority legitimized the system (Kallio, 2012, 14). Belonging to the system gave access to the Chinese markets but the ultimate pre-condition was to recognize Chinese superiority (Zhang, 2009: 550). This gave China the power to define the rules and norms of the system and, especially, to dictate how others should interact with it (Wang, 2012: 130). However, members were autonomous actors within the system with their own internal and external policies (Ren, 2010: 104).

Applying *tianxia* theory to BRICS cooperation, China's increasing economic and partly also military power are the factors that draw others into closer relations with China. It may not be entirely feasible to talk about China's superiority, but it is hard to deny that China is a key actor within BRICS. In joining BRICS, members had to accept their differences. China is also the core actor in unification against the West and Western values and in the NDB there is also a chance to create new rules for international cooperation. The idea that within a common system an enemy might become a friend could explain how India and China could cooperate within an institution like BRICS, in spite of conflicting interests.

Mandala theory has roots in over 2,500 years of Hindu philosophy. As a systematic theory it was formulated by Kautilya in his *Arthasastra* (loosely translated from Sanskrit as 'The Science of Politics'), in the third century BC. *Mandala* theory also understands the political system as a series of concentric circles. In the centre there is a hypothetical conqueror whose intention is to become a universal power while the circle around conqueror consists of its natural enemies. The next circle consists of the enemies of the states in the first circle and therefore potential allies of the conqueror. However, geography is not the only factor that defines enmity and amity. The relations between the states within the system are also defined by the balance of power and interests of the states (Rangarajan, 1992: 506–8; Gautam, 2013: 99–100; Mishra, 2016: 79).

In addition to friends and foes, a middle state and a neutral state belong to the system. A middle state is the neighbour of the conqueror and its enemy. The neutral state is the strongest state in the system (Rangarajan, 1992: 517; Gautam, 2013: 55; Mishra, 2016: 91). All alliances have to serve the interests of the conqueror and increase its power in relation to its potential enemy (Rangarajan, 1992: 510; Kangle, 2014: 255). In general, alliances are a means to increase the welfare and power of the state (Mishra, 2016: 87). When the conqueror is not strong enough to become a universal power, it has to prevent anybody else becoming a universal power (Gautam, 2013: 52, 55).

In the context of *mandala* theory, it is possible to have China and India as challengers for the position of a universal power. Russia is a middle state and the US the neutral one. In this situation, cooperation with China in BRICS is a rational choice for India. It increases India's potential power while simultaneously preventing China's rise to become a universal power in Asia. Tension with China is not a factor that would make cooperation with China impossible. Simultaneously, partnership with the US as a neutral power serves the same purpose.

Conclusion

This chapter has discussed BRICS as a paradox. In doing this, we have discussed how different interpretations of BRICS seem indeed either debatable or paradoxical and, thus, that attempts to define the nature of the BRICS are equally as difficult as those to define the future world order. These challenges notwithstanding, we have also sought to present BRICS in more theoretical light based on *tianxia, mandala* and structural imperialism theories. We suggest that these alternative avenues might offer new insights into the geopolitics of BRICS. More broadly, this implies that perspectives from other civilizations and cultures on international affairs can increase our understanding of current politics in an increasingly globalized world.

The idea of BRICS as a challenge to the world order may be arising from the US fear of losing its dominant position. Indeed, in current world affairs it is not the authoritarian states of Russia and China but the world's leading democracy that is not respecting the rules of international institutions. The US president Donald Trump has tweeted that 'trade wars are good, and easy to win' (Rushe and Haas, 2018). Trump is paralysing the WTO dispute settlement system (by not appointing new members to the Appellate Body) and has also withdrawn the US from the Paris Agreement on climate change mitigation. In consequence, it appears the challenge and threat is coming from the West rather than from 'the Rest'. The undermining of global governance in a shift from international cooperation to great power competition is being promoted by the current US presidency rather than by any member of BRICS.

In addition, in terms of the global economy, BRICS does not seem to be proposing alternative economic or developmental policies, even if they would like to have a greater share of the existing economic pie. For example, the investment profiles of BRICS members (individually) do not really differ from the extractive profiles of developed countries. While the BRICS investors have not demanded policy reforms, they have maintained a good track record on profits. According to some scholars, BRICS is as much about resource extraction, environmental degradation and capitalist power asymmetries as any developed country and more than any of the Northern countries (see for instance Moyo, 2012; Carmody, 2013; Bond, 2016). In a similar manner, some of the conflicts at the WTO result not only from the developed countries requiring enhanced patent protection for their big pharmaceutical companies, but also from the fact that higher regulations that the developed countries seek simultaneously imply higher costs, particularly for the developing countries: even the regulatory objective in itself would be approvable (like environmental rules or labour standards) (e.g., Hopewell, 2016; Juutinen and Käkönen, 2016).

It seems to be safe to conclude that BRICS at least complements existing international structures. But it also might represent a new kind of system in global governance, especially in the form of the NDB, by challenging the hegemony of the West. Further, there is a chance that BRICS symbolizes the fading out of the Western-centric order and the dawn of the non-Western-centric order. However, there is not enough evidence, yet, to say what a possible new order might look like. Or perhaps the classic *tianxia* or *mandala* approach to political systems gives a hint about the future. While BRICS promotes a more pluralist, multi-polar international order, it does not yet have the status of a hegemonic institution as it lacks the authority to set norms and rules of global governance. Nevertheless, it may shift some power from the minority to the majority of the world.

Finally, it appears that BRICS is one of those initiatives that can maintain and consolidate cooperation even in heavily stressed relationships. Paradoxically enough, in the context of significant challenges to globalization itself, BRICS may thus offer dearly needed lessons about leadership and governance. To understand these lessons, if any, we, too, may need to replenish our theoretical toolboxes.

Note

1 Minor parts of the present chapter derive from two earlier publications: Juutinen (2019) and Käkönen (2018), to which texts the authors are the copyright holders.

References

Acharya, A. (2016) The future of global governance: fragmentation may be inevitable and creative. *Global Governance*, 22: 453–460.

Babb, S. (2013) The Washington Consensus as transnational policy paradigm: Its origins, trajectory and likely successor. *Review of International Political Economy*, 20(2): 268–297.

Bond, P. (2016) BRICS banking and the debate over sub-imperialism. *Third World Quarterly*, 37(4): 611–629.

BRICS (2015) *Ufa Declaration and Action Plan*. 7th BRICS Summit. July 8–9, Ufa, Russia. Available at www.brics.utoronto.ca/docs/150709-ufa-declaration_en.html.

BRICS (2017) *Xiamen Declaration and Action Plan*. 9th BRICS Summit. September 3–5, Xiamen, China. Available at www.brics.utoronto.ca/docs/170904-xiamen.html.

BRICS (2018) *Johannesburg Declaration and Action Plan*. 10th BRICS Summit. July 25–27, Johannesburg, South Africa. Available at www.brics.utoronto.ca/docs/180726-johannesburg.html.

BRICS (2019) *Brasilia Declaration*. 11th BRICS Summit, November 14, Brasilia, Brazil. Available at www.brics.utoronto.ca/docs/191114-brasilia.html.

Callahan, W. (2008) Chinese visions of world order: post-hegemonic or new hegemony. *International Studies Review*, 10: 749–761.

Carmody, P. (2013) *The Rise of the BRICS in Africa. The Geopolitics of South-South Relations*. London: Zed Books.

Cunliffe, B. (2017) *By Steppe, Desert, and Ocean: The Birth of Eurasia*. Oxford: Oxford University Press.

D'Sa, D. and Bond, P. (2018) Why the Durban harbour project will be horrible blunder. IOL. 10 June. Available at www.iol.co.za/dailynews/opinion/features/why-the-durban-harbour-project-will-be-horrible-blunder-15376796

Duggan, N. (2015) BRICS and the evolution of a new agenda within global governance, pp. 11–25 in M. Rewizorski (ed.) *The European Union and the BRICS. Complex Relations in the Era of Global Governance*. Heidelberg: Springer.

Frankopan, P. (2015) *The Silk Roads. A New History of the World*. London: Bloomsbury.

Fourcade, M. (2013) The material and symbolic construction of the BRICs: Reflections inspired by the RIPE Special Issue. *Review of International Political Economy*, 20(2): 256–267.

Galtung, J. (1971) Structural theory of imperialism. *Journal of Peace Research*, 8(2): 81–117.

Gautam, P. K. (2013) *One Hundred Years of Kautilya's Arthasastra*. IDSA Monograph Series No. 20. New Delhi: Institute of Defense Studies and Analysis.

Global Trends: Paradox of Progress (2017) National Intelligence Council. Washington. Available at www.dni.gov/nic/globaltrends

Global Trends to 2035: Geo-Politics and International Power (2017) Brussels: European Parliamentary Research Service. Available at https://espas.secure.europarl.europa.eu/orbis/sites/default/files/generated/document/en/EPRS_STU%282017%29603263_EN.pdf

Hopewell, K. (2016) *Breaking the WTO: How Emerging Powers Disrupted the Neoliberal Project*. Stanford: Stanford University Press.

Ikenberry, J. G. (2001) *After Victory: Institutions, Strategic Restraint, and the Rebuilding of Order after Major Wars*. Princeton: Princeton University Press.

IMF (2018) IMF members' quotas and voting power, and IMF Board of Governors. Washington: International Monetary Fund. Available at www.imf.org/external/np/sec/memdir/members.aspx.

Jiang, Y. (2014) Vulgarisation of Keynesianism in China's response to the global financial crisis. *Review of International Political Economy*, 22(2): 360–390.

Juutinen, M. (2018) Kautilyan foreign policy analysis: Sino-Indian dynamics in South Asia and the Indian Ocean region. *Journal of the Indian Ocean Region*, 14(2): 206–226.

Juutinen, M. (2019) Leadership for a pluralistic order? Assessing BRICS and development finance, pp. 301–320 in A. Heikkinen, A. Kangas, J. Kujala, H. Laihonen, A. Lönnqvist and J. Bethwaite (eds.) *Leading Change in a Complex World: Transdisciplinary Perspectives.* Tampere: Tampere University Press.

Juutinen, M. and Käkönen, J. (2016) *Battle for Globalisations? BRICS and US Mega-Regional Trade Agreements in a Changing World Order.* New Delhi: Observer Research Foundation.

Käkönen, J. (2018) The first decennia of BRICS. Pluralist World Order blog, March 15. Available at https://blogs.uta.fi/pluralistworldorder/project/

Käkönen, J. (2020) Tracking the past in the Chinese and Indian regional cooperation initiatives, pp. 31–51 in É. Féron, M. Juutinen, J. Käkönen and K. Maïche (eds.) *Shedding Light on a Changing International Order: Theoretical and Empirical Challenges.* Tampere: TAPRI Studies in Peace and Conflict Research, No. 104.

Kallio, J. (2012) *Watching a dragon's egg hatch. The making of Sinocentric world.* FIIA Working Paper 74. Helsinki: Finnish Institute of International Affairs. April. Available at www.fiia.fi/en/publication/watching-a-dragons-egg-hatch

Kangle, R. P. (2014) *The Kautilya Arthasastra Part III.* New Delhi: Motilal Banarsidass.

Katzenstein, P. (1996) Regionalism in comparative perspective. *Cooperation and Conflict*, 31(2): 123–159.

Lukin, A. and Xuesong, F. (2019) What is BRICS for China? *Strategic Analysis*, 43(6): 620–631.

McNally, C. (2012) Sino-capitalism: China's re-emergence and the international political economy. *World Politics*, 64(4): 741–776.

Mielniczuk, F. (2013) BRICS in the contemporary world: changing identities, converging interests. *Third World Quarterly*, 34(6): 1075–1090.

Mishra, M. (2016) Kautilya's Arthasastra: restoring its rightful place in the field of international relations. *Journal of Defence Studies*, 10(2): 77–109.

Moyo, D. (2012) *Winner Take All. China's Race for Resources and What it Means for Us.* London: Penguin.

Muhr, T. (2016) Beyond 'BRICS': ten theses on South–South cooperation in the twenty-first century. *Third World Quarterly*, 37(4): 630–648.

National Security Strategy (2017) *National Security Strategy of the United States of America.* Washington, DC: The White House. Available at www.whitehouse.gov/wp-content/uploads/2017/12/NSS-Final-12-18-2017-0905.pdf.

National Defense Strategy (2018) *Summary of National Defense Strategy of the United States of America.* Washington, DC: Department of Defense. Available at https://dod.defense.gov/Portals/1/Documents/pubs/2018-National-Defense-Strategy-Summary.pdf.

NDB (2014) Agreement on the New Development Bank. Available at www.ndb.int/wp-content/themes/ndb/pdf/Agreement-on-the-New-Development-Bank.pdf

NDB (2017) *NDB's General Strategy 2017–2021.* New Development Bank. Available at, www.ndb.int/wp-content/uploads/2017/07/NDB-Strategy-Final.pdf

Novikov, D. and Skriba, A. (2019) The evolution of Russian strategy towards BRICS. *Strategic Analysis*, 43(6): 585–596.

Nölke, A., ten Brink, T., Simone, C. and May, C. (2015) Domestic structures, foreign economic policies and global economic order: implications from the rise of large emerging economies. *European Journal of International Relations*, 21(3): 538–567.

ORF (2015) The New Development Bank: identifying strategic and operational priorities, *ORF Policy Brief 17.* New Delhi: Observer Research Foundation, August.

Pant, H.V. (2016) Rising China in India's vicinity: a rivalry takes shape in Asia. *Cambridge Review of International Affairs*, 29(2): 364–381.

Rangarajan, L. N. (ed.) (1992) *Kautilya: The Arthasastra*. New Delhi: Penguin.

Ren, X. (2010) Traditional Chinese theory and praxis of foreign policy. A re-assessment, pp. 102–116 in Y. Zhang (ed.) *China and International Relations. The Chinese View and the Contribution of Wang Kungwu*. New York: Routledge.

Rushe, D. and Haas, B. (2018) Trump trade tariffs: Europe threatens US bikes, bourbon and blue jeans. *The Guardian*, 3 February.

Schmalz, S. and Ebenau, M. (2012) After neoliberalism? Brazil, India, and China in the global economic crisis. *Globalizations*, 9(4): 487–501.

Stephen, M. D. (2014) Rising powers, global capitalism and liberal global governance: a historical materialist account of the BRICs challenge, *European Journal of International Relations*, 20(4): 912–938.

Stiglitz, J. (2002) *Globalization and its Discontents*. New York: Norton & Company.

Stuenkel, O. (2014) The BRICS and the future of R2P. Was Syria or Libya the exception? *Global Responsibility to Protect*, 6: 3–28.

Tammen, R., Kugler, J., Lemke, D., Stam I., Allen C. Alsharabati, C., Abdollahin, M., Elfrid, B. and Organski, A. F. K. (2000) *Power Transition Strategies for the 21st Century*. Washington: CQ Press.

Thakur, R. (2014) How representative are BRICS? *Third World Quarterly*, 35(10): 1791–1808.

Van der Pijl, K. (2012) Is the East still red? The contender state and class struggles in China. *Globalizations*, 9(4): 503–516.

Wang, Y. (2012) Managing regional hegemony in historical Asia: the case of early Ming China. *The Chinese Journal of International Politics*, 5: 129–153.

Woody, C. (2018) Tensions are still simmering a year after the world's two biggest countries almost clashed over a border at the top of the world. *Business Insider*, August 22.

Xi, J. (2017) *Secure a Decisive Victory in Building a Moderately Prosperous Society in All Respects and Strive for the Great Success of Socialism with Chinese Characteristics for a New Era*. Report at the 19th National Congress of the Communist Party of China, October 18.

Zhang, F. (2009) Rethinking the tribute system: broadening the conceptual history of historical East Asian politics. *Chinese Journal of International Politics*, 5: 3–36.

2
SHIFTING PARADIGMS IN COMMUNICATION RESEARCH

Muniz Sodré, Raquel Paiva, Kaarle Nordenstreng and Leonardo Custódio

This chapter – an essay based on perspectives raised by *The Science of the Commons* (Sodré, 2019) – examines the impact of technological changes in communication on paradigms in communication research, in particular issues raised for media studies with respect to cultural expression and creative labour. In this analysis the topic of mediatization becomes central, mainly in the essential connections between social institutions and media technology, wherein subjectivity is prone to being influenced by cultural codifications performed by media devices. We suggest that mediatization is not a metaphor for a material totality, but rather a concept related to the dynamics of qualitative shifts in social patterns through the interconnection of electronic technology and human life.

The new system of social interaction created by the Internet and social networks has been metaphorically linked to the human limbic system, that is, to the medial brain surface, which accounts for behaviour, learning, memory and motivation. In other words, media technology is no longer confined to words and print, but now includes emotions and feelings in a new kind of social inter-media environment. As for the academic field of communication, it is precisely this conception of an eco-logically integrated structure that reveals profound shifts in the current paradigms.

Decades ago, a large part of post-modernist criticism was based on the hypothesis that the emerging media, both written and audiovisual, was equivalent to a *monopoly of speech*, that is, to the impossibility of a strong, symbolic response by the receiver. Thus, there was no possible response to the unilateral nature of the messages. This could be understood as the construction of a system of economic monopoly by corporate media. This system was always present as a multifaceted reality, heavily scrutinized, in fact, by analysts from various theoretical tendencies, from economics to sociology. In reality, it was not only the socio–economic, though basically cultural, aspect of the monopoly by which the decision-making power over the discourse was supported by the centres of the relation between speaker and listener, or the broadcaster; not the discourse of power, but the power of the monopolistic discourse. The communication paradigm was supported by analogue and linear information platforms, which allowed the distance between broadcaster and receiver to shine through.

The Internet era, however, seemed to show initially that interactivity provided a solution to this problem; the connection between users of the electronic network would break the monopoly of speech. The media were becoming intercommunicative thanks to unmediated feedback. The hypothesis of an electronic democracy arose from this technical possibility of instantaneous, global communication, supposedly capable of introducing difference into a dialogic game.

In the second decade of the twenty-first century, the situation has been shown to be far more complex. In the expanding environment of 'mediatization' (the articulation of media with social organizations and institutions), the electronic network has introduced a new paradigm to reflect a structure of invisible interconnection, in which everything is simultaneously both connection and gateway. One can now electronically respond to a receiver, just as on a telephone. Digital social networks have amplified this circuit of discursive exchange; the circulation of speech seems to have broken the communicative monopoly. There is, however, an enormous difference between the technical aspect of the tool and the cultural *device* of communication. As a device, the network is configured as a technological matrix capable of *increasing* the physical space-time, amplifying space and shortening time.

Thus, there is no symbolic response from the user to the centralized, electronic network, where the monopoly has culturally shifted, or rather, where it has transferred itself from the differentiated means of communication to the network. It is true that the network, besides its technical-financial aspect, includes a symbolic dimension which may be associated with a 'technology of the spirit', that is, a normative technology of attitudes and behaviours. 'Symbolic' response refers to an autonomous behaviour by the user in relation to the data it seeks to access on the network. However, the messages circulating among individualized users on social networks have not indicated any break with the unidirectional nature of broadcasting, or rather, they do not react dialogically (with the exception of the short-circuit aggressiveness of the messages), which gives primacy to the merely quantitative circulation within the electronic system. In other words, the networks do not constitute a public sphere of dialogue (where thesis, antithesis and synthesis exist dialectically), but rather a mere circulating space for messages.

At the same time, from the economic and organizational point of view, the technology for processing and storing data – the name of the product which sustains the brave, new industry of this century – strides in the direction of private oligopolies, so-called *Big Tech*, expressed in corporate logos such as Google, Amazon, Facebook, Microsoft and IBM, administrators of big data, that is, of the great masses of data which manipulate complex algorithms of artificial intelligence.

If, in traditional media, manipulation consisted of the unilateral repetition of messages – which was always the basic resource of ideological, political and religious propaganda – now it consists of the combination of digital patterns which feeds artificial intelligence. The adequate model of the phenomenon is no longer that which is oriented toward the individual target of a process of persuasion, but towards institutions and organizations in which the bases of social functioning are situated. This is no simple monopoly of speech, but rather a true oligopoly, both economic and cultural, of the variables which compose the existence of a subject in their everyday life.

The liberal ideas of free trade thus give way to the power of competitive capitalism supported by the free market, in which the state has presented itself as the guardian of the new rules without relinquishing the old, structural advantages, such as its symbolic power and military force. In front of the executive backdrop, hollow formulas are repeated which hybridize state policy, demagoguery and advertising. Thus, in the face of the growing dominion of social life by economy (finance) and technology, it is pertinent to investigate whether politics in the broad sense, that is, as the event essential to human plurality in communities, together with journalism, is still demonstrably an institutional path open to civil society.

Journalistic liberalism has always been a partner along this path, in that it mimicked, as an ideological guideline, the balance of power instituted by a democratic system of government. Hence the pertinence of speculating, together with politics, on the possibility of an independent journalistic practice – understood as: independence as a reasonable balance between the economic corporation and the position of social class – capable of intervening with a mediating function relevant to the public agenda and with socio-political effects. This function is institutional, a point midway between the central aspects of civil society and the organizational aspects of corporate media.

Mediation performs the symbolic transit, or the 'communication' of property from one element to another, by means of a third party, which is a means of articulating two diverse elements. Thus, there exists an implicit dualism in the idea of mediation, reinforced by the notion which results from 'intermediation', or rather, from the approximation, by means of a mediator, between speaker and listener. In the public space, this intermediary may consist of 'small groups' (opinion leaders) and gatekeepers (informational filters). The traditional press, a hybrid entity of productive organization and an institution that cherishes civil freedom of expression, has been sociologically characterized as a 'gatekeeper' – in practice, an intermediary between the citizen and the public sphere.

It is possible, however, that this intermediation has been affected by the decomposition of democratic politics occurring simultaneously with the emergence of new social forms and institutional embryos. In fact, the prestige of the written press stems from a mediation politically compromised by eighteenth-century liberalism, oriented toward the question of the *limits* of the state. The press was proposed to uncover and combat the secrets of state power. On the other hand, it is the cultural heritage of the Enlightenment, which contributed much to the renovation of the standards of living through the defence of rational discourse and scientific investigation.

Since the beginnings of European republicanism, it has fallen to the press to ensure the representation in citizens' words of their personal thoughts, thus guaranteeing a good, namely the civil liberty of publicly expressing or manifesting oneself. In the second half of the nineteenth century, journalism was fundamental to perfecting the liberal conditions of discussion and persuasion, opening the way to a democracy of opinions in a public space consistent with the Industrial Revolution and political and economic liberalism. Journalism was a republican entity.

Within this scope, it would be possible to conceive of journalism as a greater political project than the 'journal' in itself: journalism should go beyond the mere objective reporting of events (the model in which the press 'reports' and the reader consumes) to become a means of education and public debate. Favouring direct dialogue between citizens and journalists, journalistic activity, more than 'reporting', would have at its core the promotion of a public 'conversation'. For example, in covering a political or economic crisis, journalism could go beyond detailed newscasts – supposedly capable of presenting a general radiograph of the occurrence – and become a civil dialogue which envisions, in the interpretation of the fact in its totality, the virtual outcome of the crisis. This is a virtuality in which the dogmas of the 'sovereignty of the people', which underlie the modern idea of the nation, increase.

This function, which is the intrinsic virtue of the press, ethically underpins the implicit pact of communication in the relationship between the means of information and its receiving community. Whether in written or electronic journalism, journalists' duty to their reader-public (therefore, their ethical commitment) would be to tell the truth, recognized as such by common sense provided that the statement is consistent with fact.

The virtue in this public regime of the expression of truth stems from the precept of civil liberties instituted by the Declaration of the Rights of the Man and of the Citizen, but also results from the definition of and commitment to the liberals of the Enlightenment, to whom the only liberty that could not be suspended was that of the press, as it is an effective precondition for all others. It was thus that the free press could be recognized as a work of the modern, objective spirit and, in this way, could constitute an ethical-political backdrop which would make the phenomenon of sensationalist journalism scandalous to the liberal conscience in any part of the world, or would make the distortion or covering up of truth reprehensible to the moral conscience of a journalist.

The dissemination of the dogmas of the 'sovereignty of the people' demanded the free passage of ideas, which generated the concept of public space. Strengthened in Europe throughout the eighteenth and nineteenth centuries as a place for the manifestation of the 'general will' and not of 'private desires', public space, supposedly the natural place to express public opinion, was, therefore, always simultaneously political and cultural, a combination of politics and the arts (in the broadest sense, not only of literature and words). The connection between parliament and arts was quite familiar to eighteenth-century intellectuals.

To the political institution, what was very important, if not essential, as John Dewey stated, was the improvement of the methods and conditions of debate, discussion and persuasion. That for him was 'the problem of the public' (Dewey, 1927). Or rather, without a particular rhetoric, conditioned to a specific culture and, thus, capable of expressing the language of the masses in a public space, pure reason would simply be another instrument of domination. Behind this rhetoric is found the education system. But the 'rhetoric in itself' – or rather, pure discursive technique, detached from cultural and political creativity, therefore, from civic activism – was already the embryo of the industries of cultural diffusion, the cultural industry, together with the public at large.

The cultural industry creates another reality for informational diffusion and allows for the hypothesis that liberal discussion on the civil right to freedom of expression may not entirely coincide with the functioning of the press, which is classically linked to the liberal principle of parliamentarianism as a 'government for publicity and discussion', but which is today inseparable from the informational system as a whole, governed by the same logic of the circulatory speed of the markets, to that which is called 'real time'.

Within this system, the very concept of 'occurrence' may depend more on an algorithmic model than on symbolic negotiations between social actors who traditionally compete in the game of language or the 'agenda' of the newsworthy. It is possible to formulate a hypothesis of an essential differential between 'publication' (the mere technical registration of occurrences, whether in print or digitally) and 'publicization', understood as the communication of the fact of a 'real public', therefore, a group which is live and interactively active in that which is related to questions pertinent to the commons of citizenship.

A new juncture

At this new historical juncture, hegemonic communication has imposed itself for decades as the code of the new social order. To the discourse and practices behind the generalized attack on the social state and behind the enthronement of the new socio-economic order inherent in financialization, the codification of speech and consciences immersed in the range of devices and practices pertinent to the new way of the government of people is indispensable.

Other terminology in the discussion of this topic consists of referring to the practical normativity which accompanies the neoliberal renovation of classical capitalism. Whether codification or new social rationality, however, there is no longer any doubt that therein is found the core of a modernization focused on the market as the 'mouth of the world', that is, as the principal organizer of the social totality, and centred equally on the degradation of the institutions inspired by ancient humanist virtues.

It is politically imperative, however, to rid this theoretical diagnosis of the imposition of the communicational code from any apocalyptic perspective. It is worthwhile for the critical eye to note that, in the commitment of the hegemony to the part of this code – 'mouth of the market as the world', in its turn – affords entry to that which has been called the 'counter-hegemonic' struggle or to that which could also be designated as social counter-movements. Here communication approximates the Greek concept of *pharmakon*, which is paradoxically understood as either the 'venom' or the 'cure'. Thus, by changing the spaces open to communications technology, it might be possible to co-ordinate them with novel counter-movements related to society and culture. Communication would then in principle be separation and bridge.

This is admissible when considering that the academic field of communication is much affected by the socio-cultural context in which it is developed, as verified in the concepts disseminated by the American sociology of communication. From this springs the incipient practical and theoretical preoccupation with the communicational question, in that the circulation of information is indispensable in the urban space ruled by the market and by representative democracy.

An intellectual base for this approach was the Chicago School of Sociology from the 1910s with American philosophers such as William James, John Dewey, George Mead and Charles Sanders Peirce, but also that of European sociologists such as Gabriel Tarde and Georg Simmel, who proposed social theories distinct from the Durkheimian, Weberian and Marxian perspectives.

The Chicago School became a famed centre of empirical and micro-sociological (analysis of particular or local situations) study on the phenomena of communication, privileging the themes of 'human community', of the city as a 'social laboratory', and opening itself methodologically to disciplinary plurality in the field of social science. Max Weber, however, was not only another father of German sociology but also a particularly influential promotor of communication studies: as co-founder of the German Sociological Association he presented in its first congress in 1910 a comprehensive programme for the 'scientific study of the press' whereby newspapers were understood as something more than 'simply capitalist business with the desire for profit, but also political organizations which functioned as political clubs' (Weber, 1979).

In practical terms, communication was an industrial reality already established by a formidable technological apparatus sustained by the market. In the United States, since the post–World War II era, this apparatus has been described as 'mass communication', which, probably due as much to the influence of Nazi propaganda as that of American mobilization propaganda during the conflict, suggested that the 'masses' were driven by the competent rhetoric of the broadcasters. The knowledge which was truly desired was that of the media's discursive power over the population. In truth, since the first decade of the twentieth century, the questions to which scholars sought to respond regarding communicational phenomena originated in private media corporations such as journals, marketing agencies, strategic planners and consumer research institutes. Demand for communication knowledge was always prioritized by the market.

The idea of transmission and persuasion, established in the technical devices enabling social discourse to flow, consequently received by the broad and hetero-geneous public, is initially responsible for the 'effects paradigm' in the academic approach to communication. The expression 'functional communication' is shown to be quite adequate, in that this paradigm belongs entirely to the persistent functional positivism of the American sociological school.

This is, in fact, the theoretical path pioneered by the majority of research on communication, whether in the US or in Latin America. It is a small paradigm, which, as a dominant conceptual system, is the place where one locates the theories, that is, the presuppositions, which give origin to the hypotheses, understood as suppositions on the relationships between variables. In the case of communication, these are recorded from the ancient hypotheses to the most recent, such as those of active audience, the impact of media messages on the organization of opinions and beliefs, etc. Even the politically activist or *praxiological* conceptions of communication (which view communication as an instrument for the attainment of social ends) belong to this paradigm.

The enlargement of technological power in the sphere of communication currently demands far more of academic methodology, which is still excessively connected to the old analogue media.

The demands stem from computational thinking, relative to new fields of study and practical innovations, with a potentially great impact on the immediate future.

At the level of cultural autonomy, it is worth noting that if in traditional media, manipulation consisted of the unilateral repetition of messages – an old, basic recourse for ideological, political, or religious propaganda – now it is the combination of digital patterns in artificial intelligence that can be used to manipulate the subject. The prevalence of digits or numbers (*quantity*), therefore, leads to a trend toward the equalization of the places of speech, in which agents are oriented by the equal, in a systematic rejection of the expressive *quality* of differences.

Not the simple monopoly of speech, therefore, but rather a true oligopoly of variables – economic and cultural – but *predominantly mechanical* – determine the subject's existence in their everyday life. The potential autonomy of these algorithms opens the path toward subterranean and discourses outside human control, in that the digits amplify their generative capacity from a separated reality, gifted with its own logic and 'language', toward a new *bios*, specifically a virtual one. *Bios* is an Aristotelian and Platonic concept used for designating the spheres of existence within the Polis: *bios politikos* (political-social relations), *bios theoretikos* (knowledge, comprehension) and *bios apolaustikos* (the sensory, pleasure). Contemporary communication has introduced a fourth sphere, the virtual bios, which has technologically materialized in information devices (Sodré, 2019).

This computational thinking in the realm of communication is continually expanding and is the most recent developmental step in the automation that evolved throughout the twentieth century by the accumulative pressure of monopolistic capitalism in order to save time during production. This time-saving seeks, on the one hand, the productive ideal of an uninterrupted work process and, on the other, to compensate for the limitations of the human body in obtaining fast results. This implies a greater process speed and less use of *constant capital*, that is, of the part of capital converted into the means of production. From an economic perspective, labour productivity – understood as the real economic production divided by the number of hours worked – is key to the growth of economies, for the improvement of standards of living and for the control of inflationary processes. General automation signifies the reduction of labour costs and incomes.

Faith in the acceleration of productivity in the industrialized countries is placed in the productive promises of digitalization or robotics. Moreover, the marketing of productivity by a mere technological shortcut limits itself to the argument that, without this, younger generations will experience lower standards of living. Speed is the connecting factor between the incipient automation of the past century and modern robotics, present in state-of-the-art technology, media and financial services. Consequently, electronic technology (robotics, high tech) is the scene of a disquieting, implied mutation in the erosion of the limits between the real and the virtual, between human and machine.

Virtual or augmented reality and the machine are emerging symptoms of conceptual ambiguities in the academic field, which push towards a reformulation of the paradigm in which communication studies are traditionally supported. In general, the new juncture of our time means an instant, simultaneous and global communication that virtually remakes the planet's geography, dislocating the subjects and objects from their traditional places, destabilizing human interactions and demanding new forms of intelligibility (Sodré, 2019).

The rise of the *commons*

With the gradual epistemological shift of communication to other regions of the world – especially to Latin America, marked by the predominance of insertion into the consumptive sphere – there began to arise research perspectives supposedly capable of contesting the colonial nature of Euro-American academic power, as well as circumventing the supposed semiotic control of social discourse by the hegemonic media. This shift also implied a distancing from the strict sociological perspective, which prioritized the exterior aspects of society (businesses, technologies and their effects) in favour of the sociability inherent in the fabric of quotidian relations and concrete communication among individuals. In other words, communication as perceived from within by the social actors.

In truth, society is an historic, modern notion developed in the sphere of legal relations between subjects and diverse in that which is implied by notions such as *ritual* or *communal*, and in which predominates an intersubjective linkage generally ignored by sociological analysis. A notable exception to this mainstream analysis is the comprehensive sociology of Simmel, in which he makes *understanding* – the original phenomenon of connecting the individual with the world – the methodological instrument not only of historical knowledge, but also the base of intersubjective interaction in social life (Simmel, 1895). To him, 'society' or 'the social' are terms which are not sufficiently explanatory for socialization because they do not touch upon the structure of reciprocal action, which includes mental processes; or rather, socialization is a psychological phenomenon initiated by the representation *a priori* of one individual by another (typification or reciprocal anticipation of personal characteristics), which basically consists of understanding.

The term *connection* can be suggested as a communicational re-description of the phenomenon of understanding. From the communication perspective, it inscribes the psycho-sociological dimension onto the field of the human sciences. Through connection, therefore, or through the symbolic, fundamental interweaving of the social being, arise the institutions capable of functioning as the operators of human identity. Connecting are the discourse, the fictions and myths of the historical, communal foundations, which preside over identification with the nation-state, with the values (community, family, work, etc.), and with the ethos or the collective, emotional atmosphere.

In general, to connect (different, therefore, from simply relating) is far more than a mere interactive process, for it presupposes the social and existential insertion of the individual from the imaginary dimension (latent and manifest images) into the deliberations on practical guidelines for conduct, that is, to values. Connection is properly symbolic in the sense of a radical demand for sharing existence with the Other, therefore within a deep logic of duties to the *socius*, beyond any instrumental rationalism or shared functionality.

It is understood as follows: humans maintain with each other an existential connection, in its turn coordinated by a social totality, which designs the space-time of a social formation. The mediation between connection and society is operated by something that the German philosopher Alfred Sown-Rethel called 'social synthesis' (Sohn-Rethel, 1977), that is, a series of institutional functions that guide behaviour and attitudes. They are structures of thought socially necessary to an era strictly linked to the forms assumed by social synthesis. Social synthesis is not a temporal slice closed off in a sociological reduction, but rather a multidimensional perspective on the complexity of social representations of a group, historically apprehended in its institutional dynamic.

On the border between the individual and the collective, social representations constitute a form of practical knowledge – the concrete content of norms or regulations operating in a specific group – guided toward the understanding of the world and toward communication. On the strictly institutional plane, the way of being of a behaviour has to do with the ontology of the human modes of perceiving and realizing something in the world. The acts of perceiving, feeling, thinking, knowing, committing and doing imply bringing oneself to the meeting of a *commons*, that is the unifying centre of the institution.

This is no 'essence' of social life, but rather a convergence of actions which institute a sense of collectivity and belonging. For Christian Laval and Pierre Dardot, *commons* is the principle which animates the collective activity of individuals while simultaneously presiding over the form of political and local self-government (Laval and Dardot, 2015). This concept continues to dominate the theoretical preoccupations of philosophers, jurists and economists, who, according to Laval and Dardot, have multiplied their work, thus constituting, little by little, the increasingly rich dominion of *commons* studies. However, the challenge consisted of passing from the concrete experiences of the *commons* (plural) to a more abstract and politically ambitious conception of the *common* (singular).

In summary, the *common* became the name of a regime of practices, struggle, institutions and investigations, which point to a non-capitalist future. In an attempt to circumvent the essentialism or naturalism of the theological, legal and philosophical conceptions of the common, this theoretical position exclusively circumscribes the obligation which presides over the common to the specific activity of the realization of a task (and not to belonging as unrelated to it).

On the other hand, one can also still appeal to the proposition of the Italian thinker Roberto Esposito with the same perspective that the connecting aspect is an order of duty. Esposito (1998), in his book *Communitas*, departs from the premise that, until today, we were still incapable of conceiving of community in a non-essentialist form. We have thought of the being-in-common as a body of identity. From this perspective, what defines the group is that which it has in common, whether that of individual characteristic, territory or customs.

In an attempt to break with the essentialist perspective, his proposal involves a rupture with the very language of modern, political philosophy. It involves itself with finding a hermeneutic starting point exterior to the philosophical tradition. A starting point which will transpose it into a notion of community different from that found in the etymology of the word 'community', or rather, in the Latin term *communitas*, which is formed from the roots *cum* and *munus*. The word *cum* means with. He explains that *cum* is that which places some facing others, some in relation to others, some with others – it is what launches us in the experience of being together. Therefore, *cum* is that which connected, which joins the *munus*.

The term *munus*, he explains, has three possible meanings, all related to the notion of duty, obligation, responsibility and function. They are *onus, officium* and *donum* (burden, office and gift or donation). Thus, *munus* expresses, in the relationship with men, some with others established by the *cum*, a reciprocal recognition, a common engagement, a species of communion. Esposito considers that that which members of a community have in common is not something positive, like a good or a property, nor even a belonging or an essence. To him, what is possessed in common is a *duty*, a *task*, a *debt*. That which unites people is a deficiency which obligates them to perform certain tasks. Or rather, the debt which all have to all, this obligation, born of lack, of emptiness, of the fear in all of us.

For Esposito, there has arisen in the modern age a counter-position to the idea of *communitas*, that of *immunitas*, which is also the title of another book of his. To him, *immunitas* is that which acknowledges no debt or obligation in relation to another person. He considers that it is gratitude that induces a subject to feel a debt and to pay with a donation, and that this is no longer a characteristic of modern humans. Esposito argues that modern individuals are *immunis* and are relieved of this debt that connects some to others; they are freed from the contact that threatens their identity and their individuality, and of the possibilities that expose them to a possible conflict with their neighbour.

In this sense, new perspectives on communication in all its most diverse aspects and applications should consider the preeminence of the social connection. The Italian philosopher Gianni Vattimo (1971) presupposes an affective community, maintained by collective sharing of voices and sensations. He asserts that our original way of understanding the world is based not only on the transcendental characteristics of pure reason but to a large extent on affectivity embracing each of us profoundly and dynamically.

An intensely flowing informational context where individuals are touched in real time by news from all over the world has not guaranteed a critical eye and attentiveness to the quotidian and local. The forms of communication, many of them instrumentally drawing upon the social networks locally produced by collectives, propaganda groups and minority gatherings, have demonstrated new informational opportunities in that they are constantly connected to world events, but concerned with the emergence of local issues as their fundamental agenda.

The dynamic of communication in its modern configuration renders more present than ever the essential question of the formation of the individual, of that individual's confirmation as a citizen, that which, in classical antiquity, under the name of *paideia*, associated thought and culture with school. The global education of the person inspired by the appearance of a new version of the world was an issue in classical Greece in the same way as it represents a question of social change today occasioned by communications technology. Just as the idea of the emancipation of the individual through the exercise of reason is truly modern, the idea of generalized circulation and connection through electronic technology raises the demand for the elaboration of a new conceptual field of communication, distinct from the representational schema derived from the information paradigm of the last century, in that it contemplates the socio-political and cultural differences in diverse regions of the planet.

The challenge of BRICS to the field of communication

The paradigms of communication studies have been covered above from a Latin American and Brazilian perspective but at the same time this discussion is valid for the rest of the world. The field has historically common roots in Europe and the United States and these have been adopted by dominant research traditions in Asia, Africa or Latin America.

However, communication as a subject of study has experienced several formative stages in its evolution as an academic field. 'Ferment in the field' became a concept in communication research in the early 1980s, when George Gerbner, the legendary Dean of Annenberg School of Communication at the University of Pennsylvania, as editor of *Journal of Communication* mobilized a large number of colleagues to review the field from the point of view of research paradigms and their challenges, commenting on the significance of the field by stating 'If Marx were alive today, his principal work would be entitled *Communications* rather than *Capital*' (Gerbner, 1983: 348). A new assessment of the 'ferment in the field' was made by the same journal ten years later, but it turned out to be little more than an overview (*Journal of Communication*, 1993), followed by another review by the journal a quarter of a century later charting the progress of the field, with a more diverse group of voices – unlike the previous two special issues which had no representation from the global South – but without any grand or coherent theoretical narrative (*Journal of Communication*, 2018).

Outside the dominant variants of American stream of communication scholarship, there have been more critical works to examine the 'ferments' and their histories. Surveying the evolution of the field from the 1950s to the first decade of the new millennium, Nordenstreng (2004) listed six 'ferments' in the field of communication studies, one for each decade. According to this schema the 1950s was the formative stage of modern (mass) communication research, when the field had emerged and established itself in academia, as well as in the media industry, mainly in Europe and North America. The 1960s saw a greater emphasis on social relevance and political economy as well as challenging the hegemonic status of logical positivism as an approach to the world.

In the 1970s, the intellectual offensive of the 1960s often brought the Left into an established position as the main challenger of hegemonic powers in media as well as in academia. Strong support for progressive thinking came from international institutions, above all the Non-Aligned Movement, advocating decolonization and a new international order in economy and communication. In the 1980s, the field was increasingly challenged externally by commercialization in media and culture and internally by the growing claims of cultural studies and feminism, while communication studies in the post-Cold War world of the 1990s was heavily influenced by neo-liberal and populist-conservative politics on the one hand and by new information and communication technologies on the other. Globalization and digitalization led to ICTs becoming conceptual tools in the construction of a new network theory of society.

In communication studies, critical research, primarily from the Left, has been understood as an anti-hegemonic critical force making a difference in a predominantly bourgeois-Western field. Naturally this is just one angle, which nevertheless serves as a reminder of how the notion of critical is absorbed by the political tendencies of the day. In any case the successive ferments in the field should be seen against the background of communication studies having proliferated throughout the latter part of the twentieth century perhaps more than any other academic field apart from computer science and biomedicine.

In its expansion, the field has become increasingly diversified different media (newspapers, magazines, radio, television, cinema, etc.) and different aspects of communication (journalism, visual communication, media culture, media economy, etc.) have emerged as more or less independent branches of the field, prompting some scholars to suggest that communication had become 'a post-discipline' (Waisbord,

2019). This proliferation has not been halted by the convergence brought about by the digitalization of media production and distribution, with new social media, games, etc., becoming further specialities in media studies, often gaining the status of another major subject or even a separate discipline.

As the field has gradually been consolidated in the global South – as university programmes and research institutions have proliferated, particularly in countries such as China – it has begun to articulate its own national and regional identities, typically related to the context of decolonization and attempts at cultural autonomy. It is natural, then, that communication research in the BRICS countries – not only Brazil but also in Russia, India, China and South Africa – has an ambivalent relation to the Western mainstream research tradition: its origins cannot be denied but it is increasingly approached with a critical eye. However closely the BRICS countries might be associated with the processes of globalization, they are understandably resistant to the imposition of Western patterns and, further, can offer visions for a 'post-American' world order.

Beyond a critical approach to Western mainstream, BRICS countries have a lot of potential to broaden the critical paradigms in the evolving field of communication. Russia has a rich cultural tradition, especially in literature, which waits to be elaborated for the theory of communication in the digital era. India with its unique civilization offers unlimited possibilities for developing concepts and theories of communication, and the same is true of China. South Africa with its pan-African heritage likewise has much to offer.

References

Dewey, John (1927) *The Public and its Problems.* New York: Holt.

Esposito, Roberto (1998) *Communitas – origine e destino della comunitá.* Torino: Einaudi.

Gerbner, George (1983) The importance of being critical – in one's own fashion. *Journal of Communication,* 33(3): 355–362.

Journal of Communication (1983) Ferment in the field. *Journal of Communication,* Special Issue 33(3), editor George Gerbner.

Journal of Communication (1993) The disciplinary status of communication research. *Journal of Communication,* Special issue 43(3–4), editors Mark R. Levy and Michael Gurevich.

Journal of Communication (2018) Ferments in the field: the past, present and futures of communication studies, *Journal of Communication,* Special issue 68(2), editors Christian Fuchs and Jack Linchuan Qiu.

Laval, Christian and Dardot, Pierre (2015) *Común – ensayo sobre la revoluciónen el siglo XXI,* Editorial.

Nordenstreng, Kaarle (2004) Ferment in the field: Notes on the evolution of communication studies and their disciplinary nature. *Javnost – The Public,* 11(3): 5–18.

Simmel, Georg (1895) Problems of sociology. *Annals of the American Academy of Political Science,* 6: 52–63.

Sodré, Muniz (2019) *The Science of the Commons. A Note on Communication Methodology.* London: Palgrave Macmillan.

Sohn-Rethel, Alfred (1977) *Intellectual and Manual Labour: Critique of Epistemology.* Atlantic Highlands, NJ: Humanities Press.

Vattimo, Gianni (1971) *Introdução a Heidegger.* Lisbon: Edições 70.

Waisboard, Silvio (2019) *Communication: A Post-Discipline*. Cambridge: Polity.
Weber, Max (1979) Speech to German Sociological Association, pp. 174–182 in H. Hardt, *Social Theories of the Press: Early German and American Perspectives*. Beverly Hills, CA: Sage.

3

MOVING BEYOND WESTERN MODELS IN THE STUDY OF BRICS MEDIA SYSTEMS

Savyasaachi Jain

Models of media systems do not fit the real world very well: in many cases they appear to accurately describe media systems, but in others their categories and classifications are clearly inadequate. This is especially true for media systems that lie outside the Western world. When scholars try to apply existing typologies to media systems outside the West, including of course the BRICS countries, they find they can do so only after modifying popular schema or incorporating additional factors. All too often, they have to resort to nebulous adjectives such as 'hybrid' or 'transitional' to describe media systems that fall between the cracks of the ideal types described by dominant theoretical models. Evidently, real-world diversity is far more complex than models can account for, and the constant search for newer, better fitting typologies bears testament to this.

At one level, the explanation for this conceptual incapacity is deceptively simple – dominant models are based almost entirely on the Western experience and this is why they do not describe unfamiliar media systems quite as well. This chapter argues that media systems theory has developed along a certain path, and that path is guided by the terrain on which it has been trodden, that of the West. This chapter argues that the underlying assumptions, approaches, reference points and analytical variables draw upon experience of a restricted geographical spread of media systems and that this is central to their lack of applicability. Regardless of whether models are normative in their origins or constructed on an empirical base, international perspectives are seldom incorporated and, if they are, it is in a limited manner. When models constructed on the basis of elements considered significant in Western media systems confront reality in the form of unfamiliar factors and forces that are important elsewhere, they cannot describe or account for them because they do not possess the requisite vocabulary.

This chapter examines the conceptual limitations of contemporary media systems theory as a step towards moving beyond the lack of precision inherent in labels such as hybrid and transitional. It begins with influential models of media systems and the various critiques that have emerged in response to them. These critiques and refinements facilitate the identification of the elements of existing typologies that hobble them and restrict their geographical reach. The factors identified include basic reference points and assumptions, the variables considered, and their disciplinary and geographical boundedness. Though no perfect solution is proposed here, it is suggested that the way forward for media systems theory is to seek inputs from the local end of the spectrum, that is, to identify factors emerging from multiple grounded studies of diverse national media systems and consciously incorporate them into wider comparative studies to eliminate theoretical blind spots.

Seductive normative concepts

More than six decades ago, Siebert, Peterson and Schramm summed up the foundational question of media systems theory admirably succinctly in seven, one-syllable words: 'Why is the press as it is?' (1956: 1). Their confident answer was that the nature and behaviour of the media is determined by the political rationales and philosophy that guide their respective social systems. Their analysis later came in for extensive criticism for being ideologically rooted, conceptually flawed and far too idealistic and simplistic (Nerone, 1995; Curran and Park, 2000; Hallin and Mancini, 2004; Christians *et al.*, 2009). However, it has also been acknowledged as having great 'momentum' (Nordenstreng, 1997) and being influential, especially in how journalists conceive of their professional role (Sparks, 2000).

Siebert *et al.* categorized media systems into four normative camps, as is evident in the full title of their work, *Four Theories of the Press: The Authoritarian, Libertarian, Social Responsibility and Soviet Communist Concepts of What the Press Should Be and Do* (1956). They provided a clear indication of their intention in this title – to map 'concepts of what the press should be and do'. They took a historical approach that traced various political philosophies and how they conceived of the role of the media and its relationship with the state. Their theories of the media were, in substance, based on a classification of political systems.

A number of other normative theories of media systems followed, as enumerated in Nordenstreng's account (1997). Merrill and Lowenstein proposed a four-part typology in 1971: Authoritarian, with negative government control; Social-centralist, with positive government control; Libertarian, without any government controls; and Social-libertarian, with minimal government controls. They later added a fifth category, Social-authoritarian. Hachten's five-part classification in 1981 consisted of Authoritarian, Communist, Western (combining Siebert *et al.*'s libertarian and social responsibility theories), Revolutionary and Developmental media systems.

Picard (1985) brought another model to the mix – the Democratic socialist model, based on the relationship between the state and the media in northern European countries. In his view, the media of the Western world could be described as subscribing to the Libertarian, Social responsibility or Democratic socialist models, while the rest of the world was covered by a mix of Siebert *et al*'s Authoritarian and Communist models and Hachten's Developmental and Revolutionary models. Altschull (1995) proposed a different internationally comparative basis for understanding media systems, corresponding to the concept of the First, Second and Third Worlds or, as he calls them, the Market-oriented, Marxist and Developing countries. On this basis, he proposed a three-fold classification of Market, Communitarian and Advancing media in an attempt to eliminate value-laden terminology.

In addition to these American variations, Nordenstreng (1997: 101) reminded us of the typology of four communication systems devised in the 1960s by the British cultural historian Raymond Williams: Authoritarian, Paternal ('an authoritarian system with a conscience'), Commercial and Democratic. The most prominent European scholar in the field, Denis McQuail for his part adopted Siebert *et al*'s four theories and expanded upon them by proposing a six-part typology consisting of the Authoritarian, Free press, Social responsibility, Soviet, Development and Democratic-participant theories of the media (1983: 84–98). This classification was carried on until the third edition of his *Mass Communication Theory* (1994), but was dropped in subsequent editions because he felt media systems theory was not adequately explanatory or descriptive:

> While attempts are still made to improve the original typification of press theories [...], the goal of formulating consistent and coherent 'theories of the press' in this way is bound to break down sooner or later. This is partly because the theories formulated are more about societies than the media. [...] It also partly stems from the complexity and incoherence of media systems and thus the impossibility of matching a press theory with a type of society.
>
> *(McQuail, 2005a: 178)*

Nordenstreng, meanwhile, following the Polish scholar Karol Jakubowicz (1990), drew a distinction between the 'ideal' and 'real' levels of media theory, separating the normative approach, which has 'usually been taken for granted, without questioning its foundations', from the media sociology approach, which describes 'the real role and impact of media in society' (Nordenstreng, 1997: 106). He proposed a 'new beginning', with a typology of five normative 'paradigms' that often coexist in real-world media systems: the Liberal-individualist, Social responsibility, Critical, Administrative and Cultural negotiation paradigms.

This was a prelude to a cooperative project, *Normative Theories of the Media* (Christians *et al.*, 2009), proposing a typology of four traditions seen as the 'most appropriate for describing and evaluating a complete media system at a given historical period': the Corporatist, Libertarian, Social responsibility and Citizen participation traditions. Each of these 'paradigmatic traditions' represents an internally coherent set of values that have developed in specific historical and political contexts. They are avowedly normative in their approach and are linked to models of democracy and the role of journalists in society.

International and empirical perspectives

Though comparative political and geo-political frameworks inspired by *Four Theories* have persisted through several generations, they have also sparked efforts to better understand and describe the manifest behaviour of media systems outside the West. Downing, for instance, called for:

> communication theorizing to develop itself comparatively, acknowledging in particular that to extrapolate theoretically from such relatively unrepresentative nations as Britain and the United States is both conceptually impoverishing and a particularly restricted version of even Eurocentrism.
>
> *(1996: xi)*

Others, too, have questioned the acceptance of Western meaning making as universal (Ngugi, 1987; Nyamnjoh, 1999; Hepp and Couldry, 2009). There were a number of other voices that were not convinced of the need to adopt international perspectives, which was seen as a form of exceptionalism (see, for instance, Ma, 2000; Lee, 2000).

A concerted effort to move beyond the theoretical dominance of what Thussu (2009) later called the 'anglobalized' media was made by Curran and Park in their *De-Westernising Media Studies* (2000). They adopted an empirically grounded approach to advance media systems theory beyond the cul-de-sac in which it found itself, classifying media systems along economic and political factors. They used an economic axis ranging from Neo-liberal to Regulated and a political axis running from Democratic to Authoritarian to classify media systems into four quadrants. They then added a miscellaneous category into which they placed those media systems that did not fit neatly into other categories – countries that were undergoing transformations and regions that had mixed regimes.

Interestingly, they chose to begin their discussions with this miscellaneous category, which they called 'transitional and mixed societies'. This amorphous category – the equivalent of the 'hybrid media system' that often appears elsewhere – yielded, by their own admission, the most significant and interesting perspectives on the relationship between media and society, so significant that they decided to consider it before the four main categories arising from the four quadrants they defined. This was a striking testament to the complexity of real-world media systems and the inadequacy of current media theory in producing empirically verifiable generalizations at the global level.

Another intervention that has informed the critique of models of media systems, ideologically if not substantially, is that of 'Asian theories' of media and communication, also an articulation of unease with the dominance of Western paradigms. This approach advocates the espousal of guiding principles such as 'Asian values', Confucianism or Islam as conceptual frameworks to replace 'Western values'. It is driven politically, ideologically and philosophically, is often influenced by seminal tracts such as Edward Said's *Orientalism* (1978), and is marked by resistance to the claimed universality – and superiority – of the values and narratives of the European Enlightenment to the exclusion of other cultural perspectives and practices. There is a strong element of reconnecting with undervalued tradition, asserting identity, overcoming the legacy of colonialism and what Gunaratne calls the 'oligopoly of social science powers' (2010: 474). Among other things, the attempt is to avoid adopting 'the distortions of the West as reality about their own cultures' (Wang, 2011: 7). Despite a number of attempts to formulate frameworks of Asiacentric, and indeed Afrocentric, communication (Chu, 1985; Asante, 1980; Nyamnjoh, 1999; Dissanayake, 2003; Banerjee, 2009; Miike, 2002; Chen and Starosta, 2003), non-Western scholars have not managed to establish the centrality of their value systems in the study of media systems.

The field was reinvigorated in 2004 with the publication of Hallin and Mancini's *Comparing Media Systems: Three Models of Media and Politics.* They, too, focused primarily on the relationship between media and politics, but spurned the conceptually seductive normative approach in favour of an empirical approach. They analysed the historical development of 18 national media systems in Europe and North America, examining their linkages with the political, economic and social systems within which they existed, but focusing principally on the possible existence of 'systematic connections' between political structures and media systems. Their comparative analysis yielded sets of common characteristics that then became the basis of their models.

They proposed four major dimensions or variables for comparing media systems (2004: 21–45). The first, 'development of media markets', focuses on the development of newspapers with mass circulation, which they saw as an indicator of the relationship of newspapers to their audiences and whether their role emphasised mass- or elite-oriented communication. The second, 'political parallelism', takes into account the manner and degree to which journalists and newspapers indulge in political advocacy or embrace the values of neutrality between competing political narratives. Their third dimension concerns itself with the level of professionalism among journalists and comprises three factors – the autonomy of journalists, distinct professional norms and the level of orientation to the ethic of public service. They contrast professionalization with the instrumentalization of journalism, though they focus largely on political rather than commercial or other forms of external control and influence. Their fourth dimension examines the extent and nature of state intervention in the media system, whether in the form of public service broadcasting, state ownership, subsidies or legal and regulatory frameworks.

It is worth noting that Hallin and Mancini's four dimensions conceptually resemble a framework proposed by Blumler and Gurevitch in 1995:

> [W]e propose a framework, consisting of four dimensions, by reference to which political communication arrangements of different states could be profiled, and their further consequences for the production, reception and wider repercussions of political messages could be hypothetically specified: (1) degree of state control over mass media organizations; (2) degree

of mass media partisanship; (3) degree of media–political élite integration; (4) the nature of the legitimizing creed of media institutions.

(Blumler and Gurevitch, 1995: 62)

Apart from the four dimensions for comparing media systems, Hallin and Mancini also considered a number of variables to describe various characteristics of political systems: late versus early democratization; patterns of conflict and consensus (polarized versus moderate pluralism); whether pluralism is organized or individual; the role of the state (including to what extent a welfare state exists); and clientelism versus the existence of a rational-legal authority (Hallin and Mancini, 2004: 46–86).

They defined their three models of the media by combining these attributes of political systems with the four dimensions of media systems and labelled their three models: 1) Polarized Pluralist, 2) Democratic Corporatist and 3) Liberal. Each of them is also identified with a specific geography, the first with the Mediterranean region (France, Greece, Italy, Portugal and Spain), the second model with North and Central Europe (Austria, Belgium, Denmark, Finland, Germany, the Netherlands, Norway, Sweden and Switzerland), and the liberal model with the North Atlantic (Britain, the US, Canada and Ireland).

The Mediterranean or Polarized Pluralist model is marked by strong state intervention; periods of censorship; high levels of political parallelism; low newspaper circulation; an elite and politically oriented press; commentary-oriented journalism; weaker professionalization, and the instrumentalization of journalism. The Democratic Corporatist or North/Central European model is typified by newspapers that developed mass circulation early; have reached high levels of penetration; a strong party-political press that shifted towards a more neutral commercial model; strong and autonomous public broadcasting, and professionalized and institutionalized journalism that benefits from state interventions to protect freedom of the press. The Liberal or North Atlantic model is characterized by an early development of the mass media; medium newspaper circulation; a neutral commercial press; information-oriented and professionalized journalism, and non-institutionalized self-regulation.

Testing Hallin and Mancini's models

Hallin and Mancini's method and typology rapidly developed a narrative power approaching, if not rivalling, that of Siebert, Peterson and Schramm. It catalysed a number of theoretical explorations and studies of media systems, which variously tested their models, extended their applicability or sought to transcend them. These studies expanded the geographical and conceptual boundaries of media studies.

A number of detailed case studies tested and applied their models on various national media systems from Eastern Europe, Africa and Asia (among them Jakubowicz, 2007; Terzis, 2008; Dobek-Ostrowska and Glowacki, 2010; Hadland, 2012; Kraidy, 2012; Vartanova, 2012 and Zhao, 2012). These studies added to a growing body of research that enriched the theoretical debate but it simultaneously became apparent that most countries refused to fit neatly into one or the other of their categories. Hallin and Mancini later confirmed the conceptual difficulties inherent in extending their model to cover unfamiliar media systems:

> First, we want to underscore the point that our analysis is tied to the 18 cases we analyzed, and we did not intend it to be 'applied' beyond those cases; we believe that new theory applying to other media systems will have to arise, as our framework did, out of concrete analysis of those systems.
>
> *(Hallin and Mancini, 2012a: 217)*

Some scholars also sought to transcend Hallin and Mancini's models by suggesting alternate typologies and theoretical frameworks. Though the debate on Asian values has remained on the margins of mainstream Western media scholarship, a number of other frameworks have been proposed to study media systems from cultural, historical, institutional and processual perspectives (Koltsova, 2006; Hepp and Couldry, 2009; Humphreys, 2011; Roudakova, 2012). Another important contribution by the Swiss scholar Roger Blum, lesser known because it was published only in the German language, proposes six models: an Atlantic–Pacific Liberal model, a Southern European Clientelism model, a Northern European Public Service model, an Eastern European Shock model, an Arab–Asian Patriot model and an Asian–Caribbean Command model (2005).

Although no overarching typologies have emerged to rival the conceptual power of either Hallin and Mancini or their predecessor theorists, Siebert, Peterson and Schramm, theoretical explorations of how these iconic models can be transcended do yield a number of interesting and relevant perspectives. Voltmer (2012) points out that 'trajectories of the past' in the form of legacy media institutions, even after they are re-imagined, mean that media systems in new and emerging democracies are unlikely to fit models developed on the basis of the experience of Europe and North America; they are 'unique' and best described as 'hybrid'. This conception is similar to Curran and Park's (2000) category of 'transitional and mixed societies'.

These efforts to test, apply, extend and transcend the established typologies of media systems reinforced their status as iconic models and simultaneously broadened the debate and expanded its theoretical and geographical boundaries. Even though they have not resulted in models with enough descriptive power to characterize complex and diverse media systems such as those of the BRICS countries, they have highlighted inconsistencies, contradictions, visible or invisible perimeters, and provided a host of pointers to methodological and conceptual limitations.

So, what can these deliberations tell us about factors that serve to limit the study of diverse real-life media systems like those of the BRICS countries? Among the many aspects that can be identified, four conceptual concerns have been chosen for consideration here:

1.   Western media systems as reference points
2.   The myth of universal applicability

3. Narrow disciplinary boundaries
4. Missing variables

Western media systems as reference points

As the preceding section shows, scholars have sought to incorporate a number of international inputs in the form of both perspectives and empirical data, so it might be reasonable to conclude that comparative research has developed significantly since the days of Siebert *et al.*, who were castigated by Curran and Park (2000: 3) for how little they 'felt they needed to know' about the media in other countries. There have been frequent calls for de-Westernizing and internationalizing media studies (among them Downing, 1996; Curran and Park, 2000; Thussu, 2009), but scholars have consistently found that the dominant narrative continues to be Western in orientation and origin. Pfetsch and Esser (2004) felt that communication research lacked an international orientation comparable to that of political science, while Gurevitch and Blumler (2004) called for the adoption of comparative methods. As Hanitzsch (2019: 214) puts it, 'Western researchers often take it for granted that their work is relevant to readers around the world, while researchers from non-Western contexts often have to defend their choice of countries and country-specific literatures'.

The psychologists Henrich, Heine and Norenzayan (2010) proposed the acronym WEIRD to refer to 'Western, Educated, Industrialized, Rich, and Democratic' when they examined whether such populations, which are the subjects of most psychological experiments, are representative of humanity at large. It must be noted that they were focusing on behavioural aspects such as fairness, cooperation, inferential induction, moral reasoning and reasoning styles, which is admittedly very different from the study of media systems. However, their finding that members of WEIRD societies are frequently outliers rather than representative, and 'are among the least representative populations one could find for generalizing about humans', gives reason to rethink the viability of attempts to study diverse media systems around the world on the basis of models that are constructed largely or entirely on specific Western realities.

While it is evident that numerous theoretical refinements have taken place, it is also clear that dominant models are still rooted in the restrictive frameworks of the pioneers. Siebert *et al.* adopted a historical approach, with a focus on ideology and the development of political thought. Their reference point or benchmark was the US media system, which they considered modern and evolved because it is underlaid by classic liberalism as opposed to communism or fascism. As shown by Nerone (1995), they were unabashedly normative in their approach – the clear proposition of *Four Theories* was that other media systems should aspire to become more like the liberal media.

Hallin and Mancini's iconic model emerged from the study of 18 developed democracies, all Western. They took an empirical approach, as opposed to Siebert *et al.*'s historical-philosophical approach, but in essence their reference point has been the same – the Anglo-Saxon, Anglo-American or liberal model of media.

The liberal model is the most studied model of the media, the de facto standard, and the implicit if not explicit normative reference point. However, this type of media emerged in a unique historical context. Among other things, Britain and the US have enjoyed a long spell of uninterrupted democracy, now running into centuries. Their relatively unusual combination of stability and specific political and economic conditions is a rarity in the real world, even within the West. Most other countries have undergone – or are still undergoing – sharp disjunctures, most of them political in nature, but also social and economic.

An important consequence of using the liberal model as a pivotal reference point is the tendency to ignore features and characteristics that are either concealed under its idealized form or have been bred out of this model during its long uninterrupted development. Media systems in transition, or experiencing demo-cratic disjunctures, may display distinct characteristics or be driven by influences that are not found in the relatively stable liberal model. This is at the heart of the rationale of calls for de-Westernization, internationalization, Afro-centricity and Asia-centricity: that the characteristics that are most significant in defining the behaviour of other media systems are not even a part of the analytical framework built around the liberal model.

The myth of universal applicability

The second conceptual concern also arises from the fact that models emerging from the West are the norm in media studies, but the characteristics of the media systems of the West are not the norm at the global level. They are outliers among the huge diversity of national media systems across the world. Examining non-Western media systems for the absence – or presence – of characteristics found in Western media arguably includes an assumption that the Western media represent a 'developed' form, which the media in other parts of the world should aspire to or should be measured against.

At a deeper level, it represents a limiting framework, one that restricts the approach and thus the field of vision of inquiries into the reality of media systems. In effect, this sets the conceptual perimeter of inquiry at the known world of structures, influences and underlying ideologies observed in Western media. Factors that may play a defining role in other cultures or media systems but are outside the experience of the liberal media system or its scholars are excluded; typologies fail to recognize that other media systems may be shaped by factors other than those that are significant in Western media systems.

The Indian media system, for instance, has been characterized since the 1990s by factors that are wholly outside the experience of Western media, among them the rapid multiplication of outlets and their reach, high voltage jostling for attention, a continental scale of linguistic diversity and marked internal differences of scale as well as professional practice (Jain, 2015). Media theory based on Western cases simply does not possess the conceptual vocabulary to account for these factors, but it is nevertheless applied.

Hallin and Mancini were considerably less confident than Siebert, Peterson and Schramm about claiming the universal applicability of their models. They tempered ambition and vision with a strong measure of caution and recognized the geographical and historical specificity of their models, acknowledging that they had undertaken a limited study of 'most similar systems' in Europe and the North Atlantic in countries with roughly similar economic development and which shared a common history and culture to some extent. They stressed that they had rejected the normativism and universalism seen in *Four Theories of the Press* precisely because of its limited applicability to other national media systems, which had developed along diverse trajectories and logics. However, they simultaneously claimed an explanatory – and even predictive – power for their approach and models, claiming that models that prevail in Europe and North America 'tend to be dominant globally' and so would be useful to scholars elsewhere 'not only as an example of how to conduct comparative research but also because these models have actually influenced the development of other systems' (2004: 6). They also suggested that a process of convergence to the liberal model of the media was under way:

> It is clear, however, that the differences among these models and in general the degree of variation among nation states, has diminished substantially over time. In 1970 the differences among the three groups of countries characterized by our three models were quite dramatic; a generation later, by the beginning of the twenty-first century, the differences have eroded to the point that it is reasonable to ask whether a single, global media model is displacing the national variation of the past, at least among the advanced capitalist democracies discussed in this book.
>
> *(Hallin and Mancini, 2004: 251)*

This construct has been contested. Humphreys (2011: 170), for instance, points out that a number of studies have refuted the convergence hypothesis, pointing to the durability of national models of capitalism and stressing the crucial mediating role of national institutions. Humphreys suggests that though Hallin and Mancini touch upon the concept of path dependency, they do not adequately explore its implications, and that applying historical–institutional analysis to national media systems would reveal divergence rather than convergence.

Hallin and Mancini later also claimed that their polarized pluralist model was the one most relevant to the study of a remarkable range of national media systems:

> [I]t is probably the Polarized Pluralist Model, more than the other two we outline here, that is most widely applicable to other systems as an empirical model of the relation between media and political systems. We suspect that scholars working on many parts of the world – Eastern Europe and the former

Soviet Union, Latin America, the Middle East and all of the Mediterranean region, Africa, and most of Asia will find much that is relevant in our analysis of Southern Europe.

(Hallin and Mancini, 2012b: 306)

Thussu views claims such as these as 'parochialism' and dismisses them as 'untenable' in his *Internationalizing Media Studies* (2009: 1). He theorizes internationalization as the third important intervention in the 'anglobalized' embodiment of media studies, the first two being feminism, and race and ethnicity (2009: 2–3). Hanitzsch and Esser also weigh in against them, saying that studies that assume methodological and theoretical universalism 'are vulnerable to the production of out-of-context measurement' (2012: 503).

Using concepts that emerge from the West to characterize other media systems is often no more than a negative exercise – the vocabulary of scholars is limited to the features that exist in the West so they look for these features elsewhere and, more often than not, do not find them to be central to the systems they are studying. This results in the strange situation of widely varying media systems being described as polarized pluralist or, worse, labelled with the nebulous adjectives hybrid and transitional.

Narrow disciplinary boundaries

The third concern is about how widely theory spreads its net in attempts to model reality. Siebert, Peterson and Schramm incorporated economic perspectives into their analysis, but mainly in the form of the types of ownership of media tolerated by various political systems. For them, the economic system acted merely as a dependent of the political system and was secondary. Scholars who followed them have proposed a number of amendments to add detail and definition to their broadbrush strokes, but, more often than not, they, too, base their classifications on the basis of political and economic systems.

Blumler and Gurevitch (1995) mainly considered dimensions relating to political systems, but one of their dimensions encompassed media institutions and processes. Altschull (1995) claimed to have given prominence to economic variables, but his first-second-third world typology essentially followed the pattern of existing geopolitical blocs and was thus also linked to political ideology. Various other models and schema proposed by other scholars of political communication have also given primacy to political variables. Those from the political economy tradition have, of course, included economic forces in their analyses.

Sparks draws upon the characteristics of post-communist media in Eastern Europe to posit that a close relationship between economic and political actors is a more accurate reflection of the reality in most countries. He favours the position that there is substantial interpenetration between political and economic power, and that the two forms of power merge into a single form of social domination. He suggests that analysing the relationship between the media and its audiences would be much more productive than examining political and economic factors but does not offer a model that puts this into practice.

Curran and Park's (2000) clean, two-variable analysis utilized one political system variable (democratic vs. authoritarian) and one economic system variable (neo-liberal vs. regulated). They gave almost equal importance to political and economic systems and used both variables to categorize media systems but, as has been observed, their 'transitional and mixed societies' category, which supplied the most interesting insights fell outside the four basic categories that emerged from their two variables. At one point, they seemed to promise a wider inquiry into 'social relations', but this promise did not mature into additional variables for their analysis and classification:

> But perhaps the key point to emphasize is that media systems are shaped not merely by national regulatory regimes and national audience preferences, but by a complex ensemble of social relations that have taken shape in national contexts. It is precisely the historically grounded density of these relationships that tends to be excluded from simplified global accounts, in which theorists survey the universe while never straying far from the international airport.
>
> *(Curran and Park, 2000: 10)*

Similarly, Hallin and Mancini also tantalizingly indicate the possibility of a wider field of inquiry, but rapidly retreat into the comforting confines of political science perspectives:

> Comparative analysis of media systems is about understanding those systems in the context of history, culture, and social and political structure more generally, and this means that scholars of communication need to be in dialogue with other fields, including comparative politics, political sociology, and political anthropology.
>
> *(Hallin and Mancini, 2012a: 217–218)*

No formal rationale has been forthcoming for why they shrank media systems into one-dimensional entities that possess only one primary relationship – with the political system – that is worth exploring. The result is an inexplicable neglect of the media systems' interactions with social, cultural and value systems. Interestingly, other efforts to define media behaviour do take such factors into account. For instance, the five filters of Herman and Chomsky's propaganda model (1988) – ownership, advertising, sourcing, flak and anti-communism – encompass institutional, commercial, cultural, ideological and professional factors.

There does seem to be, however, a simple reason for the field's theoretical affinity with political science – path dependency. The scholarship on media systems intersects to a very large extent with that of political communication because many prominent scholars come from the field of political communication. Indeed, many of their classifications, concepts and methods are sourced directly from political communications and, by extension, from the study of political systems.

Viewed in this light, it is easier to understand the cacophony of criticism – some of it in fairly strong language – of Hallin and Mancini's models. Many scholars have found that models based on only one discipline (in this case, political communication) are evidently incapable of describing, accounting for, perhaps even noticing the characteristics that seem most prominent to those who study those systems. As Norris notes: 'It is not apparent whether the four dimensions identified by Hallin and Mancini are indeed the critical ones that define the major contrasts today among contemporary media systems' (Norris, 2009: 331). Norris also separately notices Hallin and Mancini's questionable claim to the territory of 'media systems' and calls it a 'misleading conceptual classification'. She points out that Hallin and Mancini are in fact trying 'to define a *system of political communications*, which is a very different animal' (2009: 328–329; emphasis in original).

It is significant that there is little consideration of media-related variables in the analysis of media systems. There is a lack of agency ascribed to the media; the media is considered as if it were determined entirely by the ideological, political or economic structures that surround it. In reality, the media not only has a symbiotic relationship with society, culture and politics, its behaviour is also influenced by its internal dynamics. Hallin and Mancini's four dimensions (2004) do focus upon the media, but three of the four dimensions consider the relationship between the media and the political system, and only one – levels of professionalism in journalism – examines the working of the media itself. A notable exception was Chakravartty and Roy's (2013) intense focus on the relationship between ownership and political partisanship in their proposal of an alternative typology of India's linguistic media systems. However, their two categories – partisan and network media systems – also do not go beyond emphasizing the media–politics relationship.

Missing variables

The fourth conceptual concern relates to the question of which aspects of the reality of media systems are considered significant in modelling them. The debate around what variables are significant reveals a gulf between the understanding of those who have formulated models and those who have sought to apply them. It is significant that the critical voices covered earlier in this chapter have emphasized areas such as culture, society, religion and values. A case can be made that while the media and political systems continue to be distinct systems, the media's intersection with society and culture is far more intermeshed and marked by feedback loops rather than mere influence.

The analytical frameworks used in extant models cover only some of the factors that one intuitively associates with the media. Take, for instance, observations on press freedom or independence of the media, which one might use while characterizing a media system. These are broad concepts, but they are usually represented narrowly in existing typologies. Hallin and Mancini take them into account through the dimensions of political parallelism and the degree and extent of state intervention, but they are in fact far broader. There can be many other threats to the independence of the media, including from commercial imperatives, owners, and social, cultural or religious factors.

However, Hallin and Mancini are confident that their choice of variables is a good fit for the rest of the world:

> In fact, we were struck by the fact that the list of variables we proposed to compare the relationship between mass media and politics in the Western world seemed to hold up reasonably well as we shifted to a 'most dissimilar systems' design, at least in the sense that the participants were almost always able to tell a coherent and interesting story about how their cases could be understood in relation to those dimensions.
>
> *(Hallin and Mancini, 2012b: 5)*

Other scholars have between them produced a long list of variables that they consider important. Jakubowicz (cited in Nordenstreng, 1997), like Curran and Park, proposed two axes that resulted in four quadrants, but considered different variables. One of the two axes, autonomy or subordination of the media with respect to the power structure, was political, while the other measured the media system in terms of dominance versus pluralism of content. McQuail (2005b) and Remington (2006) have mentioned country size and patterns of regionalism; others have suggested media consumption and market size (Hardy, 2012). Yakovenko (2000, cited in Koltsova, 2006) has an intense focus on media freedom, and Norris (2009) also repeatedly returns to press freedom and the enabling legal framework.

The studies that have sought to apply Hallin and Mancini's models to other media systems also underscore a number of country-specific variables. Peri (2012), for instance, identifies security considerations and the media's commitment to nation building as central to understanding Israeli media, while Balčytienė (2012) points to cultural protection and national resistance as driving forces in the Baltic states. De Albuquerque (2012) finds that Hallin and Mancini's variables cannot adequately describe important aspects of the Brazilian media system. The variables he proposes to add are: whether a media system is central or peripheral with reference to other national media systems and, in common with Voltmer (2012), whether the system of government is presidential or parliamentary. De Albuquerque also suggests disaggregating the dimension of 'political parallelism' into two variables – the strength of political parties and the level of involvement of media in political activity.

Hadland (2012) proposes to expand the scope of Hallin and Mancini's 'state intervention' dimension to include the type of coercive intervention that can be seen in young democracies. McCargo (2012), drawing upon his earlier studies of the media in East and South-East Asia (2000, 2003), proposes the concept of 'partisan polyvalence' as a working label for many of the media systems in the Asia-Pacific region. This term points to the multiplicity of voices as well as the high levels of contention between state-sanctioned and unauthorized voices in those media systems, but is not intended as an alternate model:

> Media in the new democracies, illiberal democracies, and semi-authoritarian nations of Pacific Asia are commonly characterized by intense partisanship, persistent state interference, ambiguous modes of ownership, and questionable profitability. Although these features are too miscellaneous to amount to a model, there is ample scope for comparative research concerning the ways in which similar media characteristics recur around the region.
>
> *(McCargo, 2012: 223)*

Humphreys (2011) proposes a comprehensive list of variables, including: history (continuity/disjuncture); market size; levels of media concentration; ethnic/linguistic structure; ideological polarization; majoritarian or consensual governance on three dimensions (unitary/federal, party/government, interest intermediation); state tradition; influence of judicial law making/constitutional-legal rulings and the legal tradition.

Such a large number of variables would be too much to incorporate into any reasonable analysis, but their perceived need delivers a clear message – that the tools used to study media systems should conceptually be able to take into account a wider range of factors.

Conclusion

As we have seen, there is often a mismatch when models of media systems are sought to be correlated with real-world media systems. Scholars who apply models to diverse media systems find that theoretical models frequently cannot account for observed behaviour because their frameworks do not include the forces and influences responsible for observed behaviour. The use of labels such as 'hybrid' is the result of this poor fit between models and empirical reality.

If the study of diverse systems, such as those of the BRICS countries, is to be made more meaningful, there is a need to move beyond studying media systems for their similarity to or convergence with Western models. The perspectives encapsulated in this chapter have identified various dimensions of the problem, which include the aspects that extant models are overwhelmingly based in specific Western realities, they largely limit their ambition to political and economic factors and they privilege normative considerations and structural factors over empirical inputs.

So, how can BRICS media systems be studied and described with greater accuracy and granularity? Here, three broad approaches are proposed as worthy of attention: first, to move beyond the focus on political and economic systems; second, to deepen the inquiry past the normative and structural levels and, third, to undertake grounded studies of media systems.

The imperative of moving beyond political and economic considerations has been demonstrated by the large number of studies of different media systems that have found other factors significant in influencing the nature of the media. One important area is culture, which has a strong symbiotic relationship with media, but seldom features among the primary variables used for constructing models. Many of the noteworthy characteristics of media systems that remain unaddressed by theory fall under the broad label of culture and range from cultural values, historical contexts, tradition, religion and social relationships, to linguistic cultures, attitudes to knowledge, and corruption and impunity both within the media and in its social context. Another such area is the state and practices of institutions that govern, regulate or empower the media.

Second, it is important to go beyond normative and macro-level structural factors to consider variables that account for the instrumental forces and relationships within the media. These cover a wide range and include the media's growth or decline; business imperatives and practices; power relationships within the media and the pressures on journalism and journalists. It is also in some cases important to take into account the agency that the media exercises in resisting the pressures of other systems and structures. Attempts to define a media system without factoring in such information can only result in incomplete descriptions because a media system is not unidirectionally determined by external systems alone. It is relevant here that variables within the media system are not being proposed as an alternative to those at the macro level, they are proposed in addition.

Third, is the need to undertake grounded case studies of media systems. Grounded studies offer an alternate to macro-level approaches and usefully supplement them. Normative and structural approaches yield relevant data, but they tend to be deductive and top-down in nature. Grounded approaches are inductive by nature and thus focus more on manifest behaviour than on prior expectations. They have a greater explanatory power because they build upwards from lower structural levels, as is evident from many of the studies that have proposed fresh variables for consideration. Grounded studies also enable a disaggregation of the media system so that it can be studied at various levels ranging from that of the individual journalist to that of media organisations rather than merely at the level of the system as a whole.

An additional advantage of grounded case studies is that they can focus not only on normative considerations, but also on deviations from the norm. There is a specific advantage in studying systemic ethical or behavioural fault-lines in media systems – typically system-wide aberrations from the normative expectations. These deviant cases reveal critical information about the functioning of media systems. Whether it is phone-hacking in the UK or the rapid institutionalization of paid political news in India, these fault-lines act as intriguing sites for the study of the forces and influences that drive the real behaviour of media organizations and personnel. This proposition has clear methodological implications for the study of media systems.

The recommendations above do not represent an attempt to either create a template for the study of media systems, or to propose a fresh set of models applicable to BRICS countries. At the moment it is questionable whether such a set of models is at all feasible or meaningful. This answer can emerge only on the basis of a number of grounded studies and depends on whether or not patterns that fall within a coherent framework emerge as the result of such an exercise. The intention here is merely to find a way to advance beyond the intellectual cul-de-sac of repeatedly applying unsuitable Western models to media systems such as those of BRICS countries with inconclusive results that do no more than suggest an undefined hybridity. A series of deep inquiries into the tangible observed behaviour of varied media systems seems to be the way forward, and this could lead to more generalizable approaches and characterizations that allow the bridging of conceptual gaps.

References

Altschull, J. H. (1995) *Agents of Power: The Media and Public Policy*, second edition. White Plains, NY: Longman.

Asante, M. K. (1980) Intercultural Communication: An Inquiry into Research Directions, pp. 401–410 in D. Nimmo (ed.) *Communication Yearbook 4*. New Brunswick, NJ: Transaction.

Balčytienė, A. (2012) Culture as a Guide in Theoretical Explorations of Baltic Media, pp. 51–71 in D. Hallin and P. Mancini, (eds.) *Comparing Media Systems Beyond the Western World*. Cambridge: Cambridge University Press.

Banerjee, I. (2009) Asian Media Studies: The Struggle for International Legitimacy, pp. 165–174 in D. K. Thussu (ed.) *Internationalizing Media Studies*. London: Routledge.

Blum, R. (2005) Bausteine zu einer Theorie der Mediensysteme. *Medienwissenschaft Schweiz* 2005(2): 5–11.

Blumler, J. G. and Gurevitch, M. (1995) Towards a Comparative Framework for Political Communication Research, pp. 59–72 in J. G. Blumler and M. Gurevitch (eds.) *The Crisis of Public Communication*. London: Routledge.

Brants, K. and Voltmer, K. (eds.) (2011) *Political Communication in Postmodern Democracy: Challenging the Primacy of Politics*. Basingstoke: Palgrave Macmillan.

Chakravartty, P. and Roy, S. (2013) Media Pluralism Redux: Towards New Frameworks of Comparative Media Studies 'Beyond the West'. *Political Communication* 30(3): 349–370.

Chen, G. M. and Starosta, W. J. (2003) Asian Approaches to Human Communication: A Dialogue. *Intercultural Communication Studies* 12(4): 1–15.

Christians, C. G., Glasser, T. L., McQuail, D., Nordenstreng, K. and White, R. A. (2009) *Normative Theories of the Media: Journalism in Democratic Societies*. Chicago: University of Illinois Press.

Chu, G. (1985) In Search of an Asian Perspective of Communication Theory. In: AMIC-Thammasat University Symposium on Mass Communication Theory: The Asian Perspective, Bangkok, 15–17 October. Singapore: Asian Mass Communication Research & Information Centre.

Couldry, N. (2007) Researching Media Internationalization: Comparative Media Research as if We Really Meant it. *Global Media and Communication* 3(3): 247–250.

Couldry, N. and Hepp, A. (2012) Comparing Media Cultures, pp. 249–261 in F. Esser and T. Hanitzsch (eds.) *The Handbook of Comparative Communication Research*. London: Routledge.

Cunningham, S. and Flew, T. (2000) De-Westernizing Australia? Media Systems and Cultural Coordinates, pp. 210–220 in J. Curran and M. Park (eds.) *De-Westernising Media Studies*. London: Routledge.

Curran, J. and Park, M. (eds.) (2000) *De-Westernising Media Studies*. London: Routledge.

de Albuquerque, A. (2012) On Models and Margins: Comparative Media Models Viewed from a Brazilian Perspective, pp. 72–95 in D. Hallin, and P. Mancini (eds.) *Comparing Media Systems Beyond the Western World*. Cambridge: Cambridge University Press.

Dissanayake, W. (2003) Asian Approaches to Human Communication: Retrospect and Prospect. *Intercultural Communication Studies* XII(4): 7–37.

Dobek-Ostrowska, B. and Głowacki, M. (2010) *Comparative Media Systems: European and Global Perspectives*. Budapest: Central European University Press.

Downing, J. (1996) *Internationalizing Media Theory: Transition, Power, Culture – Reflections on Media in Russia, Poland and Hungary 1980–95*. London: Sage.

Esser, F. and Pfetsch, B. (eds.) (2004) *Comparing Political Communication: Theories, Cases and Challenges*. Cambridge: Cambridge University Press.

Gunaratne, S. (2010) De-Westernizing Communication/Social Science Research: Opportunities and Limitations. *Media Culture & Society* 32(3): 473–500.

Gurevitch, M. and Blumler, J. G. (2004) State of the Art in Comparative Political Research: Posed for Maturity? pp. 325–343 in F. Esser and B. Pfetsch (eds.) *Comparing Political Communication: Theories, Cases and Challenges*. Cambridge: Cambridge University Press.

Hadland, A. (2012) Africanizing Three Models of Media and Politics: The South African Experience, pp. 96–118 in D. Hallin and P. Mancini (eds.) *Comparing Media Systems Beyond the Western World*. Cambridge: Cambridge University Press.

Hallin, D. and Mancini, P. (2004) *Comparing Media Systems: Three Models of Media and Politics*. New York: Cambridge University Press.

Hallin, D. and Mancini, P. (2012a) Comparing Media Systems: A Response to Critics, pp. 207–220 in F. Esser and T. Hanitzsch (eds.) *The Handbook of Comparative Communication Research*. London: Routledge.

Hallin, D. and Mancini, P. (eds.) (2012b) *Comparing Media Systems Beyond the Western World*. Cambridge: Cambridge University Press.

Hanitzsch, T. (2019) Journalism Studies Still Needs to Fix Western Bias. *Journalism* 20(1): 214–217.

Hanitzsch, T. and Esser, F. (2012) Challenges and Perspectives of Comparative Communication Inquiry, pp. 501–516 in F. Esser and T. Hanitzsch (eds.) *Handbook of Comparative Communication Research*. London: Routledge.

Hardy, J. (2012) Comparing Media Systems, pp. 185–206 in F. Esser and T. Hanitzsch (eds.) *The Handbook of Comparative Communication Research*. London: Routledge.

Henrich, J., Heine, S. J. and Norenzayan, A. (2010) The Weirdest People in the World? *Behavioral and Brain Sciences* 33(2–3): 61–83.

Hepp, A. and Couldry, N. (2009) What Should Comparative Media Research Be Comparing? Towards a Transcultural Approach to 'Media Cultures', pp. 32–47 in D. K. Thussu (ed.) *Internationalizing Media Studies*. London: Routledge.

Herman, E. and Chomsky, N. (1988) *Manufacturing Consent: The Political Economy of the Mass Media*. London: Vintage.

Humphreys, P. (2011) A Political Scientist's Contribution to the Comparative Study of Media Systems in Europe: A Response to Hallin and Mancini, pp. 157–176 in N. Just and M. Puppis (eds.) *Trends in Communications Policy Research*. Bristol: Intellect.

Jain, S. (2015) India: Multiple Media Explosions, pp. 45–165 in K. Nordenstreng and D. K. Thussu (eds.) *Mapping BRICS Media.* London: Routledge.

Jakubowicz, K. (2007) *Rude Awakening: Social and Media Change in Central and Eastern Europe.* Cresskill, NJ: Hampton Press.

Koltsova, O. (2006) *News Media and Power in Russia.* London: Routledge.

Kraidy, M. (2012) The Rise of Transnational Media Systems: Implications of Pan-Arab Media for Comparative Research, pp. 177–200 in D. Hallin and P. Mancini (eds.) *Comparing Media Systems Beyond the Western World.* Cambridge: Cambridge University Press.

Lee, C. C. (2000) State, Capital and the Media: The Case of Taiwan, pp. 10–123 in J. Curran and M. Park (eds.) *De-Westernising Media Studies.* London: Routledge.

Ma, E. K. (2000) Rethinking Media Studies: The Case of China, pp. 17–28 in J. Curran and M. Park (eds.) *De-Westernising Media Studies.* London: Routledge.

McCargo, D. (2000) *Politics and the Press in Thailand: Media Machinations.* London: Routledge.

McCargo, D. (2003) *Media and Politics in Pacific Asia.* London: Routledge.

McCargo, D. (2012) Partisan Polyvalence: Characterizing the Political Role of Asian Media, pp. 201–223 in D. Hallin and P. Mancini (eds.) *Comparing Media Systems Beyond the Western World.* Cambridge: Cambridge University Press.

McQuail, D. (1983) *Mass Communication Theory: An Introduction.* London: Sage.

McQuail, D. (2005a) *McQuail's Mass Communication Theory.* Fifth edition. London: Sage.

McQuail, D. (2005b) Review of Hallin and Mancini, *Comparing Media Systems: Three Models of Media and Politics.* Cambridge University Press, 2004. *European Journal of Communication* 20(2): 266–268.

Miike, Y. (2002) Theorizing Culture and Communication in the Asian Context: An Assumptive Foundation. *Intercultural Communication Studies* XI(1): 1–21.

Nerone, J. C. (ed.) (1995) *Last Rights: Revisiting Four Theories of the Press.* Chicago: University of Illinois Press.

Ngugi, W. (1987) *Decolonising the Mind: The Politics of Language in African Literature.* Harare: Zimbabwe Publishing House.

Nordenstreng, K. (1997) Beyond the Four Theories of the Press, pp. 97–109 in J. Servaes and R. Lier (eds.) *Media and Politics in Transition: Cultural Identity in the Age of Globalisation.* Leuven/Amersfoort: Acco.

Norris, P. (2009) Comparative Political Communications: Common Frameworks or Babelian Confusion? *Government and Opposition* 44(3): 321–340.

Nyamnjoh, F. (1999) African Cultural Studies, Cultural Studies in Africa: How to Make a Useful Difference. *Critical Arts: South-North Cultural and Media Studies* 13(1): 15–39.

Peri, Y. (2012) The Impact of National Security on the Development of Media Systems: The Case of Israel, pp. 11–25 in D. Hallin and P. Mancini (eds.) *Comparing Media Systems Beyond the Western World.* Cambridge: Cambridge University Press.

Pfetsch, B. and Esser, F. (2004) Comparing Political Communication: Reorientations in a Changing World, pp. 3–22 in F. Esser and B. Pfetsch (eds.) *Comparing Political Communication: Theories, Case and Challenges.* Cambridge: Cambridge University Press.

Picard, R. G. (1985) *The Press and the Decline of Democracy: The Democratic Socialist Response in Public Policy.* Westport, CT: Greenwood.

Remington, P. (2006) Comparing Media Systems: Three Models of Media and Politics. *Global Media Journal: Mediterranean Edition* 1(1): 141–144.

Roudakova, N. (2012) Comparing Processes: Media, 'Transitions,' and Historical Change, pp. 246–277 in D. Hallin and P. Mancini (eds.) *Comparing Media Systems Beyond the Western World.* Cambridge: Cambridge University Press.

Said, E. (1978) *Orientalism.* London: Routledge.

Siebert, F., Peterson, T. and Schramm, W. (1956) *Four Theories of the Press: The Authoritarian, Libertarian, Social Responsibility, and Soviet Communist Concepts of What the Press Should Be and Do*. Chicago: University of Illinois Press.

Sparks, C. (2000) Media Theory After the Fall of European Communism: Why the Old Models from the East and West Won't Do Any More, pp. 29–42 in J. Curran and M. Park (eds.) *De-Westernising Media Studies*. London: Routledge.

Terzis, G. (2008) *European Media Governance: National and Regional Dimensions*. Bristol: Intellect.

Thussu, D. K. (ed.) (2009) *Internationalizing Media Studies*. London: Routledge.

Vartanova, E. (2012) The Russian Media Model in the Context of Post-Soviet Dynamics, pp. 119–142 in D. Hallin and P. Mancini (eds.) *Comparing Media Systems Beyond the Western World*. Cambridge: Cambridge University Press.

Voltmer, K. (2012) How Far Can Media Systems Travel? Applying Hallin and Mancini's Comparative Framework Outside the Western World, pp. 224–245 in D. Hallin and P. Mancini (eds.) *Comparing Media Systems Beyond the Western World*. Cambridge: Cambridge University Press.

Wang, G. (ed.) (2011) *De-Westernizing Communication Research: Altering Questions and Changing Frameworks*. London: Routledge.

Zhao, Y. (2012) Understanding China's Media System in a World Historical Context, pp. 143–173 in D. Hallin and P. Mancini (eds.) *Comparing Media Systems Beyond the Western World*. Cambridge: Cambridge University Press.

PART II

Media and communication structures and systems

4

THE BRAZILIAN MEDIA SYSTEM IN A TURBULENT ENVIRONMENT

Fernando Oliveira Paulino and Liziane Soares Guazina

This chapter examines the Brazilian media system in its regional, geographic and historical context. In particular, it considers the impact of the turbulent political environment since 2013 on the media system and on how information is disseminated to and shared by the public. In recent years, as will be presented below, political mobilizations and technological phenomena, such as increased access to the Internet, have influenced the ways of production, distribution and access to the media, especially with regard to the impact of the growth of the media on policy debates and decisions.

The Latin American context

As the biggest country in Latin America, occupying over 40 per cent of the land mass with over 8.5 million square kilometers, Brazil is the most important country in the region – as well as a formidable media power. With a population of 209 million (34 per cent of the population of Latin America), 84 per cent of whom live in 5,570 cities across 27 states, with one official language (Portuguese), its media has a huge domestic market and wide-spread presence in the Lusophone world, especially in the field of television entertainment – telenovelas – in which Brazil is the world leader (Straubhaar, 2012; Sinclair and Straubhaar, 2013; Rosas-Moreno, 2014; Davis, Straubhaar and Cunha, 2016). With the growing use of digital media, circulation of such content has grown exponentially both in Brazil and abroad, as the number of people with access to information and communication technologies, especially mobile phones, has rapidly grown in the past decade.

Historically speaking, the media system in Brazil has been characterized by the predominance of a handful of very powerful commercial media groups – notably Rede Globo – which championed pro-business and pro-military causes for most of the period Brazil was under military rule (1964–1985) (Martins da Silva and Paulino, 2007; Albuquerque, 2012). In such an institutional and ideologically conservative framework, the Brazilian media system has largely failed to establish a diverse and democratic discourse in a vast and diverse, multi-racial and multi-cultural country, representing one of the world's most unequal societies (Birman and Lehmann, 1999; Matos, 2008). The dynamic between media and religion is also an important component of the media system in a country where both Catholicism and evangelical Christianity have great influence in shaping public opinion, something which politicians of all ideological orientation have used for retaining or gaining power (Birman and Lehmann, 1999; Reis, 2006; Biller and Watson, 2018). After 21 years of dictatorship, when the military rule ended in 1985, Brazil adopted a multi-party political system, holding regular elections. Although electoral politics reflected social diversity, media democratization has generally lagged behind. Matos notes that democratization 'involves a change in citizens' understandings of, uses of and approaches to the media. Thus, demands are placed on media systems to provide better quality information, to make an increased commitment to representing political diversity and giving voice to different groups in society, and to pay greater attention to professional standards' (Matos, 2012: 13). However, today, the political system is fragmented, with nearly 30 political parties in the Brazilian Congress and consequently Brazil has faced significant political and economic crises in recent years, reflected in anti-establishment protests (Davis and Straubhaar, 2012). From 2014, the '*Lava Jato*' ('Car Wash') investigation imprisoned more than 100 people for corruption, implicating important players in the government, including former president, Luiz Inácio Lula da Silva. Between 2015 and 2018, President Dilma Roussef was impeached, while the Vice President Michel Temer assumed the leadership of the country (Albuquerque, 2017).

In the 2018 Presidential Elections, voters elected the far-right-wing populist politician, Jair Bolsonaro as President for four years, reflecting the new international trend towards populist and authoritarian governments (Norris and Inglehart, 2019). Right-wing groups played a fundamental role in organizing protests against Rousseff's government and her Workers Party, and supported the impeachment process, using both social media (Nalon, 2018), as well as the country's leading and right-wing network, TV Globo (Van Dijk, 2017). Such traditional media are also powerful political actors in a country where large private media groups support conservative governments (Matos, 2008; Porto, 2011; 2012).

Brazil's economy is driven mainly by services, industrial production and export of goods. After a period of accumulated growth between 2001 and 2014, the economy declined by 4.5 per cent in 2015 and 3.6 per cent in 2016, generating 14.2 million unemployed (more than 13 per cent of Brazil's population). The largest decline, in 2016, was seen in the farming sector (6.6 per cent), whereas industry declined 3.8 per cent and services 2.7 per cent. This was the deepest recession in Brazil's history since 1948 when records to measure such economic activities began. As a result of the economic crisis, nearly 66 per cent of families were without a regular income and there were severe cuts in government expenditure, affecting social programmes such as the *Bolsa Família*, cuts to public funding for research and universities. In

2017, the Brazilian GDP grew by just 1 per cent reaching $2.05 trillion (nearly 45 per cent of the GDP of Latin America).

Because of its geographical and economic importance, Brazil is considered to be Latin America's economic engine, influencing the rest of the region, with which it shares a common colonial past. In other words, its territory did not necessarily belong to the majority of its inhabitants, with the economy based on commodities. Unlike the conventional stereotype, the region is quite urbanized, with about 80 per cent of the population living in cities, making Latin America the world's most urbanized region. Brazil is known for huge income inequality and a considerable level of illiteracy (8.7 per cent of the population). The UN Human Development Indexes, for example, show that this is true across the region, which has a high level of income concentration. In the words of the World Economic Forum, 'although the region achieved considerable success in reducing extreme poverty over the last decade, its still-high levels of income and wealth inequality have stymied sustainable growth and social inclusion'. In other words, Latin America is still the world's most unequal region where most of the time democracy and ideas of equality, social justice and dignity are not well understood (Matos, 2008). As the region further integrates with the rest of the world thorough trade, tourism and cultural exchange, the awareness for greater equity and democratization might grow (Matos, 2012).

After a period of relative euphoria in the first decade of the twenty-first century, the years since 2010 have been marked by a lack of hope in Brazil and other Latin American countries. The decrease in commodity prices in key products such as oil and soy, coupled with a credit crisis with a large number of people in debt, have harmed the political system in almost all Latin American countries, especially Brazil, Argentina and Mexico, which are all important for the regional economy. These economic troubles have also revived ideologies from the past, which threaten democracy and demonstrate the vulnerability of Latin America's fragile political systems. Over the last twelve years, for example, there have been changes in presidencies, without elections, in countries such as Honduras, Paraguay and Brazil.

Shifts in the political system have led to elected governments that reduce social spending and worsen social indexes without any prospect of improvement. In Brazil, for instance, the Michel Temer government has approved in 2016 a constitutional amendment to put a freeze on health and education spending (Phillip, 2017). In reality, that means a reduction in funding as the annual budget does not recover the annual inflation. The recent economic and political crises have reinforced the practices of *patrimonialismo* (patrimonialism), *personalismo* (personalism), *coronelismo* (a form of persecution and protection) and *caciquismo* (despotism), so typical of the political practices in the region where landowners have traditionally ruled. In short, the confusion between public and private power continues in the political system of Brazil.

The Brazilian media system

Against this background we can begin to understand the media system in Brazil as the country moved towards democracy after almost three decades of military rule. The degree to which democracy develops within a society depends directly on the plurality and diversity of ideas and values circulating within it. It has been suggested that Brazilian telenovelas (soap operas) have had a important impact on shaping Brazilian society and identity in terms of creating a pan-national sentiment, while keeping the citizens entertained, a product which has found transnational audiences, being exported to more than 100 countries (Mattelart and Mattelart, 1990; Joyce, 2012; Straubhaar, 2012).

The media's role in the public sphere and its accessibility, guaranteeing freedom of expression and the right to information are crucial to support democracy. Therefore, monitoring the level of media development in a country becomes a key component in monitoring the level of development of its democracy. The relationship between communication and democracy can be investigated using numerous approaches. In an era of profound transformation for liberal democracies, the limits and challenges of participation are some of the most important indicators of the health of democracy and public debate. Peter Dahlgren points out that democratic values and procedures are often overridden by economic values, thus limiting the space for effective political participation (Dahlgren, 2009: 6–7).

The primary objective of journalism has been defined as 'to provide citizens with the information they need to be free and self-governing' (Kovach and Rosenstiel, 2001: 17). These words, as McQuail has reminded us, carry a responsibility with them (McQuail, 2003), which media organizations and professionals should adopt in order to moderate the power they wield over their audience and society at large. Keeping track of how this responsibility is met is at the core of accountability practices (McQuail, 2003; Paulino, 2009; Fengler *et al.*, 2014).

With regard to the prominent role mass media play in modern societies, a growing number of media scholars, over the past few decades, have emphasized the urgent need to hold this media accountable (see for example, Curran, 2002; Waisbord, 2013; Vincent and Nordenstreng, 2016). This sentiment has been echoed by concerned media professionals and discussed worldwide in cases like the 2012 *News of the World* scandal in Britain. Observers agree that the quality of the media has to be monitored due to its unique role in democratic societies (McQuail, 1992; Schudson, 2018). They create a public sphere, where controversial arguments regarding political (and other) matters can be exchanged and acted upon by authorities.

The lack of an independent regulatory body for broadcasting services means Brazil did not have a centralized collection of data on the media sector, so information is not always accurate or robust. It was only in 2012 when the Ministry of Communications began to report data. Anatel (*Agência Nacional de Telecomunicações – the National Agency of Telecommunications*), the institution responsible for technical regulation, does have a grant system but the information thus provided is not always reliable or necessarily credible.

The main institutions in Brazil for the collection and organization of statistical data also do not have a history of covering communication. In 2010, the Institute for

Applied Economic Research (IPEA) established the 'Panorama of Communication and Telecommunications in Brazil' in partnership with Socicom (the Brazilian Federation of Scientific and Academic Associations of Communication). The same year marked another important effort to organize information on the media in Brazil using UNESCO's Media Development Indicators. A group of specialists from UNESCO, *Coletivo Intervozes*, the Laboratory of Communication Policies of the University of Brasilia, the Nucleus of Transdisciplinary Studies on Communication and Conscience of the Federal University of Rio de Janeiro, and the National Network of Press Observatories RENOI) collected and reported data on Brazilian media (Barbosa *et al.*, 2017). Some data is available from the private sector, in particular, on the Internet, data which is organized systematically and can be used for research, for example, by the Study Centre on Information Technology and Communication (Cetic.br), in conjunction with CGI.br, the Brazilian Internet Steering Committee.

In Brazil, the media system has economic strengths arising from the commercial sector, which has been successfully growing since the 1960s, but the weakness is that this development has occurred without a regulatory body to guarantee pluralism and diversity and without stimulus to the operation of Public Service Media. This economic strength arises from an almost universal system of commercial television and radio broadcasting, which generates a considerable amount of revenue. Even though newspapers, including major ones such as *O Estado de S. Paulo*, *Folha de S. Paulo* and *O Globo*, do not share this same economic strength (though the latter is part of the Rede Globo group – Brazil's biggest and one of the world's leading media conglomerates), they have benefited from a broader consumer market until the political crisis of recent years.

Of the more than 500 television channels on air, around 80 per cent are connected to large media conglomerates. In terms of audiences and advertising revenue, the four largest broadcasters – TV Globo, SBT, Record and Band – total more than 70 per cent and 90 per cent of the market share, respectively. In reality, the private media power was directly responsible for stimulating a group of networks out of partnerships with large national media groups and state political and economic groups. Around a third of the members of the Brazilian National Congress have some kind of connection to television and radio broadcasters, whether directly or indirectly. In addition to television, in 2018 there are nearly 4,600 community radio stations operating under license, while another 20,000 were still awaiting theirs. (Barbosa *et al.*, 2017). Public commercial, community and state channels are only available for those who can afford pay TV. The Brazilian Telecommunications Code has not been updated in a long time, while most articles of the country's Constitution dealing with Social Communication have not yet been implemented. Pluralism and diversity, which are important reference points for communication systems in many countries, are not covered by legislation in Brazil and are practically ignored as public policies. There is no legislation making the state responsible for strengthening and operating small circulation media outlets or public and community ones.

Media regulation in Brazil

The 1988 Constitution, like many international treaties ratified by Brazil, determines freedom of expression and the press in accordance with international codes. It protects access to information, the right of reply and privacy, and prohibits any kind of political, ideological or artistic censorship. The Constitution states that expressions of an intellectual, artistic, scientific and communicative manner are freedoms, independent of censorship or licensing, and it guarantees access to information for all.

However, legislation is too inconsistent to effectively guarantee freedom of expression and the situation has become worse in recent years. Campaigns are created by civil society, like the 2016 campaigns *Calar Jamais* ('*Shut up never*') based on cases of muzzling of media and harming journalists. Indicators show that the effects of the abuse of defamation laws have inhibited public debate and this represents a risk to freedom of expression. The OEA's Special Report on Freedom of Expression in 2019 included the cases of journalists who were being persecuted politically for looking into allegations of irregularities in public funds (Inter-American Commission on Human Rights, 2019). There is no legislation which supports censorship, but there are cases in which legal proceedings have created mechanisms blocking the treatment of certain issues or the citation of some names, creating a *de facto* censorship.

Access to information is upheld by law as part of the scrutiny of State and public institutions, but there is no ombudsman in public administration appointed to handle appeals. The culture of transparency and ethics in relation to the public's right to access information is still a fragile one in Brazil. The main regulatory bodies relating to media and communication (Anatel, the Ministry of Communication, Ancine – Brazilian Film Agency, CADE – Administrative Council for Economic Defense and the Ministry of Justice) are not sufficient: there is a need for constant and permanent monitoring to prevent broadcasting services from being exploited by partisan interests. In addition, there are no opportunities for public participation, whether that is for creating public policies or for receiving state grants. The only body under Constitution that could discharge this role in the sector is the Council on Social Communication, which serves only to support Parliament.

Monopoly or oligopoly with regard to ownership of the means of communication is formally prohibited in Brazil by the 1988 Constitution, which states that only one body can provide one type of radio broadcast service in the same area. However, the failure to impose limits on creating networks and the lack of effective monitoring for conflicts of interest with relatives or partners of media company owners are all examples of how the constitution is not enforced. Even though Article 223 of the Constitution imposes the principle of complementarity on the broadcasting sector, in order to maintain diversity between private, public and state systems, it has never been enforced through regulation. Anatel, the regulatory body responsible for channel distribution, does not consider pluralism when allocating frequencies, which, in turn, results in a prevalence of commercial broadcasters.

A law published in 2011 reaffirmed the position on ownership by permitting telecommunication companies to invest no more than 30 per cent of their capital in producing programmes, at the same time limiting investment by producers and programmers in telecommunications companies to 50 per cent of their capital. The law also established quotas for the transmission of national content: a minimum of 3.5 hours weekly in a primetime slot, half of which should be produced by an independent Brazilian producer. These obligations are due to cease in 2022.

Granting concessions and permissions are determined through licensing processes, also defined by law, which state that the more influence and reach a broadcast service has, the more it can charge. As the decision not to renew a license is dependent on 40 per cent of the Congress' votes (even if some serious irregularity has been committed) in roll-call vote, the licensee faces the possibility of being named and shamed, therefore making it very difficult to get back full legal right to its airwaves. In 2012, the Ministry of Communication published for the first time an annual plan for monitoring broadcasting services and license renewals became almost automatic. The only requirement made of license holders was to pay their taxes on time.

A maximum of one frequency channel per community radio station is permitted in each city. The combination of the one radio frequency per community, a maximum broadcast radius of 1 km, and the minimum distance of 4 km between broadcasters' results in a maximum of only 20 per cent coverage within the municipality, even if the radio stations were distributed in the best way possible. These limits can make it difficult to reach marginalized communities and prevents many communities from having a community radio station (Barbosa *et al.*, 2017).

There are no positive economic measures to promote community media. Quite the opposite, legislation prohibits spreading commercial advertising. The station *Canal Cidadania* made it possible for community members to participate in the operating of municipal channels, but they have yet to make it a sustainable reality. However, FM radio transmitters with multiple frequencies have been deployed by civil society groups to create political awareness and community communication and media literacy across the country (Novaes and Caminati, 2019).

The range of community television is smaller still, since such stations do not have guaranteed space in the spectrum allocated to public television. Due to the limited reach of its signal, and being available only in a few municipalities, there is a low access rate to public broadcasting. Commercial broadcasters have a much larger reach. Although only 11 per cent of the municipalities have television generators, due to the relays and repeaters, television is available in 95 per cent of Brazilian municipalities.

Television digitalization has been mostly through pay TV. At the end of 2013, more than 28 per cent of subscribers were already watching channels in high definition. Complete changeover occurred in 2018, two years later than anticipated. Regarding radio, Brazil has not yet determined which digitalization standard will be adopted. In 2012, an Advisory Board was formed to discuss the standard of digital radio, but the Radio Digital conversion is still without definition.[1]

With regard to official advertising, there have been advances in the distribution of public funds from the state, trying to promote transparency and diversification. From 2003 to 2013, the number of media enterprises that received public funds from the federal government grew from 499 to 9,663. However, this was concentrated on TV channels, at 69 per cent of resources, and Rede Globo companies alone received nearly 74 per cent of these resources.

Public service, public trust and attacks on journalists

It has only been since 2008 that the complementarity set out in the Constitution gained ground in the national public-service media system. There is, however, some confusion between public service and state systems reflected in both the management of the *Empresa Brasil de Comunicação* (EBC – Brazilian Enterprise of Communication) and in the more than 20 other state educational and cultural broadcasters. The reach of the EBC is quite limited, considering its objective of being a national public communications company and President Bolsonaro announced the intention, during the 2018 election campaign, to end the activities of the EBC. Already at risk, EBC has been fighting against restructuring since 2016: Temer's government proposed and Congress approved a law abolishing the Council of the EBC, with the effect that the Brazilian President would appoint the president of the EBC, compromising the independence and autonomy of the EBC in relation to the content and procedures of public TV, radio and news agencies (Fraga and Durazo-Herrmann, 2019).

In terms of media self-regulation, even though the media companies maintain internal codes of ethics and journalistic practice, there are few self-regulation mechanisms in the field of communication. One exception is advertising, which relies on CONAR (the National Council of Public Self-Regulation) and is often criticized by civil society organizations for its lax attitude towards excessive commercialization.

An important number of journalists point to ethics as a major factor in journalism quality, pointing out that the main national media and communication associations do not have an ombudsman, capable of dealing with allegations and complaints from the public about ethical violations within media outlets (Leal Filho *et al.*, 2012). The right to response is a fundamental right upheld in the Brazilian Constitution, yet this is not generally applied, due to media companies that do not uphold it, but its application is costly and often used by those who have more financial resources, such as politicians.

According to the Social Trust Index, measured by the IBOPE, the public's trust in media has declined and is at the lowest level since the beginning of this survey in 2009 (*IBOPE inteligencia*, 2019), which reflects the rise of social media, especially in the context of elections. The index has gone down from 71 points in 2009 to 51 in 2018. This trend was noticed in 2014 with data from the Secretary of Social Communication for the Presidency of the Republic, which commented that people did not have a high level of trust in news and commercials on television, radio, newspapers, magazines, sites, blogs and social media: only 41 per cent said they always or mostly trusted news on these media.

There has also been an increase in physical and verbal aggression against journalists, political activists and politicians. Data from FENAJ (the National Federation of Journalists) shows a large number of attacks being directed towards politicians or government authorities and 42 per cent are related to political issues or public administration. In January 2019, FENAJ presented its 'Report on Violence against Journalists and Press Freedom in Brazil, 2018'. In addition to the general number of cases of violence, journalist Ueliton Bayer Brizon was murdered in Rondônia State. There was also an increase in the number of murders of other communication professionals compared to the previous year when a blogger was murdered. Four radio journalists also lost their lives because of their professional activities (*Federação Nacional dos Jornalistas*, 2019)

Physical aggression was the most common violence mentioned in the Report, repeating the trend of previous years. There were 33 cases, which victimized 58 professionals, against 29 occurrences in 2017, an increase of 14 per cent. But there was a greater increase in the number of verbal assaults, threats/intimidations and impediments to professional practice. In 2018, verbal assaults and impediments to professional practice increased by over 100 per cent compared to the previous year; threats/intimidation cases grew by about 87 per cent (ibid.).

This significant growth is directly related to the presidential election of 2018 and the events associated with it, such as former President Lula da Silva's appeal to a Federal Regional Court and his subsequent imprisonment. Of the recorded cases of violence, 27 were directly related to the election and 16 to former President Lula. The supporters of the populist politician and ex-army Captain Jair Bolsonaro of the far-right *Partido Liberal Social* – and now President of the country – were responsible for most of the violence committed. In second place were the truck drivers who, during a strike, also assaulted journalists in several states.

Journalists were also victims of politicians, police officers, judges, businessmen, football team leaders and fans. In addition to murder, physical and verbal aggression, threats/intimidation (especially on social media) and impediments to professional practice, there were also cases of restrictions on freedom of the press due to judicial decisions, censorship, attacks, imprisonment and practices against the trade union organization of the category (Ganter and Paulino, 2020). Data from the InterAmerican Press Society and from Article 19 point to an increase in the cases of journalists being murdered. Research in 2018 from the Committee for Journalist Protection (CPJ), a New York-based advocacy group, demonstrates that Brazil is the country with the 10th highest number of journalist murders in the world that go unpunished. Between 1992 and 2018, 42 journalists were killed in Brazil: 40 of those were targeted for murder, and 28 of those were murdered with impunity (CPJ, 2018).

In 2020, FENAJ published a new report denouncing that President Bolsonaro was responsible for 58 attacks against journalists and media in Brazil in 2019, 17 per cent of the total, most of them made during official pronouncements. Since then, threats against the free press and the number of aggressions against journalists have been increasing in the country, reflecting the polarized environment, lack of political and social stability and absence of dialogue and agreement.

Journalism training

There are hundreds of courses related to journalism, and more broadly, communication in Brazil – many have journalism training and skill development at the core of their teaching. The country has more than 50 post-graduate programmes in communication (for a list see www.compos.org.br/programas.php). Data from IPEA and Socicom show a great increase in the number of courses in this field. The number of registrations for communication courses in public and private institutions demonstrates a growth both in the number of courses available and the number of registrations, which reached 186,000 in 2012.

The indicators show that curriculum guidelines only superficially cover issues of media rights, ethics, regulation and public policies. The relation between media and the promotion of democracy and human rights is not even directly mentioned in Social Communication curriculum guidelines. This is why media education requires two graduation courses: either in secondary schools or in civil society organizations. The media companies are also responsible for capacity building programmes. However, studies from RENOI (National Network of Press Observatories) indicate that awareness of the importance of pluralism and the relationship between journalism and the expansion of democracy among journalists is weak, and there is a lack of consensus among media professionals around fundamental values of diversity and plurality, which has a direct impact on the quality of journalism.

The important role of trade unions and professional organizations is indicated by the guarantee of professional and union memberships and the consolidated organization of journalists and broadcasters across the country. Unions and the National Federation are recognized as actors to be heard. There are at least two dozen civil society organizations, which monitor content and media ownership in order to promote pluralism and diversity. Many groups focus on media criticism and defending human rights, including representation of marginalized groups such as Black people, women and children. In the field of public service media and community communication there are also various bodies as well as a large number of organizations that deal with issues related to the Internet.

Lastly, academic institutions have also been following issues about media policies, ethics and professionalism, as well as broader aspects of digital connectivity through various surveys and studies. Two such highlights are Laboratory of Communication Policies and the SOS-Imprensa at the University of Brasilia, working on the subject since the 1990s. Another is the Brazil Chapter of the Latin Union of Political Economy Information, Communication and Culture (ULEPICC–Brazil), as well as the Brazilian Society of Interdisciplinary Communication Studies (Intercom).

The rise of the Internet and social media

In 2018, the Internet was reaching 67 per cent of the country's households, 64 per cent of them having broadband connections, according to data from the *TIC Domicílios 2017* survey from the Center of Studies on Information and Communication Technologies (CETIC.br), published at the end of 2018 (Telesintese, 2019). The study points out that inequalities by socio-economic class and by urban and rural areas persist: Internet access is present in 30 per cent of economically poor households (proportion was 23 per cent in 2016) and 34 per cent of rural households (in 2016, it was 26 per cent). Among middle and upper middle classes, this proportion is, respectively, 99 per cent and 93 per cent. In addition, 19 per cent of connected households do not have a computer, which represents 13.4 million households.

The *TIC Domicílios 2017* survey indicates that half of the connected population accesses the Internet exclusively by mobile phone, which represents 58.7 million Brazilians. For the first time in the history of this annual survey, the study showed that the proportion of users accessing the network only by mobile phone (49 per cent) surpassed those using both mobile phone and computer (47 per cent). The profile of exclusive use of a mobile phone is more common among low-income citizens (80 per cent) and those who live in rural areas (72 per cent). According to the study, the price of the connection was the main reason mentioned for the absence of the Internet in homes: 27 per cent of respondents said that the service was too expensive. This perception reinforces the need for investment in infrastructure and public policies that allow everyone to have access to the Internet in their homes. In 2010, the government created the National Broadband Programme with hopes of promoting access. However, by the end of 2014, the programme had not reached its goals. The issue of Internet quality is seen as an industry problem but there are prospects of improvement after Anatel had approved a regulation in 2011 requiring operators to ensure good broadband speed.

The growth of Internet access in Brazil has been accompanied by the popular use of social media as a source of information. According to the *Digital Media Report 2018*, published by the Reuters Institute, about 50 million Brazilians use Instagram and 130 million use Facebook. The country is one of the world's most enthusiastic social media users: two-thirds (66 per cent) of respondents to their survey use social media as a source of news. About 120 million Brazilians use the WhatsApp application (Reuters Institute, 2018). The popularity of the app and its use for political purposes, including during the last presidential election campaign, opened up an important discussion about the dissemination of fake news as an instrument of electoral propaganda against political opponents. Right-wing groups have been particularly good at using hostile and aggressive messages, memes, personal narratives and direct channels of mobilization against progressive politicians and activists (Chagas, Modesto, and Magalhaes, 2019). In 2014, Brazil passed the *Marco Civil da Internet* or Brazilian Civil Rights Framework for the Internet (the 'Marco Civil'), which establishes 'principles, guarantees, rights and obligations for the use of the Internet in Brazil' and 'provides guidelines' for all levels of Brazilian government to follow when regulating this use (Souza, Viola and Lemos, 2017). Expanding the fibre network to the interior regions of the country and installing submarine cables is part of government plan to improve digital communication. There has been a notable growth in cable and fibre optic use in recent years, though the speeds of connections remain poor and the government has implemented a number of Internet expansion and improvement programmes.

Conclusion

As can be seen in this chapter, on the one hand, the decade since 2010 demonstrates significant changes in the processes of production, distribution and access to communication in Brazil, brought about by technological changes, including the growth of the Internet, and economic and social changes, influenced by the political turbulence that the country has experienced with even greater intensity after 2015. On the other hand, during this period, some important initiatives were established but are running down and are at risk of being closed, such as the initiative of a Public Service of Media, which is likely to be discontinued and its organizational structure used for governmental purposes.

In summarizing the character of the current media system in Brazil, according to official data, television remains the main source of information. However, with more Brazilians using the Internet every day, the media system and access to media have changed, especially for youth and others who use the Internet on mobile phones, particularly for social media. These characteristics have altered the relationship between media and politics, creating a more complex media environment.

In addition, there are doubts about the role of the media during the far-right-wing Bolsonaro government, which has been openly supporting one of the leading television networks (Biller and Watson, 2018). Bolsonaro, for instance, promised to and did change the criteria for distributing official advertising funding, benefiting companies with editorial content more aligned with his party's policies. This concern is especially relevant to print media because leading newspapers have been labelled as the 'enemies of the people' by the President and are suffering, more than other media, the effects of the political and economic crisis.

Other important point is related to the impacts of digital changes. In recent years the main question has been and will be: how will the Internet change the current Brazilian media system? In addition, the political context is also important: what will be the effects of the Bolsonaro government on the media landscape in Brazil and on Brazilian political culture? In such polarized and turbulent times, there are more questions and doubts than answers and prospects.

Note

1 www.mctic.gov.br/mctic/opencms/legislacao/portarias/migracao/Portaria_MC_n_365_de_14082012.html?searchRef=abratel&tipoBusca=expressaoExata

References

Albuquerque, A. (2012) On models and margins: Comparative media models viewed from a Brazilian perspective, pp. 72–95 in D. Hallin and P. Mancini (eds.) *Comparing Media Systems Beyond the Western World*. Cambridge: Cambridge University Press.

Albuquerque, A. (2017) Protecting democracy or conspiring against it? Media and politics in Latin America: A glimpse from Brazil. *Journalism*, 20(7): 906–923.

Barbosa, B., Paulino, F.O., Pereira, S., Amorim, A.P., Bandeira, O., Moysés, D., Ouriques, E. and Brant, J. (2017) Brasil e seu desenvolvimento mediático: síntese e análise da aplicação dos indicadores da unesco. *Infoamerica: Iberoamerican Communication Review,* 11: 75–95. Available at https://dialnet.unirioja.es/servlet/articulo?codigo=6435758'

Biller, D. and Watson, R. (2018) Bolsonaro makes Upstart Evangelical Network Brazil's must-see TV. *Bloomberg News*, 18 November.

Birman, P. and Lehmann, D. (1999) Religion and media in a battle for ideological hegemony: The universal church of the Kingdom of God and TV Globo in Brazil. *Bulletin of Latin American Research,* 18(9): 145–164.

Calar Jamais (2016) *Calar Jamais* Campaign. Available at www.youtube.com/watch?v=T6k22KCGkJs

CPJ (2018) *Getting Away with Murder*. New York: Committee to Protect Journalists, October. Available at https://cpj.org/reports/2018/10/impunity-index-getting-away-with-murder-killed-justice.php

Chagas, V., Modesto, M. and Magalhaes, D.O. (2019) Brasil vai virar Venezuela: medo, memes e enquadramentos emocionais no WhatsApp Pro-Bolsonaro. *Esferas*, 14: 1–17.

Curran, J. (2002) *Media and Power*. London: Routledge.

Dahlgren, P. (2009) *Media and Political Engagement: Citizens, Communication, and Democracy*. Cambridge: Cambridge University Press.

Davis, S. and Straubhaar, J. (2012) Producing *Antipetismo*: Media activism and the rise of the radical, nationalist right in contemporary Brazil. *International Communication Gazette,* 82(1): 82–100.

Davis, S., Straubhaar, J. and Cunha, I. F. (2016) The construction of a transnational Lusophone media space: A historiographic analysis. *Popular Communication: The International Journal of Media and Culture,* 14(4): 212–223.

Federação Nacional dos Jornalistas (2019) *Violência contra Jornalistas e Liberdade de Imprensa no Brasil*. Relatório 2019. Brasilia: Federação Nacional dos Jornalistas. Available at: https://fenaj.org.br/wpcontent/uploads/2020/01/relatorio_fenaj_2019.pdf

Fengler, S., Eberwein, T., Mazzoleni, G., Porlezza, C. and Ruß-Mohl, S. (eds.) (2014) *Journalists and Media Accountability: An International Study of News People in the Digital Age*. New York: Peter Lan.

Fraga, M. and Durazo-Herrman, J. (2019) The challenges of Public Broadcasting Service: a study of *EmpresaBrasil de Comunicação*. *Journalism*. https://doi.org/10.1177/1464884919871139.

Ganter, S. A. and Paulino, F. O. (2020) Between attack and resilience: the ongoing institutionalization of independent digital journalism in Brazil. *Digital Journalism*, DOI: 10.1080/21670811.2020.1755331

IBOPE inteligencia (2019) *Confiança do brasileiro nas instituições é a mais baixa desde 2009*. IBOPE inteligencia. Available at www.ibopeinteligencia.com/noticias-e-pesquisas/confianca-do-brasileiro-nas-instituicoes-e-a-mais-baixa-desde-2009/

Inter-American Commission on Human Rights (2019) *Annual Report of the Office of the Special Rapporteur for Freedom of Expression*. Inter-American Commission on Human

Rights. Office of the Special Rapporteur for Freedom of Expression. pp. 65–80. Available at www.oea.org/en/iachr/expression/docs/reports/annual/IA2018RELE-en.pdf

Joyce, S. (2012) *Brazilian Telenovelas and the Myth of Racial Democracy*. New York: Lexington Books.

Kovach, B. and Rosenstiel, T. (2001) *The Elements of Journalism: What Newspeople Should Know and the Public Should Expect*. New York: Three Rivers Press.

Leal Filho, L., Paulino, F. O. and Martins da Silva, L. (2012) Radio ombudsman services of Brazilian Public Radio (EBC) as media accountability instruments. *Central European Journal of Communication*, 2: 275–283.

Martins da Silva, L. and Paulino, F. O. (2007) Media accountability systems: models, proposals and outlooks. *Brazilian Journalism Research* 3(1): 137–153. Available at https://bjr.sbpjor.org.br/bjr/article/view/103.

Mattelart, A. and Mattelart, M. (1990) *A Carnival of Images: Brazilian Television Fiction*. New York: Bergin and Garvey.

Matos, C. (2008) *Journalism and Political Democracy in Brazil*. Lanham, MD: Lexington Books.

Matos, C. (2012) *Media and Politics in Latin America: Globalization, Democracy and Identity*. London: I. B. Tauris.

McQuail, D. (1992) *Media Performance: Mass Communication and the Public Interest*. London: Sage.

McQuail D. (2003) *Media Accountability and Freedom of Publication*. Oxford: Oxford University Press.

Nalon, T. (2018) Did WhatsApp help Bolsonaro win the Brazilian presidency? *Washington Post*. 1 November.

Norris, P. and Inglehart, R. (2019) *Cultural Backlash: Trump, Brexit and Authoritarian Populism*. Cambridge: Cambridge University Press.

Novaes, T. and Caminati, F. (2019) Nomadic transmitter: public sphere and aesthetics in Brazilian media activism. *Westminster Papers in Communication and Culture*, 14(1): 81–93.

Paulino, F. O. (2009) *Responsabilidade social da mídia: Análiseconceitual e perspectivas de aplicação no Brasil, Portugal e Espanha*. Brasília: Casa das Musas. Available on: https://repositorio.unb.br/handle/10482/5175

Philips, D. (2017) Brazil senate approves austerity package to freeze social spending for 20 years. *The Guardian*, December 13.

Porto, M. (2011) The media and political accountability, pp. 103–126 in T. J. Power and M. M. Taylor (eds.) *Corruption and Democracy in Brazil: The Struggle for Accountability*. Notre Dame, IN: University of Notre Dame Press.

Porto, M. (2012) *Media Power and Democratization in Brazil: TV Globo and the Dilemmas of Political Accountability*. London: Routledge.

Reis, R. (2006) Media and religion in Brazil. *Brazilian Journalism Research* 2(2): 157–172.

Reuters Institute (2018) *Digital News Report 2018*. Oxford: Reuters Institute for the Study of Journalism.

Rosas-Moreno, T. (2014) *News and Novela in Brazilian Media: Fact, Fiction, and National Identity*. New York: Rowman & Littlefield.

Schudson, M. (2018) *Why Journalism Still Matters*. Cambridge: Polity.

Sinclair, J. and Straubhaar, J. (2013) *Television Industries in Latin America*. London: BFI/ Palgrave.

Souza, C., Viola, M. and Lemos, R. (eds.) (2017) *Brazil's Internet Bill of Rights: A Closer Look*. Rio de Janeiro: Institute for Technology and Society of Rio de Janeiro. Available at https://itsrio.org/wp-content/uploads/2018/02/v5_com-capa__pages_miolo_Brazil-Internet-Bill-of-Rights-A-closer-Look.pdf

Straubhaar, J. (2012) Telenovelas in Brazil: From traveling scripts to a genre and proto-format both national and transnational, pp. 148–77 in T. Oren and S. Shahaf (eds.) *Global Television Formats: Understanding Television Across Borders*. London: Routledge.

Telesintese (2019) Acesso À Internet Chega A 67% Dos Domicílios Brasileiros, Diz Cetic. Br. Available at www.telesintese.com.br/acesso-a-Internet-chega-a-61-dos-domicilios-brasileiros-diz-cetic-br/

Van Dijk, T. (2017) How Globo Media manipulated the impeachment of Brazilian President Dilma Rousseff. *Discourse & Communication*, 11(2): 199–229.

Vincent, R. and Nordenstreng, K. (eds.) (2016) *Towards Equity in Global Communication?* Second edition. New York: Hampton Press.

Waisbord, S. (2013) *Reinventing Professionalism: Journalism and News in Global Perspective*. Cambridge: Polity.

5
A POST-ANALOGUE HYBRID MEDIA SYSTEM

The Russian case

Elena Vartanova

BRICS media offer an interesting case for understanding how contemporary processes are affected by very specific national political and economic conditions and historically and culturally diverse contexts and for assessing how applicable the established concepts in Western media studies are. The discourse of the latter has been challenged by such approaches as de-Westernization, Internationalization or even Easternization (De Smaele, 1999; Curran and Park, 2000; Thussu, 2009; 2018; Waisbord and Mellado, 2014). Given current geopolitical power shifts and digital transformations of national socio-cultural contexts, BRICS media systems can provide fresh empirical evidence for constructing new media models.

The key processes to consider here are: the digitalization of and convergence in media industries, which in less developed industrial economies should be understood in the context of digital globalization (Thussu, 2018: 55); shifts in traditional 'media-state-politics' paradigms under the influence of 'democracy' and 'free market' concepts, including business models of media enterprises different from the theoretically dominant, Western ones (Noam, 2016); the clash between old and new regulatory systems in national media policy-making processes, bringing together a range of policy streams and multiple stakeholders (Nieminen, 2019: 58–60), and, finally, in relation to journalism practice, the interplay of national and global standards and ethics in the construction of professional cultures and identity (Paasti and Ramaprasad, 2017). Each BRICS country can provide an illustrative case, even if its impact on media theory-making is a matter for debate.

The BRICS countries represent dynamically developing media contexts, less explored by media scholars, but which are characterized by strong links with a country's economic position, territorial diversity, complex ethnic and linguistic structures and, particularly, the specific path of its historical development and the diverse roles the media played in societal dynamics (Hallin and Mancini, 2012; Nordenstreng and Thussu, 2015). Compared to the Western media systems rooted in market-based democratic political systems (Hallin and Mancini, 2004; Hardy, 2008; 2012; Curran *et al.*, 2009; Flew and Waisbord, 2015), BRICS countries represent alternative, though different historical trajectories in which such issues as post-colonialism, socialism and post-socialism, path dependency, social inequalities, multi-ethnicity and multiculturalism need to be taken into account. The interrelations between the conceptual positions of Western media studies and realities in media systems beyond the Western world do exist, but in more complex and controversial ways than in the Western world. Recent debates on the typology of media systems, their homogeneity and/or hybridization initiated and continued by Hallin and Mancini (2004; 2012) have become a theoretical challenge for countries outside the 'Western' world.

Scholars have elaborated the empirical basis of typology-building by adding more variables or emphasizing the role of national contexts, both in defining the nature of national media system or their influence on the particular work of established or new variables (Dobek-Ostrowska *et al.*, 2010; Büchel *et al.*, 2016). The study of BRICS media systems has opened new ways to explore the concept in entirely different national contexts, as well as to contribute to defining universal and nationally specific variables of a media system (Nordenstreng and Thussu, 2015).

The Russian case

In Russia, while the media structures have been adjusting to the processes of global digitalization and adapting national legislative and economic regimes to mega-changes, the nationally determined culture and socially diverse value systems have continued to strongly influence media. The contemporary Russian media system is diverse and contradictory, reflecting the multi-layered structure and the geographical and socio-economic complexity of modern Russia. It is unique for a number of reasons. Russia is the largest country in the world and unevenly populated, with 11 time zones from the Baltic Sea in Europe to the Pacific Ocean in the far east of Asia. Its highly diverse, multi-ethnic population speaks more than 100 languages apart from the official Russian. Thus, the media and broadcasting system, using terrestrial and satellite networks, is very much determined by geography and ethnography: in addition to the dominant federal television channels, there is a need to maintain media in a high number of minority languages (Vartanova, 2019).

The fall of the USSR (1991) marked a new period in Russian media history: post-Soviet society introduced new social structures and practices, including competitive elections, the abolition of the Communist ideological monopoly, a decrease in state control over the national economy and culture. For media, this resulted in prohibition of censorship, legislation to protect freedom of the press, privatization of state-owned media companies and a shift to an advertising-based business model, as well as gradual adaptation to global standards of journalism. Important was a breakdown of the centralized and pyramid-form Soviet media system and the rise of horizontal, regionally structured media markets. But the media transformation process in Russia, though common to many transitional media systems in Central and Eastern Europe, looks quite different, due to specific features of the social changes in Russia (Splichal, 1994; Sparks and Reading, 1998; McNair, 2000; Nordenstreng *et al.*, 2002; Rantanen, 2002; Toepfl, 2013).

It is obvious that the Russian media system has been changing under the pressures of globalization, economic neo-liberalization and digitalization, as media systems elsewhere in the world. These changes were also an intrinsic part of more profound societal transformations. Nevertheless, despite these large-scale political and economic transformations, Russian society and media have kept many traditions and practices rooted in the country's history. The relationship between the state and media has always defined the functioning of the media system. Since 1703, when Tsar Peter the Great established the first Russian newspaper, *Vedomosti*, the strong ideological and economic relations between the Russian state and journalism continued for almost two centuries (Ivanitsky, 2010: 56). The paternalistic tradition of state–media relations can be seen in the state regulation and state media policies influencing the developing legislative frameworks of a multi-ethnic and multi-linguistic Russian society (Gladkova *et al.*, 2019). This chapter aims to analyse current processes in the Russian media system at three institutional dimensions of the Russian media system, that of the media industry, social media and media regulation, thus focusing on the work of currently influential 'agents of change' in the Russian media in the first two decades of the second millennium.

The Russian media industry: digitalization as a driver

The Russian media industry today is the result of the multi-layered and controversial post-Soviet processes of deregulation, privatization and shift to a market economy (Vartanova, 2015). However, its present state is much more complex compared to earlier transformational stages. The transition of the Russian media to new economic, organizational and technological systems was an integral part of the large-scale social transformations that started in the 1990s and continued with the digitalization of media production and consumption in the 2000s. This has resulted in a permanent restructuring of the Russian media industry in many different dimensions. While in the 1990s it moved from the rigid state-controlled planned economy to private ownership and market-driven commercial business models, with almost no anti-trust and foreign ownership regulation, in the 2000s the Russian media industry expanded due to the growth of the advertising market stimulated by domestic economic growth, paralleled by an increased audience demand for news and entertainment, as well as a rapid audience shift to online media (Ivanitsky, 2010; Makeenko and Vyrkovsky, 2013; Vartanova, 2015).

The number of media companies registered by *Roscomnadzor* (the Federal Service for Supervision of Communications, Information Technology and Mass Media, RKN), the national media regulator, has grown substantially. However, the most visible growth is seen in digital media, with increasing penetration all over Russia. As a result of digitalization since the 1990s, by 2019 the Internet and social media were accessible through broadband and mobile networks to more than 75

TABLE 5.1 Changes in the Russian media industry, 2000–2019

Indicators	2000	2019
Population (in million)	146.3	146.8
Federal TV channels penetration (as per cent of the population)	98.1	98.6
FM and AM radio stations penetration (as per cent of the population)	64.2	89.9
Internet users (in million)	3.1	95.8
Personal computers per 1000 households	60	800
Mobile phones per 1000 people	22	1,969
.ru domains	250,000	4,951,205
.рф domains (since 2010)	0	742,285
Advertising market (in billion $)	0.8	7.6
Internet advertising (in billion $)	0.03	3.9
Average number of terrestrial TV channels per household	7	80
Average number of radio channels per household	11	n/a
Time of average daily media consumption	4 hours 29 minutes	9 hours 40 minutes

Sources: Vartanova, 2019; Rosstat, 2020; Mediascope, 2020a; AKAR, 2020; Deloitte, 2019.

per cent of Russian households, providing them with Russian-language content in the .ru domain. In the 2010s, Russia became one of the most advanced countries in terms of Internet use for information and recreation and the digital media became one of the crucial parts of the Russian media system. In qualitative terms the Russian media industry is quite large though uneven (see Table 5.1).

However, the different levels of the Russian media industry – national, regional and local – remain rather unequal in terms of the distribution of economic resources. While the bulk of advertising revenues are concentrated on the national media based in Moscow, local media businesses continue to find it difficult to attract local advertising. As a result, the poor financial state of media companies in small cities and their uneasy relations with local governments, which often formally or informally finance local newspapers, are among the worst factors affecting the Russian media industry (Shchepilova and Burianova, 2014).

In the 2010s, the Russian media industry was challenged by media digitalization and new patterns of media consumption, especially among young urban digital Russians representing 'Generation Z' (Dunas and Vartanov, 2020; Vyugina, 2017). Also, there has been a clear shift in media policy from deregulation to reregulation by the government to restrict foreign ownership in the media industry and tighten state control over the digital infrastructure (Galkina and Lehtisaari, 2016; Vartanova, 2019).

At present the Russian media industry with its uneasy combination of the old and the new, the analogue and the digital, might be described by several important characteristics. First, in the last three decades national terrestrial television has become and still remains the core of the industry, accumulating a comparatively large share of financial and audience resources. According to the Communication Agencies Association of Russia, the total advertising revenues of terrestrial TV channels in the mid-2010s were about 1.5 times higher than the revenues of their closest competitors, the online media. The majority of Russians get their news from national free-to-air channels and, according to many surveys, television remains the main source of daily news for 57 per cent of Russians (Makeenko and Vyrkovsky, 2013).

The dominance of national television has even strengthened in the Russian digital switch-over, i.e. the national implementation of the federal programme for the 'Development of Television and Radio Broadcasting in the Russian Federation in 2009–2015'. As a result of this digital switch over, 20 television channels became free and universally available for the national audience via the first digital multiplex. About 99 per cent of Russians have access to these channels broadcast in digital format – a huge change from having on average only four free channels previously. For the majority viewers this has also resulted in an improved quality of broadcasting signal and, while regional broadcasting markets have shrunk and their news content reduced, the supply of news and entertainment from national broadcasters has substantially increased.

Second, the advertising-based business model is the most prevalent in all segments of the Russian media industry, regardless of ownership structure. Whether private, state-owned or hybrid in terms of ownership, all media companies struggle for advertising revenues, which is reflected in the unequal national distribution of economic resources in the industry. Though less widespread, but promising, is the audience-based model, still strong in the market for glossy magazines and in the subscription-based model for cable and satellite channels. However, the audience-based model is mostly present in large urban centres with higher living standards than in other regions (Vartanova *et al.*, 2017: 40).

Third, there is a high level of concentration in leading segments of the media industry, along with an enhanced state media ownership. During the 2000s, there was a decrease in private investment in the media business, paralleled by a growth in state and hybrid (state and private, non-media) media ownership. At the same time, the number of small and medium size media companies has decreased. The largest media companies are currently owned either by state-controlled organizations (VGTRK, Gazprom-Media) or by powerful private conglomerates with their main interests outside the media sector, including banking or heavy industry (National Media Group) (Smirnov, 2014; 2016).

Fourth, given that most financial and labour resources are centralized in Moscow, almost all major Russian media outlets are also based in the Russian capital and they continue to dominate advertising, audience share and news agendas. Regional media holdings are much smaller in terms of revenues and audiences and cannot compete in national or even regional markets (Ershov, 2012; Makeenko and Vyrkovsky, 2013; Smirnov, 2016).

Digitalization

As in the other BRICS countries, the media industries in Russia, too, are going through a period of digital transformation, driven by new processes such as the constantly growing supply of digital media content and the increase in audience demand for news and entertainment on new digital platforms. A study based on interviews with 50 senior managers in the media industry identified four main possible scenarios for the media industry, which, through its rapid development, could significantly influence the contours of the Russian media system (see Figure 5.1) (Vartanova *et al.*, 2017).

The scenarios, though not unique for Russia, are shaped by two recent trends. The first is the rapid change in media consumption patterns and audience behaviour. Within a decade, media consumption is expected to change with new generational media cultures, since young Russians representing a 'digital' generation become older and are expected to replace audiences who formed their media consuming habits in the pre-digital era. As many surveys demonstrate, more than half of 18–45 year old Russians consume news online, while less than one third of 45–64 group do (Dunas *et al.*, 2017; Dunas and Vartanov, 2020), resulting into a move away from watching linear TV and reading print media. A top-manager representing print media remarked: 'the audience will migrate online. There is an audience born online and it will remain there'. Another CEO from a production company assumed that in ten years 'we'll see the change of generations – coming of the people who have been living the whole life with the Internet or linked to media consumption and changing business models, mobile device and content search are a new reality, not just a TV screen or a button' (Vartanova *et al.*, 2017: 42). However, a few managers expected continuation of some type of traditional media consumption patterns.

The second trend is the shift from the advertising-driven business model, which currently dominates the industry, to a model based on content sales. As

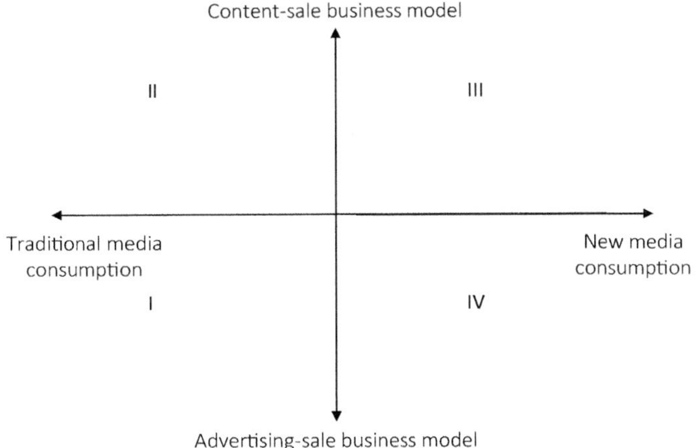

FIGURE 5.1 Scenarios of Russian media industry development

the editor-in-chief of a major content aggregator stated, 'The future is surely in favour of the paid subscriptions, but for the time being, the audience, moreover, the Russian one, is not ready for that' (Vartanova *et al.*, 2017: 42). Nevertheless, revenues from advertising sales (at least, in their traditional forms) are going to decrease in the Russian media. An editor-in-chief of a major online media in Russia predicted: 'Sooner or later, the quality niche media will be the first in need to collect some cash from its users, which would lead to decrease of their overall number but also to the revenue growth' (Ibid., 2017: 43).

The four scenarios can be described as follows:

I   **'Inertial'** – continuation of existing practices of media consumption retaining the advertising model as the key one in media business;
II   **'Nonlinear television-based'** – relies on revenues from content sales with the preservation of the traditional media consumption model, based on watching TV;
III   **'Revolutionary'** – mass rejection of old media consumption practices and simultaneous rapid content sales growth;
IV   **'Customization-oriented'** – spread of a new media consumption model while retaining the advertisement-driven model (Vartanova *et al.*, 2017: 43–44).

Although all these scenarios are possible on the basis of the empirical data, the majority of top managers believed that the 'inertial' scenario was the most probable. While caution should be exercised with any prediction, this research has shown that digital transformation will continue to reshape the contours of Russian media business and digitalization as a process will define both transformation of business models and the development of digital media.

Digital media reshaping the media system

The Russian Internet has been developing since 1993 and the number of users has been increasing rapidly, initially in large industrial cities but, in the past decade, more evenly across the country, reaching an Internet penetration rate of 72 per cent in 2018 (Mediascope, 2020b). As in many other countries, mobile telephony has played a major role in this expansion of digital media. In the early 2010s, mobiles proved a cheap and effective mechanism for accessing the Internet, becoming a major driver for Internet penetration in large cities and among young Russians: between 2011 and 2015 the number of Russian Internet users doubled annually (Internet v Rossii v 2018, 2019).

The rising penetration of the Internet, together with growth of digital literacy and increasing amount of content and services has made it the most serious challenger to legacy media: television, radio and the press. As a result, the majority of media outlets have moved some distribution to the Internet: by 2017 the audience of the Internet sites of popular print media outnumbered the circulation of print editions of Kp.ru (10.5 million), AiF.ru (5.9 million) and Mk.ru (5.7 million).

Many popular online media such as Gazeta.ru or Lenta.ru have ceased their print operations. Even major broadcasters such as the national 'Big Three' – *Rossija 1*, *Pervyi Kanal* and *NTV* – have their online presence, and provide viewers with newscasts, documentaries, children's programmes and, especially, drama serials on their websites (Vartanova, 2019: 29–30).

A significant role in transforming the Internet into a digital media space was played by the shift of advertising revenues to Internet companies. In 2012 the domestic search engine Yandex out-performed the most popular free-to-air television channel, *Pervyi kanal*, in terms of advertising income. Other new players of the emerging Russian digital media ecosystem – Mail.ru, Vkontakte (VK) and Odnoklassniki social networks and the Telegram messenger – have acquired the largest audience and advertising flows, forming an integral system of production and distribution of digital content between authors, producers, media companies and users. The role of legacy media in this new digital environment is steadily decreasing (Veselov, 2017).

Recently, there has been a big increase in the use of social media: search engines, social networks and messengers are the most popular Internet resources for Russian users Google became the most used Internet platform with a monthly audience of 82.5 million, overtaking its main competitor the Russian search engine Yandex (81.2 million), while YouTube had a monthly audience reach of 81.2 million, in comparison with popular Russian social networks – Vkontakte (69.8 million) and Odnoklassniki (52.3 million) (Mediascope, 2020a). Among message services, WhatsApp was the clear leader, with more than 41 per cent of Russians using it. However, the rapid success of Telegram, a messenger created by Pavel Durov from Russia, was a surprise success in 2018, with about 10 per cent of Russians using it. With 22 million monthly users, Instagram, too, was very popular among Russians (Internet v Rossii v 2018, 2019).

Another important trend in the digital media landscape is the popularity of user-generated content accessed through LiveJournal, Zen.yandex, YouTube and Telegram. A large number of bloggers, including professional and non-professional authors, compete with the legacy media for audiences and advertising on several digital platforms. Russian blogger Iliya Varlamov, for example, was one of the top authors on Telegram and his photo blog on LiveJournal, as well as on his own online media, attracted two million visitors per month. Russian language video blogs on YouTube, producing a variety of entertainment and infotainment content, are also extremely popular among the young demographic. Well-known journalists – notably Yury Dud, Leonid Parfenov and Maxim Shevchenko – have started new careers on YouTube with socially significant interviews and documentaries, analysis of political issues or film and book reviews, for a discerning audience.

The growth of content available on social media and digital platforms has also affected digital audiences in several ways. First, there is a clear trend towards diversification and complexity of the audience structure and digital media usage compared to the early years of the Russian Internet, when users were mostly the younger and wealthier urban population. Currently, digital audiences include an increasing number of females (more than a half of all users), as well as members of various ethnic and linguistic groups and residents of small towns and villages (Internet v Rossii v 2018, 2019). Second, the younger segment of the Internet audience has grown substantially: in Russian cities with a population over one million, about 70 per cent of youngsters aged under 22 are active users. Surveys have shown that almost all schoolchildren and students from large and medium sized cities access Internet through mobile and social networks, which have become a new 'entry point' into the digital media landscape and communication space (Dunas *et al.*, 2017).

The communication behaviour and media consumption of young Russians is different to that of older age groups, and scholars have focused on the media consumption of the 'generations' X, Y and especially Z, as particular communities united not only by common media habits but also by lifestyles and values (Vyugina, 2017). As Dunas and Vartanov argue, their primary reasons for such consumption patterns 'are associated not only with socialization as the adoption of prevailing norms and values but with the satisfaction of the need for attachment and involvement in a specific community, the approval of its members and integration into that community' (Dunas and Vartanov, 2020: 8). In the last decade, the online media environment has also begun to play a crucial role in public communication, making an impact on election campaigns, public debates, agenda setting and discussions on economic, social, cultural and ethnic issues (Davydov, 2020). It might be argued that, as a consequence of Internet expansion, the structure of the Russian Internet audience resembles and even replicates the structure of society, indicating the societal significance of digital media.

Digital divides

Digital inequalities reflect the existing inequalities between regions in terms of their economic prosperity, development of telecommunication infrastructure, differences in legal systems, etc. In a country of multi-ethnic and linguistic diversity, comprising 190 ethnic groups speaking more than 170 languages, the Russian Federation remains a kaleidoscope of plurality, despite a centralized polity dominated by one powerful leader. The digital divide is the result of a complex set of factors including the socio-economic status of users, their education, location, etc. (Ragnedda and Muschert, 2013). Inequalities as a result of limited access to digital infrastructure and digital capital are also related to ethnicity through a complex of dependent variables, as many ethnic minority groups live in economically less developed regions of the country (Gladkova *et al.*, 2019).

The government has a responsibility to promote equality on ethnic, cultural and linguistic grounds and overcome the digital divide, through political programmes and setting a policy framework for federal and regional levels. These include such federal laws as 'On Languages of the Peoples of the Russian Federation' and 'On Securing Rights of Small Indigenous Peoples of the Russian Federation', as well as programmes, notably, 'Strengthening of the Unity of the Russian Nation and the

Ethno-cultural Development of the Peoples of Russia (2014–2020)'. They all aim to strengthen the role of the media in building intercultural dialogue and provide media content in different languages of Russia's ethnic groups. However, given the current legal regulation of Russian media and the multiplicity of strands within media policy (discussed below), there are questions about the efficacy of the state as the sole policy maker, as well as the effectiveness of regulation to prevent digital inequality (Timofeyev, 2019).

The growing importance of the Internet within the Russian media system has challenged traditional media in relation to political agenda-setting and news and entertainment provision. Growing social media networks today provide audiences with a huge variety of journalistic and user-generated content. Different and radically opposite views and ideologies are widely represented in the digital sphere: not only political parties and official state agencies, but also numerous personal sites of opposition leaders create a diversity of political and cultural views. While some scholars consider this digital landscape to be intolerant, ignorant and incompetent (Samartsev, 2017), others underline the importance of the variety of viewpoints, essential for an informed citizenry (Davydov, 2020).

Media policy-making: analogue to digital

As a theoretical area within Russian media studies, media policy differs from international approaches in a number of ways, as 'media policy' is not a widely used Russian term or concept. Russian political discourse prefers the term 'state information policy', thus establishing it within a conceptual framework as a state-driven policy, primarily with regard to the role of the state in the regulation of the production and distribution of, primarily, journalistic content.

The legacy media in Russia continue to be influenced by the basic forms of national regulation covering audio-visual media, ownership restriction, copyright protection and preventing harmful content for audiences (Rickhter, 2007; Pankeyev, 2019). Moreover, the regulation of content production and editorial processes within traditional media companies also involves 'self-regulatory' mechanisms, from codes of journalistic ethics and editorial charters to informal rules and culturally and historically defined taboos (Pankeyev, 2019; Roudakova, 2017). The widening digitalization of the Russian media has stimulated the emergence of new policy approaches with a particular focus on the universal access to Internet, demands for no regulation of the networked media, for open source and the appeal for a user-generated content media model (Gureyeva and Samorodova, 2019).

Over the last two decades, Russian media policy has developed through various phases. In the early stages, Russian media policy was concentrated on protecting freedom of speech and was seen by the society and journalism professionals as developing a legal framework for a 'free press', especially because it was a part of the socially broader transformation process aimed to replace the Soviet legal system (Rickhter, 2007). For the media system in general there was a clear need to change Communist, top-down, ideologically based media regulation to a more liberal regulatory and policy framework in line with the new democratic values of the media field (Nordenstreng *et al.*, 2002).

The philosophy of the new market-driven economy defined media policy in the 1990s, with an emphasis on the de-politicization of the media resulting in media deregulation. In addition, in relation to professional regulation, the reconceptualization of journalism with regard to the principle of the freedom of the press (and the complete abolition of the censorship) became a dominant process. This was also supported by the mainstream neoliberal approaches of the Russian media market (Ivanitsky, 2010). In the 1990s and 2000s the changing economic structures of the Russian media industry through privatization and commercial advertising-based business models called for state withdrawal from the media ownership and media market (Rantanen, 2002; Shchepilova, 2010).

In the 2000s, Russian media policy-making embraced multiple pressures and diverse actors in a response to institutionalization of emerging social institutions and processes. For instance, media industry regulatory frameworks – professional journalistic, corporate managerial, have set new editorial norms and a number of professional practices with the focus on the social responsibilities and accountability of journalism (Anikina, 2014).

Many internal contradictions, mostly consequences of the post-Soviet 'transitional period', also influenced media regulation, including a growing misunderstanding between journalists, politicians and other segments of society about the scope and limits of the freedom of press and journalism autonomy, resulting in a high degree of audience distrust of the media (Anikina, 2015; Paasti and Ramaprasad, 2017). This reflected differences in views between media professionals and audiences, varying priorities of social and cultural agendas, leading to a demand for a balance between standards of global news reporting and Russian journalistic cultures, including questions about professionalism (Anikina, 2015). Added to these misgivings were concerns about an emerging Russian advertising market, with newly-privatized media businesses building sometimes questionable strategies to attract investment (Ivanitsky, 2010; Vartanova *et al.*, 2017). The introduction of financial support to weak regional and local media, mostly print, contradicted a deregulation policy at the national level in order to maintain the local press as PR-instruments of the local government agencies (Shchepilova and Burianova, 2014).

Other complicating factors included new information and communication developments, digitalization and the rise of mobile technology. The digital telecom environment became the focus for the rise of a neoliberal philosophy in the Russian economy, regardless of the crucial role of the state in controlling the core technological infrastructure (especially fixed telephone lines, analogue transmission of TV signal and satellites). This role remained important as in previous periods, but in the 2000s digital production and distribution were generally paid little attention by state legislators. With little regulation of digital content distribution for two decades, film piracy through widely privatized cable networks led to the creation of a huge pirate content market with little regard for copyright, a trend which has accelerated in the Internet age. Another big concern for regulators was the growing availability of harmful content, including access for underage groups to pornographic and violent material. As a consequence of the developments during the first decade of the century, several 'agents of change' within media policy-making can be identified, showing that the process was being driven by particular logics – of the state, industry, professional community and public 'agents of change'.

State-driven logic

Legal regulation of media by the state has traditionally been the most important area of media policy. Strong state-media relations are one of the strongest historical traditions of the Russian media, and this continues to have a significant impact on the media system (Galkina and Lehtisaari, 2016; Minaeva, 2018; Vartanova, 2019). The role of the state in media regulation is also an area of much controversy. Policy approaches shift from one extreme to the other, ranging from one of the most liberal press laws in the world – the 1991 'The Law on Mass Media' – to restrictions on press freedom enshrined in the 2006 Law on Terrorism. The state is the most powerful actor, for example planning the shift to digital infrastructure or providing economic support for certain types of media content (for minorities or particular cultural products). The policy on information security of children was the first attempt to introduce the protection of minors with emphasis on 'traditional' family values. Another dimension of the state concern is copyright regulation to minimize piracy in the digital environment.

Other state media policy developments have concerned the protection of the domestic media market with the 2014 Law on the Limits on Foreign Ownership in Russian mass media, also covering information security policy and protection of national economic and political interests. This can be seen in the amendments to many recent laws, including the Law on Communications, the Federal Law on Counteraction of Terrorism (2016), the Internet Libel Bill (2018), the Fake News Law (2019) and the Sovereign Internet Law (2019). The Federal Service for Supervision of Communications, Information Technology and Mass Media (*Roskomnadzor*, RKN) plays a crucial role not only in monitoring Internet space but also in making lists of websites with illegal content that must be blocked by Internet service providers.

State regulation remains the only instrument to support the public service obligations of the media. On the one hand, this is realized through several recent documents like the 'Decree on the Creation of Public Television Channel in Russia' and the 'Law on Protection of Children from Information Harmful to Their Health and Development', both passed in 2012, and the 2018 'Law on Protection of Journalists in the Hot Spots'. The 2017 amendments to the Administrative Code, to the Law on Information and to the Law on Communications, which cancelled the 2014 'Bill on Bloggers' – requiring popular bloggers on the Internet with more than 3,000 unique visitors to register as media – demonstrate the controversial nature of present media policy-making.

However, in the context of a commercialized media industry and relatively under-developed civil society, the state remains the only power that can support non-commercial and publicly oriented media. The Federal Agency for Press and Mass Communication (*Rospechat*) under the Ministry of Digital Development, has financially supported the production of socially important content by Russian media companies. For instance, state support for regional and local newspapers in 2017 was about 349 billion roubles, in 2018 it grew to 549 billion roubles (*Rossiyskiy rynok periodicheskoy pechati v 2018*, 2019). Thus, while describing the state-driven logic of Russian media policy-making, it could be argued that the role of the state as the main driver remains a very uneven, controversial one. However, there are negative vs. positive forms of regulation as well as federal vs. regional and local levels of media policy.

Industrial/market-driven logic

This kind of regulatory logic has rather short history in the Russian media system. The major motivation for economic regulation is profit, and therefore policy making is realized through adoption of particular laws to define the scope of economic activities, and the major one has been the 'Advertising Law' (2009, 2019). Another legal document initiated by film and television producers in order to protect their copyright ownership, was the 2013 'Anti-Piracy Law', which was an important document for the digital media as well. Another form of policy making has become the lobbying activity of employers' associations such as *Natsionalinaya Associatsija Veshatelei* (National Association of TV and Radio Broadcasters), *Gildiya izdatelei periodicheskoi pechati* (Guild of the Press Publishers) and *Assotsiatsiya kabelnogo televideniya Rossii* (Cable Television Association of Russia).

As with the state-driven logic, there are several layers in the industry logic, such as old vs new media (demands for press subsidies, negation of copyright ownership, free-on-air vs. subscription – cable, satellite); federal vs regional (in protection of economic interests of regional or federal broadcasting companies), Russian vs foreign capital, which is represented in the debate about limits for foreign ownership in Russian media companies. It is obvious that the most influential business forces affecting media regulation are represented either by large national companies or by emerging digital media giants – both from content production and distribution segments (Martynov and Os'kin, 2015).

Professional/corporate logic

This kind of logic reveals itself mostly through self-regulatory mechanisms or charters/editorial standards approved by certain media companies, for instance, by publishing houses, *Kommersant* and *Vedomosti* or the news agencies, TASS and Interfax. In terms of professional standards or journalistic ethics, documents such as the 'Charter of the Russian Union of Journalists', the 'Code of Professional Ethics of the Journalist' and the 'Moscow Charter of Journalists' – both adopted in 1994 – remain guiding principles.

Another case of adopting self-regulatory instruments was closely linked to the terrorist attacks in the early 2000s. The introduction in 2003 of the 'Anti-terrorism Charter' by the Industrial Committee, which united CEOs and top-managers of leading media companies, along with the broadcasters' 2005 charter 'Against Violence and Cruelty', signed by six national TV channels, were protective measures against legal restrictions. Many experts underlined that both documents were a response to the public and political criticism of the media coverage of terrorist attacks in Moscow in 2002 and in Beslan in 2004.

Arguably, a more effective form of professional self-regulation is provided by media critics and the work of popular journalists who review television programmes or newspaper content, considered as a form of professional accountability. The layers of professional regulatory logic involve professional standards and values, ranging from the statist (historical Russian journalistic tradition) to the liberal (Europe/ Anglo-Saxon objective news reporting) and accountability models, varying from social to corporate or ideological accountability. However, the regulatory civil/ public logic remains the weakest, with not many cases, though they do encourage public discussions about media performance and accountability.

Reviewing the Russian media policy-making process, there are two particular aspects to highlight. First, though newer drivers such as the media industry and professional community have begun to play a role in the policy-making process, the traditional 'top-down' logic leaves the leading role for the state. The latter remains the key driver in setting the legal regulatory framework through positive (safeguarding socially and culturally significant media, subsidizing them) and nega-tive (restrictions for foreign ownership, protection of information security) policies. Second, there is almost no economic regulation in the media system, though the business interests of the media industry have been growing recently. Also, technical regulation still remains outside the media system, and legislators have only just started to pay attention to technical issues in the last few years in the context of information security.

Conclusion

After almost three decades of change, the key features of the Russian media system are: the central role of television – setting the news agenda, providing mass entertainment and maintaining national identity; the crisis of print media with newspapers' declining circulation and advertising revenue, out-of-date and ineffi-cient print technology and distribution systems, and the growing popularity of the Internet and social media (Vartanova, 2012; 2015). The development of Russian media continues to be increasingly influenced by digitalization. Competition of legacy media with social media and the digital media landscape in general is growing. Online media have broadened the scope of available media content, providing a huge amount of entertainment as well as parallel and alternative news agendas competing with mainstream television and press. Changing patterns of media use by young Russians prove the importance of the digital environment both in terms of an emerging digital media ecosystem and importance of digital media literacy.

Russian media policy-making is deeply integrated into processes of state, society and national identity-building and this has become a defining area for the future development of the media system. The exceptional role of the state in 'top-down' policy-making has been determined not only by the specific nature of the state relationship with the Russian media business, but also by socio-cultural traditions of Russian society. Thus, the first clash of controversies in media policy-making has been shaped by a confrontation of new institutions and old social and cultural practices rooted in history. The complexity of challenges and objects for national media policy-making has become more noticeable with the digitalization of the media industry and changes in media consumption. Poorly established principles of the normative media policy are challenged by the rise of the neoliberal philosophy of the digital online media environment requiring minimal regulation.

The new tensions within the Russian media system have articulated the conflicts between the national and the global, between the political, the cultural and the economic. Digitalization, a driving force of the current media system, demonstrates the particular path of development of the Russian media system, while being influenced by dominant global trends.

References

AKAR (2020) Association of communication agencies of Russia. Available at www. akarussia.ru.

Anikina, M. E. (2014) Journalism as a Profession in the First Decades of the 21st Century: The Russian Context, *World of Media: Journal of Russian Media and Journalism Studies*, 233–252.

Anikina, M. E. (2015) Ideals and values of modern journalists: the search for balance, pp. 153–178 in G. Nygren and B. Dobek-Ostrowska (eds.) Journalism in Change: Journalistic Culture in Poland, Russia and Sweden. New York: Peter Lang.

Büchel, F., Hamprecht, E., Castro-Herrero, L., Engesser, S. and Brüggemann, M. (2016) Building Empirical Typologies with QCA: Toward a Classification of Media Systems, *International Journal of Press/Politics*, 21(2): 209–232.

Castro-Herrero, L., Hamprecht, E., Engesser, S., Brüggemann, M. and Büchel, F. (2017) Rethinking Hallin and Mancini Beyond the West: An Analysis of Media Systems in Central and Eastern Europe, *International Journal of Communication*, 11: 4797–4823.

Curran, J. and Park, M. J. (eds.) (2000) *De-Westernizing Media Studies*. London: Routledge.

Curran, J., Iyengar. S., Brink Lund, A. and Salovaara-Moring, I. (2009) Media System, Public Knowledge and Democracy. A Comparative Study, *European Journal of Communication*, 24(1): 5–26.

Datareportal (2020) *Digital 2020: The Russian Federation*. Moscow. Available at https:// datareportal.com/reports/digital-2020-russian-federation.

Davydov, S. (ed.) (2020) *Internet in Russia: A Study of the Runet and Its Impact on Social Life*. Cham: Springer.

De Smaele, H. (1999) The Applicability of Western Media Models on the Russian Media System, *European Journal of Communication*, 14(2): 173–189.

Deloitte (2016) *Media Consumption in Russia 2016. Key Trends.* Available at www2.deloitte. com/ru/en/pages/technology-media-and-telecommunications/articles/media-consumption-in-russia-2016.html.

Deloitte (2019) Trends in content monetization on the Internet. Media consumption in Russia – 2019. Available at www2.deloitte.com/ru/ru/pages/technology-media-and-telecommunications/articles/media-consumption-in-russia.html.

Dobek-Ostrowska, B., Glowacki, V., Jakubowicz, K. and Sukosd, M. (2010) *Comparative Medias Systems: European and Global Perspectives.* Budapest: CEU Press.

Dunas, D., Cherevko, T. and Tolokonnikova, A. (2017) Aktualnye kontseptualnye podkhody k rassmotreniyu protsessa mediapotrebleniya [Current conceptual approaches to the process of media consumption], *VestnikMoskovskogoUniversiteta*, 10(5): 30–50.

Dunas, D.V. and Vartanov, S. A. (2020) Molodezhnyi segment auditoriyi SMI: teoreticheskie podhodyo techestvennyh mediaissledovatelei [Youth as Media Audience: Theoretical Approaches in Russian Media Studies], *Theoretical and Practical Issues of Journalism*, 9(1): 106–122.

Ershov, Y. M. (2012) *Televidenie regionov v poiske modeley razvitiya* [Regional Television in Search of Development Models]. Moscow: Moscow University.

Internet v Rossii v 2018 (2019) *Sostoyanie, tendentsii i perspektivy razvitiya. Otchet* [The Internet in Russia in 2018. Condition, Trends and Development Prospects. Report]. Moscow: FAPMC.

Flew, T. and Waisbord, S. (2015) The Ongoing Significance of National Media Systems in the Context of Media Globalization, *Media, Culture & Society*, 37(4): 620–636.

Galkina, M. and Lehtisaari, K. (2016) Prognozi zmeneniya gosudarstvennogo regulirovaniya rossijskih SMI [Forecast of changes in state regulation of Russian media], *Mediascope*, 4. Available at http://www.mediascope.ru/2243.

Gladkova, A., Aslanov, I., Danilov, A., Danilov, F., Garifullin, V. and Magdeeva, R. (2019) Ethnic Media in Russia: Between State Model and Alternative Voices, *Russian Journal of Communication*, 11(1): 53–70.

Gureyeva, A. N. and Samorodova, E. V. (2019) Mediaregulirovanie v Rossii: izmenenija mediapolitiki v uslovijah transformacii obshhestvennyh praktik [Media Regulation in Russia: Changes in Media Policy under Transformation of Social Practices], *Mediascope*, 4. Available at www.mediascope.ru/2596.

Hallin, D. and Mancini, P. (2004) *Comparing Media Systems: Three Models of Media and Politics.* Cambridge: Cambridge University Press.

Hallin, D. and Mancini, P. (eds.) (2012) *Comparing Media Systems Beyond the Western World.* Cambridge: Cambridge University Press.

Hardy, J. (2008) *Western Media Systems.* New York: Routledge.

Hardy, J. (2012) Comparative Media Systems, pp. 195–206 in F. Esser and T. Hanitzsch (eds.) *Handbook of Comparative Communication Research.* London: Routledge.

Ivanitsky, V. L. (2010) Modernizatsiya zhurnalistiki: metodologicheskiy etyud [Modernization of Journalism: methodological attitude]. Moscow: MediaMir.

Makeenko, M. and Vyrkovsky, A. (2013) Economic Effects of Convergence in Russian Daily Press, pp. 144–162 in *World of Media. Yearbook of Russian Media and Journalism Studies.* Moscow: Faculty of Journalism.

Martynov, D. and Os'kin, A. (2015) *Gosudarstvennaya podderzhka SMI za rubezhom v tsifrovoy vek* [Support for Media Abroad in the Digital Age]. Moscow: Sobesednik.

McNair, B. (2000) Power, Profit, Corruption, and Lies: The Russian Media in the 1990s, in J. Curran and M. J. Park (eds.) *De-Westernizing Media Studies.* London: Routledge.

Mediascope (2020a) Top-10 Resources. Available at https://webindex.mediascope.net/top-resources.

Mediascope (2020b) Total Internet Audience. Available at https://webindex.mediascope.net/general-audience.

Minaeva, O. (2018) *Istoriya otechestvennoy zhurnalistiki 1917–1945* [History of national journalism. 1917–1945]. Moscow: Aspekt Press.

Nieminen, H. (2019) Inequality, Social Trust and the Media: Towards Citizens' Communication and Information Rights, pp. 43–66 in J. Trappel (ed.) *Digital Media Inequalities: Policies Against Divides, Distrust and Discrimination*. Göteborg: Nordicom.

Noam, E. M. (ed.) (2016) *Who Owns the World's Media? Media Concentration and Ownership Around the World*. Oxford: Oxford University Press.

Nordenstreng, K. and Thussu, D. K. (eds.) (2015) *Mapping BRICS Media*. London: Routledge.

Nordenstreng, K., Vartanova, E. and Zassoursky, Y. (eds.) (2002) *Russian Media Challenge*. Helsinki: Aleksanteri Institute.

Paasti, S. and Ramaprasad, J. (eds.) (2017) *Contemporary BRICS Journalism: Non-Western Media in Transition*. London: Routledge.

Pankeyev, I. A. (2019) *Pravovoe regulirovanie* SMI [Legal regulation of the media]. Moscow: Aspekt Press.

Ragnedda, M. and Muschert, G. W. (2013) *The Digital Divide: The Internet and Social Inequality in International Perspective*. New York: Routledge.

Rantanen, T. (2002) *The Global and the National. Media and Communications in Post-Communist Russia*. Lanham: Rowman & Littlefield.

Rickhter, A. G. (2007) *Svoboda massovoy informatsii v postsovetskom prostranstve* [Freedom of Mass Information in the Post-Soviet Space]. Moscow: VK Publication.

Rossiyskiyrynokperiodicheskoypechati (2019) *Sostoyanie, tendentsii I perspektivyrazvitiya. Otchet* [Russian Periodical Press. Condition, Trends, and Development Prospects. Report]. Moscow: FAPMC.

Rosstat (2020) Federal State Statistics Service. Available at https://rosstat.gov.ru/folder/14478.

Roudakova, N. (2017) *Losing Pravda: Ethics and the Press in Post-Truth Russia*. Cambridge: Cambridge University Press.

Rykov, Y., Nagornyy, O. and Koltsova, O. (2017) Digital Inequality in Russia Through the Use of a Social Network Site: A Cross-Regional Comparison. *Communications in Computer and Information Science*, 745: 70–83.

Samartsev, O. R. (2017) *Tsifrovaija real'nost. Zurnalistika informatsionnoj iepokhi: factory trnsfor matsiji, problemy i perspektivy* [Digital Reality. Journalism of the Information Age: Factors of Transformation, Problems and Perspectives]. Moscow: Izdetel'skiyeresheniya.

Shchepilova, G. G. and Burianova, M. V. (2014) Vzaimodejstvie SMI i vlastnyh struktur v rossijskih regionah [Interaction between the Media and Power Structures in the Russian Regions], *Mediaskop*, 4: 1–8.

Shchepilova, G. G. (2010) *Reklama v SMI: istoriya, tekhnologii, klassifikatsiya* [Advertising in Mass Media: History, Technologies, Classification]. Moscow: Moscow University Press.

Smirnov, S. S. (2014) *Mediakholdingi Rossii: natsionalnyyo pyt kontsentratsii* SMI [Russian Media Holdings: National Media Concentration Experience]. Moscow: MediaMir.

Smirnov, S. S. (2016) Osobennosti razvitiya krupneyshikh regionalnykh mediakholdingov Rossii [Features of the Development of the Largest Regional Media Holdings in Russia]. *Mediaalmanakh*, 5: 6.

Soldatova, G. U., Rasskazova, Y. I. and Nestik, T. A. (2017) *Tsifrovoye pokoleniye Rossii: kompetentnost' I bezopasnost* [The Digital Generation of Russia: Competence and Security]. Moscow: Smysl.

Sparks, C. and Reading, A. (1998) *Communism, Capitalism and the Mass Media*. London: Sage.

Splichal, S. (1994) *Media Beyond Socialism. Theory and Practice in East-Central Europe*. Boulder, CA: Westview Press.

Televidenie v Rossii v 2018 (2019) *Sostoyanie, tendentsii i perspektivy razvitiya*. Otchet [Television in Russia in 2018. Condition, Trends and Development Prospects. Report]. Moscow: FAPMC.

Thussu, D. K. (ed.) (2009) *Internationalizing Media Studies*. London: Routledge.

Thussu, D. K. (2018) A New Global Communication Order for a Multipolar World, *Communication Research and Practice*, 4(1): 52–66.

Timofeyev, A. A. (2019) Tendencii gosudarstvennogo regulirovaniya mediasfery v Rossii i za rubezhom v 2018–2019 gg [Trends in Government Regulation of the Media Sector in Russia and Abroad in 2018–2019], Mediaalmanah, 2: 20–30.

Toepfl, F. (2013) Why Do Pluralistic Media Systems Emerge? Comparing Media Change in the Czech Republic and in Russia After the Collapse of Communism, *Global Media and Communication*, 9(3): 239–256.

Vartanova, E. (2012) The Russian Media Model in the Context of Post-Soviet Dynamics, pp. 119–142 in D. Hallin and P. Mancini (eds.) *Comparing Media Systems Beyond the Western World*. Cambridge: Cambridge University Press.

Vartanova, E. (2015) Russia: Post-Soviet, Post-modern, Post-empire, pp. 125–144 in K. Nordenstreng and D. K. Thussu (eds.) *Mapping BRICS Media*. London: Routledge.

Vartanova, E. (2019) Russian Media: A Call for Theorising the Economic Change, *Russian Journal of Communication*, 11(1): 22–36.

Vartanova, E. L. (ed.) (2015) *Mediasystema Rossii* [Media System of Russia]. Moscow: Aspekt Press.

Vartanova, E. L., Vyrkovskiy, A. V., Makeenko, M. I. and Smirnov, S. S. (2017) *Industriia rossiiskikh media: tsifrovoe budushchee* [The Russian Media Industry: The Digital Future]. Moscow: MediaMir.

Veselov, S. V. (ed.) (2017) Rossijskij reklamnyj ezhegodnik – 2016 [Russian Advertising Yearbook – 2016]. Moscow: AKAR.

Vyugina, D. M. (2017) Osobennosti mediapotrebleniya tsifrovogo pokoleniya Rossii [Features of media consumption of the digital generation of Russia], *Mediascope*, 4. Available at www.mediascope.ru/2386

Waisbord, S. and Mellado, C. (2014) De-westernizing Communication Studies: A Reassessment, *Communication Theory*, 24(4): 361–372.

6

MEDIA SYSTEMS AND STRUCTURES IN INDIA

B. P. Sanjay

In discussing systems of media and communication, media studies as a field has borrowed concepts from social sciences in relation to the structures of power (politics), society (sociology) and economics (structures). In the so called 'Third World', the legacy of colonization, modernization and development, and their relative democratic status have been the foci of media studies scholars. The New World Information and Communication Order debates of the 1970s, for example, analysed world media systems in terms of colonial, historical, cultural and technological parameters (MacBride Commission, 1980). These dimensions are essential in understanding the media system in India, in particular the historical framework, in which to assess the long experience of colonialism and its impact on the development of media and communication.

The history and development of print (Kesavan, 1997; Venkatachalapathy, 2012) and broadcasting media (Masani, 1976; Baruah, 2017) have been the focus of much research. British colonization has been the subject of intense interrogation and the nationalist struggle for independence has highlighted the role of the press (Ram, 2011). While the growth of broadcasting during the British administration was of short duration it was nevertheless significant in laying the foundation for India's government-owned system.

This chapter will focus initially on print and broadcasting media and, later, a more integrated view of India's media ecology will be presented. For example, the economic liberalization of the 1990s enables us to look at the media system more holistically (Athique *et al.*, 2018). The introduction of social media in the first two decades of the twenty-first century adds a new digital dimension to the Indian media system. The dramatic increase in the use of mobile phones, buoyed by comparably low data and voice rates has enhanced the spread and use of social media, whose role and impact in elections has become significant (Sardesai, 2019). The new media, in addition to allowing consumption of media-generated content, have also spurred user-generated content and have transformed commerce, governance and a range of digital services.

Broadcasting, with its amateurish beginnings in radio in the 1920s, was taken over by the colonial government in the 1930s and was then transferred to the Indian state after Independence in 1947. Building on the telecoms infrastructure developed in the 1980s, including satellites, technological developments were rapid and, after liberalization and privatization in the 1990s, the broadcasting system grew exponentially, from one state-owned broadcaster, *Doordarshan* into a vast network of both public and private radio and television stations. The print medium, specifically newspapers, however, has a much longer trajectory in India, from its colonial origins.

Print culture in India and the colonial context

Printing came to India in the sixteenth century, with the Portuguese colonizers of Goa and their Jesuit missionaries: 'The art of printing entered India for the first time on September 6, 1556. Its advent was like a happy accident. Generally, it was as an aid to proselytization that the printing press was taken outside Europe' (Priolkar, 1958). The subsequent spread of book publishing, initially in Indian languages and later in English have been the subject matter of extensive inquiry in cultural history (Venkatachalapathy, 2012). Before print, India had a rich culture of manuscripts in Sanskrit, Pali, Persian, Arabic and many regional Indian languages, written on palm leaves and hand-made paper. This practice continued till the end of the nineteenth century, when the printing press became more widely used, with the development of fonts for Indian languages. It took until the eighteenth century before the first newspaper in India was produced. Since then, for nearly two centuries, newspaper and print journalism in its broadest sense has gone through several phases, characterized by the interaction with colonialism and nationalist struggles (Murthy, 1966; Ram, 2011).

Pre-newspaper publications such as newsletters disseminating information existed during the pre-Mughal as well as the Mughal era (Rau, 1968). The work of news writers was an essential source of information for rulers and courts (Natarajan, 2017: 10) and their services were also used by the East India Company (EIC) (Fisher, 1993). Although the Company started using printing presses around 1674 in Bombay and elsewhere, it was not until 1780 that the first English-language newspaper, the *Bengal Gazette*, was published. Its founder, James Augustus Hicky had his own reasons to start a newspaper: his business had failed, he was jailed for debt and he wanted to expose the Company's maladministration (Otis, 2018). He was persecuted for criticizing Church and the State when the Company made other publications toe the line. Reluctance to encourage or start newspapers, disgruntlement with Company officials, using newspapers as vehicles to promote interests or settle scores, and indirect company patronage of friendly publications – all this characterized newspaper journalism in its first few decades (Natarajan, 2017: 11). However, about ten Anglo-Indian and 25 Indian-language newspapers were in existence in 1857 at the time of the 'First War of Independence'.

The Indian language press: social reforms and resistance

Indian-language journalism in the colonial era had to develop within the framework of the dual attitude of the EIC towards English and the vernacular press. This language press was motivated by regional and sectarian issues and readership (Codell, 2004). Early accounts of the development of the Indian-language press in the nineteenth century, in Bengal to begin with and subsequently in other regions, describe the colonial attitudes towards journalism and partisan attitudes towards the Indian-language press and a host of press laws and restrictions (Chatterjee, 1929). The colonial experience of the Indian-language press was not a deterrent for its growth despite the low levels of literacy that limited their circulation.

A proliferating commercial print culture, a new generation of administrators and editors, missionaries and elites open to new ideas led to demands for a free press, as opposed to the repressive attitude of the EIC. The easing of censorship in 1818 is said to have heralded the publication of journals in Bengali by missionaries, as well as the local elite. The EIC's attitude to and control of the press allowed for daring responses by social reformers such as Rammohan Roy and marked the beginning of a new type of political activity: 'This forgotten chapter of protest focused on the idea of a free press provides a key insight into the continuation of politics as the dominant theme in Indian journalism today' (Sonwalkar, 2015).

The colonial era saw both the loyalist and nationalist press expressing demands for social reforms, particularly within a Hindu religious framework. Many nationalist leaders such as Tilak, Gokhale, Ambedkar, Nehru and Gandhi (Natarajan, 2017: 143) articulated their views through their journals (Israel, 1994). They also sought the services of senior journalists to be their editors. Many industrialists, who owned newspapers, supported the Independence struggle and aligned with various ideological strands of what became the largest anti-colonial movement in history (Israel, 1994; Guha, 2003; Rau, 2016; Pol, 2018).

The nationalist leader in Bombay, Bal Gangadhar Tilak was instrumental in creating nationalistic awareness both among the English-speaking elite as well as the majority population, which speaks Marathi. In 1881, he published a newspaper in Marathi called *Kesari*, to cater to the 'mass of ignorant population who generally have no idea of what passes around them and who therefore must be given the knowledge', and the English-language *Mahratta*, aimed at the educated segment of the community (Natarajan, 2017: 143). Indian-language newspapers were edited by a host of literary figures in their respective regions, who provided the local nationalist flavour of the movement. The Indian press became increasingly vocal about political authority and nationalism from 1880 onwards (Codell, 2004: 107).

Radio and nascent nationalism

By the time radio evolved in the 1920s, the nationalist movement was firmly established. However, it was clear that radio was 'intended to serve as a medium for imperial propaganda' (Zivin, 1998). Its origins and development before Indian independence are indicative of a significant lack of interest on the part of British administration (Pinkerton, 2008). However, the National Planning Committee, set up in 1938, recognized broadcasting as a necessity and described its functions as news, adult education, propaganda by the State and entertainment. Recognizing communication and broadcasting services as a monopoly of the state, it recommended it be continued but 'run on commercial principles' (Shah, 1948: 58, 85). The empire broadcasting services during World War II created interest in news and a fondness for the Reithian model for broadcasting in post-independence India (Chatterji, 1987; Rudolph, 1992).

Post-Independence media

By 1947 when India gained Independence, radio broadcasting had taken shape as a state-owned medium, while the print media were privately owned. According to the first Press Commission report, in 1953 there were 370 daily newspapers in India, of which 41 were in English and the rest in Indian languages. However, the 41 English dailies had a circulation of about 0.65 million copies out of the total 2.50 million of all dailies circulating in India (Govt. of India, 1954: 15). The English-language press had an advantage as advertisers were willing to pay better advertising rates, as circulation was significantly higher. English newspapers also offered better perks to their journalists than their Indian-language counterparts. In contrast, the Indian press system, classified as big, medium and small based on circulation, were constantly seeking support from the government (Mani, 1952).

It is to the credit of the Indian press, both English and the Indian language press, that they maintained their adversarial role after Independence. The Press Laws Enquiry Committee was set up to look into the laws governing the functioning of the press and noted at least 12 laws that restricted press freedom (Govt. of India, 1948). Prime Minister Nehru's belief in the freedom of the press shaped the constitutional provisions for press freedom in Article 19 of the Indian constitution (Rau, 2016). However, the addition of reasonable restrictions in the Article, including many qualifiers, limited the initial liberal enthusiasm. Both Nehru and his then Home Minister Sardar Patel worked together to bring in the first amendment to place restrictions on the press (Daniyal, 2015). In the absence of any meaningful opposition to the ruling Indian National Congress party that held sway over most of India from independence until the 1970s, the critique provided in the newspapers did keep the readers' (albeit elite) faith alive in what they considered as democracy.

Broadcast media

The adversarial attitude of the privately owned Indian press, by default, compelled the establishment to develop and depend on other mass media, particularly broadcasting. Broadcasting from the very beginning was subsumed in the framework of the archaic Indian Telegraph Act that allowed the state to adopt licensing and regulatory regime. Radio in India operated through the public broadcaster, All

India Radio, with a vast network of 470 stations covering the entire country with about 92 per cent of the area and 99 per cent of the population.

The Nehruvian approach towards the press and its freedom did not apply to broadcasting (Rau, 2016). It found it convenient to let radio remain under government control. The state television broadcaster, *Doordarshan*, inaugurated in 1960s, was also state controlled. A summative look at communication policy during that era suggests that the Nehruvian period had an overwhelming belief in mass media and its perceived role in development and nation-building. The planning approach it adopted for development posited a publicity role for mass media (Vidyalankar, 1963).

By 1967 when a comprehensive committee had examined the matrix of communication and media system in India, it was evident that its expansion was not commensurate with what was needed. Disappointment with government control of broadcasting was constant. 'Broadcasting should hereafter be entrusted to autonomous corporations, to be constituted separately for radio and television'. The hesitant expansion and unimaginative use of the media was highlighted, including the lament that its development was not considered as a basic facility (Chanda Report, 1966: 44).

Development mantra and broadcast media

As well as the importance of the media in 'nation-building', the relationship between communication and development was characterized in India, as a developing country from the 1950s to the 1990s, through the prevailing modernization paradigm. Radio Rural Forums and the Delhi School Television Project were examples of media use for national development. The Finance Ministry was disinclined to give any funding for television as it considered the medium to be merely a status symbol and not as important for a poor country (Luthra, 1986: 56). Strong advice from UNESCO and fortuitous access to a Philips transmitter (left behind after an industrial fair) persuaded India to adopt communication satellites as a means of bypassing terrestrial limitations to expansion. This experimental TV service in India was launched in 1959. The Ford Foundation (Lerner *et al.*, 1977), and diffusion studies in health and agriculture indicated the potential role for satellites in development through visual media in a country with very low levels of literacy, especially in rural areas (Rogers, 1978; Melkote and Steeves, 2015).

The Satellite Instructional Television Experiment (SITE) (1975–1976) was a significant policy shift for India: reversing the usual pattern of urban first and rural later, it took television directly to about 2,400 villages in six states of India. The planning for SITE was part of India's atomic energy policy that was subsequently hived off into a space programme (Chander and Karnik, 1976). The experiment lasted for only a year and its evaluation was a mammoth exercise involving a host of institutions engaged in education, broadcasting and technology development, including the Planning Commission, the then highest planning think tank in India.

The experiment also formalized television research in India across the academia and policy circles.

The comprehensive evaluation of the SITE experiment was to form the basis for a decision to adopt satellite technology as the means for broadcasting and telecommunication needs. The decision was made even before the experiment ended. The commercial interests of US satellite manufacturers provided the reason for strictly adhering to the one-year experiment despite India wanting an extension. It may be pointed out that the first Indian National Satellite systems were built by Ford Aerospace and Communications Corporation. Ford Foundation India was an active think tank that among other things advocated and promoted television.

The trajectory of television growth in India after the SITE experiment did not realize the hoped-for potential for development. Numerous scholars and committees have commented on the failure to meet its goals (Joshi, 1985; Sanjay, 1991). Comprehensive analysis of evaluation reports shows that the main result was to confirm that the technological basis for television expansion in India should be through satellite transmission (Agrawal, 1981). Later analysis states explicitly that the technology imperative had guided the educational or developmental agenda more than any other macro assessment of need (Patel, 1999).

Impact of the internal emergency on the media

The internal emergency in India (1975–1977), imposed by Prime Minister Indira Gandhi coincided with the SITE experiment, complicating some of the state's policy objectives (Sanjay, 1991). During this 'dark period' for India's media history, strict censorship was introduced, opposition newspapers were closed and journalists and political leaders detained. The government used the 'security of the state' and 'promotion of disaffection' as its defence for imposing strict control on the press. And with the airwaves already under government ownership, Indira Gandhi 'successfully controlled the mass communication system in India' (Singh, 1980: 40). The government also tried to restructure the newspaper industry with more friendly chairpersons on various boards and also to integrate the country's four major news agencies into one news agency for better control and dissemination (Grimes, 1975).

After the emergency was lifted and Gandhi lost power, committees instituted by the Janata (people's) Party coalition government held an inquiry into the internal emergency period and its excesses, including the abuses of the mass media. A White Paper provided details of the systematic attempt to muzzle the press and persecution and prosecution of journalists, as well as complete control of broadcast media (Dass, 1977). The new government focused on the restoration of the pre-emergency status to the Indian press and autonomy to broadcast media that had lingered as a constant demand. Dismantling the authoritarian media structure in India was advocated as policy framework and it included a corporate structure for broadcasting media, advisory to newspapers to perform as public utilities and 'not profit only enterprises' (Verghese, 1977: 731).

Post-emergency India also saw the launch of many periodicals/magazines with multi-colour printing and better layouts, enhancing the appeal and readership base for the print media. It also was the beginning of the rise of the Indian-language press. In 1978, the circulation of the language press, notably the Hindi press, surpassed the circulation figures of the English media. The first non-Congress government did not complete its five-year term and multi-party jostling for power led to the return of Gandhi in 1980. With Indira Gandhi at the helm again, India saw the introduction of colour television to coincide with hosting of the Asian Games in 1982. The then Director General of *Doordarshan* summarized it as metaphor for switchover to high technology and creation of an ambition for nationwide satellite television. Gandhi's loyalists felt that the games 'helped her to discard the opprobrium of the Emergency' (Mehta, 2014). This phase also coincided with the abolition of licence fees for both radio and TV sets in 1985, a revenue model that had been in place since independence (Luthra, 1986).

Liberalization of the media in the 1990s

The post-structural reforms or the liberalization of the Indian economy was an inevitable response to the dynamics of globalization and the economic reforms of the early 1990s. A far-reaching judgement by the Supreme Court of India questioned the government monopoly of broadcasting. The country's highest court ruled that the airwaves were public property and implied that they did not belong to the government alone. This judgement, apart from opening up airwaves to the growth of broadcasting in the private sector, also brought in a wave of changes in the media landscape, with television occupying the centre stage of consumption of entertainment and news, more of the former (Govt. of India, 1995).

The resultant unregulated growth of cable TV systems across the country was the beginning of last-mile distribution of television content (Naregal, 2000). The broadcast media has grown since then at a phenomenal pace in terms of the exponential increase in terms of television sets and households, private television stations for news and entertainment and multiple forms of distribution of content. In the newspaper industry, too, phenomenal growth has been seen in Indian-language newspapers, a phenomenon attributed to improved technology, enhancement of literacy levels and purchasing power, as well as hyper-localized content (Jeffrey, 2000).

While the sustained growth of newspaper circulation and readership in India intrigues observers from North America and Europe, in reality India's rising literacy levels (around 74 per cent), low cover prices and local content contributed to the rise in circulation of the Indian-language print media. The readership profile, too, has changed affecting the erstwhile perception of what a newspaper ought to be. The trend has continued in all sectors of Indian media, including digital spaces. The metrics for measurement has changed to readership now as opposed to circulation that was a more rigorous audit carried out by the Audit Bureau of Circulation. The readership for newspapers – in English and particularly in Indian languages – has also grown with neo-literates and new consumers in small towns and rural parts of the country.

The Indian media system today

The sustained growth of print and broadcast media has not necessarily ensured or promoted healthy practices in journalism. The post-liberalization media is accused of neglecting the deprived sections of India's population. Critics call it the hidden hand of media censorship, referring to the absence in the news of farmers' distress, growing unemployment and inequity (Gupta, 2005). The overwhelming lament pertains to the position and role of journalists in the media as their working conditions are increasingly precarious with contractual rather than full-time employment. Because the editor responsible for news content needs to be more responsive to the advertising and marketing needs of news organization, there is a trust deficit about ownership dynamics and the so-called corporatization of Indian media. The circulation and price wars referred to by Samir Jain, the owner of the Times of India Group, one of India's leading media organizations, in the dictum that newspapers are a commodity bought and sold in the marketplace, has considerably affected both content and editorial practices (Auletta, 2012). Large sections of dominant media in India are increasingly veering towards entertainment-driven content (Chadha, 2017), a trend visible elsewhere in the world (Thussu, 2007).

The credibility of newspapers has been further substantially eroded by the phenomenon of 'paid news', which has become more acute during elections. A detailed report outlined practices that deny candidates even basic media coverage if they do not or cannot pay, and recommended that the Election Commission issue specific guidelines (Guha-Thakurta, 2013). Despite prevalent aberrations in media practices, there is resistance across all sections of the media towards any regulation by the government. The need for self-regulation is stressed, but print media content continues to be innocuously regulated by the Press Council of India. In the context of changes in the media scene and the spread of social media, the Council wants an expanded Media Council of India (PTI, 2017).

In the state legislature elections leading up to the general elections of 2019, even more than paid news, the issue of fake news and its spread through social media was predominant (IFJ, 2019: 40). However, at least a few mainstream newspapers adhere to basic journalistic practices and principles. *The Hindu*, for example, has institutionalized the role and functions of a Readers' Editor – the first newspaper in India to do so. One of India's most serious newspapers, it has taken a definitive stand against paid news, sting operations and other practices, including recognition of the fast changes in technology and concerns such convergence brings to the profession (Panneerselvan, 2019).

In the case of television news, the News Broadcasting Standards Authority looks into violations of the code of ethics laid out by the News Broadcasters Association. However, membership of this self-regulatory body is voluntary. Only about 60 news channels out of the over 400 channels are members, leaving the majority of news channels outside the ambit of any regulatory mechanism (Prateek, 2017). News on the radio, however, is still confined to the state-owned All India Radio and not yet allowed in the private sector FM stations or community radio, despite considerable pressure by the stations (Rajagopal, 2017).

Media ownership in India and implications for journalists

The news-gathering operation of many newspapers, including many significant Indian-language newspapers, is dependent on freelance contributors, including citizens and part time journalists (stringers), often paid according to the length of stories sent or accepted. In many situations, the journalists are also local agents for procuring media advertisements. Such practices have implications for coverage in areas where livelihoods are affected by corporate presence and activities. The journalists' dependence on seeking advertisements and accepting low salaries has eroded their editorial priorities (Seshu, 2016). The media are also increasingly dependent on government support from advertising. For example, the Narendra Modi government, currently in its second successive term, has spent three times more on government advertisements than its predecessors. Critics feel that the funds could have been better used to support social sector spending (Raman, 2018). The Press Council of India has noted in its comprehensive review of Indian news media the impact of corporatization on democracy (Ray, 2009). The National Alliance for Journalists has stated in its appeal to parliamentarians, that 'conditions in the print, the digital and in the electronic media are deteriorating. Media workers today have no protection whatsoever and are caught in a wave of layoffs with little remedy' (National Alliance of Journalists, 2019).

In the present Indian ecosystem, more than 800 television channels offer a range of content in a wide variety of genres, including news channels, movies, music, youth, sports, kids, infotainment, lifestyle, devotional, teleshopping and general entertainment (BARC, 2018). Observers often query as to whether all the channels are viable regarding their economics. More than profits, political parties and economic interests own media in order to gain political influence. A recent analysis has noted that the actual number of television channels has increased but does not mean that all the channels are profitable: the motivation for owning a channel is for the political and economic access it provides (Ajith, 2019).

Ownership and threats of shrinking public sphere

India's diversity, plurality and democracy are being undermined by the nature and structure of media ownership in the country. It is concentrated in a few companies with cross-media and non-media interests (Rangnekar, 2018). The concerns are similar, for example, to those in the US about media ownership and monopolies that limit access to information (Lancia, 2009), and around the world (Noam, 2016). It has been suggested that more media does not necessarily mean or reflect India's plurality and diversity. In this sense, the Habermasian concept of the public sphere appears to be eroding in the world's largest democracy as growing concentration of media power among a shrinking number of corporate and political interests can undermine political processes (TRAI, 2014). The government occasionally attempts to curb cross-media ownership with very little effect on the legislative front, as a review by the Law Commission of India demonstrated, noting the comprehensive lack of restrictions on cross-media ownership (Law Commission, 2014).

The media industry, on the other hand, looks at ownership from the point of investment. There is strong lobby for enhancing foreign direct investment (FDI) in India, with a few well-articulated responses for restrictions in the news sector. For example, in the print sector FDI is limited at 26 per cent and the digital media has opened up to 26 per cent in 2019. Between 2000 and 2019, foreign direct investment in the Indian media sector that includes entertainment, news, carriage and distribution, was $8.38 billion (IBEF, 2020). In a note to the government, the Confederation of Indian Industry had a perceptive analysis and reasoning as to why the amount of FDI allowed in the electronic news sector should be increased from 26 to 49 per cent. Even though there are a large number of 24x7 news channels, most of these exist for extraneous and collateral reasons to boost the power and influence of certain domestic groups having interests in other unrelated businesses. Also, news channels are primarily dependent on advertisement revenues in the absence of a viable subscription-based business model (CII, 2010).

The non-media interests of many media companies are also a cause for concern (Bhattacharjee and Agrawal, 2018: 56). For example, Mukesh Ambani's Reliance group owns Network 18 and its multiple television channels, reaching more than 800 million people in India. Its media footprint traverses movie production, digital content and commerce, print magazines, mobile content and allied services. Its subsidiary news network, TV 18, owns 20 channels in 15 Indian languages and claimed nearly 11 per cent of news viewership in 2019, while its digital services, Jio, with 307 million subscribers, had 34 per cent of the telecom pie. The company, India's largest conglomerate, owns refining, petrochemicals, oil and gas, retail in addition to media and digital. The consolidated turnover of the company was nearly $82 billion with media and entertainment segment worth $674 million and digital services $619 million. Together the communication segment constituted 8.28 per cent of their turnover (Reliance, 2019). In April 2020, Facebook acquired a 10 per cent stake in Jio as part of a mutually beneficial communication strategy (*Business Today*, 2020). A dominant political party in southern Tamil Nadu state owns a media conglomerate under the Sun group; Bennet Coleman & Co. owns the flagship newspaper *Times of India* that claims the highest readership among English newspapers.

Prominent Indian politicians and corporate entities are increasingly making under-hand investments in news media affecting media's ability to serve as an unbiased tool for information, as one observer noted 'media outlets in India are openly owned and controlled by political and business conglomerates, which are using the media to undermine the relevance of their opponents with scant regard for overall national interest' (Jha, 2016).

More recently, there is also a trenchant criticism of Indian media particularly television, for its near alignment with the government and the ruling party (Jain, 2020). The divisive agenda, particularly by a few television news channels, have come in for sharp criticism (Pande, 2019). The intersection of social media and mainstream media is further highlighted for the significant rise of a majoritarian agenda and perceived insecurity for India's Muslim minority (Mirchandani, 2018).

The legacy media, referring to the print and broadcasting sectors, retain their relevance and presence. The January 2020 Indian Readership Survey indicates a slight dip in readership (estimated at 425 million) but suggests that the legacy media are holding their own (IRS, 2020), despite competition from online media. The slight dip in print readership is viewed with alarm by a few dominant groups. They feel it is time for them to re-think their strategy (Joseph, 2020). The IRS 2020 places the population usage of media as follows: television (76 per cent), newspapers (38 per cent), radio (20 per cent) and Internet (35 per cent). Convergence has allowed for changes in the business and content models of the legacy media but the adaptation is not complete. The most robust growth in Indian media is in entertainment industry (IRS, 2020).

Looking ahead with a new media system

The digital revolution, which has transformed media and communication around the world, has even greater impact on a country of the size and scale of India. The euphoric celebrations of the digital era into which the Asian region and its sub-variants, the Asia Pacific, the ASEAN and South Asia have leaped is reminiscent of many such parallels in the past. Both colonial and post-colonial developments have highlighted the techno-centric dimension of media. The earlier conceptions of media imperialism formulated by scholars such as Herbert Schiller were largely US-centric. With the significant rise of media in Asia, the observation is that 'Asianness is colonising international communications markets, influencing the production of hardware' (Liu *et al.*, 2017: 1).

The growth and spread of telecommunications in India has gone beyond the historical perception of the telephone as not only a luxury but also expensive. The tele-density as of February 2020 was 90 per cent, with more mobile users than landline. Modi government's 'Digital India' programme launched in 2015 intends to build on the expansion and further reach out to remote and rural areas to make it inclusive and universal. At least two factors of the relationship of developments in telecom to legacy media are recognized. The adaptation of digital media opportunities by the print and broadcasting, and increasing use of social media by different sections of the population needs to be underscored. The print media have adapted to digital formats and transmission (Aneez and Neyazi, 2019). In social media, disinformation, also referred to as fake news, is a more serious problem (Alisha, 2018). Concerns about the spread of rumours in volatile situations have led to Internet shutdowns across the country's sensitive and troubled areas (Rampal, 2019). Journalists and reputable media institutions are worried about this rumour-mongering, including the responsibility they have to disseminate verified and credible news (Panneerselvan, 2019).

Colonial origins and experience have considerably influenced the media system and structures in India. The nationalist cause codified their functions including formalizing the Indian language media as an important element. Post-independence, the media system, including broadcasting, was shaped by political and economic factors, including responses to globalization that have led to corporatization of the media. The public-broadcasting system is tenacious and valiantly trying to discharge its social sector obligations. Recognizing this complex interplay, the Sectoral Innovation Council of the Ministry of Information and Broadcasting has articulated the need for a comprehensive media policy that integrates all existing media segments, including the need for regulation to address new ground realities (Swaroop, 2012). In the current economic conditions, we cannot ignore the exclusionary realities of the digital media system. The unfolding policy dynamics of digital India faces challenges of social and economic exclusion, not only with regard to media but in financial and governance matters.

References

Agrawal, B. (1981) *Evaluation: Results, Experiences and Implications*. Ahmedabad: Space Applications Centre.

Ajith, A. (2019) You cannot have Ambani owning TV channels when he owns half the nation: Journalist Sandeep Bhushan. *The Caravan*. June 18. Available at https://caravanmagazine.in/media/sandeep-bhushan-book-the-indian-newsroom

Alisha, S. (2018) How fake news spreads in India. *The Diplomat*, April 9.

Aneez, Z. and Neyazi, T. (2019) *India Digital News Report*. Oxford: Reuters Institute for the Study of Journalism. March 25.

Athique, A., Parthasarathi V. and Srinivas, S. V. (2018) *The Indian Media Economy (2-volume set) Vol. I: Industrial Dynamics and Cultural Adaptation Vol. II: Market Dynamics and Social Transactions*. New Delhi: Oxford University Press.

Auletta, K. (2012) Citizens Jain: Why India's newspaper industry is thriving. *The New Yorker*. October 8.

BARC (2018) *News and Media—BARC India*, July 26. Available at www.barcindia.co.in/AnnouncementDetails.aspx?ID=127

Baruah, U. L. (2017) *This is All India Radio*. New Delhi: Publications Division, Ministry of Information and Broadcasting.

Bhattacharjee, A. and Agrawal, A. (2018) Mapping the power of major media companies in India. *Economic and Political Weekly*, 53: 47–57.

Business Today (2020) Facebook buys 10% stake in Reliance Jio: Here's what Mark Zuckerberg, Mukesh Ambani have to say. *Business Today*, April 22.

Chadha, K. (2017) The Indian news media industry: Structural trends and journalistic implications. *Global Media and Communication*, 13(2): 139–156.

Chanda Report (1966) *Radio and Television: Report of the Committee on Broadcasting and Information* (Ashok K. Chanda, Chairman). New Delhi: Ministry of Information and Broadcasting.

Chander, R. and Karnik, K. (1976) *Planning for Satellite Broadcasting*. Paris: UNESCO.

Chatterjee, R. (1929) Origin and growth of journalism among Indians. *The Annals of the American Academy of Political and Social Science*, 145: 161–168.

Chatterji, P. C. (1987) *Broadcasting in India*. New Delhi: Sage.

CII (2010) *FDI in Media and Entertainment*. New Delhi: Confederation of Indian Industry. Available at https://trai.gov.in/sites/default/files/CII.pdf

Codell, J. F. (2004) Introduction: The nineteenth-century news from India. *Victorian Periodicals Review*, 37(2): 106–123.

Daniyal, S. (2015) Why Nehru and Sardar Patel curbed freedom of expression in India. *Scroll.In*, January 13. Available at https://scroll.in. https://scroll.in/article/700020/why-nehru-and-sardar-patel-curbed-freedom-of-expression-in-india

Dass, K. K. (1977) *White Paper on Misuse of Mass Media*. New Delhi: Government of India, August.

Fisher, M. H. (1993) The office of *Akhbār Nawīs*: The transition from Mughal to British forms. *Modern Asian Studies*, 27(1): 45–82.

Govt. of India (1948) *The Press Laws Enquiry Committee Report*. New Delhi. Available at https://ia801900.us.archive.org/14/items/in.ernet.dli.2015.40249/2015.40249.Press-Laws-Enquiry-Committee-Report-1948.pdf

Govt. of India (1954) *Report of the Press Commission Part 1*. New Delhi: Publication Division.

Govt. of India (1995) *Supreme Court Judgement on Airwaves*. New Delhi: Ministry of Information and Broadcasting. Available at https://mib.gov.in/document/supreme-court-judgement-airwaves

Govt. of India (2018) *Press in India, 2017–18: 62nd Annual Report, Registrar of Newspapers for India*. New Delhi: Ministry of Information and Broadcasting.

Grimes, P. (1975) India seeking to tighten control over the press. *The New York Times*. December 21.

Guha, R. (2003) Gandhi the journalist. *The Hindu*, June 8.

Guha-Thakurta, P. (2013) Why paid news is a threat to Indian democracy. *Firstpost*, December 5. Available at www.firstpost.com/politics/why-paid-news-is-a-threat-to-indian-democracy-1268751.html

Gupta, S. (2005) Post-liberalisation India: How free is the media? *South Asia: Journal of South Asian Studies*, 28(2): 283–300.

IBEF (2020) *Media and Entertainment Industry in India*. New Delhi: India Brand Equity Foundation, January. Available at www.ibef.org/industry/media-entertainment-india.aspx

IFJ (2019) *Truth vs. Misinformation the Collective Push Back South Asia Freedom Report 2018–19*. Paris: International Federation of Journalists.

Israel, M. (1994) *Communication and Power: Propaganda and the Press in Indian Nationalist Struggle 1920–1947*. Cambridge: Cambridge University Press.

Jain, A. (2020) Modi's love affair with Western liberal media has finally ended. *HuffPost India*, January 25.

Jeffrey, R. (2000) *India's Newspaper Revolution: Capitalism, Politics and the Indian-language Press, 1977–99*. London: Hurst.

Jha, R. (2016) *India's Free Press Problem: Politics and Corporate Interests Invade Journalism*, June 22. Toronto: Canadian Journalists for Free Expression. Available at https://www.cjfe.org/indias_free_press_problem

Joseph, A. T. (2019) Why Mukesh Ambani's reliance may be looking to exit the media business. *Newslaundry*, December 4. Available at www.newslaundry.com/2019/12/04/mukesh-ambanis-reliance-exit-media-business

Joseph, A. T. (2020) Is India's newspaper industry dying? *Newslaundry*, February 3, Available at www.newslaundry.com/2020/02/03/is-indias-newspaper-industry-dying

Joshi, P. C. (1985) *An Indian Personality for Television*. New Delhi: Publications Division, Ministry of Information and Broadcasting.

Kesavan, B. S. (1997) *History of Printing and Publishing in India*. New Delhi: National Book Trust.

Lancia, P. (2009) *The Ethical Implications of Monopoly Media Ownership*. The Institute for Applied & Professional Ethics, July 27. Available at www.ohio.edu/ethics/2001-conferences/the-ethical-implications-of-monopoly-media-ownership/index.html

Law Commission (2014) *Consultation Paper Media Law*. New Delhi: The Law Commission. Available at https://cis-india.org/internet-governance/blog/consultation-paper-media-law.pdf

Lerner, D., Nelson, L. M. and Schramm, W. (1977) *Communication Research: A Half-century Appraisal*. Honolulu: East-West Center-University Press of Hawaii.

Liu, J., Sandvik, K. and Mortensen, C. H. (2017) Media and communication in Asia in early 21st century: Changes, continuities, and challenges. *MedieKultur: Journal of Media and Communication Research*, 33(62). Available at https://tidsskrift.dk/mediekultur/article/view/26255

Luthra, H. R. (1986) *Indian Broadcasting*. New Delhi: Publications Division, Ministry of Information and Broadcasting.

MacBride Commission (1980) *Many Voices, One World: Towards a New, More Just, and More Efficient World Information and Communication Order*. Paris: UNESCO.

Mani, A. D. (1952) The Indian press today. *Far Eastern Survey*, 21(11): 109–113.

Masani, M. (1976) *Broadcasting and the People*. New Delhi: National Book Trust.

Mehta, N. (2014) The story of how an Asiad remade a city. *The Economic Times*, September 18.

Melkote, S. R. and Steeves, H. L. (2015) *Communication for Development: Theory and Practice for Empowerment and Social Justice*, Third edition, New Delhi: Sage.

Mirchandani, M. (2018) *Digital Hatred, Real Violence: Majoritarian Radicalisation and Social Media in India*. New Delhi: Observer Research Foundation, July 29.

IRS (2020) *Indian Readership Survey Q3 2019*, January 20, Mruc.Net, Available at https://mruc.net/uploads/posts/195a27e70e0ddae2aa3601970e191531.pdf

Murthy, N. K. (1966) *Indian Journalism: Origin, Growth and Development of Indian Journalism, From Asoka to Nehru*. Prasaranga: University of Mysore.

Naregal, V. (2000) Media reform and regulation since liberalisation. *Economic and Political Weekly*, 35(21–22): 1817–1821.

Natarajan, J. (2017) *History of Indian Journalism* (third reprint). New Delhi: Publications Division, Ministry of Information & Broadcasting.

National Alliance of Journalists (2019) Save the messenger, save journalism, *The Citizen*, February 11.

Noam, E. M. (ed.) (2016) *Who Owns the World's Media?: Media Concentration and Ownership around the World*. Oxford: Oxford University Press.

Otis, A. (2018) *Hicky's Bengal Gazette: The Untold Story of India's First Newspaper*. New Delhi: Westland.

Pande, M. (2019) Bloodlust TV: Calling out India's hate media, *Newslaundry*, October 21, Available at www.newslaundry.com/2019/10/21/bloodlust-tv-calling-out-indias-hate-media

Panneerselvan, A. S. (2019) The elements of engaged journalism. *The Hindu*, December 9.

Patel, I. (1999) *Education Television Broadcasting in India: A Policy Perspective*. Anand: IRMA (Institute of Rural Management, Anand), Working Paper. Available at www.irma.ac.in/uploads/randp/pdf/986_61121.pdf

Pinkerton, A. (2008) Radio and the Raj: Broadcasting in British India (1920–1940). *Journal of the Royal Asiatic Society*, 18(2): 167–191.

Pol, P. (2018) The journalistic legacy of B.R. Ambedkar, the Editor. *The Wire*, April 14.

Prateek, S. (2017) Why press freedom is on the decline in India. *HUFFPOST*, May 5.

Priolkar, A. K. (1958) *The Printing Press in India, its Beginnings and Early Development.* Bombay: Marathi Samshodhana Mandala.

PTI (2017) *Press Council Wants Social Media Under Its Ambit.* New Delhi: Press Trust of India, May 16.

Rajagopal, K. (2017) Why can't FM stations broadcast news, asks SC. *The Hindu*, January 16.

Ram, N. (2011) *The Changing Role of the News Media in Contemporary India.* Key-note address at the Indian History Congress 72nd Session. Patiala: Punjabi University. Available at www.thehindu.com/multimedia/archive/00863/Contemporary_India__863821a.pdf

Raman, S. (2018) Rs 4,800 cr spent by BJP govt on ads could have fed 46 million children midday meals for a year, built 6 million toilets. *Firstpost*, August. Available at www.firstpost.com/india/rs-4800-cr-spent-by-bjp-government-on-ads-could-have-fed-46-million-children-midday-meals-for-a-year-built-6-million-toilets-4936701.html

Rampal, N. (2019) More than 350 Internet shutdowns in India since 2014. *India Today*, December 18.

Rangnekar, S. (2018) The fate of press freedom in India over the years. *The Wire*, November 16.

Rau, M. C. (1968) *The Press in India.* New Delhi: Allied.

Rau, M. C. (2016) The press after Nehru. *National Herald*, November 14.

Ray, G. N. (2009) *The Changing Face of Indian Media.* New Delhi: Press Council of India. Available at http://presscouncil.nic.in/OldWebsite/speechpdf/November%2016%20 2009%20Hyderabad.pdf

Reliance (2019) *Reliance Report 2019.* Mumbai: Reliance Industries, July 2. Available at www.ril.com/ar2018-19/reliance-at-a-glance.html

Rogers, E. (1978) The rise and fall of the dominant paradigm. *Journal of Communication*, 28(1): 64–69.

Rudolph, L. I. (1992) The media and cultural politics. *Economic and Political Weekly*, 27(28): 1489–1496.

Sanjay, B. P. (1991) *The Role of Institutional Relationships in Communication Technology Transfer: A Case Study of the Indian National Satellite System (INSAT).* National Library of Canada.

Sardesai, R. (2019) *2019: How Modi Won India.* New Delhi: Harper India.

Seshu, G. (2016) Disowned by their own: The disturbing pattern about the murders of independent journalists. *Scroll.In*, May 18. Available at http://scroll.in/article/808293/disowned-by-their-own-the-disturbing-pattern-about-the-murders-of-independent-journalists

Shah, K. T. (ed.) (1948) *National Planning Committee Series Communications.* Bombay: Publication Division. Available at http://archive.org/details/in.ernet.dli.2015.85676

Singh, I. B. (1980) The Indian mass media system: Before, during and after the national emergency. *Canadian Journal of Communication*, 7(2): 38–49.

Sonwalkar, P. (2015) Indian journalism in the colonial crucible: A nineteenth-century story of political protest. *Journalism Studies*, 16(5): 624–636.

Swaroop, A. (2012) *Sectoral Innovation Council.* New Delhi: Ministry of Information and Broadcasting.

Thussu, D. K. (2007) *News as Entertainment: The Rise of Global Infotainment.* London: Sage.

TRAI (2014) Recommendations on issues relating to media ownership. New Delhi: Telecom Regulatory Authority of India. Available at https://main.trai.gov.in/sites/default/files/Recommendations_on_Media_Ownership.pdf

Venkatachalapathy, A. R. (2012) *The Province of the Book.* New Delhi: Permanent Black.

Verghese, B. G. (1977) The media in a free society: Proposals for restructuring. *Economic and Political Weekly*, 12(18): 731–740.

Vidyalankar, C. A. N. (1963) *Report of the Study Team on Five Year Plan Publicity.* New Delhi: Ministry of Information and Broadcasting.

Zivin, J. (1998) The imagined reign of the iron lecturer: Village broadcasting in colonial India. *Modern Asian Studies*, 32(3): 717–738.

7
BEYOND CONVERGENCE

Rethinking China's media system in a global context

Zhengrong Hu, Deqiang Ji, Peixi Xu and Kriti Bhuju

If we take a close look at the multiplicity of media development in the contemporary world, China certainly represents one of the most distinctive, complex, adaptive and fastest-growing media systems. At the same time, driven by the national policy of improving China's image and cultural influence abroad and the economic motivation to connect with more markets, China's state-run media and private media companies are going global while international media and communication companies are increasingly operating in China (see essays in Thussu, de-Burgh and Shi, 2018; Keane, Yecies and Flew, 2018, among others). In doing so, intensive cross-border connectivity has been built between media systems in China and beyond, encapsulated in the overarching themes of the Belt and Road Initiative and the building of 'A Community with Shared Future for Mankind', which underpin connectivity, including both in infrastructure and culture, as a pillar for an inclusive and dialogical approach towards development and prosperity.

In the arena of international communication, ranging from infrastructure building to discursive interaction, there are certainly many debates surrounding China's state-driven soft power initiative, such as digital authoritarianism (Feldstein, 2020), neo-imperialism/neo-colonialism (Hadland, 2012; Zhu, 2017), the geopolitics of platforms (van Dijck, 2018), and global power shifts (Zhao, 2014). Amid this ongoing process, it is hard to gauge the actual consequences of China's active involvement in international communication, just as with the complexity of media transformation inside China. As a result, any analysis of China's media system should avoid static and one-dimensional assumptions that may detract from understanding the ongoing dynamic processes by which the media in China have been re-defined, re-invented, re-organized and re-located in an increasingly connected, massively digitized, datafied and globalized Chinese society.

However, for both Chinese and overseas scholars, it is theoretically unhelpful to continually emphasize that China is an exception: this approach implies either an ethno-centric perspective or a reductive binary logic that isolates China in comparative media studies and leads to a lack of understanding. Instead, just as China's overall model in development has been conceptualized over the last 40 years, for example, as 'Socialism with Chinese Characteristics', there have also been differing articulations of the model, from outside and inside, against China's opening-up and economic reform policies.

This pragmatism dates back to the early years of the People's Republic of China. When Chairman Mao Zedong was invited to attend the celebrations of the 40th anniversary of Russia's October Revolution in 1957, he said to the leaders of communist parties from more than 70 countries, that the experiences of both October Revolution and USSR's socialist construction should provide a model for China. Equally important, he emphasized that China should articulate those experiences with its own concrete social circumstances in order to find the most appropriate way for each socialist country. This spirit of pragmatism continues today and is expected to maintain its central position in China's policy-making in the decades to come.

With regard to media studies, such articulations have happened on both theoretical and practical levels. During the twentieth century, there was a historical shift in developing media studies through influences from outside China (Hu, Ji and Zhang, 2015: 381–382). Before the end of the 'cultural revolution' was officially announced in 1977, media studies, or more accurately, press or journalism theories, were influenced overwhelmingly by the Soviet communist model, articulated with a rich history of propaganda practices by the Chinese Communist Party. With the opening-up and reform era, and after regular encounters with American mass communication theories, the press was redefined in a 'scientific' and 'neutral' way as media (*meijie* or *meiti*), in order to reduce the close association with political dogmas of propaganda. Media studies quickly gained popularity as an independent discipline amidst the rebuilding of the broader social sciences in China.

Over the past four decades we have seen the complex formulation of media theories from internationalization to domestication to help understand the changing media landscape in China. At a practical level, undoubtedly, China's media system has kept its domestic features that continue to differentiate it from the dominant models of the Western, and more specifically, Anglo-American tradition. Meanwhile, its connection with the outside world is also intensified in the context of the multi-phased globalization in which China has been playing a changing but increasingly important role. Evidence of this can easily be found, including state-run media's global outreach, joint venture capital in audio-visual content industries, and China's social media going global as an alternative force that drives the transformation of communication and its 'platformization' in a digitizing world (Nieborg and Poell, 2018: 4275). Despite continuing disputes surrounding the expansion of China's digital/Internet power, such as the ownership of China's Internet giants and their relationship with the state power, it cannot be easily denied that the Internet world is changing with China's participation, even with many contradictions and uncertainties.

Therefore, this chapter suggests that there should be more scholarly attention paid to the fast-changing media landscape in China and to how the state power has tried to contain the dynamics of transformation and its consequences through a series of both active and reactive policies. With this in mind, the chapter will first concentrate on 'Media Convergence', a key concept imported from Western academic and policy discourses, and one that has been consistently appropriated by Chinese policymakers and practitioners in their efforts to achieve concrete technological, economic and political goals. Second, after contextualizing this concept within the evolving framework of the current industry and policy, we will address an old question concerning the possibility of re-introducing China into comparative media studies by building dialogue with Daniel Hallin and Paolo Mancini's seminal work on the three models in media and politics within the framework of media systems. If media convergence is regarded as a technological appropriation by China in order to pursue an alternative path of development for its traditional media system in a digitizing world, comparing this with the three models may offer a way of understanding both the continuities and discontinuities in China's media system.

Reforming China's media system in a digital age: convergence from the top

As elsewhere in the world, the defining features of media system in China have been deeply affected by the tremendous and fundamental changes in the media and communication industries, mainly driven by the transformation of information and communication technologies, together with the rise of private Internet companies, which have rapidly built a new information infrastructure for the digital and mobile era. As mentioned earlier, any major reform in China's media system should be understood from both outside and inside. In the past four decades, the Communist Party of China has taken a pragmatic approach in order to maintain the dominant position of traditional media in sustaining the 'commanding heights' on the one hand, and to marketize the media industries in pursuit of advertising subsidies on the other. As a result of this pragmatism, the media system has become an integral part of China's political, economic and social transformation and has in the process internalized the dynamic power reconfigurations between the party and media elites. In order to analyze this interdependent relationship, it is argued that a holistic view of Chinese society in a globalizing context is of great importance for investigating any changes in the media system.

It is helpful to start with a chronological reading of the recent policy-driven or politics-driven restructuring of China's media system, which aimed to strengthen the capacity of traditional media to regain people's attention, or at least share people's attention with private digital platforms and offer good public services by building public digital infrastructures in the new era of multiple media. Against this background, the traditional media are defined not only as including news organizations, content providers or publishers, but also platform builders such as Douyin, Weibo,

Didi and WeChat, which have already taken a leading role in shaping people's digital lives.

Ever since 18 August 2013, when General Secretary of the Communist Party of China and President Xi Jinping delivered a milestone speech at a meeting of the Central Leading Group to Deepen Overall Reform, 'media convergence' (*meitironghe*) has become the buzzword in China's policy making with regard to the strategic aim of the state-owned, 'mainstream media' (in the official language) to adapt successfully to the new media and communication environment. Even more important is the aim to achieve 'mastery' in the age of digitization, datafication and platformization. Understanding the multiple-layered meanings of 'media convergence' is key to mapping the challenges of media development that the Party faces in pursuing smart and effective governance in a fast-changing, instantaneously and globally connected and increasingly datafied society.

Borrowed from an intellectually imagined Western context, media convergence was translated into Chinese as early as 2003 (Li, 2003: 10), providing a vision of the future of media and even the future of a digitally connected society. Since then the concept has spread widely among scholars and started to draw attention from media industries. In 2013, when Xi Jinping officially used this concept in the top-level political meeting mentioned above, he defined it in a very concrete way, which was eventually translated into specific, practical requirements for state-run media to follow in order to be digitally competent. However, in order to encourage people to engage with discussion and practice surrounding media convergence, a series of meta-narratives were also mobilized to support the legitimacy of convergence in policy-making and academic deliberation, which takes us back to the afore-mentioned holistic view of China's reform era.

First, media convergence was categorized as a new phase in the development of China's media system. Following an evolutionary logic, convergence was in line with the informatization of the Chinese economy and digitization of Chinese society. In other words, the idea of convergence in China's media system is framed within a developmentalist mindset.

Second, there is an intrinsic nationalism that drives China to catch up with the advanced West in the technological revolution. Media convergence is thus seen as necessary and even pressing in the twenty-first century because in Western countries like the United States it is already underway, regardless of the fact that different countries may face different challenges and develop different models of transition. Any delay in the technological revolution could reinforce people's anxieties that China lags behind again, which is unacceptable due to the history of the twentieth century when the country was passively involved in a Western modernization process and struggling to find an alternative path towards technical autonomy.

Third, technological rationality is a major element in the conceptualization and application of media convergence. Perhaps different from previous technological terminologies, convergence entails a much broader discussion among both traditional media and new media industries. The latter mainly refers to Internet companies, which subsequently transformed to platform companies, rather than telecommunication companies. The involvement of platform companies could be a major change in the convergence of media from that of previous decades. For example, in the 1990s, questions about convergence were largely associated with the mutual and conflicting relations between broadcast media and telecommunication companies. Last but not least, convergence is a reaction from media itself to deal with the financial crisis of the advertising-dominant business model, though it seems to be not successful until now.

As a normative concept, media convergence has a two-fold meaning for media systems: namely the extension of commodification towards new media platforms and non-media platforms. The latter meant a dynamic new space, which is formerly not classified as a media profession, such as Internet, big data, cloud computing, artificial intelligence and their systematic application in the entire social informational system. On the basis of these narratives, media convergence is considered as the most inclusive terminology that creates a greater space for imagining a better future for traditional media system and introduces a new way in which the Party can manage the changing media landscape by enabling its communication arms.

On 19 February 2016, Xi Jinping led the politburo on a visit to the headquarters of the *People's Daily*, Xinhua News Agency and China Central Television in Beijing, all on the same day. A meeting with high-level propaganda officials and leaders of these flagship media organizations was convened right after the visit. In his talk to both media managers and publicity officials, Xi re-emphasized the importance of journalism and propaganda for the Party in the context of a historical continuum and firmly tasked the state-owned media to catch up with the new information and communication technologies. Otherwise, given the dramatic decline in advertising income and the corresponding crisis of the advertising-centered financial model of the past four decades, traditional or 'legacy' media would lose the battle with the new communication platforms to serve and influence the people, who were migrating in large numbers to those new platforms for their information, as well as to express and exchange attitudes and ideas.

Reading Xi's words, it is clear that the Party seems most concerned about the potential threat to its political and cultural leadership from the lack of strong technological support required for effective mainstream media in the new digital and mobile era. This new ecology of mediated and networked communication has not grown organically within the traditional media system, but outside, where private and capital-rich Internet companies are the major players. Based on Xi's directives to the state-owned media system, it is also clear that the Party recognizes the weakness of its propaganda organs in the rapidly changing information environment. However, the pragmatic nature of the Party in the reform era means it can respond to this new situation in a timely manner, without challenging or upsetting the status quo.

Nearly two years later, on 25 January 2019, Xi led the politburo again to visit the new media mansion of the *People's Daily*. In contrast to his previous talks, this time Xi focused on the conceptualization of media convergence in more detail, covering vertical integration, 'mobile-first' strategy, the adaptation of artificial intelligence, Internet regulation, as well as coordination and collaboration between different media organizations, such as legacy media and new media, central media and regional media, mass media and professional media.

It is worth mentioning that, since 2018, media convergence at regional, county level has been given a higher priority in policy discourse. Beside the need for central-level media to catch up with technological trends and sustain their leading position in setting media and public agendas, in his speech at the National Conference on Propaganda and Ideological Work in August 2018, Xi also highlighted the importance for county-level governments to build convergent media systems and convergent media centres. The aim is that the population will be better served by the mainstream media, with improved provision of public information in an increasingly connected society. At the same time, with the technological support of, for example, big data analytics, country-level government will be able to move towards a smart governance model, which is central to the national policy of building a modern governance system. In other words, county-level media convergence aims to reclaim the public-service functionality of traditional media in the fragmented and highly competing information market.

Integral to the systematic transformation of the Chinese media system, new regulatory frameworks are also being formulated in response to the continuing convergence of media architecture. As a result, the leadership of the publicity department of the Party of journalism and its influence on public opinion has been enhanced. For example, two bureaus subordinate to the former State Administration of Press, Publication, Radio, Film and Television (SAPPRFT), have been reorganized into the Publicity department of the Party's Central Committee, namely the Bureau of Press and Publication, and the Bureau of Film. The prefectural, city and township governments underwent the same reorganization with regard to media governance. The SAPPRFT is now reduced to SART, only responsible for the development and regulation of radio and television, which are on the frontier of technological and market convergence and facing perhaps the biggest survival challenges among all traditional media forms. In other words, the regulation system is very likely to experience another big change in the coming years if the physical and organizational boundaries between traditional media and new media platforms blur further or eventually disappear.

Thus, since 2013, the discursive focus of media convergence in China has shifted from a technological and market/industry agenda towards a more political agenda. Media convergence, as a top-down policy-making process, aims not only to empower the Party to maintain its commanding position in a fast-changing information environment, with growing complexities and uncertainties, but also to contribute to the overall deepening reform in contemporary China led by the Party in pursuit of the 'modernization' of the national governance system. In addition, alongside the convergence turn in media development and governance, there is a growing concern over the technological innovations needed to build China's national image and international communication capacity in a global context.

Short videos are the preferred form in which to share Chinese stories across national and cultural boundaries, while social media platforms, particularly those from the West, such as Facebook and Twitter, are considered to be more effective strategic tools to reach people across the world, compared to traditional media networks. More interestingly, TikTok, a short-video social media application from the Chinese platform company Byte Dance, has been gaining consumers beyond China. Due to its unexpected success in connecting global users, TikTok is also regarded as a new media to channel China's voice to the world. In doing so, as a long-term national strategy, China's media going global is hoping to take advantage of the success of new media forms to broaden access to and soften the tone of Chinese stories for an unfamiliar global audience.

Three conclusions could be made with regard to the strategic goals and implementation of this policy: first, convergence from the top is designed to sustain the leadership of the Communist Party of China of a fast-changing media system, particularly the state-owned media. Second, in order to strengthen or even rebuild communicative relationships between the Party and the people, who are, in great number, migrating to digital platforms, innovative communication strategies are required. These include building convergent media centres to customize content for multiple channels and carefully monitor and provide for the youth's media use. Such strategies are central to the transformation of the state-owned media from a patriarchal mindset to cater to a new generation of digital natives using digital platforms. Third, the approach to media governance is also in transition from a single directive model to a multi-sided negotiation model, as the state cannot directly control all the various media platforms but desires to contain and deploy all possible media platforms to achieve its political, economic and cultural purposes.

China's media system and Hallin and Mancini's three models

Moving from normative grouping to empirical analysis, Hallin and Mancini formulated three models of the relationship between media and politics in carefully selected Western European and North American democratic societies:

> The Liberal Model is characterized by a relative dominance of market mechanisms and of commercial media; the Democratic Corporatist Model by a historical coexistence of commercial media and media tied to organized social and political groups, and by a relatively active but legally limited role of the state; and the Polarized Pluralist Model by integration of the media into party politics, weaker historical development of commercial media, and a strong role of the state.
>
> *(Hallin and Mancini, 2004: 11)*

In addition, the three models also have geographical connections: 'the Liberal Model, which prevails across Britain, Ireland, and North America; the Democratic Corporatist Model, which prevails across northern continental Europe; and the

Polarized Pluralist Model, which prevails in the Mediterranean countries of southern Europe' (ibid.). By comparing the media systems of selected societies, Hallin and Mancini unpacked the concept of the 'West', and simultaneously downplayed the impact of a simple Western-centric, West-East framework, which has been underpinning international and global communication research over a long period of time.

For historical and political reasons, China's media system is not like any of the three models. As Zhao has noted: 'to bring the Chinese media system into a world-wide comparative project is to bring one of the "most dissimilar systems" into the messy picture of non-Western empirical reality' (Zhao, 2012: 143). In her dialogical and reflective piece on Hallin and Mancini's three models, Zhao highlights the asymmetric power relations in the world media structure. She documents in detail the historical linkages that define China's media system as one undergoing constant hybridization and contestation, such as between the Leninist and Maoist legacies, state power beyond intervention, and tensions between political instrumentalization and professionalization. In so doing, the analysis of the media system in China is situated in a historical context rather than a comparative framework. As a continuum of this kind of dialogue, our goal here is that instead of simply verifying the suitability of these models for China, or reducing China's experiences in order to fit into them and reinforce a Western-centric perspective, we aim to develop a state-of-the-art analysis about the current changes in China's media system. In short, Hallin and Mancini's three models offer an approach to study the national media system from three interrelated dimensions, namely state, market and society, together with their different power configurations.

The commercial operation of traditional media has been dominant in China since the early 1980s and has been accelerated by the introduction of private, capital-driven Internet industries. No matter how much political control can be exercised in the daily operation and practice of Chinese media, the profit motive is always a core purpose, as the outcome of four decades' of marketization. Ian Weber has situated the political economy of China's media system in 'a framework of controlled commodification, in which the state constitutes the most determining influence over media operating in a commercial, profit-oriented socialist market economy' (Weber, 2005: 792).

Resonating with this conceptualization, we will emphasize two dimensions of media power in China, which explain the boundaries of 'commercialization'. Vertically, media in China is owned and run by a four-tiered Party and government system. There is thus a clear management line between the media and their bosses. Horizontally, media is located in geographically diverse, economically uneven and culturally different administrative regions. The political and economic power of the media relies to a great extent on the political influence and economic strength of each region, which, in turn, nurtures the distinctiveness of media economics, management, regulation and professional practices. As a result of these multi-faceted political economic articulations, the media receives directives from a highly controlled, clearly layered and geographically segmented political communication system, but simultaneously enjoys different degrees of freedom in commercialization due to economic unevenness between regions.

The only exception to this is the central media group, which is owned either by the Central Committee of the Party or the central government. They have national influence and, accordingly, access to the country's vast national market. However, these absolute advantages are also facing challenges from both the national digital migration and emerging competitors from several developed regions, including Hunan, Jiangsu, Zhejiang and Shanghai, where some of the media are growing beyond their regional markets and gaining popularity among the national audience. In a word, controlled commodification happens at different levels and embodies regional diversities.

There are two new visible trends with regard to the funding of traditional media. Due to the sharp decline in advertising income, arising from the impact of new digital platforms on the advertising market, the Party decided to resume the subsidy of traditional media and reclaim their mouthpiece role as state-owned media. However, this process has not been even. As mentioned earlier, the financing capacity of different regions varies significantly. As to central media and media in affluent regions, with strong political support, they can easily mobilize all possible resources to maintain their monopolistic position in both traditional and new platforms.

For example, in order to consolidate its flagship advertising platform in the national market, China Central Television (CCTV) launched the Chinese Brands Build Strong Nation (*pinpaiqiangguo*) project to appeal to both Chinese companies and domestic audiences with nationalist sentiments. For Chinese companies, this was not new, because having advertisements on CCTV channels meant the quality of those products and services or simply the company's image were not only recognized, but also endorsed by the state media. Due to the intervention of the state media, these companies gain a market advantage. Besides, by launching this new project, CCTV uses its advantage as central-level media to absorb and reconfigure the remaining advertising market values and forces competitors to explore other advertisers or move to digital platforms.

This is one side of a growing divide between media at different levels and in different regions. In poorer regions, traditional media, together with their overseeing governments, are struggling to find a way out of this 'freezing cold winter' (*handong*), due to the fact that advertising income has so dramatically reduced. As a result, they continuously attempt to fulfill the political requirements from the top, including daily and key event propaganda, while mobilizing all available resources to collaborate or merge with other media outlets – and even other industries – under the banner of 'media convergence'. This potentially entails a shift in the dependence of traditional media on their usual advertising market to a more diverse capital market.

In 2019, we investigated media convergence experiments in two county-level media organizations: Pizhou County in Jiangsu and Changxing County in Zhejiang. The two cases were selected as they are widely believed to be successful in terms of profit-making and technological and organizational innovations. Both counties have hosted their peers from other counties or cities in China, who came to learn how to undertake media convergence and so meet the requirements of their superiors. The findings were that they shared three key characteristics:

First, they both built and ran highly efficient media convergence centres, which increased their capacity to reach the audience through digital means. Second, they were keen to develop mobile applications to integrate media functions, particularly the public-information service provided by the government. In doing so, they were contributing to the digital transformation of the governance system, popularly defined as e-governance, by facilitating information sharing between government and public and among government departments, at the same time as building an Internet public-user base. Third, due to the strength of their local economies, both of them explored the potential of collaboration with other sectors, such as exhibitions, tourism and e-commerce, seeking additional opportunities for profit-making, and they were successful. This reinforces the above-mentioned regional unevenness in economic development, which is a key factor in media economics. Therefore, these successful models of convergence, whether in the media or beyond, cannot simply be imitated in other regions, which again demonstrates the complexity of the media market and how commercialization interacts with the political economy of different localities in China.

Hallin and Mancini's Democratic Corporatist Model is mainly found in wealthy Nordic countries, where press freedom is the major legal framework, there are higher literacy rates, the public-service media and commercial media co-exist, political parallelism is high, and society is moderately pluralist. In this sense, there is, in principle, no compatibility between China's media system and the Democratic Corporatist Model in the West. However, this model prompts us to look beyond political control and economic impact to shed light on the dynamic formulation of Chinese society in a digital age.

Huge innovations in communication and organization have led to a restructuring of media power. In contemporary China, due to the history of revolutionary mobilization and political-economic restructuring under state socialism, the power of society is highly constrained and systematically monitored by the state and increasingly hostage to the market hegemony. In addition, the differentiation, even segmentation, of Chinese society has accelerated after four decades of neoliberal transformation. Various interest groups have emerged, exemplified by the forging of both an urban middle class and a new working class (i.e. migrant workers), which have jointly reshaped social differentiation and diversification or confrontation of voices in today's China. This trend is accelerated due to the prosperity of social media platforms and the pervasiveness of mobile technologies across all regions and social classes. In 2019, Internet penetration in China was higher than the global average at 61.2 per cent, which means appropriately 854 million Chinese are using the Internet on a regular basis, most of them on mobile devices (CNNIC, 2019).

The Internet has become a central part of the infrastructure of China's economy and society for both top-down policy making and people's everyday lives. The

Internet is utilized by the state in organizing an increasingly mobile society and by different social groups to respond to national policies and organize themselves for different purposes. A multi-layered virtual society is now emerging, which creates enormous tensions with the offline society. Therefore, not only the differentiation of social structure, but also the segmentation between online and offline society are shaping public opinion in China.

The Party has recognized this development and has required all publicity officials to pay attention to it. As President Xi crystalized in a talk on cyber security and informatization in 2016, in order to build social solidarity, online and offline should become concentric circles. While admitting the diversity of online expressions, the core of Internet governance is to make sure the Party is at the centre of these concentric circles. This is, according to Xi, not only about a 'purified cyberspace', but also about determining whether the Party can win the trust of the people. Xi's linguistic creation highlighted a crucial fact that the Internet/cyber/virtual society is driving China towards a future characterized by communicative uncertainties. For a political party that has long built its ruling legitimacy on mass communication and mobilization, the Internet is posing unexpected challenges to maintaining the Party's political and cultural leadership. With such a sense of crisis, 'self-revolution', a concept from the past, is now widely penetrating into the propaganda system of the Party.

Along with the differentiation of Chinese society, whether online or offline, disputes rather than consensus have become the new normal in China's information environment. Against this backdrop, traditional media have been trying to contain the increasing diversity of voices, while private, capital-driven Internet platforms are playing a major role in allowing different opinions to be voiced. Convergence and divergence coexist in this process. In addition, a new public-private alliance is also being widely discussed in China to demonstrate how the state power is collaborating with platform companies like Alibaba to implement a new model of governance in a connected and datafied society. As part of the global map of 'post-truth', the role of social media in producing fake news and misinformation is also attracting attention and critique. The declining trust of the public in cyberspace too has had a negative impact on the power of the state, which is in the middle of a digital 'self-revolution'. Therefore, it is still too early to say that a new order is emerging, be it a further centralized model or a pluralist model like the Nordic countries.

However, there might be one inspiration that we can draw from Hallin and Mancini's Democratic Corporatist Model to analyse China's media system – that is the moderate, autonomous regional media. Whether in ancient imperial dynasties or in modern, twenty-first-century China, the power structure of Chinese society has always been two-sided. One side is the imperial or state power centralized on the capital city and central governing body, while, on the other side, are the regions, which were always allowed a certain amount of autonomy in terms of self-governance, in order to organize such a geographically large and ethnically diverse country.

Therefore, if we take a look at the county-level governments and their media systems, as we discussed above, more heterogeneity than homogeneity can be found. The role of the media in creating regional political and cultural solidarity is of great importance, let alone the fact that the regional economies are the major support system for their own media's survival and development. This is relevant for both traditional media and new media. If the Democratic Corporatist Model is based on a high level of independence of society and a diverse self-organization of different active social groups, China certainly has less of this, but offers an interesting case to see how the state power tries to reduce, even contain, the diversity of voices on the one hand, and how a balance between different levels of the political system is being maintained despite these enormous challenges.

China's media system perhaps shares more elements with the Polarized Pluralist Model, including weak professionalization and strong state intervention. The political imperative to influence and even control the media is obvious in this model and related societies. Arbitrary powers over the media system could come from political parties, economic elites and their alliance. What clearly differentiates China from this model is a single ruling party system and a relatively more unified and culturally homogenized society. However, it may be worth looking at another dimension of this system, which could be called 'internal pluralism' within the political system. In addition to the autonomy of regional governance, the split of political beliefs is also creating more internal pluralism in the system and even contestation. Inside the party-state, at least three contesting beliefs can be found, namely, the liberal, the old left and the new left. Their voices are carried by different traditional media affiliated with their respective organizations and amplified by various social media platforms.

Last but not least, we also need to think about the applicability of the four dimensions that structure Hallin and Mancini's three models: media market, political parallelism, professionalism and state intervention. First, the media market, particularly the newspaper industry, is a relatively neutral and de-contextualized category. China's newspaper penetration is comparatively low. As elsewhere in the world, this industry in China, too, is now facing a huge decline in both circulation and advertising income. Second, in general, political parallelism is very high in China largely because of the Party's monopolistic, constant and strict supervision over the media entities. But it should be noted that political parallelism could also be found inside the party-state due to its rival political-ideological camps.

Third, there is indeed a space for professionalism in China's media system despite the Party's systematic control, but the issue is not the extent of professionalism, be it strong or weak, but the specific organizational contexts in which professionalism struggles to build legitimacy. The question also remains who are the major proponents for journalistic professionalism and the structural forces behind them. Last, state intervention or, more accurately, state control is always central to the explanation of China's media system, but this does not merely refer to a coercive power. State control over the media system in China acts both as a protector (in terms of supporting and sustaining media organizations and thus reducing market dependence) and regulation (which has switched from one side to another over the history of opening up and reform).

'One System, Two Operations' is still a useful term in explaining the ambiguous or hybrid nature of China's media system since the 1980s, no matter how many changes there have been in recent decades as a result of economic, political and technological transformations, as discussed above. After almost 40 years of articulating Western concepts in Chinese academia and introducing China's experience in media development to the international academic community, it is still difficult to place this locally-created concept in international comparative media systems research. Furthermore, the changing landscape of China's media system and its global expansion has made it more challenging for global perception. Thus, this dialogue with Hallin and Mancini's framework in trying to understand media transformations in China is just a small step forward to enrich the representativeness of the human story (Sparks, 2013: 121). Convergence could be the future of China's media system, but understanding the meaning of convergence should incorporate the multiplicity of media power in China and diverse appropriations of this concept in practice. A deeply rooted pragmatism underpins the policy-making logic in China's media system, while academic discussions about China and its rapidly globalizing media are contributing to a new 'ferment in the field' of international communication.

References

CNNIC (2019) *Statistical Report on Internet Development in China*. Beijing: China Internet Network Information Center (CNNIC), August. Available at http://cnnic.com.cn/IDR/ReportDownloads/201911/P020191112539794960687.pdf

Feldstein, Steven (2020) *When It Comes to Digital Authoritarianism, China is a Challenge—But Not the Only Challenge*. Washington: Carnegie Endowment for International Peace. Available at https://carnegieendowment.org/2020/02/12/when-it-comes-to-digital-authoritarianism-china-is-challenge-but-not-only-challenge-pub-81075

Hadland, Adrian (2012) If the Hat Fits: Revisiting Chinese Neo-Imperialism in Africa From a Comparative Historical Perspective. *Asian Politics & Policy*, 4(4): 467–485.

Hallin, Daniel and Mancini, Paolo (2004) *Comparing Media Systems: Three Models of Media and Politics*. Cambridge: Cambridge University Press.

Hu, Zhengrong, Ji, Deqiang and Zhang, Lei (2015) Building the Nation-State: Journalism and Communication Studies in China, pp. 369–395 in P. Simonson and D. Park (eds.) *The International History of Communication Study*. New York: Routledge.

Keane, Michael, Yecies, Brian and Flew, Terry (eds.) (2018) *Willing Collaborators: Foreign Partners in Chinese Media*. London: Rowman & Littlefield.

Li, Chunyu (2003) Local TV Station's Survival Strategies in the Age of Media Convergence. *Journalism & Communication*, 2: 10–13.

Nieborg, David and Poell, Thomas (2018) The Platformization of Cultural Production: Theorizing the Contingent Cultural Commodity. *New Media & Society*, 20(11): 4275–4292.

Sparks, Colin (2013) Global Media Studies: Its Development and Dilemmas. *Media, Culture & Society*, 35(1): 121–131.

Thussu, Daya Kishan, de-Burgh, Hugo and Shi, Anbin (eds.) (2018) *China's Media Go Global*. London: Routledge.

van Dijck, José (2018) The geopolitics of platforms: lessons for Europe, Keynote Speech at ECC 2018, Lugano, Available at www.ecrea2018lugano.eu/jose-van-dijck/

Weber, Ian (2005) Digitizing the Dragon: Challenges Facing China's Broadcasting Industry. *New Media & Society*, 7(6): 791–809.

Zhao, Yuezhi (2012) Understanding China's Media System in a World Historical Context, pp. 143–173 in D. Hallin and P. Mancini (eds.) *Comparative Media Systems beyond the West*. New York: Cambridge University Press.

Zhao, Yuezhi (2014) Communication, Crisis and Global Power Shifts: An Introduction. *International Journal of Communication*, 8: 275–300.

Zhu, Jie (2017) Rebutting the Charge of Neo-Colonialism: China's Need for Soft Power in Namibia. Johannesburg: China-Africa Project. Available at https://chinaafricaproject. com/migrated-posts/china-namibia-africa-soft-power-colonialism-jie-zhu/

8

SOUTH AFRICA

Beyond democratic deficit in public service broadcasting

viola candice milton and Winston Mano

South African media have much in common with media in BRICS and other countries in the global South, in the sense that its media systems inherited frameworks from the colonial era that are either no longer applicable or are urgently in need of reform. In South Africa the re-emergence of debates on the decolonization of knowledge and culture has revived interest in the tenuous link between democracy and the country's post-apartheid media institutions. This chapter argues that there is an urgent need to interrogate, uncover and unsettle power in the existing media models. The experience of democratization in South Africa demonstrates the necessity for a contextually embedded approach to the role of media in transitioning societies. Crucially, the chapter draws attention to the tensions between Southern African understandings and visions of democracy and those which have been articulated by global North paradigms, which are not always transferable to the different contexts of the BRICS countries. Through the case of the South African Broadcasting Corporation (SABC), the chapter examines how public service broadcasting in a transitional democracy raises questions about the nature of democratic participation. By rooting the analysis of democratic participation within local histories, practices and contexts, the chapter argues for a contextually driven framework for understanding the role of media systems in democracy in Southern Africa.

Media in Africa are increasingly discussed in terms of their relationship to the liberal democratic concepts of media freedom, freedom of expression and media accountability. For some African scholars, the notion of democracy is wedded to the context and aspirations of Western modernity (Conway and Singh, 2011: 689); hence they argue that the concept and its concomitants are incompatible with African political and social systems. Yet, as can be seen in places ranging from Hong Kong to the streets of Zimbabwe, the citizens of the global South have repeatedly demonstrated their desire for 'the rights and freedoms that democracy offers'

(Friedman, 2019: ix, 59). However, the democracy that the global South desires, 'neither emulates a model of democracy based on the Western "norm", nor rejects elements of what might be described as liberal democracy' (Brooks, Ngwane and Ranciman, 2020: 20).

Thus, it is not surprising that the South African mediascape differs from media models in the global North. There is inevitable discomfort with the notion that in order to 'legitimize' a particular media set up, it has to be evaluated in relation to what it is not, rather than for what it is and might mean within its own particular contexts. So, in South Africa the media might adopt universally agreed upon principles (such as media freedom and freedom of expression) but will (and should) do so on their own terms. This is in part because, where media policy is concerned, socio-political considerations are key. In this regard, Mano and milton (2021) argue for self-standing African media theories that are informed by locally relevant epistemologies and ontologies.

What is at stake in the above are crucial questions linked to ongoing debates about reformulating media frameworks in changing postcolonial societies. At issue are the ways in which the global North continues to be an unspoken or silent normative assumption underpinning the frame of reference for doing media studies in the global South. In this respect, it has been suggested that one should question whether the 'comparing media systems' approach in the tradition of Hallin and Mancini (2004) is useful for discussing mediascapes in the global South. In fact, the very notion of thinking of the media in terms of 'systems' is antithetical to the extreme heterogeneity of media spaces and their usage in the global South. This raises questions about *whose* gaze or epistemological vantage point is invoked when we attempt to identify something as a media *system* (Shome, 2017: 67)?

What this means for us is that an uncontextualized analysis of media in BRICS, which simply juxtaposes them against an invisible global North, might fail to consider the media in these global South contexts for what they are. Such an approach would exacerbate what Grosfoguels (2007) has described as a 'colonial matrix of power' – that is a global system of asymmetric power relations which can be analysed in terms of who is speaking (body politics of knowledge) and from where (geo-politics of knowledge). The global South is rarely listened to – by which we mean that their voice is not taken seriously – especially in policy frameworks, given the in-built continuities in the existing structures of communication and education. The approach here argues for rethinking from and at the margins of the world system to allow other possibilities to emerge.

In relation to the academic discipline of media and communication, this has been approached in terms of 'de-Westernising' media studies (Curran and Park, 2000); internationalizing media studies (Thussu, 2009), and internationalizing cultural studies (Abbas and Erni, 2004). In each of these, the idea is to go beyond the global North cultural and intellectual ambit. Yet, as milton and Mano (2021) argue, despite these laudable ethical origins, which sought to foster cross-cultural and inter-cultural solidarity, these efforts to internationalize and 'de-Westernise' communication studies to bring everyone and everything into the fray, ironically, still largely neglect and misrecognize perspectives from the global South. What is needed are bold and valid epistemological frameworks from the global South which are recognized as such within the pluriverse of knowledge (Mano and milton, 2021). As will be argued in this chapter, a contextualized study of the SABC will illuminate the need for the shift in epistemological thinking proposed above. Like most media in South Africa, the SABC is both a product and victim of the apartheid context from which it emerged.

Media-democracy dynamic

The democratization process in transitional societies around the world – and also in Africa – has been far from uniform. There is a need to question the extent to which changes in these countries constituted a thorough-going transformation of society or whether instead this has resulted in the repositioning of, or partnerships between, elites (Sparks, 2009). Spark's analysis of media in countries moving from authoritarian to democratic rule finds significant continuities in 'both institutions and personnel between the old regime and the new' with 'highly politicised interventions into broadcasting and a highly partisan press' and 'licensing of new commercial broadcasters' in a manner that favours those connected to 'political power' (Sparks, 2009: 196). Close attention should also be paid to 'how media institutions that emerge from transitions are strongly influenced by the political elite'. Sparks uses this to argue that 'the degree of democratisation, if any, is secondary' and in the case of South Africa in particular he notes that the '… South African media has a fair degree of fit with the elite continuity model', with some modifications needed to the model arising from the specific context (ibid.: 197, 213).

It can be noted that in the immediate aftermath of apartheid, there was a general mood of 'never again' in the reconstruction of South African media policy, i.e. never again would the media be used as a tool for powerful elites, never again would censorship be allowed to deter the voices of the most vulnerable, never again would the public broadcaster function as an organ of state. However, as observed by Sparks above and will be shown below, the South African public-service broadcaster's emergence from apartheid seems to belie this affirmative approach to transform. Amongst others, it reveals a changing dynamic in the negotiation of power in the representation of party politics (as well as the politics of identity) in South Africa.

The political transition in South Africa has had a noticeable influence on media democracy that emphasizes the need to adequately assess and account for the specificities of the post-apartheid context, especially as it pertains to the media landscape. South Africa's media issues, as with media in other BRICS contexts, challenge generalizations about the media-democracy link common in the field of media and communication. Berger's questioning of the media-democracy relationship is especially apropos here:

> [m]any writers (but not enough) have sounded warnings about lifting concepts like media and democracy from Western conditions and applying

them unthinkingly to Africa … Most striking of all is the reliance in much of the writing upon unreflective, conventional wisdom about the way that 'media' is an important element in 'democracy' – which 'wisdoms' in turn tend to be limited to a liberal pluralist paradigm … [whose] suitability to Africa is questionable.

(Berger, 2002: 21)

Berger argues that there is a need to look at alternative paradigms of democracy and of media in Southern Africa. Nyamnjoh (2011) agrees but advocates caution in this regard, noting that, despite the critique of the dominant, normative, liberal-democratic paradigm, one should avoid the trap of an idealization of Africa. He advises against a blind, romantic essentialism of 'African values' that, according to him, many proponents of Afrocentric thought are prone to. Instead, a 'flexible theoretical position is needed … one which takes into account the multiple, overlapping spaces and flows in the era of globalization yet refuses to gloss over global power imbalances and material inequalities' (Nyamnjoh, 2011: 20).

Clearly, a one-size-fits-all approach to the concept of democracy creates problems. The above critiques are not meant to suggest that democracy and media democratization are alien to Africans. For example, freedom of expression, a vital aspect of democracy and economic development, is, in our view, consistent with the African concept of *ubuntu* as it enables people to be the most they can be, facilitating the establishment of communities (Chasi, 2015: 91). Hence, we argue that the democratization of broadcasting is essential for citizen participation in the African democratization process.

In Southern Africa, not least as a result of the great economic divide, free-to-air public broadcasters still attract the majority of the viewing and listening audience, but questions about public-service broadcasting are being articulated ever more loudly. Commentators, including civil society organizations, print media and academics, question African public-service broadcasting's purpose, how it should be defined and who it should be accountable to (milton and Fourie 2015; Mano, 2016). For our purpose, we have to question what the role or place of media – and here specifically public-service broadcasting – is and/or should be in relation to democracy, without falling prey to 'fortress journalism syndrome' (Nordenstreng, 2004). A nuanced analysis, in our view, necessitates an understanding of the interplay between media transformation and broader societal change. More importantly, it requires 'engaging, and even sometimes building, epistemological references and frames for understanding media, its scope (that is, what may count as media) that thus far may not exist' (Shome, 2017: 70).

In South Africa – as elsewhere on the continent – the most important factor that has influenced the development of broadcasting is the varying shades of colonial legacy (Eko, 2000: 87). Colonialism not only placed broadcasting and other public institutions outside African life, it also, crucially, positioned them as vehicles for taking Africans out of a rural, subsistence existence, which had hitherto been dominated by traditional philosophies, practices and personality types. Eko maintains that the modernization process dismissed African life and saw broadcasting as a way to diminish its role in public life. The institutions of public-service broadcasting were part of a well-orchestrated modernization approach that aimed to condition African populations to distrust traditional knowledge and 'Africanness' as a precondition for development (Eko, 2000). Hence, it could be argued that the problem with public-service broadcasting in South Africa is that it is linked to apartheid and failed modernization programmes from the 1950s and 1960s, which sought to bring 'Western-type' development by destroying local knowledge and traditions (West and Fair, 1993; De Beer and Tomaselli, 2000).

Following Mararike's (1998) work on African philosophy and development, Mano (2005) has used the metaphor of '*kudyiswa*' in Shona, '*ukudhliswa*' in Ndebele, '*guthaiga*' in Gikuyu or '*miti*' in Kikamba to discuss this damaging conditioning of media in Africa (Mano, 2005). Each of these terms refers to the administering of a traditional love potion to one's lover in order to ensure that they remain devoted in their love for you in a myopic manner. The overall effect of the '*kudyiswa*' process is to create a client out of someone. We see this as relevant to the discussion of how colonialism's embeddedness in modernization thinking refused to acknowledge an Africanist ethos in approaches to public broadcasting. As Mararike boldly states:

> [the] '*kudyiswa*' process … must be seen as 'conditioning' a practice of 'knowing' that constructs an object as 'external' to the 'knower' and 'independent of him or her.' The role …. is to create and preserve conceptions and means of description for the world as it is for those who have power rather than 'as it is' for the ruled and power-less. The '*kudyiswa*' process … is a process of 'mental conditioning' or 'ideological indoctrination' and 'brainwashing'.
>
> *(Mararike, 1998: 90)*

The '*kudyiswa*' process arguably shaped the development of public service broadcasting (PSB) in Africa and was effective on the basis of side-lining locally-generated historic knowledge, local actors and processes. This heritage might explain why postcolonial broadcasters have struggled to find a social fit. As institutions, they remain subservient and serviceable to modernization agendas (ostensibly in service of the 'developmental state' of the emerging democracies) that were decidedly against the local. It is our argument that current public-service broadcasters, including the SABC, need to overcome restrictive media policies, including undemocratic, colonial developmental legacies.

Alhassan and Chakravartty concur, noting that '[m]edia and communication policy for nations and societies in Africa, Asia and Latin America is "deeply embedded" in discourses and practices of development and modernisation', which can be traced 'to a longer history of colonial, national and international governance' (Alhassan and Chakravartty, 2011: 366). For them, 'the legacy of the colonial encounter … is visible in the ways in which the actual state practices of policy-making often betray … the unresolved fundamental questions of inequality and exclusion, upon which national discourses of development are founded' (ibid.).

There is therefore a need to re-theorize the role of the postcolonial state in discussions of media and communication policy in emerging postcolonial nation states to be more in step with actual conditions on the ground.

A re-theorized PSB framework needs to encourage participation through all its structures and processes. Chasi and Rodney-Gumede (2016) argue in this regard that we need to re-imagine PSB in ways that will speak to our (African) realities. In essence, we are arguing here for a destruction of the 'crooked room', which, in our view, will allow something else to emerge. This metaphor is utilized by Melissa Harris-Perry (2011) to explore the particular epistemology that Black women face in 'white spaces'. Perry argues that, when Black women are confronted with race and gender stereotypes, they are standing in a 'crooked room', and that they have to figure out which way is up. When they find themselves being inundated with warped and distorted images of their humanity, some Black women tilt and contort themselves in order to 'fit' the distortion rather than stand up straight in a space that is extremely disorienting and uncomfortable.

We borrow this metaphor to elucidate on the strictures to reform media in the global South arising from hostile, colonial-era structures. We argue that, in these cases, many behave in a way that compels them to fit the alien world around them, a world which then rewards them with accolades about how well behaved they are, but which never quite meets their need to be more appreciated and respected. At core is a question about their misrecognition and denial of dignity. Scholars from the global South cannot give up; they need to produce more knowledge informed by and capable of informing their (un)changing media context. We will illustrate this by unpacking our primary argument, i.e. that public-service broadcasters must engender democratic participation and inclusive democratic communication aligned to the needs and realities of African lived experiences.

Public-broadcasting policy frameworks in African contexts veer towards inward-looking policy structures, which complicates policy-negotiation. Contemporary broadcast policy in Africa, we argue, is shaped by the process of 'kudyiswa'. Civic groups, for example, have not been sufficiently involved in media policy-making because of the centralization of processes by the state, specifically the overzealous involvement of Ministries of Information. Where civic groups do engage, they by and large tend to fall back on an elitist, paternalistic, Reithian-perception of the public-service ethos, negating in their deliberations a thorough focus on, or in some cases even any acknowledgement of, an African ethos. This is in part a result of the ways in which Africanist media models such as 'journalism for social change', 'communal journalism' and 'journalism inspired by oral discourse' (Skjerdal, 2012: 637) have been misused by autocratic governments to serve their own political ends, instead of the common good – or, to phrase this in PSB language, the public interest. However, it is also primarily a manifestation of the lack of consensus about what an Africanist ethos in PSB might entail (Berger, 2002; Skjerdal 2012).

To get out of this quagmire, there is need for democratization to step in line with Afrokology in a process of 'gutahiko' or 'kuritsiswa', i.e., the expunging of colonial thought or then, the decolonization of PSB in Southern Africa. We propose Afrokology as a key African-facing heuristic toolkit that can counter the '*kudyiswa*' process (Mano and milton, 2021). If '*kudyiswa*' is an expression of the colonization that 'continues to be administered to the African population and is producing more damaging results than before' (Mararike, 1998: 93), then the process of '*kurutsiswa*' can neutralize, expunge and ultimately insulate against the '*kudyiswa*' effects, and herein lies the lesson for an Afrokology of PSB. First, the causes of the problems with PSB and the frameworks within which they operate need to be identified clearly.

Following this, there is a need to rid Africa of the problem by administering the right kind of medicine at the right time and in correct quantities. Finally, permanent preventative measures must be put in place. To this end then, we appreciate Berger's assertion that '… if much African media has historically played a political propagandist role or a developmentalist role, it does not serve any explanatory purpose to hold up a watchdog model and measure Africa's historic deficit. What needs to be explained is not what did not happen, but rather what did' (Berger, 2002: 21–22). We offer a contextually driven explication of the South African Broadcasting Corporation's emergence from apartheid era state apparatus to contemporary (fledgling) public-service broadcaster with a broader democratic mandate.

The case of the SABC

The democratization process in transitional societies globally – including in Africa – has been 'far from uniform', and one needs to question the extent to which changes in these countries constituted thoroughgoing transformation of society or rather resulted in the repositioning of, or partnerships between, elites, as mentioned above (Sparks, 2009). In South Africa for example, the democratization of the political sphere, ushered in an ostensibly transformed broadcasting mediascape with the SABC leading the changes in its move to transform itself from a state to a public broadcaster (Duncan, 2000). The SABC developed and implemented transformation strategies in key areas such as programming and news and current affairs. These changes supposedly marked a radical break with the ethos of the old apartheid-era state broadcaster.

Duncan, however, is sceptical about the extent to which these changes have been effective. She notes that it is less acknowledged that there are many continuities between the old and the new order that involve '… an eerie convergence of interests … [that] severely curtails the Corporation's ability to become a bona fide public broadcaster' (Duncan, 2000: 53). Added to this, the commercialization of the public broadcasting space means a continuation of audience segmentation, possibly reflecting a reconstitution of old apartheid identities, which goes against the stated post-apartheid commitment to non-racialism (Jacobs, 2004). In fact, the numerous problems facing PSB as an institution in post-apartheid South Africa are well documented.

Recent years have for example seen a downward spiral of financial woes for the public broadcaster, coupled with increasing concerns about political interference (milton, 2018; Khosa and Khosa, 2019). Its editorial code emphasizes the SABC's autonomy, including journalistic, creative and programming independence of its staff. It gives special importance to protecting the freedom of expression of the SABC's audiences. However, faith in the SABC's autonomy is dwindling, with scholars suggesting that '[a]lthough care should be taken not to overstate the case of government interference in broadcasting in South Africa, it would appear that a number of high-profile incidents between 2002 and 2008, are suggesting a shift for the SABC from public broadcaster into his master's voice' (Louw and milton, 2012: 267).

In the face of threats to media freedom and freedom of expression in the past two decades, South African civil society has organized and picketed the SABC. They also instituted court cases to challenge the broadcaster's approach to censorship and journalistic freedom. A case in point is when, in 2016, civil society joined journalists in approaching authorities to rule on the lawfulness of a decree by the then Chief Operating Officer of the SABC to ban political and service delivery protests. The fall-out of this de-facto censorship resulted, perhaps for the first time in 30 years, in public interest from the broader community of viewers in the role and function of the SABC. Media workers joined with viewers and civil society to protest by picketing and disregarding decrees that interfered with journalistic freedom and professionalism. When the latter resulted in the SABC firing the journalists involved in the protest, there was a defiant show of solidarity when their colleagues wore black on the very same broadcasts.

The pressure resulted in a temporary cease-fire. The former COO was forced to reverse his belligerent position and had to agree to stop censorship of images related to protest action and to reinstate the fired journalists. These responses and their resultant impact on the threats to media freedom and freedom of expression, demonstrate that South Africa's democracy is very much alive and kicking. As such, the SABC can be seen as a metaphor for South African society: it is unsettled, it is in transition and is, in many ways, not unlike the society it represents and reflects. Take, for example, the policy contradictions inherent in the SABC's editorial policies, which mirror the shifts and changes in the fledgling post-colonial democratic context.

SABC's 2014 editorial policy review process

The SABC's editorial policy review process of 2014 was introduced in line with South Africa's principle of consultative/participative democratic practice, which requires an extensive consultative process with stakeholders, citizens and civil society all making verbal and written contributions. milton (2014) contributed to that process on behalf of the Media Policy and Democracy Project – a joint project between the University of South Africa and the University of Johannesburg. Key to the contribution was the idea about journalistic credibility. A revised editorial policy, it was argued was needed to rebuild the trust in the editorial integrity and credibility of the broadcaster's content and the process by which it was produced and distributed. The submission to the SABC's Editorial Policy review was particularly concerned about governance and the relationship between management and editorial oversight, which was complicated by the so-called 'upward referral' clause in the existing editorial policy.

This clause gave the broadcaster's General Chief Executive Officer (GCEO) the final say on editorial matters. Given the politics of the board nomination and implementation process in South Africa, where board members (especially the GCEO) are often political appointees, this blurring of the necessary distinction between management roles and editorial roles opened the SABC to undue external commercial, political, religious and other influences. In this situation, there was potential for a conflict of interest, with the GCEO ignoring the SABC's accountability to the general public. It was argued that allowing the GCEO to also be editor-in-chief contradicted the SABC's claims of 'editorial independence' and 'freedom from undue influence' – be that influence from the market or from politics. Issues such as the SABCs blacklisting of journalists and commentators, and unilateral decisions by the GCEO to 'can' television and radio programmes critical of government or the ruling party illustrate that when management roles and editorial roles collide, freedom of expression is inhibited and journalism suffers.

In the submission, milton (2014) also observed that 'upward referrals' endangered the editorial policy of commitment to content diversity given that distribution on the SABC was being dominated by a single point of view. Apartheid and a colonial-era type of control in the institution narrowed down the performance of the SABC. What was needed was content diversity that furthered the goals of a democratic society by enhancing public access to the full range of ideas, information, subject matter and perspectives required to make informed judgements about issues important to South Africans. It also reflected the public service broadcaster's 'special mandate to serve many different and discrete audiences' (ibid.). The goal of diversity thus requires ongoing efforts to ensure that the broadcaster's content fully reflects the pluralism of South African society, including for example, appropriate representation of linguistic and other minorities. Upward referral thus poses a threat to public service broadcasters being usurped by political appointees who, under the guise of development, use the institution for political gain (milton and Fourie, 2015). It is worth noting that, when upward referral was first introduced into the SABC's editorial policy, its inclusion in the editorial code was debated at length and at that stage it was argued that it was consistent with international practise in this regard. At issue here is the legacy of broadcasting administration structures, in service of 'international best practice' that are not adequately suited to media democratization in post-authoritarian contexts.

milton's (2014) submission to the review process proposed that it was good governance practice to separate the duties of the SABC Board from that of professional management. It was submitted that the GCEO should concern him/herself with ensuring a proper business platform to enable content providers and journalists to do their job. The Editor-in-Chief's role, it argued, was to protect the reputation of the SABC and its journalism: hence, neither the GCEO nor any other board member should be engaged in editorial decision-making. Board members should adopt policies and procedures that enabled professional management to operate in a way that would give the public full confidence in the editorial integrity of the broadcaster's content/programming. The submission suggested that the SABC should make every effort to ensure that the content it distributed satisfied editorial standards to ensure integrity. It should lead in demonstrating to both citizens and public policy makers that its 'programming is free from undue or improper influence'. The submission's proposals were echoed by other civil society actors such as SOS: Support Public Broadcasting and the Right-to-Know Campaign.

PSB as partner in participation

The transformation of the SABC, as the title of a book by Louw and milton (2012) suggests, was about bringing 'new voices to the air'. This is in line with the aim of public-service broadcasters to engender democratic participation and inclusive communication, reflecting the diversity of the community. However, the problem with 'bringing new voices' to the table is that it assumes that the 'table' is fine and that all we need to do is bring new voices. For example, in the South African context, a preoccupation with the 'numbers game' in effect re-racializes society in ways that the non-racial ANC of the 1960s and 1970s probably did not envision (Chasi and Mboti, 2016).

How then do we participate if, in Chasi and Mboti's (2016) words, 'inclusion' as envisioned in contemporary transformation discourse is not the way? Indeed, what would an Africanist participation theory look like? In 2015, a group of African scholars organized a pre-conference at IAMCR (International Association for Media and Communication Research) where they retheorized 'participation' from an African vantage point. The Africanist participation studies approach was proposed as a counter-weight to conventional communication frameworks of enquiry. Chasi and Mboti (2016) submitted that the main objection to conventional communication theories that are in use in communication departments in (South) African universities and governments is not necessarily that such theories are non-African in their original ethos. Rather, the objection is that such theories do not always adequately march in step with qualitative transformations in the everyday lives and lived realities of Africans. At base, this is a question about relevance (ibid.).

Thus, when arguing in the abstract that public-service broadcasters must engender democratic participation and inclusive communication, this is the participation we have in mind. One that marches in step with qualitative transformations in the everyday lives and lived realities of the Africans in whose interest it ostensibly operates. This question of relevance was also behind the 2013 'Continental Conference on Media Legislative Reforms and Transforming State Broadcasters into Public Broadcasters in Africa' held in Midrand in South Africa, at the Pan-African Parliament (PAP). The conference was co-hosted by the Africa Governance Monitoring and Advocacy Project (AfriMAP), the Open Society Initiative of Southern Africa, Article 19 and the Media Institute of Southern Africa. It attracted a new constellation of local and international organizations, including consultants, universities, politicians, journalists and high-level international partners, to find resolutions for the ongoing problem of state control over public broadcasters. The conference culminated in the 'Midrand Call to Action: Media Freedom and Public Broadcasting in Africa' (Mano, 2016).

Noting the dire state of broadcasting in Africa, it called on all African institutions, decision-makers, civil society and social justice organizations and publics to promote media freedom on the African continent as well as commit to actively playing their part in transforming and strengthening all state broadcasters into public broadcasters (Afrimap, 2013). The Midrand Call to Action focused in particular on the [accountability] role that each sector should play, noting with regard to National Public Broadcasters that these should, amongst others, '… develop, through an inclusive public process, editorial and programme guidelines that adhere to public broadcasting principles and promote public interest programming …' and 'use digital technologies to promote broader access and public participation in the development of editorial policies' (ibid.: 6).

Of particular relevance to this discussion is that the delineations of PSB as envisioned within the African context above, is congruent with a PSB ethos that submits that, for a PSB to be useful within a democratic framework, it should adhere to the widely accepted core goals for PSBs, summarized by Barr as being: (1) universal accessibility (geographic); (2) contribution to a sense of national identity and community; (3) distance from vested interests; (4) direct funding and universality of payment; (5) competition in programming rather than for numbers; (6) guidelines that liberate rather than restrict programme makers and (7) universal appeal (general tastes and interests) (Barr, 2000: 66).

Clearly these principles have changed little since the beginning of public service broadcasting in Britain. Murdock notes that, for much of its history, public service broadcasting:

> was designed to demonstrate how the distinctive qualities of the nation, and by extension of the Western Christian tradition, found their highest expression in works that had entered the official canon. Reith was adamant that one of public broadcasting's central missions was to ensure that 'the wisdom of the wise and the amenities of culture are available without discrimination …', but he took it for granted that what constituted 'wisdom' and 'culture' would be defined by intellectual and creative elites.
>
> *(Murdock, 2010: 180)*

Reith's core elements of a national, non-commercial service that is directly funded by government are still important aspects of the services provided by the BBC and remains one of the most contested aspects of PSB funding in South Africa (cf. Louw and milton, 2012; milton and Fourie, 2015).

In spite of aspirations for alternatives, wholesale mimicking of global North frameworks is still widespread in Africa. Even when transformation in service of

African ideals is discussed, there is still a tendency to revere templates and reference points that are alien. Mano and milton (2020), for example, with regard to their participation in the Midrand-Conference, note that, apart from a few notable exceptions, the experts from the North framed and dominated the policy conception phase. African stakeholders were largely included at the operationalization stage and as implementers. At issue here is that the global North remained an invisible and, due to the nature of the event, at times a very visible point of reference for the conference deliberations and outcomes. Their experience as participants in the conference processes led Mano and milton to conclude that a more inclusive collaboration is needed whereby the voice of African stakeholders are *listened to* in PSB reform (ibid.). Here it is worth noting that African-developed charters have much to offer to the ethos of PSB. Most laudable is the defined commitment towards a participatory PSB environment that pays specific attention to emancipation, human dignity and dialectical processes of voice and listening. These commitments are geared towards ensuring deeper participation, especially for marginalized communities.

In general, what is at issue in attempts to theorize from the African metropolis, is how do we 'reorient the media content (to change the focus to stories which have genuine relevance for the African context); transform the presentation style (emphasising processes and dialogue rather than breaking news) and reorganise the structural outlook of the media (where it is argued that, rather than serving as an isolated Fourth Estate, the media should work together with other parties in society for national development)' (Skjerdal, 2011). What is evident in this is the emphasis placed on participation as a necessary component of communicative theory and practice. This is interesting also in the light of recent efforts towards emphasizing the importance of participation in PSB globally – perhaps influenced by marketization, digitization and the increasing popularity of social networking. Lowe (2010), for example, notes that contemporary discussions about renewal in PSB has focused increasingly on public participation, although what that means for practice remains uncertain and why it matters is largely framed in ethical terms. He notes that '[a]s an "altruistic imperative", public participation is important among media theorists concerned about growing marketisation that may threaten the vitality of the public sphere for contemporary democracy' (Lowe, 2010: 9).

When discussing contra-flows in theorizing, it should be noted that concepts shift and change across continental borders, languages and political contexts. Sometimes it merges with so-called concepts from the global North (for example there is some overlap between the concept of *ubuntu* and the more Western-defined communitarianism), while at other times theorists themselves insist on interrogating the concepts through a Western lens, hence rendering the concept powerless before it is even considered. The argument is raised that the political economy of African mediascapes is still guided and dominated by views from the global North. Values related to ownership, control, management and journalism practices, and freedom of expression as well as public opinion and public interest are therefore inevitably discussed from the viewpoint of an assumed universal gaze (milton and

Fourie, 2015). We conclude by considering what value could be added by looking at PSB from an Afrokological vantage point.

An Afrokology of public-service broadcasting

Afrokology is presented by Mano and milton (2021) as a heuristic toolkit, which can provide a basis for an indigenous approach to African media and communication that resonates with conditions on the continent. Here, we look at whether and how PSB and PSB practices can be situated within an indigenized theoretical framework for media, based on an African ethos. To interrogate these, we turn our attention to two attempts at 'indigenizing' media theory in general and PSB theory specifically, from the Southern African context. The first is Blankenberg's (1999) attempt to redefine media theory in the context of *ubuntu* and the second is Banda's (2007) project to redefine PSB within the context of development journalism.

PSB as 'ubuntu'

Ubuntuism can be understood as a moral philosophy, a collective African consciousness deeply embedded in African culture's expression of communal (collective or shared) compassion, reciprocity, dignity, harmony and humanity in the interest of a community (traditionally the tribe or clan), with justice and mutual caring for all (cf. e.g. Nussbaum, 2003: 1). As such, it differs from the emphasis on the individual of mainstream Eurocentric moral philosophy, which Nyamnjoh singles out as 'harmful' to the African communard (Nyamnjoh, 2004: 2011). *Ubuntuism* views the essence of being as participation with other humans. Unlike Western individualistic democracy, which insists on freedom of the self from intrusion by others, *ubuntuism* sees a person's freedom as dependent on their personal relationships with others. A person is first and foremost a participatory being dependent on others for his/her development. *Ubuntuism* therefore places a high premium on negotiation, inclusiveness and tolerance (cf. Fourie, 2008; milton and Fourie, 2015).

Taking this basic understanding of *ubuntu* into consideration, Blankenberg argues that the philosophy of *ubuntu* could be used as a foundation for and a legitimation of a liberation journalism that attempts to unite the role of the media – and for our purpose, particularly PSB – to serve the basic tenets of democracy (Blankenberg, 1999: 44). The tenets of democracy underlined by Blankenberg include, first, the creation and preserving of a space within which people are able to voice their opinions on the future of their nation and, second, that the media has a strong role to play in the creation and recognition of a civil society, a public space and a common culture. To this he adds that the media is integral to 'the modern day liberation project, as a facilitator to ensure widespread participation in the political system and all aspects of the public sphere, as a "catalyst" for critical consciousness, and as a storyteller, creating and litigating public cultural rituals for negotiating cultural conflicts and agreeing on common values' (ibid.).

For Blankenberg, liberation media combine the best elements of development journalism, participatory communication and other theories of media to come up with a concept of journalism that best addresses the needs of many African communities. He concludes that the philosophy of *ubuntu*, combined with a Freirean philosophy of critical consciousness, principles of Third Cinema and a spirit of participation, provide a foundation for a journalism applicable certainly to Africa but also globally (ibid.). It is further noted that the *ubuntu*-ethos as explicated here, chimes with UNESCO's definition of public broadcasting, which sees it as a meeting place where all citizens are welcome and considered equals. It is an information and education tool, accessible to all and meant for all, whatever their social or economic status.

This has far reaching theoretical and practical consequences as pointed out by Fourie (Fourie, 2008). First, the implications of this view of the ontology and epistemology of contemporary Southern African thinking about the media are clear. 'The West' focuses on media primarily in terms of its information, surveillance, entertainment and educational role; journalism's freedom and right to protection in order to be able to fulfil its social responsibility, and the individual's right to information, surveillance, entertainment and education. *Ubuntu* shifts the focus towards the media's role in community bonding and dialogue towards reaching consensus based on the cultural and social values and morals of a community. Of course, it has to be noted that this idea of the media sphere is not that different from Habermas' perception of the public sphere (the latter's many problems notwithstanding). The emphasis thus moves from the media as informant, gatekeeper, interpreter and educator, to the media as mediator; from the media as observer, to the media as participant and negotiator, from the media as a watchdog to the media as a guide-dog.

Fourie therefore raises five questions about *ubuntu* as a normative framework for journalism. He points out the significant consequences such a framework may have for journalism in its Western-defined libertarian–democratic ideal of an 'objective representation of the world'. The questions speak to concerns about the relevancy of *ubuntuism* in the context of the changed nature of traditional African culture; the claim that *ubuntuism* is distinctively an African moral philosophy; moral philosophy's vulnerability to political exploitation; *ubuntuism* as a normative theory in a globalized world and changed media environment, and the implications an *ubuntu* approach may have for journalism practice (Fourie, 2008). Yet, as pointed out by Chasi (2015: 98) locating *ubuntu* within a liberal constitutional framework is not necessarily counter-intuitive, 'especially if one recognizes that ubuntu can be read as a moral philosophy that does not eschew recognition of individuals ... and that ubuntu has, for example, been found to be consistent with Ralwsian liberal thought ...' (ibid.).

Blankenberg was not oblivious to the issues highlighted by Fourie. In his conclusion he noted that many obstacles stand in the way of the realization of the ideal of an *ubuntu*-inspired liberatory media. Notably, he singled out the interests of those who benefit from a libertarian journalism that enforces the status quo and is elitist in nature, as a key obstacle. In this respect he acknowledges the importance of buy-in from different role-players in the search for a model journalism that aspires towards mainstreaming – cautioning therefore against a journalism that is 'relegated to only marginalised "grassroots" development' (Blankenberg, 1999: 60). Echoes of such a line of reasoning can be found in West and Fair's work, who argue that:

> Only … by locating media within the sphere of social relations of power and by historically situating media forms … will we see clearly that what is at issue in using communication for development purposes is not merely the success or failure of 'development', but rather the ability of people in African societies to construct, advance, contest, transform, and resist visions for the future direction of their own communities'.
>
> *(West and Fair, 1993: 95)*

PSB as development journalism

Development journalism, notwithstanding its many problems, appears to be making a comeback, notably in the work of Banda, in his attempt to reconceptualize development journalism within the new African reality, specifically aiming at a synthesis between development journalism and public-service broadcasting ideology. Banda's effort, read in conjunction with Blankenberg's explication of so-called *ubuntu*-journalism, presents some interesting pointers for an 'Afrokology' of PSB (Banda, 2007). He notes that the demonization of development journalism (resulting from a discourse embedded in Western notions of press freedom) has diverted attention from important questions about how journalism can contribute to participatory democracy, security, peace and other humanistic values.

Banda demonstrates first, the relevance of the development journalism paradigm to PSB and second, how the principles of the paradigm can be implemented within the context of PSB. He points to five key areas of similarity between development journalism and PSB. First, development journalism stresses the free will of the journalist, which resonates with the requirement of PSB to be independent from vested interests. Second, PSB's notion of 'universality' (i.e. universal accessibility and universal appeal) is implied in development journalism's concern with providing access to marginalized members of society and enhancing their participation (through, for example, having their voices heard on a range of issues) and its holistic view of 'development' as 'appealing to all'. Third, PSB's structure of regional houses and its insistence on a people's representative body to which it is accountable, assumes that PSB is there to service the needs of the people and not a particular political elite. Fourth, both development journalism and PSB value cultural and community identity as a counter-hegemonic force against any local or foreign hegemonic cultural encroachment and, last, both development journalism and PSB are infused with a concern for the development of societies in their entirety (Banda, 2007: 164).

Banda expands on this list in a comparative table where he also points to similarities between the two concepts' perceptions of content i.e. both emphasize good, quality programming content, with development journalism specifically highlighting the importance of infusing grassroots voices as well, and both value independent programme-making and independent and democratic participation. A distinguishing feature of Banda's attempt to redefine PSB within the context of development journalism, is not necessarily its insistence that the media exists for the people and must therefore have emancipation as its ultimate goal, but rather its downplaying of the role of the state and its focus on the potential of citizens in media making (an aspect that is also gaining traction in contemporary 'Western' discussions of citizen participation in media-making in a digitalized PSB environment).

Conclusion

What does this discussion of PSB in Africa tell us about the way in which the media-democracy link in post-apartheid South Africa can be theorized? The challenges faced by the media system in South Africa, in particular facing SABC as a public-service broadcaster, reflect structural issues in the global media system, which is still dominated by the West. South Africa is not alone in facing this need to find a culturally appropriate path to develop its media. BRICS could provide a framework within which to create a shared strategy that mobilizes for the liberation of media institutions in the global South. Such an intervention might be similar to the establishment of the BRICS Bank in terms of bringing an alternative model for global media governance, one that can be inspired by relevant indigenous knowledge and experiences in the South. However, no one wants to exchange one master for another, so vigilance is required to prevent the imposition of new controls.

Universally, the challenge for PSB has, from the beginning, been characterized by dialectical relations seemingly inherent in linking organizational egoism and orientational altruism (Lowe, 2010). This holds true for the SABC as well. Under apartheid, the SABC operated as a monopoly in a constrained context in which it wished to make a difference – albeit a difference for groups that were narrowly defined in line with first colonial and thereafter postcolonial political and economic interests. It saw at its core the necessity for a developmental function in service of nation building but it remained vulnerable to the political party and government of the day in this respect. For this broadcaster to truly provide a participatory democratic sphere, there is need for a concerted effort to limit government influence.

In our view, a reconceptualised PSB is not necessarily African-centric or Afrocentric. Rather, it is located within a global context that goes beyond the centrism of the global North. This ethos takes precedence in both Blankenberg's attempt to theorize media within the context of *ubuntu* and Banda's aligning development journalism and public-service broadcasting. Both operate within a policy framework that places the emancipation of the African people at the centre of media and PSB principles. Notably, both emphasize the necessity for free and independent media, although they do not necessarily see the role of the media as an objective observer. Instead, they place PSB as an actor in a participatory civil society with an emphasis on what Nyamnjoh calls 'conviviality', in the pursuit towards different and competing individual and/or collective goals within negotiated socio-cultural arrangements (Nyamnjoh, 2013: 128).

References

Abbas, A. and Erni, J. N. (eds.) (2004) *Internationalizing Cultural Studies: An Anthology.* Oxford: Blackwell.

Afrimap (2013) The Midrand Call to Action: Media Freedom and Public Broadcasting in Africa. Available at www.afrimap.org/english/images/report/AfriMAP%20-%20Midrand%20Call%20to%20Action%20 Final.pdf

Alhassan, A. and Chakravartty, P. (2011) Postcolonial media policy under the long shadow of empire, pp. 366–382, in R. Mansell and M. Raboy (eds.) *The Handbook of Global Media and Communication Policy.* Oxford: Blackwell.

Banda, F. (2007) An appraisal of development journalism in the context of public-service broadcasting. *Communicatio: South African Journal for Communication Theory and Research,* 33(2): 154–170.

Barr, T. (2000) newmedia.com.au: *The changing face of Australia's media and communications.* Sydney: Allen & Unwin.

Berger, G. (2002) Theorizing the media-femocracy telationship in Southern Africa. *Gazette: The International Journal for Communication Studies,* 64 (1): 21–45.

Blankenberg, N. (1999) In search of real freedom: Ubuntu and the media. *Critical Arts,* 13(2): 42–65.

Brooks, H., Ngwane, T. and Runciman, C. (2020) Decolonising and re-theorising the meaning of democracy: A South African perspective. *The Sociological Review,* 68(1): 17–32.

Chasi, C. (2015) Ubuntu and freedom of expression: Considering children and broadcast news violence in a violent society. *Journal of Media Ethics: Exploring Questions of Media Morality,* 30(2): 91–108.

Chasi, C. and Mboti, N. (2016) *Towards a participation studies: A concept note.* Unpublished.

Chasi, C. and Rodny-Gumede, Y. (2016) Smash-and-grab, truth and dare …. *The International Communication Gazette,* 78(7): 694–700.

Conway, J. and Singh, J. (2011) Radical democracy in global perspective: notes from the pluriverse. *Third World Quarterly,* 32(4): 689–706.

Curran J. and Park M. J. (eds.) (2000) *De-Westernising Media Studies.* London: Routledge.

De Beer, A. S. and Tomaselli, K. G. (2000) South African journalism and mass communication scholarship: Negotiating ideological schisms. *Journalism Studies,* 1(1): 9–33.

Duncan, J. (2000) *Broadcasting and the National Question. South African Broadcast Media in an Age of Neo-Liberalism.* Braamfontein: Freedom of Expression Institute.

Eko, L. (2000) Public broadcasting in a changing regulatory environment: The case of Africa. *Equid Novi: African Journalism Studies,* 21(1): 85–100.

Fourie, P. J. (2008) Ubuntuism as framework for South African media practice and performance: Can it work? *Communicatio: South African Journal for Communication Theory and Research,* 34(1): 53–79.

Friedman, S. (2019) *Power in Action: Democracy, Citizenship and Social Justice.* Johannesburg: Wits University Press.

Grosfoguel, R. (2007) The epistemic decolonial turn: beyond political-economy paradigms. *Cultural Studies,* 21(2/3): 211–223.

Hallin, D. C. and Mancini, P. (2004) *Comparing Media Systems: Three Models of Media and Politics.* Cambridge: Cambridge University Press.

Harris-Perry, M.V. (2011) *Sister Citizen: Shame, Stereotypes, and Black Women in America*. New Haven: Yale University Press.

Jacobs, S. (2004) Mapping the Public Sphere after 1994: The Media Set-up. Available at www.newschool.edu/tcds/Sean%20Jacobs.pdf

Khosa, R. M. and Khosa, M. (2019) Policy, regulation and implementation of advertiser-funded programming in South Africa: A case of the South African Broadcasting Corporation. *Journal of African Media Studies*, 11(1): 81–101.

Lowe, G. F. (2010) Beyond altruism: Why public participation in public service media matters, pp. 9–36 in G. F. Lowe (ed.) *The Public in Public Service Media*. Göteborg: Nordicom.

Louw, E. and milton, v. c. (2012) *New Voices over the Air. The Transformation of the South African Broadcasting Corporation in a Changing South Africa*. New York: Hampton Press.

Mano, W. (2005) Exploring the African view of the global. *Global Media and Communication*, 1(1): 50–55.

Mano, W. (2016) The state and public broadcasting: Continuity and change in Zimbabwe, pp. 190–205 in T. Flew, P. Iosifides and J. Steemers (eds.) *Global Media and National Policies: The Return of the State*. London: Springer.

Mano, W. and milton, v. c. (2021) Afrokology of Media And Communication Studies: Theorising from the margins, in W. Mano and v. c. milton (eds.) *Routledge Handbook of African Media and Communication Studies*. London: Routledge.

Mano, W. and milton, v. c. (2020) Civil society coalitions as pathways to PSB reform in Southern Africa. *Interactions*, 11(2): 135–158.

Mararike, C. G. (1998) African philosophy and human factor development, pp. 87–95 in V. G. Chivaura and C. G. Mararike (eds.) *The Human Factor Approach to Development in Africa*. Harare: University of Zimbabwe Publications.

milton, v. c. (2014) *Submission on the SABC Editorial Policy Review on behalf of the Media Policy and Democracy Project*. Unpublished document.

milton, v. c. (2018) South Africa: Funding the South African Broadcasting Corporation, pp. 181–202 in C. Herzog, H. Heiko, L. Novy and O. Torun (eds.) *Transparency and Funding of Public Service Media – Die deutsche Debatteiminternationalen Kontext*. Wiesbaden: SpringerVS.

milton, v. c. and Fourie, P. J. (2015) South Africa: A free media still in the making, pp.181–201 in K. Nordernstreng and D. K. Thussu (eds.) *Mapping BRICS Media*. London: Routledge.

milton, v. c. and Mano, W. (2021) Afrokology as a transdisciplinary approach to media and communication studies in W. Mano, and v. c. milton (eds.) *Routledge Handbook of African Media and Communication Studies*. London: Routledge.

Murdock, G. (2010) Public broadcasting and democratic culture: Consumers, citizens and communards, pp. 174–198 in J. Wasko (ed.) *A Companion to Television*. Cambridge: Wiley-Blackwell.

Nordenstreng, K. (2004) Ferment in the field: Notes on the evolution of communication studies and its disciplinary nature. *Javnost*, 11(3): 5–18.

Nussbaum, B. (2003) Ubuntu: Reflections of a South African on our common humanity. *Reflections*, 4(4): 21–26.

Nyamnjoh, F. (2004) Africa in 2015: Interrogating Barbie democracy, seeking alternatives. *Democracy & Development*, 4(2): 107–112.

Nyamnjoh, F. (2011) De-Westernizing media theory to make room for African experience, pp. 19–31 in H. Wasserman (ed.) *Popular Media, Democracy and Development in Africa*. London: Routledge.

Nyamnjoh, F. (2013) From quibbles to substance: A response to responses. *Africa Spectrum*, 2: 127–139.

Shome, R. (2017) Going South and engaging non-Western modernities. *Media Theory* 1(1): 65–73.

Skjerdal, T. S. (2011) Development journalism revived: The case of Ethiopia. *Ecquid Novi: African Journalism Studies*, 32(2): 58–74.

Skjerdal, T. S. (2012) The three alternative journalisms of Africa. *International Communication Gazette*, 74(7): 636–654.

Sparks, C. (2009) South African media in transition. *Journal of African Media Studies*, 1(2): 195–220.

Thussu, D. K. (ed.) (2009) *Internationalizing Media Studies*. London: Routledge.

West, H. G. and Fair, J. E. (1993) Development communication and popular resistance in Africa: An examination of the struggle over tradition and modernity through media. *African Studies Review*, 36(1): 91–114.

PART III

BRICS and global strategic communication

9

BRAZIL AND CORPORATIST SOFT POWER

Joseph Straubhaar

This chapter argues that Brazil has developed considerable soft power in the world, particularly from commercial cultural industries in television and music, but also from government initiatives like the building of its new capital Brasilia in the 1950s and the initiatives to host the World Cup and Olympics in the 2010s. It also argues that the soft power originating from Brazilian cultural industries has a distinct flavour, albeit one similar to other Latin American countries, in the way that cultural industries have developed key export genres, such as telenovelas, in a corporatist form of interaction with a series of national governments. These governments have delegated much of their internal ideological work on national identity to the cultural industries, particularly in music, from the 1930s on and in television, from the 1970s.

Soft power

The term soft power is often evoked in foreign policy debates as a measure of state or national strength. Soft power is a crucial component of state (or 'national') influence and control that attempts to attract or persuade other states or their publics to act in the interests of the country exercising the power. This is opposed to hard power of military or economic might, which may be able to force another country to change its policies, such as the United States and European efforts to force Iran to change its nuclear policies through an economic boycott. Soft power is often based on the foundation of communication and media industries and mass media technologies. As originally defined by Nye (1990), soft power consists of a wide range of cultural and informational resources, including both government public diplomacy aimed at publics beyond classic official diplomacy, and the export or extension abroad of a variety of products and activities by a range of civil-society actors, such as foundations, universities, unions and churches, as well as cultural industries of news, film, television, music, plastic arts, classical music and dance.

State soft power might be thought of as based in resources that the state directly controls, such as official media, like the Voice of America or RT (formerly Russia Today), as well as official exchanges, like the Fulbright Programme or Peace Corps. In contrast, I argue here that, depending on the nature of the state and economy of a country, much of its soft power is likely to be generated by private, commercial national cultural industries, which produce most of the news, information and cultural exports of many nations, reflecting the broader nation as opposed to directly expressing the will of the state.

For example, the first book on Brazilian national communication policy, produced as part of a UNESCO project to encourage nations to articulate clear national policies in the 1970s, noted that Brazil had a historic tendency for the state to delegate most of national media production to private enterprises and cultural industries (Camargo and Pinto, 1975), rather than have the state create or take over its own media. There are, however, some historic exceptions to that, particularly the takeover of the main national radio network by the authoritarian populist regime of Getúlio Vargas in the 1930s (Haussen, 2005). Below I will theorize this tendency as a form of media corporatism, in which the state delegates some crucial functions to private commercial entities, such as relying on private media to create the media content that will largely serve the state's interest, or delegate some activities to non-profit groups, such as relying on churches for aspects of education and health (Malloy, 1977).

This chapter concentrates on Brazil as one of the BRICS, a group of large, emerging powers (Brazil, Russia, India, China and South Africa). Within that group, two of the largest powers are present (China) or former (Russia) communist states with a continuing history of strong central control over media, information and most forms of cultural production. If one looks at the most prominent media expressions of China and Russia abroad, they reflect state activities, such as RT or China Global Television Network (originally known as CCTV-9). By contrast, in the other three, including Brazil, most media and cultural activity is produced by different forms of civil society and cultural industry, including television, radio and the print media that are commercially profitable. In some of these countries, the state does sometimes step in to subsidize arts activity, including film, but in India, for example, film is a vibrant cultural industry that thrives economically on a commercial basis. The face of these countries abroad is dominated by private media, like TV Globo from Brazil or Bollywood from India. Brazilian soft power is, therefore, of a different kind, based in national culture, consumerism and politics, but simultaneously friendly to regional and global capitalism. While the first wave of Brazilian music exports for soft power in the 1930s showed a guiding government hand, most subsequent soft-power flows, particularly after the 1970s, have come from cultural industries, but often in a corporatist dialogue with the state.

Cultural industry and corporatist soft power

As is common in Latin America, in Brazil there has often been an articulation of cultural industry and government via corporatism. Corporatism includes both ways of representing people and groups upwards to the state, and ways of expressing state control downwards, either directly or through propaganda and persuasion. In terms of how people and interests are represented within and to the state, Schmitter says, 'I have found it useful to consider corporatism as a system of interest and/or attitude representation, a particular modal or ideal-typical institutional arrangement for linking the associations and organized interests of civil society with the decisional structures of the state' (Schmitter, 1974).

Corporatism in Latin America is often seen as inheriting Italian and Iberian tendencies toward patrimonial, hierarchical politics and economy in which society is divided into major organizations by activity (Malloy, 1976). These are frequently private, like regional groupings of corporations, or powerful individual corporations, such as television networks. They can also be independent powers, for example the Catholic Church, which often found this mode of organization sympathetic, since the state recognized and worked with the Church as a major power in society (Wiarda, 1978). Sometimes they are chartered, organized and controlled by the state, like the official unions, or syndicates, developed after the model of Italian fascism in several Latin American countries, including Brazil.

In the 1930s, corporatism was particularly dominant, as strongmen in several countries, like Juan Peron in Argentina and Vargas in Brazil, looked for alternatives to formal democracy and Western competitive capitalism, admiring the ways that fascist societies in southern Europe (Italy, Portugal and Spain) in particular organized labour and capital in harmony with authoritarian politics. In some ways this was a renewed wave of post-colonial influence from Portugal and Spain, which had lost much of their economic and political influence in Latin America to Britain and the United States, and most of the cultural and intellectual influence to France and the US. Wiarda found it useful to distinguish 'between "natural corporatism" as a powerful historical, political-cultural ingredient still shaping Iberic-Latin politics, and "corporatism" as a manifest ideology of the interwar period, currently (then 1978) reviving, designed in part to harness rising labour movements' (1978: 310).

Corporatist forms of connecting government to powerful social corporations can co-exist with democratic forms of governance, as a way of connecting powerful institutions, such as the Church, dominant companies, or major media, directly to central or regional governments, bypassing electoral politics. This can be seen as one systemic explanation for how media-state relations developed in a number of Latin American countries. Media in Latin America have tended to be privately owned, often by family economic empires sometimes based primarily in media and sometimes part of larger conglomerates with a variety of holdings (Sinclair, 1999). Starting in the 1930s, several Latin American leaders, such as Peron and Vargas saw the advantages of using radio, along with government-controlled labour unions, to mobilize the new working and middle classes to support their regimes (Haussen, 2005).

Vargas nationalized Radio Nacional in 1940, which became a powerful political mobilization arm for the state and also promoted and furthered a number of music and entertainment genres, including samba and radio novelas – the radio soap opera antecedent of telenovelas (McCann, 2004; Saroldi and Moreira, 2005). Some of these, like samba and telenovelas, became major aspects of Brazilian soft power abroad. Radio Nacional created an image of an enjoyable, populist Brazil via promotion of soccer and samba (Goldfeder, 1980). It helped mobilize both urban and semi-rural working classes to support Vargas, with Radio Nacional also an important industry, since the government, after taking it over, continued to run the radio broadcaster like a business, with an eye on both popularity and profitability. Vargas also established a Department of Press and Censorship, and created *de facto* partnerships with media magnates like Assis Chateaubriand (Simões, 1986; Morães, 1994).

Since the early days of television, Latin American states have tended to develop political and economic partnerships with one or two major television networks, such as Televisa's very visible cooperation with the PRI party in Mexico (Fernández and Paxman, 2001), giving them an advantage over competitors with sympathetic economic and regulatory treatment in return for favourable media coverage of government actions and policies. In this way, media can be seen as a new type of major societal corporation with strong potential power, one that needs to be harmonized with the interests of the state, for which corporatism provides a culturally-proximate solution in historical and cultural terms.

In Brazil, media corporatism returned forcefully with the military governments between 1964 and 1985. Even before the 1964 coup, the military had laid out a vision for Brazilian development that emphasized media, particularly television, as partners in creating or reinforcing an economy based on the promotion of consumer capitalism (Mattos, 2002). People in the industry were largely eager to participate, since that vision also appealed to them. For example, in the midst of the 1970s expansion of television, a major advertising executive gave a paper at the Brazilian War College, which functioned as a sort of military-civilian think tank for planning, in which he promoted television and advertising as key ways to enhance consumption and economic growth (Salles, 1975).

National propaganda and soft power

Soft power often radiates out from the export of cultural-industry or even government products designed for internal national reasons, to promote consumption or sell ideas, in a cultural frame designed to attract and gratify national sensibilities. Two of the main media bases of soft power for Brazil are the export of music and television entertainment. These media evolved primarily to reflect the evolving popular culture and interests of Brazil. Both were driven by popular culture creators who wanted to express and add to a sense of national identity and this interacted with a similar desire by governments, notably and most formatively with the populist government of the 1930s–1940s in the case of music (McCann, 2004), and the military governments of 1964–1985 in the case of television entertainment. Major artists, writers and producers worked within a political frame that was set by governments to accomplish their national objectives, but also the political, social and cultural goals and interests of the creators themselves (Mattos, 2002; Sacramento, 2012). They also worked within an economic system in which the main boundaries and goals were set by entrepreneurs within family-based media empires who were also interested in shaping social life and politics, but even more concerned with commercial success (Sinclair and Straubhaar, 2013).

For example, as commercial television was consolidated in the 1970s, content promoted consumption through advertising, product placement and plot themes about how to be upwardly mobile (Mattos, 1984; La Pastina *et al.*, 2004). While aimed at internal Brazilian development, these messages promoting commercial development became part of the message exported, when television exports started in 1975–1976, forming a major base of Brazilian soft power.

Brazilian music, as well as film, news and television, have all taken in a lot of influence from abroad, particularly the US. As we will see below, much of that influence was creatively hybridized into Brazilian media. Perrone and Dunn examine a 1959 song, '*Chiclete com Banana*' ('Chewing gum with bananas'), which playfully acknowledges how much Uncle Sam is influencing Brazil, but wants to speak back to the US, to have Uncle Sam hear and even play Brazilian music, too. They see that as a metaphor for the desire of Brazilians to have others, in the US and elsewhere listen to (and watch) their culture, of which they are very proud (Perrone and Dunn, 2002). Thus, artists and those at the creative end of civil society in Brazil also want to export their culture, as a kind of grassroots urge for soft power as something not only driven by cultural attaches or industry executives.

Soccer, samba and hybrid beauty

The soft power of a nation abroad is affected both by how people and institutions within the culture try to represent it to themselves and to others abroad, and by how people from abroad, explorers, colonists, travelers, artists, writers and media creators represent it. This is particularly true of relatively new nations, like Brazil, which have been extensively imagined from both within and abroad (Sadler, 2008). Sadler argues that Brazil has long been imagined both at home and abroad in terms of race and nature, both positively and negatively, of noble savages and cannibals, of Edenic nature and a green hell of impenetrable jungle, particularly in the first couple of centuries after its 'discovery' by Europeans. As Brazil became more modern in the nineteenth and twentieth centuries, Brazilians had to deal with these received images, as when the early twentieth-century poet, Oswald de Andrade deliberately seized on the cannibal image to celebrate Brazil's creative hybridity (Andrade, 2001; Sadler, 2008). In a related manifesto of the same era, de Andrade also calls for 'poetry for export', not only to absorb and rework foreign culture, but to create culture that can be exported back to other modern nations, since much of this wave of thought was about how to create modern art in Brazil. Dunn argues that this movement and idea helped shape later tropicalist Brazilian music and other culture for export (Dunn, 2001).

By the twentieth century, Brazil had more tools with which to shape its own image, internally and externally, such as poetry and fiction, art, music, sports, developed versions of popular culture festivals, radio, film and television. However, Brazil still had to struggle with images made about it by neighbours like Argentina, its former colonial power Portugal and global powers like France, Britain and, particularly, the US, as both a regional and a global power, and the dominant image-maker of the twentieth century (Shohat and Stam, 1994; Perrone and Dunn, 2002; Sadler, 2008). For example, as the US tried to engage with Brazil to win goodwill and a military alliance during the Good Neighbor Policy era of World War II, the State Department asked Walt Disney to make films about Argentina, Brazil and Mexico (*Saludos Amigos*, 1942; *The Three Caballeros*, 1944) to show them in a positive light, but ended up creating lasting stereotypes about them internationally (Goldman, 2013).

Key aspects of the cultural base for what would become Brazilian soft power began in the 1920s. Theoretically, a good way to understand this phase of Brazilian culture was the articulation through artists of an ethnically and culturally hybrid set of practices and ideas for making music, arts, writing, poetry, popular culture such as festivals and holidays, and sports. Much of the dynamism of Brazilian popular culture, particularly music, festivals like Carnival (a large pre-Lenten festival with European roots, but a large Afro-Brazilian influence through music and dance), and sports, came from Afro-descendent or mixed-race performers and artists, as well as from indigenous and European traditions.

Artists from both Black and European cultures in Brazil began to proclaim the value of a hybrid culture within which to be creative. Modern Art Week in São Paulo in 1928 ended with a proclamation of 'Cultural Cannibalism', a home-grown Brazilian mix of indigenous, European and African cultures, and this was considered a desirable trend to be embraced (Andrade, 2001). It can be seen in the incorporation of indigenous, African and mixed imagery and themes in high art, like painting and sculpture, as well as in the inclusion of samba, Carnival, soccer and other aspects of popular and folk culture in mainstream media and government promotion of mass culture as a means of unifying national identity (McCann, 2004). The poetry, literature and art that came out of this movement was hailed abroad, as were samba, soccer and Carnival, reaching a celebratory status in foreign films like *Flying Down to Rio* (1933) and *Black Orpheus* (1959), which form part of Brazil's soft power in the world.

Government promotion of samba at home and abroad

Due to a climate partially influenced by European scientific racism, samba and Carnival had been repressed as undesirable 'Black' culture in the late nineteenth and early twentieth centuries. Hermano Vianna noted the rapid transformation of samba from repressed and despised Black culture in 1910 to the primary symbol of Brazilian national identity in the 1930s–1940s, as well as one of its first big cultural exports (Vianna, 1999). That came in part as a number of European descended intellectuals and cultural intermediaries, such as artists, writers, government officials and cultural industry managers, began to admire and promote samba culture, Carnival, and the careers of Black musicians (Vianna, 1999; McCann, 2004).

The Brazilian government under Getúlio Vargas saw the promotion of samba music, through Carnival, events, recordings and radio, as a way of unifying the nation (McCann, 2004). Vargas also began to see it as a form of soft power, paying the travel expenses to send Carmen Miranda to the US in 1939 to create a good impression and, reportedly, to sell more Brazilian coffee in the US (Sadler, 2008). The Brazilian government had earlier sent an orchestra of samba musicians to Europe in 1925, so this idea of promoting Brazil abroad through popular music was not entirely new to Vargas (Perrone and Dunn, 2002). However, the promotion of Carmen Miranda as the embodiment of Black Brazilian samba – a white woman, born in Portugal, who came to be seen as its most famous interpreter – privileging white performance of Black music, demonstrated, in both the creation and export of some of the most visible kinds of samba, a racial tension and ambivalence that was also common in the US in this era (Johnson, 2003).

Brazilian music was also recorded and distributed internationally, particularly in the Americas, as another part of the US Good Neighbor Policy 'to attract markets and support in the World War II effort' (Perrone and Dunn, 2002). US recording artists and technicians were sent to record Brazilian music for release in the US. Orson Welles, who had been sent along with Walt Disney teams to Brazil to make films, presented Brazilian music to Americans on the radio. This was an interestingly complex operation in public diplomacy, to create goodwill in Latin America by making other Americans more aware of their popular cultures, particularly their music.

Brazilian and US government and private commercial motives overlapped. For example, Carmen Miranda was invited to the US by a US music agent, but the trip was paid for both by Vargas and the US State Department (Perrone and Dunn, 2002). The US film industry benefited, with the films starring Carmen Miranda, and particularly Disney, which still has *The Three Caballeros*, starring Donald Duck, Zé Carioca (Brazil) and Pancho (Mexico), on release, and which made Brazil-only comics with the Zé Carioca character (a suave Brazilian parrot) for years. The US government benefited when Vargas, having had warm relations with both Germany and Italy in the 1930s, finally joined the Allied war effort in 1943. And Brazil gained some lasting soft power from this US-aided exposure to the world.

Radio and Brazilian identity

Brazil is a large country, composed of a number of ethnic and racial groups, with very different regional cultures and with a decentralized regional political structure.

For centuries, indigenous languages like Tupi or Guarani were the most widely used in many parts of Brazil, and Portuguese only gradually came to dominate. From Vargas onwards, at least, Brazilian governments have pushed hard to promote the use of Portuguese, making media in it available to all the remote and border areas of Brazil. The integration of Brazil through culture and language, and the promotion of a strong national identity have been major priorities, especially for broadcasting, which reaches literate and illiterate alike. In this way Brazil was like most developing countries (Katz and Wedell, 1976) but it pursued these goals particularly strongly in the 1930s–1940s and again under the military regimes of 1964–1985. The government still operates radio stations in remote areas, like the Amazon, to make sure they have Portuguese-language, Brazilian-oriented radio programmes to listen to.

Vargas saw the need both for radio, as a vehicle, and for music, e.g., samba and events like soccer, etc. as content to help create a strong national identity (McCann, 2004). Even before Vargas took over *Rádio Nacional*, its directors and programmers were already thinking about how to create a national popular culture:

> These producers had already dedicated their talents to a patriotic treatment of Brazilian popular culture before the takeover, and the tone of their programming did not change after 1940 … Most presciently, before any affiliation with the *Estado Novo* (New State), they endorsed Afro-Brazilian popular music as the 'cultural essence of the nation'.
>
> *(McCann, 2004: 38)*

Radio Nacional also played a more explicitly political role in producing the 'Hour of Brazil' ('*Hora do Brazil*'), which was mandatory for all stations to broadcast from the 1940s through the 2000s, but it was widely considered to be ineffective and unpopular, compared to the impact of popular music (de Lima Perosa, 1995). This popular music was also broadcast over an international shortwave system, aimed at North America and Europe by Vargas' Department of Information and Propaganda in 1942, announcing, in relation to Brazilian music, 'It is the voice of Brazil that will speak to the world, to tell civilized peoples of the universe what is being done here for the benefit of civilization … exhibiting all its beauty and splendor' (Perrone and Dunn, 2002).

'Tropical Modernism'

In the 1950s, Brazil had increasing interactions with the outside world, taking in influences, hybridizing them, working with international partners, and projecting new ideas, developments and media out into the world. One of the most visible and lasting was still in the area of music, *bossa nova*, which had an even bigger impact in the US and elsewhere than samba, with major US hits like *The Girl from Ipanema* (1963) and major interactions with US jazz musicians like Stan Getz. This music reflects the confidence of the presidency of Juscelino Kubitschek (1956–1960), 'who had promised "fifty years of progress in five" and then undertook to build the utopian, futuristic capital of Brasilia on the high plains of central Brazil' (Perrone and Dunn, 2002).

The new capital, Brasilia, was another dramatic expression of the optimistic era of national growth following World War II, developed by radical new Brazilian architects and city planners (De Vries *et al.*, 2012). In some ways, the soft power of Brazil in this era reflected the fact that Brazil seemed to be doing well within the then-widely accepted paradigm of developmentalism, not only achieving rapid economic growth but showing an ability to innovate within a modern and modernist paradigm, through things such as a cool music that blended well with the global avant-garde jazz and architecture.

The Brazilian cinema of that era was also the first to have international impact. *Cinema Novo* echoed and adapted the patterns of French New Wave and Italian Neo-Realism, but, in the tradition of Brazilian hybridity, also created its own version of genres. Several major Brazilian auteurs rose to some international prominence, for example Glauber Rocha with films like *Black God, White Devil* (1964), which echoed popular themes of messianic movements and folk bandits from the less developed northeast of Brazil, but also used them to create a political critique of the conditions of the poor in Brazil (Johnson and Stam, 1982). The goal was to create a political intervention in Brazilian politics but this film and others may well have been more popular outside Brazil than inside, creating soft power abroad more than revolution at home.

If we want to generalize about this era of Brazilian soft power, it built on the existing paradigm of industrialized cultural hybridity created by the music industry in interaction with both government and the global cultural industry. *Bossa nova* gained Brazil much soft power by succeeding and innovating within the global artistic hierarchy of jazz and within the global music industry, without much government intervention required. The creation of Brasilia on the other hand was both a national and international intervention by the state itself to create a new focus for economic development in a somewhat empty part of the country, while also creating a very visible international symbol of Brazilian innovation. Both reflect the national base of transnational cultural power.

TV Globo and the soft power of the telenovela

The articulation of cultural industries and government through corporatism definitely applies to the television era of both national communication and external soft power in Brazil, as does another important concept for understanding the relationship of media to government in Latin America, clientelism. These ideas apply, particularly, to TV Globo, which became the dominant agent of Brazilian national identity and soft power from the late 1960s on, though there was an important era of Brazilian television in the 1950s–1960s before Globo. The rapid growth of the middle class increased demand for high-quality television news and entertainment. Several television networks, including some that ultimately failed, like TV Tupi and TV Excelsior, created vital genres, including the telenovela, the live variety show, music shows, distinctive patterns of comedy, etc. (Bucci, 1996; Silva Júnior, 2001).

Many of these genres were the result of complex interactions with both the US and other Latin American countries in the 1950s and 1960s, such as the telenovela, which was created in Cuba at the behest of Colgate-Palmolive in the 1950s to sell soap in Latin America (Rivero, 2009), but which was radically adapted and hybridized, first in Cuba and then further as it spread by scripts, émigré professionals and local adaptations to the rest of Latin America (Sinclair and Straubhaar, 2013). Brazil's version of the telenovela, along with Mexico's, was to become a huge export product and source of soft power, first within Latin America, then for Brazil in the Portuguese-speaking world, and for both in much of the rest of the world, starting in the 1990s (Sinclair and Straubhaar, 2013). The key to that was the rise of TV Globo and its version of the telenovela.

In terms of the continuity of corporatist relations between media and the state, TV Globo was the favoured partner of the military governments between 1964 and 1985. TV Globo's owner, Roberto Marinho had favoured the initial military coup, as did many in the business elite of Brazil and was a personal friend of some of the leaders in the Castello Branco-Geisel-Figueiredo wing of the military governments (Wallach, 2011). More than anything, they shared a Cold War capitalist vision of Brazilian development, in which government, media, advertising and industry cooperated to expand the consumer economy so that Brazilians would be attracted to it rather than to the ideas of socialism (Salles, 1975; Mattos, 1982). They also shared the goal, noted above for radio, to expand television coverage so that all Brazilians had a Portuguese-language national network to watch.

In terms of the corporatist relationship, TV Globo provided ideological support for and promotion of a consumer society, while the military governments provided the technological infrastructure: expanding television signals across Brazil, government advertising and favourable treatment of Globo initiatives that were illegal or unpopular. For example, the military government ignored the fact that the initial joint venture between TV Globo and Time-Life Inc. violated the Brazilian Constitution's provisions against foreign ownership of media. The military tolerated the joint venture from 1964 to 1970, until TV Globo was up and running then applied pressure to get Time-Life to withdraw (Wallach, 2011).

The military governments provided a rapidly widening telecoms infrastructure of microwave towers and satellite coverage to enable TV Globo and others to reach genuine national coverage, as local businessmen and even mayors in the 1970s set up stations to re-broadcast satellite signals, a phenomenon highlighted in the popular film, *Bye Bye Brasil* (1980). For its part, aside from TV Excelsior, which the military shut down over political differences with its owners, TV Globo was the only network with a clear commercial vision of a national market and networked operations to sell national advertising. It took quick advantage of this infrastructure to create national coverage, while Chateaubriand's TV Tupi floundered amid a decentralized and poorly managed network, and went bankrupt in 1981 (Straubhaar,

1984). The government also steered advertising toward TV Globo, at a point where government companies, trading companies and holding companies were involved in nearly half the overall economy (Mattos, 1984).

TV Globo represented another phase of creating cultural power by hybridizing Brazilian culture with both commercial and artistic forms and practices from the US. Key to the process was Joe Wallach, who came from Time-Life to TV Globo, becoming Globo's head of commercial operations, advertising and network development. He dumped Time-Life's initial strategy of showing US-imported programmes and invested their money instead in hiring Brazilian programmers, producers, directors and writers to create Brazilian programming that would be more popular (Wallach, 2011). They started with live music and variety then focused on telenovelas, bringing in skilled but controversial left-wing scriptwriters, like Dias Gomes, from 1969 (Sacramento, 2012) to make the telenovelas more focused on key national themes and images, right at the peak of increased military regime censorship. The military permitted this, while keeping censorship fairly tight, gambling along with TV Globo's management that, even though these writers would be critical of Brazilian politics and a number of issues, they would also help modernize the content of television, promote the idea of Brazil as an enjoyable lively culture and create high quality programmes to carry the advertising and product placement that would promote a consumer economy and an acceptance of consumer capitalism (Sacramento, 2012).

This new pattern was consolidated between 1969 and 1974. Many of Brazil's best writers came to work for Globo and the company emphasized the drama to improve the quality of programming, what they called the Global pattern of quality (Oliveira Sobrinho, 2011). For the writers, many of whom had been involved with left wing popular theatre, this opportunity was 'the popular theater of their dreams' (Gomes, 1998). Their shows proved very popular, expanding both Globo's audience and the advertising market, consolidating a consumer economy and indirectly preparing for a wave of telenovela exports by creating a distinctive telenovela. They were so valuable to Globo that, when the writers were threatened by military officials, unhappy with their criticisms of the regime, Globo's owner, Roberto Marinho, reportedly faced down the officials, saying, 'You take care of your communists, I'll take care of mine' (Wallach, 2011).

Although the regional market for television in Latin America had been created and first dominated by telenovela scripts from Cuba between 1950 and 1959 (Rivero, 2007; Straubhaar, 2011), that phase ended with Fidel Castro's take-over and transformation of Cuban television into a supportive vehicle for his revolution (Rivero, 2015). The early peak of telenovela popularity came in 1974–1975 with *O Bem Amado* (The Well Beloved), by Dias Gomes. It was the first telenovela in colour, depicting a mythical small town with a corrupt mayor (symbolizing the military and authoritarian government) and many colourful characters. It was a huge hit both in Brazil and in much of the rest of Latin America, starting in 1975. This began an era in which Brazil and Mexico rose to be top of a pyramid of television flow in Latin America as the dominant exporters to the region (Roncagliolo, 1996), while importing fairly little, except from the US, which was shown mostly outside prime time (Straubhaar, 1984).

As the two largest economies in Latin America, Brazil and Mexico had the market base for mass television production (Sinclair *et al.*, 1996; Sinclair and Straubhaar, 2013). They also had prolific theatre, film and music industries to draw on, as well as leading television networks, Televisa and TV Globo, with corporatist relationships with governments that helped them grow in export power. Argentina and Venezuela were the next most prolific producers in the 1980s and 1990s in Latin America (Roncagliolo, 1996). Since then Chile and Colombia have risen into the second tier (Straubhaar, 2007, Piñon, 2014) while Venezuela has fallen in production (Acosta-Alzuru, 2013).

Although Brazilian telenovelas and other programmes had to be dubbed into Spanish, they were much more similar to and relevant to the rest of Latin America than were those from the US, as the theory of cultural proximity predicted (Straubhaar, 1991). Even after translation, the jokes made more sense, the people and landscapes looked more similar, and there was a great deal of common history to draw on. However, US exports continued to be very popular, often more popular than imports from the rest of Latin America, building on the long history of familiarity with imported US culture in the region. Although Brazilian and Mexican soft power rose considerably in Latin America from the 1970s on through the export of television, US soft power through television continued very strong in the region as well.

Dominating Lusophone transnational popular culture

The Portuguese empire, along with the Spanish, were the original empires on which the sun never set, leaving a legacy of countries who still speak Portuguese or Spanish, shaped by those colonial histories and cultures, and often very interested in new cultural producers who spoke those languages and reflected those shared heritages. The Portuguese moved first along the African coasts in the fifteenth century, creating lasting imprints in Guinea Bissau, Cabo Verde, Angola and Mozambique (Russell-Wood, 1998). In 1500 they landed in Brazil, soon after in India, maintaining a colony in Goa into the twentieth century. Then they colonized parts of Southeast Asia, leaving a Portuguese-speaking colony in East Timor that would break away from Indonesia in 1999, and Macao, which became part of China in 1999. In other places they were dispossessed of their colonies by the Dutch or English early enough so that little lasting influence remains (Russell-Wood, 1998). The empire began to transform when the Portuguese emperor's son stayed in Brazil and declared it independent in 1822, while most of the other colonies did not become independent until after World War II, mostly in the 1970s after the fall of the Salazar dictatorship in Portugal in 1974.

Brazil had already had considerable economic and cultural development, including thriving music, film, publishing and television industries, while the African colonies of Portugal were still struggling for independence, which many

Brazilians actively supported. In the 1940s and 1950s, Portugal actually promoted the example of Brazil in its African colonies, as a sort of successful Luso-Tropicalism, showing how Portugal was a beneficent colonial power that helped development (Davis *et al.*, 2016). However, Portugal had not encouraged much media development in its empire. Local or native print media were forbidden in Brazil until the Portuguese court arrived there in 1808, fleeing an invasion by Napoleon. In other colonies, it was developed only by and for the religious or colonial authorities (ibid.). Brazilian music, magazines and television had a fairly open field to move not only into the former Portuguese colonies in and near Africa, but also into Portugal itself, establishing Brazil's area of almost dominant soft power, in the Lusophone cultural linguistic space. Portugal has tried hard to regain primacy in this space in television with a special branch of its public television aimed at Africa, with magazines aimed at the Lusophone world.

Brazil had begun to be present in the music and magazine spaces in Portugal, too, as the Lusophone cultural space evolved. They became even more dominant in television (Sinclair and Straubhaar, 2013; Davis *et al.*, 2016). Not long after TV Globo exported *O Bem Amado* to Latin America in 1975, it exported its next big hit, *Gabriela* (1976), adapted from an already internationally well-known novel popular in the Lusophone world, to Portugal, where it was broadcast by the public television channel, RTP. According to Isabel Ferrin Cunha, it was a smash hit in Portugal. Stores, restaurants and even the national legislature would stop, so everyone could watch it (Cunha, 2011).

After the deregulation of TV in Portugal in 1991, removing a monopoly for public television and allowing private competition (Traquina, 1995), the Brazilian network TV Globo entered the market as a partner in the first private television network, SIC. This was an enormous expansion of Brazilian soft power into its former colonial authority, as SIC became the most highly rated station, a source of both revenue and prestige for TV Globo and Brazil (Cunha, 1977). To some degree, SIC was also an extension of the US commercial model, as part of a larger wave of deregulation and privatization across Europe and much of the globe. However, there is an ongoing tension with nationalizing, localizing forces, so that markets once dominated by a major cultural linguistic space producer, like Brazil in Portugal, might gradually increase its own production and substitute it for what had been imported. There is an increasing tendency toward co-production, script and format sales instead of direct, finished programme sales and flows in worldwide television trade. We can see an example of that between Globo and SIC Portugal, of which TV Globo has been a part owner since its beginning in the 1980s. This has included the creation of Portuguese adaptations of several classic telenovelas, including the 1976 hit *Dancing Days*, recently remade in Portugal.

Starting in the 1980s, TV Globo also began exporting television, particularly telenovelas, to Africa. The first was *O Bem Amado*, which had been the first export to Latin America as well. The import of telenovelas from Brazil became very visible on screens in Lusophone Africa and seems to have had considerable impact in Africa. On the author's first visit to Mozambique, in 1992, I noticed that people talked a lot about the telenovelas. Quite a few children, streets and markets were named after Globo telenovela characters or towns. In a 1996 visit, which gave me more opportunity to speak to television industry directors, telenovelas were deeply ingrained in the schedule of TVM (TV Mozambique) and were very popular, according to the television professionals, as well as the regular audience members I spoke to. People talked about how you could see the impact of the Brazilian accent in the way that the Portuguese language was spoken in Mozambique, as well as in fashions and popular culture.

Brazil's direct soft power in Lusophone countries may be declining. It seems like there is some degree of searching for greater telenovela proximity within Lusofonia. Portugal is adapting Brazilian scripts to bring the resulting production closer to its reality. Portuguese telenovela exports to Africa have also been increasing since 2000, by RTP International, TVI, SIC. A Portugal telenovela co-production with Angola has been very successful, also generating huge social media reactions (Davis *et al.*, 2016).

Another interesting factor in the larger picture of Brazilian influence in Portugal and Africa is the expansion into these areas by Rede Record, now the number two network in Brazil, owned and operated by the Universal Church of the Reign of God. Their strategy integrates stations and networks owned by the church in developing nations, plus Portugal, and channels aimed at their members plus the Brazilian diaspora. The number two network in Mozambique is also owned by Rede Record and the Universal Church of the Reign of God (Straubhaar, 2014).

World exporter in deregulatory times and the satellite era

In the 1980s and 1990s Brazilian and Mexican telenovelas expanded into the larger world market, beyond the Latin America and the Lusophone world. In 1985, 10 per cent of TV Globo's income came from exports. In 1986, it was exporting its products to 130 countries. The number of Brazilian television exports increased further in the 1990s (de Melo, 1995). Brazil, particularly TV Globo, expanded into a rapidly growing global marketplace for television programmes, linked to the 1990s' waves of deregulation and privatization (Noam and Pogorel, 1994; Nanjundaiah, 1995; Traquina, 1995). This opened up spaces for new commercial television networks and privatized some existing public stations into private ones, which often then looked for more commercially-oriented, entertainment programming. The market for programmes grew further in those years with new direct broadcast satellites, which needed more programming.

Brazilian television expanded into a number of countries, including some that preferred to import television from other developing countries. For example, *Escrava Isaura* (1976), a telenovela about a story about a white woman mistakenly enslaved in the nineteenth century, was hugely popular in Russia, China, Poland and Cuba (Marques de Melo, 2010). But for a time in the 1990s, telenovelas, including *Escrava Isaura*, were also popular in Italy, France and other parts of Western Europe (ibid.).

Brazil as a BRICS member

From the late 1990s until 2012, Brazil went through a period of widespread economic growth and prosperity, which put Brazil on the list of large, emerging economies, becoming part of the BRICS grouping. That raised Brazil's profile internationally, adding to its image and probably to its soft power. The long economic boom also pumped even more money into media, and provided funds to let Brazilian governments' attempt showcase projects, like hosting the World Cup and Olympics. The government of both Fernando Cardoso (1995–2002) and Luiz Lula (2003–2010) wanted to put Brazil in a larger role on the world stage (Cervo, 2010). Like other emerging powers, such as China, the Lula administration in particular saw getting the Olympic Games to Brazil as a way of promoting international awareness of Brazil as an emerging power (Cornelissen, 2010).

However, by the time of the World Cup in Brazil in 2014, and the Olympics in 2016, there was strong internal opposition to the expenditures required, the dislocation of poor people in Rio, and also the level of corruption that was enabled by the massive construction projects that both sets of games required (Millington and Darnell, 2014), which created negative international news. Both sets of games were successful in some ways, creating certain positive images, but also quite a bit of negative news. Overall, the impact of the two sets of games on Brazil's soft power abroad had probably been ambivalent.

Conclusion

In this chapter, I argue that soft power from Brazil is primarily created and exercised by commercial cultural industries, like TV Globo, which has massively exported Brazilian culture abroad. This has particularly been in the form of the telenovela, but also magazines and music. TV Globo has extensively reached other Latin American countries and world television programme markets, but has probably had the heaviest impact in other Lusophone countries, notably Portugal and Lusophone Africa. Other major corporations like Editora Abril in magazines and TV Record in television have also been major exporters of Brazilian culture (Davis *et al.*, 2016).

TV Globo expanded abroad in classic media multinational form: primarily as an exporter of telenovelas, second, with targeted investments in Portugal, and third, with satellite channels aimed at Portuguese speaking audiences worldwide. Brazilian TV programme exports are still strong in Latin America, the Lusophone world and globally. A recent TV Globo hit, *Avenida Brasil* (Brazil Avenue, 2012), was licensed to 106 countries by 2013. Particularly in television, Brazil is a major world exporter (with the associated level of potential soft power) and its telenovelas have found new global audiences via streaming services such as Netflix. To some degree, Brazil became associated in the international television marketplace as well as in audience expectations and experience as a brand with the telenovela genre, the way that India is associated with the brand of Bollywood.

This chapter has argued that the roots of soft power in Brazil have both a corporatist and hybrid form. Although the forms of soft power most visible from Brazil are produced by cultural industries, those industries have grown in extensive cooperation with a series of governments. For example, the artists, genres and industry structures of Brazilian music, which is still a force for Brazilian soft power originally grew with extensive support and interaction with government-run *Rádio Nacional*, and TV Globo grew in even more extensive interaction with the military governments. The cultural products that became sources of soft power were originally designed by artists, industries and government to nourish national identity and address national issues. In terms of hybridity, many of these cultural forms and industries also grew and developed their genres, such as *bossa nova* in music or the telenovela itself, in fairly extensive interaction with US cultural forms and cultural industries, with some input from the US government itself. So soft power from Brazil reflects the unique forms of Brazil, and Latin America, more broadly, that reflect a distinct pattern of cultural industry development with extensive government and US influence.

References

Acosta-Alzuru, C. (2013) Melodrama, reality and crisis: The government–media relationship in Hugo Chávez's Bolivarian Revolution. *International Journal of Cultural Studies*, 17(3): 209–226.

Andrade, O. d. (2001) *Escritos antropófagos.* Buenos Aires: Corregidor.

Bucci, E. (1996) *Brasil em tempo de TV.* Rio de Janeiro: Boitempo Editorial.

Camargo, N. and Pinto, V. (1975) *Communication Policies in Brazil.* Paris: UNESCO.

Cervo, A. L. (2010) Brazil's rise on the international scene: Brazil and the world. *Revista Brasileira de Política Internacional*, 53: 7–32.

Cornelissen, S. (2010) The geopolitics of global aspiration: Sport mega-events and emerging powers. *The International Journal of the History of Sport*, 27(16–18): 3008–3025.

Cunha, I. F. (1977) *Transicao e Telenovela.* Lisboa: Universidade Catolica Portuguesa.

Cunha, I. F. (2011) *Memórias de Telenovela: Programas e recepção.* Lisbon: Livros Horizonte.

Davis, S., Straubhaar, J. and Cunha, I. F. (2016) The construction of a transnational Lusophone media space: A historiographic analysis. *Popular Communication: The International Journal of Media and Culture*, 14(4): 212–223.

de Lima Perosa, L. M. F. (1995) *A hora do clique: análise do programa de rádio Voz do Brasil da Velha à Nova República.* São Paulo: Annablume.

de Melo, J. M. (1995) Development of the audiovisual industry in Brazil from importer to exporter of television programming. *Canadian Journal of Communication*, 20: 317–328.

De Vries, G., Erumban, A., Timmer, M., Voskoboynikov, I. and Wu, H. (2012) Deconstructing the BRICs: Structural transformation and aggregate productivity growth. *Journal of Comparative Economics*, 40(2): 211–227.

Dunn, C. (2001) *Brutality Garden: Tropicália and the Emergence of a Brazilian Counter culture.* Chapel Hill: University of North Carolina Press.

Fernández, C. and Paxman, A. (2001) *El Tigre: Emilio Azcárraga y su imperio Televisa.* Mexico City: Grijalbo Mondadori.

Goldfeder, M. (1980) *Por tras das ondas da Rádio Nacional.* Rio de Janeiro: Editora Paz e Terra.

Goldman, K. (2013) Saludos amigos and the three caballeros: The representation of Latin America in Disney's 'Good Neighbor' films, pp. 23–38 in J. Cheu (ed.) *Diversity in Disney Films: Critical Essays on Race, Ethnicity, Gender, Sexuality and Disability*. Jefferson, NC: McFarland & Co.

Gomes, D. (1998) *Apenas um subversivo*. Rio de Janeiro: Bertrand Brasil.

Haussen, D. F. (2005) Radio and populism in Brazil: The 1930s and 1940s. *Television and New Media*, 6(3): 251–261.

Johnson, E. P. (2003) *Appropriating Blackness: Performance and the Politics of Authenticity*. Durham: Duke University Press.

Johnson, R. and Stam, R. (1982) *Brazilian Cinema*. Austin: University of Texas Press.

Katz, E. and Wedell, G. (1976) *Broadcasting in the Third World*. Cambridge: Harvard University Press.

La Pastina, A., Pathel, D. S. and Schiavo, M. (2004) Social merchandizing in Brazilian telenovelas, pp. 261–277 in A. Singhal, M. Cody, E. Rogers and M. Sabido (eds.) *Entertainment-Education and Social Change*. New Jersey: Lawrence Erlbaum.

Malloy, J. (ed.) (1976) *Authoritarianism and Corporatism in Latin America*. Pittsburgh, PA.: University of Pittsburgh Press.

Malloy, J. M. (1977) *Authoritarianism and Corporatism in Latin America*. Pittsburg: University of Pittsburg Press.

Marques de Melo, J. (2010) *Televisão Brasileira, Desenvolvimento, Globalização, Identidade: 60 anos de ousadia, astúcia, inovação*. São Paulo: Cátedra UNESCO/UMESP de Comunicação.

Mattos, S. (1982) *The Brazilian Military and Television*. Austin: University of Texas Press.

Mattos, S. (1984) Advertising and government influences on Brazilian television. *Communication Research*, 11(2): 203–220.

Mattos, S. (2002) *História da televisão brasileira: uma visão econômica, social e política*. Rio de Janeiro: Editora Vozes.

McCann, B. (2004) *Hello, Hello Brazil: Popular Music in the Making of Modern Brazil*. Durham: Duke University Press.

Millington, R. and Darnell, S. C. (2014) Constructing and contesting the Olympics online: The internet, Rio 2016 and the politics of Brazilian development. *International Review for the Sociology of Sport*, 49(2): 190–210.

Morães, F. (1994) *Chatô: o rei do Brasil, a vida de Assis Chateaubriand*. São Paulo: Companhia das Letras.

Nanjundaiah, S. (1995) Deregulation of television broadcast in India. *Asian Journal of Communication*, 5(1): 71–87.

Noam, E. M. and Pogorel, G. (eds.) (1994) *Assymetric Deregulation: The Dynamics of Telecommunications Policy in Europe and the United States*. Norwood, NJ: Ablex.

Nye, J. (1990) Soft power. *Foreign Policy*, 80: 153–171.

Oliveira Sobrinho, J. B. (2011) *O livro do Boni*. Rio de Janeiro: Casa da Palavra, 119.

Perrone, C. A. and Dunn, C. (eds.) (2002) *Brazilian Popular Music and Globalization*. London: Routledge.

Piñon, J. (2014) Reglocalization and the rise of the network cities media system in producing telenovelas for hemispheric audiences. *International Journal of Cultural Studies*, 17(6): 655–671.

Rivero, Y. M. (2007) Broadcasting modernity: Cuban television, 1950–1953. *Cinema Journal*, 46(3): 3–25.

Rivero, Y. M. (2009) Havana as a 1940s–1950s Latin American media capital. *Critical Studies in Media Communication*, 26(3): 275–293.

Rivero, Y. M. (2015) *Broadcasting Modernity: Cuban Commercial Television, 1950–1960*. Durham: Duke University Press.

Roncagliolo, R. (1996) La integración audiovisual en América Latina: Estados, empresas y productores independientes. *Culturas en globalización*, 41–54.

Russell-Wood, A. J. R. (1998) *The Portuguese Empire, 1415–1808: A World on the Move*. Baltimore: John Hopkins University Press.

Sacramento, I. (2012) *Nos tempos de Dias Gomes: a trajetória de um intelectual comunista nas tramas comunicacionais, Tese de Doutorado em Comunicação e Cultura*. Rio de Janeiro: ECO/ UFRJ.

Sadler, D. (2008) *Brazil Imagined*. Austin: University of Texas Press.

Salles, M. (1975) *Opinião Publica, Marketing e Publicidade no Processo Brasileiro de Desenvolvimento*, Escola Superior de Guerra.

Saroldi, L. C. and Moreira, S.V. (2005) *Rádio Nacional, o Brasil em sintonia*. São PULO: Zahar.

Schmitter, P. C. (1974) Still the century of corporatism? *The Review of Politics*, 36(1): 85–131.

Shohat, E. and Stam, R. (1994) *Unthinking Eurocentrism: Multiculturalism and the Media*. London: Routledge.

Silva Júnior, G. (2001) *Pais da TV: a história da televisão brasileira contada por*. São Paulo: Conrad.

Simões, I. F. (1986) TV à Chateaubriand. *Um país no ar*. São Paulo: Editora Brasiliense.

Sinclair, J. (1999) *Latin American Television: A Global View*. New York: Oxford University Press.

Sinclair, J. and Straubhaar, J. (2013) *Television Industries in Latin America*. London: BFI/ Palgrave.

Sinclair, J., Jacka, E. and Cunningham, S. (1996) *Peripheral Vision: New Patterns in Global Television*. New York: Oxford University Press.

Straubhaar, J. (1984) The decline of American influence on Brazilian television. *Communication Research*, 11(2): 221–240.

Straubhaar, J. (1991) Beyond media imperialism: Asymmetrical interdependence and cultural proximity. *Critical Studies in Mass Communication*, 8(1): 39–59.

Straubhaar, J. (2007) *World Television: From Global to Local*. London: Sage.

Straubhaar, J. (2011) Telenovelas in Brazil: From traveling scripts to a genre and proto-format both national and transnational, pp. 148–177 in T. Oren and S. Shahaf (eds.) *Global Television Formats: Understanding Television Across Borders*. New York: Routledge.

Straubhaar, J. (2014) *Brazil's Cultural Export to the Lusophone World as Soft Power: Desire for Shared Cultural Experience*. Stuttgart: CAMECO, Robert Bosch Stiftung.

Traquina, N. (1995) Portuguese television: The politics of savage deregulation. *Media, Culture & Society*, 17(2): 223–238.

Vianna, H. (1999) *The Mystery of Samba*. Chapel Hill: University of North Carolina Press.

Wallach, J. (2011) *Meu capítulo na TV Globo*. Rio de Janeiro: Editora Topbooks.

Wiarda, H. J. (1978) Corporatism in Iberian and Latin American political analysis: Criticisms, qualifications, and the context and 'whys'. *Comparative Politics*, 10(2): 307–312.

10
RUSSIAN SOFT POWER FROM USSR TO PUTIN'S RUSSIA

Dmitry Gavra and Elena Bykova

Soft power is about forming the preferences of other actors on the international scene so that they want what the dominant actor wants (Nye, 2004). In examining the current state of Russia's soft power, we will look at two aspects: essential and instrumental. The essential aspect is related to the culture of the country, its language, arts, science and educational systems, as well as the attractiveness of its socio-economic model as a whole. The instrumental aspect of soft power comprises the institutions through which the essential aspect can be manifested – various governmental and non-governmental organizations and charitable foundations, including the media, cultural, scientific and educational institutions, etc.

Historical context

When we talk about modern Russia, it is important to remember that today's Russian Federation is largely the successor of the Soviet Union, just as the Soviet Union was in many ways the successor of the Russian Empire, especially in relation to geo-politics and culture. In this regard, a significant part of today's Russian soft power is also based on the pre-eminently civilizational, cultural and geopolitical character of both the Imperial and the Soviet periods of its history.

The destruction of the Soviet Union, which was the leader of the Eastern bloc and enemy of the Western bloc during the Cold War, could not but affect the influence in the world of its successor, the Russian Federation. Communist ideology based on socialist values, ideas of equality and anti-colonialism were a powerful alternative to the market liberal ideology of the West (Barghoorn and Friedrich, 1956). Soviet ideology, together with the victory over Nazism, its example of industrial growth, advances in outer space and support for the 'Third World' formed the basis of the soft power of the USSR, particularly among the countries of Asia, Africa and Latin America, who, liberated from colonialism, were attracted to and guided by it (Hilger, 2017).

The Soviet intellectual and cultural investment in many developing countries during the decades of the Cold War – including Arab countries (Katsakioris, 2010), South Africa (Filatova and Davidson, 2013), India (Wishon, 2013) and China (Li, 2019) – is well documented. Numerous publications from Moscow's Progress Publishers, notably English translations of books about Marxism and Leninism, as well as great works of Russian literature, were dispatched to countries around the world, made available in many major languages, including Mandarin and Hindi. In addition, such magazines as *Soviet Union, Soviet Life, SovietLand and Misha* – in multiple translations – became ubiquitous propaganda vehicles across the developing world until the disintegration of the USSR. The communist, social democratic and left-wing forces in the countries of the West were also influenced by progressive ideas emanating from the USSR.

All this soft power was lost after the collapse of the USSR and Russia's return to a market ideology. Russia's loss of influence and global stature was intensified by the economic hardships and failures of the 1990s. On the other hand, the new Russia assumed other characteristics, generating a positive perception abroad. After Gorbachev's *perestroika* and its vital role in uniting Germany for the Western world, Russia was seen as a country moving towards democracy and human rights. At the same time the perception of Russia as a source of military threat and risk of universal nuclear destruction started to diminish.

The world had recognized the merits of the Soviet Union in the victory over Nazism during World War II. The authority of the Soviet Union in the field of space exploration also remained at a high level. However, in the 1990s, the attention to Russia's soft power from the federal authorities was minimal. The financing of the instrumental aspect of soft power had disappeared: programmes of economic aid to former allies in eastern Europe and among countries of the global South were discontinued. Public diplomacy was not developed: for example, the number of foreign students studying Russian language and culture decreased dramatically.

By the new millennium, post-Soviet Russia found itself in a difficult economic position and it lost its role as a model in socio-economic terms. Russia was rapidly losing its soft power influence not only in the world, but also in the former post-Soviet area (Sherr, 2013; Kiseleva, (2015; Lankina and Niemczyk, 2015). On the other hand, Russia maintained its image as a country transitioning to democracy, which under Gorbachev had changed attitudes towards the Soviet Union from its former Cold War enemies to become more positive. Instead, the USSR (then Russia) lost some of its former allies as a result of the change in policy.

This situation changed with the ascension to power of President Vladimir Putin. He presented the country with a new philosophy of reviving Russia's influence in the world. The period of the 2000s was a time of sharp rise in prices for hydrocarbons – the biggest export revenue source of Russia. This resulted in a strong economic recovery and rise in the living standards of the population and, as a consequence, in the sense of national identity. Putin and his team understood, however, that economic growth and defence capability were not enough to revive the country's influence. The new Russia needed an essential, substantial basis for soft power, to promote it not only to its own population, but also to external audiences.

In summary, the new ideological basis of Russian soft power rests on two foundations: the concept of a 'multipolar world' and the aim of protecting conservative values. President Putin spoke about the latter in his address to the Federal Assembly in 2013:

> there are more and more people in the world who support our position on the protection of conservative values, which for thousands years have been forming the spiritual and moral basis of civilization, of every nation: the values of traditional family, genuine human life, including religious life, not only material life, but also spiritual, the values of humanism and diversity of the world.
>
> *(PoslaniePrezidenta, 2013)*

Thus, Russia positions itself as one of the centres of the 'multipolar world', standing up against 'American hegemony' and 'globalism', which destroy national sovereignty. In addition, Russia sees itself as protecting traditional cultural patterns, national values and religious identities, and acts as an apologist for 'reasonable conservatism', opposing the 'bulldozer of cultural unification' that blurs the lines between nations, cultures and even genders. As a result, a part of the Western right-wing political spectrum began to perceive the Russian Federation as a stronghold of 'conservative values', and even 'the last hope of white Christian civilization'. For the first time since the demise of the Soviet Union, a new Russian ideology has a target audience not only within the country but also abroad, including some Western countries. Thus, today's Russia has managed to find ideological allies within the Western world among its anti-liberal forces (Polyakova, 2014). However, the reverse effect of this development was the creation of an extremely negative image of Russia in the eyes of Western liberal supporters of secularism and globalization.

In Russian discourse the term 'soft power' was first mentioned in an interview given by Foreign Minister Sergey Lavrov on the problems of interaction with foreign Russian-speaking communities in *Rossiyskaya Gazeta* in 2008. The Minister defined 'soft power' as 'the ability to influence the world through civilizational, humanitarian, cultural, foreign-policy and other attractiveness' (Lavrov, 2008). Deputy Foreign Minister G. B. Karasin, in an interview with the magazine *Free Thought* defined 'soft power' as 'the ability to project abroad the achievements in the economy, science, technological development, cultural and humanitarian sphere, thereby increasing the attractiveness of the country' (Karasin, 2010). In the *Moscow News* in 2012, Putin defined it as 'a set of tools and means to peacefully achieve foreign policy goals, by means of information and other bargaining chips' (*Moskovskienovosi*, 2012).

The foreign policy concept of the Russian Federation, approved by the Russian President in 2016, characterizes 'soft power' as a tool for solving foreign policy challenges. It is noted that the tool is based on the capabilities of civil society, information and communication, humanitarian and other means and technologies that complement traditional diplomatic means (Gerasimova, 2018). The latest version of the Russian Foreign Policy Concept recognizes the use of 'soft power' tools as an integral part of foreign policy. These 'tools' include information and communication, humanitarian and civil society capacities. The aims of this soft power include: protection of the rights of compatriots abroad; strengthening the role of Russia in the international humanitarian area (language, culture, history, cultural identity of the country, education, science, Russian diaspora); strengthening the international position of the Russian media, and fostering dialogue among cultures and civilizations.

The essential components of the modern Russian model of soft power include the Russian language, culture and the arts (music, literature, painting, cinema), universities, science and technology, especially space, and the media. Another particular aspect of Russian soft power is the event-related component, holding large global events, such as the Olympics.

Russian language and literature

In 2015 President Putin declared his intention 'to make Russian literature and Russian language the powerful factors of spiritual influence of Russia in the world' (Putin, 2015). The Russian language would be the dominant tool of soft power as a carrier and translator of the national culture. Russian is one of the global languages, being the sixth most spoken language in the world after English, Chinese, Hindi, Spanish and Arabic and is one of the six official languages of the United Nations. It has served as a means of international, inter-ethnic and multicultural communication since Soviet times. The collapse of the Soviet Union significantly weakened the influence of the Russian language in the world for a quarter of century but by 2013 Russian was spoken by over 270 million people in the world: 146 million people in Russia and 127 million in 33 countries around the world (Bovt, 2013).

Russian is also a widespread language on the Internet: 5.9 per cent of all sites in the global network are in Russian. It is the most common language on the websites of the former Soviet republics, including Belarus (87 per cent), Kazakhstan (84 per cent), Tajikistan (82 per cent), Uzbekistan (80 per cent), Ukraine (79 per cent) and Kyrgyzstan (76 per cent), which makes the Russian language a soft-power tool to reach the younger generation (Borta, 2017).

Russian language and culture are promoted through Russian Centres of Science and Culture (RCSC). The Centres are supported by the Foreign Ministry and diplomatic missions in foreign countries. In 2018, there were 67 Centres (59 plus 8 branches) in 59 countries and there are plans to build new ones in Turkey, Venezuela and Laos. At the same time, according to Ozerova, Russian is gradually ceasing to be a means of international communication in post-Soviet countries, giving way not to national languages but to English (Ozerova, 2013).

In 2007 the 'Year of Russian Language' programme was launched, in which a series of bilateral cultural events were to be held annually with different partner countries. The Year of Russian Language in China was organized in 2009. In 2014, the UK–Russia Year of Culture was held for the first time in the history of bilateral relations at the initiative of the British Council and the Ministry of Foreign Affairs of the Russian Federation. This year-long festival contributed to the mutual enrichment of cultures, the emergence of new ideas and the strengthening of relations between people and organizations of the two countries.

An important factor in the role of language in the promotion of Russian influence is the study of Russian as a foreign language, both through programmes of training foreign students in Russian universities and abroad, in the RCSCs or branches of Russian universities or other institutions. For this purpose, special programmes have been developed to train or retrain Russian language teachers from among the Russian-speaking diaspora. The Russian government aims to increase the number of students studying Russian outside Russia first to 300,000 and then to 500,000 students a year. It should be noted that these figures lag behind those of the Soviet period, when 600,000 students outside the USSR annually were taught Russian (Androssova, 2011).

The Federal Agency for the Commonwealth of Independent States, Compatriots Living Abroad and International Humanitarian Cooperation (Rossotrudnichestvo – RS Agency), together with the Ministry of Education and Science of Russia have a programme of support for Russian language education in the world. An international forum of teachers of foreign schools teaching Russian was first held in 2010 in Moscow at the Institute of the Russian Language as part of the 'Fourth Assembly of the Russian World', organized by the Russian World Foundation, the Ministry of Education and Science, the Ministry of Foreign Affairs and the Rossotrudnichestvo Agency. The forum discussed the functioning of foreign secondary schools teaching Russian and the development of foreign supplementary schools (Saturday and Sunday schools) (Androssova, 2011).

Russian culture

Russian culture is a crucial component of Russia's soft power, in its widest historical definition. The most important for promoting the image of Russia is its classical culture, developed during the Russian Empire, especially in the nineteenth and early twentieth century. The Soviet period is also important, especially in fine art and music. Among the Russian and Soviet composers who have gained worldwide recognition are Tchaikovsky, Rimsky-Korsakov, Mussorgsky, Rachmaninov, Stravinsky, Shostakovich, Prokofiev, Khachaturian and Schnittke. Russian musicians are also famous around the world: Shalyapin, Oistrach, Richter, Rostropovich. The modern ones – Gergiev, Spivakov, Currentzis, Hvorostovsky, Netrebko – perform on the best world stages.

The Russian and Soviet ballet schools throughout the twentieth century have been the gold standard in the world of classical ballet. The names of Matilda

Kshesinskaya, Anna Pavlova, George Balanchine, Maya Plisetskaya, Rudolf Nureyev and Mikhail Baryshnikov should be mentioned, among many. The Moscow Bolshoi Theatre and the Mariinsky Theatre in St. Petersburg are world-famous. The 'Bolshoi ballet' and 'Mariinsky ballet' brands always sell out concert halls.

Among the most important components of Russian culture is its world-renowned works of great literature by such writers as Alexander Pushkin, Fyodor Dostoevsky, Leo Tolstoy, Anton Chekhov, Mikhail Bulgakov, Vladimir Nabokov, Boris Pasternak, Alexander Solzhenitsyn and Joseph Brodsky. Many others have been translated into foreign languages and published outside Russia – Russian is fourth among languages which are most often translated. Five Russian writers have been Nobel laureates, including Ivan Bunin (1933), Boris Pasternak (1958), Mikhail Sholokhov (1965), Alexander Solzhenitsyn (1970) and Joseph Brodsky (1987). Leo Tolstoy was also nominated for the Nobel Prize every year from 1902 to 1906, but did not receive it (Kulturologia, 2013).

The influence of Russian literature on international culture and art has given Russia a form of soft power that has been constant, whatever the political regime and the state of international relations, boosted by numerous cinema adaptations of these great works by Western filmmakers throughout the twentieth and twenty-first centuries. This has promoted the image of Russia as a part of the European cultural tradition. The influence of Leo Tolstoy on European culture can hardly be exaggerated, as expressed by the French writer, Romain Rolland:

> Tolstoy is the great Russian soul, the light shone on earth a hundred years ago, who illuminated the youth of my generation. In the sweltering twilight of the passing century, he became our guiding star; our young hearts gravitated towards him; he was our refuge. Along with others – and there are many people in France, for whom he was more than a favorite author, but a friend, the best, or even the only, true friend among all the masters of European art.
>
> *(Rolland, 1954)*

Not surprisingly, the novels most filmed are those of Tolstoy, most notably his epic novel *War and Peace* and the doomed love story of *Anna Karenina*. The film of *War and Peace* (1956, US–Italy) directed by King Vidor was the first full-fledged film adaptation of the novel, with the main character, Natasha Rostova being played by Hollywood star Audrey Hepburn. The film received three Oscar nominations from the American Academy. A highly acclaimed Russian version of *War and Peace*, directed by Sergey Bondarchuk (1965–1967), became the first Soviet feature film to receive the 'Best foreign language film' Oscar nomination (Korsakov, 2016). In 1972, the BBC screened the longest, 20-episode dramatization of the novel, in which the role of Pierre Bezukhov was played by a young Anthony Hopkins. In 2007, a joint production by Russian, French and Italian artists was broadcast in four parts. A new version of the epic was made by the BBC in 2016, which received extensive feedback in Russia in official media and on social networks (Korsakov, 2016).

The novel *Anna Karenina* has also been filmed many times since the first silent version in 1910 (and about 10 silent film versions were made) and there are up to 30 foreign adaptations. The first was filmed not in Russia, but in Germany, six months before the death of Tolstoy in 1910, but unfortunately no reel of this has survived. Greta Garbo played the role twice, in *Love* (1927) and *Anna Karenina* (1935), receiving for the latter the NYFCC award in the 'female lead role' nomination and the Mussolini Cup in the 'Best foreign film' nomination at the Venice festival. In the UK, Vivien Leigh played Anna Karenina in 1947 and Jacqueline Bisset was the lead in the 1985 version. In the Anglo-American version of 1997, filmed in Moscow and St. Petersburg, Anna Karenina was performed by a French actress Sophie Marceau and a British film of *Anna Karenina* in 2012 had Keira Knightley as Anna.

Fyodor Dostoevsky's novels and stories have also produced a variety of screen versions. The film of the story 'White Nights' in 1957 was released by Luchino Visconti with Marcello Mastroianni in the lead role and it also inspired a 2007 Bollywood film *Saawariya*, directed by Sanjay Leela Bhansali. Akira Kurosawa, Jean-Luc Godard and Aki Kaurismaki all made films based on Dostoevsky's novels (Uznayvse.ru). The novel *Doctor Zhivago* by Pasternak has also led to cinematic adaptations, including the famous 1965 epic film directed by David Lean, starring Omar Sharif and Julie Christie.

Russian cinema can also be considered one of the crucial elements of the country's soft power. Soviet and Russian filmmakers have many times won the top prizes of the most prestigious film festivals – Cannes, Venice, Berlin and others, most notably Andrei Tarkovsky (winning in 1969, 1972, 1983 and 1986), who is widely regarded as one of the greatest masters of cinema with such internationally acclaimed and influential films to his credit as *Mirror* (1974), *Andrei Rublev* (1966) and *Stalker* (1979).

Russian fine art, especially painting, is also a positive element of the Russian image abroad and thus contributes to the soft power of the country. The most sought after in the world art auctions are the works of the Russian avant-garde school of artists of the early twentieth century, among them Nicholas Roerich, Kazimir Malevich, Vasily Kandinsky, Alexander Rodchenko, Marc Chagall and Natalia Goncharova. The value of works by these artists have increased in recent years: in 2008 'Suprematist Composition' (1916) by Malevich (1879–1935) fetched $60 million at Sotheby's and in 2013 'Madonna Laboris' (1931) by Roerich (1874–1947) was sold for $13.5 million at Bonham's, seven times higher than the estimate. At Sotheby's over the past decade, six paintings by Kandinsky (1866–1944) were sold for a total of $52 million.

The nineteenth-century Romantic artist Ivan Aivazovsky, the most expensive sold Russian artist, in 2011, for the first time, entered the top ten most expensive paintings by Russian artists. Contemporary Russian artists are also in demand in the world art market and contribute to Russian soft power, for example, Ilya Kabakov, Eric Bulatov, Semyon Faibisovich, Grisha Bruskin, Vasily Komar and Alexander Melamid, who work as a duo. Their works are sold at Sotheby's and Christie's auctions for millions of dollars (*Novosti iskusstva*, 2014).

Higher education

Traditionally, higher education has been one of the priorities of the country and has contributed to the prestige of the Soviet Union and Russia abroad. The education of foreign students in Russian universities is an indicator of the country's integration into the world community and today is a criterion for assessing the effectiveness of educational institutions in Russia. The education of foreign students in order to create an attractive image of the country has a long history. During Czarist Russia, in 1865, at a meeting of the Council under the Minister of Education, it was deemed appropriate to start training foreign citizens in Russian universities. Soon students from Bulgaria, Albania, Bosnia, Herzegovina, Serbia, etc. came to study at universities in St. Petersburg, Moscow, Odessa and at a number of other civil and religious educational institutions. The government of Emperor Alexander II appointed special state scholarships for them and foreign students were exempted from tuition fees. Nevertheless, the training of foreign students in the Russian Empire did not become widespread.

After 1918, the new Soviet government resumed inviting foreign students to study, and in the early 1920s, citizens of Turkey, Persia, Afghanistan and Mongolia studied free of charge in the Soviet Union. In 1921, the Communist University of the Toilers of the East (KUTV) was established, where foreign citizens of 44 nationalities studied (Sheregi, Dmitriev and Arefiev, 2003). After World War II, in 1960, the world's largest Peoples' Friendship University, named after Patrice Lumumba, the first President of Congo, was established in Moscow to train foreign specialists. On the eve of the collapse of the Soviet Union, there were 126,500 foreign students in the USSR, which amounted to just over 10 per cent of the global number of foreign students, putting Soviet universities at third place in the world after American and French universities in the number of foreign students, according to UNESCO (UNESCO, 1972 and 1993).

With the economic and technical assistance of the Soviet Union, 66 higher education institutions (universities, institutes, university centres, specialized faculties and branches), 23 secondary special education institutions, over 400 primary vocational education centres and five secondary schools were established in 36 countries. The Soviet Union equipped them with modern educational and laboratory tools, provided research and methodological literature, and thus contributed to the organization of the educational process by the efforts of the Soviet specialists.

The collapse of the USSR destroyed the Soviet system of supporting foreign students' education and more than 500 educational institutions in foreign countries created with the assistance of the USSR lost Russian support and passed to the guardianship of other states. According to UNESCO, in 1996, the share of foreign students Gants studying in Russia had reduced to about 5 per cent of the world's total number of foreign students (UNESCO, 1999). However, from 2005, attracting foreign students to Russian universities again became a priority for the Russian state, as a source of Russia's soft power (Torkunov, 2012). This factor is especially important for the promotion of Russian influence in the countries of the former

Soviet Union, for whom the system of Russian higher education is familiar, which facilitates academic mobility. The Russian language continues to be the second most widely spoken language in these territories. Knowledge of the Russian language gives a competitive advantage for studying in Russia compared to students from other countries.

The number of foreign students in Russian universities is growing year by year. The total number of foreign students at the universities of the Russian Federation in the 2016/2017 academic year, increased by 28,600 (14 per cent), compared with the previous year, mainly from Central Asian countries (Kazakhstan, Turkmenistan, Tajikistan and Uzbekistan) and from China and India. The largest contingents of full-time foreign students in 2016/2017 were from Kazakhstan (39,700), China (26,800) and Turkmenistan (17,300). The proportion of foreign students, funded by the Russian government, has been steadily increasing since the beginning of the 2000s, from 23 per cent in 2003/2004, to nearly 40 per cent in 2016/2017 (Obuchenie, 2018).

In order to promote Russian education and science, between 2015 and 2018, the Russian government supported the participation of more than 120 Russian universities in 92 international exhibitions. It also assisted in establishing partnerships and major projects with world-leading universities and institutions by holding seminars in Italy, Slovenia, Germany, France and Cyprus on the development of the network of Russian schools abroad and the promotion of Russian educational technologies.

Within the BRICS context, Russian-Chinese cooperation in education is developing, with joint training of staff, encouraging young people to learn each other's languages, supporting collaboration between educational institutions and increasing youth exchanges. The two countries have agreed to increase the target for student exchanges to 100,000 students by 2020. The number of Chinese students in Russia is constantly growing, due to long-term development of friendly relations between the two countries and favourable terms, including a low threshold for admissions and reasonable fees. Among all foreign students in Russian universities, the number of students from China – 22,529 in 2015–2016 – was the third largest after Kazakhstan and Ukraine, according to the Ministry of Education and Science of the Russian Federation (Russian.china.org.cn, 2017). There is also an active exchange of specialists and teaching personnel with China. The top universities of both countries, Lomonosov Moscow State University and Peking University have created a joint postgraduate school, with joint bachelors and masters in technical and humanitarian programmes (Karpov, 2013: 34).

The global presence of Russian media

Throughout the twentieth century, and particularly during the Cold War, television and radio were crucial tools of soft power, alongside hard military and economic power, as a means of propaganda and ideological influence. In recent years, with the explosion of 24/7 news channels, many states are using media to extend their influence internationally and get their points of view across. Following the Qatari channel Al-Jazeera, the Chinese CGTN (formerly CCTV), the French France 24, the Iranian Press TV have started broadcasting to global audiences, both in English and via many other targeted language channels. Russia has also been a significant part of this process. In the 'Concept of Russian Foreign Policy 2008', the goal was set 'to achieve a perspective of Russia in the world, developing its own effective means of information influence on public opinion abroad, to ensure the strengthening of the position of the Russian media in the world infosphere' (Koncepciy avneshnejpolitiki Rossijskoj Federacii, 2008). As part of this goal, the Russia Today (RT) TV company and the Sputnik News Agency were created. These projects, especially RT, have become a notable tool of Russian soft power over the last decade.

RT, formerly known as Russia Today, which started broadcasting in 2005, is the first Russian news channel with global round-the-clock broadcasting in English and other major world languages – Arabic (since 2007), Spanish (since 2009), German (since 2014) and French (since 2017) – on a non-commercial basis. Given its availability in such major languages of the world, the network is aimed at a global audience, including foreigners living in Russia and those who are interested in Russian affairs. The purpose of RT is to provide coverage of the world news from the Russian point of view. Defining its editorial position, the RT chief editor Margarita Simonyan said in an interview: 'It will be a view of the world from Russia. We do not want to change the professional format established by such TV channels as BBC, CNN and Euronews. We want to reflect Russia's view of the world and make Russia itself more understandable' (Lenta.ru, 2005). In another interview she said: 'RT shows what neither Fox, nor NBC or CBS shows. People are interested in how and what Russian people think' (Russian.rt, 2016); telling the American network NBC in a 2018 interview, 'RT's goal is to inform the audience. If you think that informing means influencing, then yes, you can say so' (Russian.rt., 2018).

The founders of the channel aimed to present the audience in English-speaking countries with the views of Russian society on the most pressing issues, to get rid of stereotypes imposed during the years of the Cold War: 'One of the key components of the Russia Today mission is a correct and balanced message to the foreign audience on the Russian view of world events' (Tupitsyna and Neymatova, 2008).

The RT television network includes three round-the-clock news channels broadcasting from Moscow in more than 100 countries in English, Arabic and Spanish, RT America and RT UK, broadcasting from their own studios in Washington and London. RT channels also exist in French and in German. In addition, it has a documentary channel and a global news agency (RUPTLY), offering exclusive material to TV channels around the world. In 2018, RT was available to 700 million viewers throughout the world around the clock. In 2013, RT became the first news channel to pass the billion views mark on YouTube and since then it has remained as the leader among the 24/7 news channels on YouTube: the total number of hits for all RT channels on the world's biggest video hosting site is about three billion. According to comScore survey, the online audience for the RT TV channel is over 32 million unique users per month. Funded by the Russian Federation, RT's 2019 published budget will amount to $340 million, much smaller than the budgets of other leading international broadcasters (Russian.rt, 2018).

RT broadcasts hourly news bulletins about the events in Russia and the world: while about 70 per cent of programming is international news, including business and sports, the channel also regularly airs documentary films and cultural programmes. Among its flagship programmes is 'Cross Talk', and a weekly exclusive show 'Politicking', hosted by well-known American journalist, Larry King. According to television ratings from Ipsos, an international market research company, in 2017, 100 million people in 47 countries watched RT every week, with the biggest growth in Latin America and the US. The weekly audience in the US grew by more than 30 per cent – from 8 million to 11 million viewers, while the number of RT.com users globally was more than 187 million, according to Similar Web (Russian.rt, 2018). RT is the only Russian TV channel to be nominated six times for the prestigious Emmy Award. In 2012, RT was a finalist of the award for coverage of the Occupy Wall Street movement in the US, while, in 2016, the nomination was received for a series of RT specials, dedicated to the 70th session of the UN General Assembly.

Since 2018, a massive information, and then political campaign against the RT and Sputnik channels, as the tools of Russian soft power, started among the policymakers and in the media of Western Europe and the US. The channels were accused of being the means of Russian propaganda, manipulating public opinion and providing fake news. The US Congress insisted that Russian channels should be included in the list of foreign agents and thus their activity would be limited. In 2018, US Congressmen presented a bill directed against the activities of RT. Such a strong reaction by Western politicians and media could be considered as recognition of the effectiveness of the RT channel in influencing the opinion of audiences in their countries, a success in terms of promoting Russia's soft power. In Britain the media regulatory authority Ofcom (Office of Communications) has fined the network for violating broadcasting protocols, while in the European Union too, concerns have been raised about the partisan perspectives that RT is allegedly promoting among its audiences – following an anti-Western editorial line.

Russian diaspora and the Russian Orthodox church

The Russian diaspora abroad, which, with about 30 million people is third in the world after that of the Chinese and the Indian, plays an important role as the subject and channel of Russia's soft power (Budaev, 2015). The Russian government's focus on Russian people abroad and support to their associations and organizations has grown in recent years, including the establishment of the World Coordination Council of Russian Compatriots Abroad in 2018. Regional and country Co-ordination Councils also greatly contribute to this process. At the same time, the Russian diaspora needs to preserve its cultural and civilizational identity in the context of increasing globalization and growing feelings of national identity in the super-ethnic groups prevalent in the countries of residence. In this regard, the Russian diaspora, in turn, needs the national soft power, which objectively contributes to the preservation of its identity and is able to be the key agent of its interests.

Another, related channel of Russian soft power is the Russian Orthodox Church and its numerous parishes abroad. Remaining for a long time almost the only core of unity and spiritual support of Russian people abroad, today the Russian Orthodox Church of the Moscow Patriarchate brings traditional Orthodox spiritual and moral ideas and values to people. This implicitly supports the actions of official government agencies to improve the image of Russia. Spiritual nourishment of members of the Russian Orthodox Church with both Russian and foreign citizenship underpins the essential moral and ethical values of Russian soft power and its civilizational mission in the world.

Soft power institutions and actors

To implement the soft power resources discussed above, there are a number of institutions, including public authorities, primarily the Ministry of Foreign Affairs and its agencies, business associations and non-governmental organizations and civil society institutions. The Federal Agency for the Commonwealth of Independent States (abbreviated as *Rossotrudnichestvo* Agency) is the main governmental institution implementing state policy in the field of soft power. The Agency was established in 2008 by a Presidential Decree and is subordinated to the Russian Foreign Ministry. It is currently represented in 80 countries by 94 institutions, including 70 Russian Centres of Science and Culture (RCSCs) in 61 countries and 24 Agency representatives in 22 embassies. In many ways, *Rossotrudnichestvo*, as a key soft power institutional agent, is similar to the US Agency for International Development. The activities of this Federal Agency and its foreign missions are aimed at the implementation of the state policy in international humanitarian cooperation and the priority area for its activities is the CIS countries. As mentioned above, the agency also provides the system of support for promoting the Russian language abroad.

Another key institution for Russian soft power is the Russian World (*Russkiy Mir*) Foundation, which was established on the models of the German Goethe Institute, the British Council and the *Alliance Francaise*, and which plays an essential role in sustaining interest in Russian culture and language. It has branches all over the world, from Jakarta and Sydney to Seattle and Buenos Aires and provides grants to support the implementation of projects launched by Russian and foreign non-profit organizations, as well as by foreign citizens on a competitive basis and dealing with the promotion of the Russian language, programmes in the Russian language, the development of cultural and humanitarian cooperation between Russia and other countries, and the support for foreign-based Russian-language media outlets.

The annual international pedagogical forums of the Russian World Foundation provide an intellectual platform where Russian and foreign Russianists discuss issues of teaching Russian language and literature. In 2018, an updated version of 'The Russian World Professor' programme was launched to systematize the work of sending Russian specialists abroad, at the invitation of their foreign partners, and to organize the teaching of the Russian language and other subjects. 'The Russian World Student' programme oversees recruitment of young students to learn the Russian language by participating in readers' libraries, children's educational centres and language camps. The Foundation also runs a grant programme (Russkiy Mir Foundation, 2015).

The key priority in the promotion of national soft power, namely its public diplomacy component, is the involvement of civil society, the Russian public and non-governmental organizations (NGOs), which have proliferated in recent years. Among the most active, and those playing a prominent role in the implementation of public diplomacy and soft power include, Public Chamber, the Council for Foreign and Defense Policy, the Centre for Political Research of Russia, the Foundation for Support of Public Diplomacy, the Russian Foreign Affairs Council and the Russian World Foundation.

In 2018, as many as 281 NGOs from Russia had consultative status with the UN Economic and Social Council, a key body for coordination with civil society organizations. Their diverse activities, not always following official opinion, are a useful addition to traditional diplomacy, bringing to Russian soft power more confidence and credibility. Civil society, its institutions and agencies are an important source of Russia's soft power, with great potential in terms of developing and strengthening relationships with compatriots, with Russian-speaking diasporas, with political elites and the general public in foreign countries.

The positioning by the Federal and regional authorities of the largest cities of the country as attractive places for the major international socio-political, economic and sports events can be considered a new element in the use of Russian soft power. In this regard, the annual St. Petersburg International Economic Forum and the Valdai International Discussion Club, the holding of G-8 leaders' summits and other events within the context of BRICS and the G20, are notable examples. In addition, Russia has recently hosted major international championships and competitions, including the World Athletics Championship in Moscow and the World Martial Arts Games in St. Petersburg – both held in 2013, the Winter Olympic Games in Sochi in 2014 and the World Cup in 2018.

The successful holding of such large-scale multilateral forums, conferences, exhibitions and competitions becomes an effective information and media channel, contributing to the creation of a positive image of Russia, the consolidation of a benevolent attitude among a significant part of the national and international community, including their specific segments (political establishment, economic and sports community, youth).

Sophisticated information technologies and Internet resources have a significant potential for the expansion of Russia's soft power, taking into account their almost unlimited opportunities to reach a wide audience, the efficiency of information transmission and the ability to communicate in real time. A good example is the web page of the Ministry of Foreign Affairs of Russia and its numerous institutions abroad, with technical capabilities to access the social networks: Facebook, Twitter and YouTube.

It is important to note that Russia has its own social network, Vkontakte, an alternative to Facebook, which is used daily by more than 140 million people, including residents of the CIS and other neighbouring countries (Leontiev, 2012). Vkontakte allows the creation of an information space in which the key position is occupied by Russian cultural values, and the main generators of content are the people who share these values. Vkontakte is also the basic social network for the Central Asian countries.

In conclusion, it should be noted that modern Russia is trying to use a range of up-to-date soft power tools and that Russia does not reject the positive historical developments inherited from the USSR. The emphasis is placed on media, universities, promotion of the Russian language and culture, global events and tourism. It should be added that the context for the implementation of Russian soft power policy in the last five years has become less favourable (Nye, 2013). This is due to growing international tensions, the negative reaction of the West to Russia's military actions in Syria and Ukraine, accusations of interference in the 2016 US Presidential elections and the 2018 case of alleged poisoning of Sergei Skripal, a former Russian military officer and double agent for British intelligence services in the UK. At the same time, the Russian Government understands that it is impossible to make do with only soft power in the intensified global confrontation between Russia and the West. Therefore, it is trying to build a balance of 'hard' and 'soft' approaches in international influence – what is been called 'smart power'.

References

Androssova, D. (2011) 'Myagkayasila' rossiinaprostranstvesng. Vyssheeobrazovanie. *Aktual'nyeproblemyEvropy* [Russian 'soft power' in the CIS. Higher education. *Actual problems of Europe*], 2: 203–218.

Barghoorn, F. and Friedrich, P. (1956) Cultural relations and Soviet foreign policy. *World Politics,* 8(3): 323–344.

Borta, Yu. (2017) 'Myagkayasila'. Luchshijsposobprodvizheniyayazyka – dialog naukiikul'tury. *Argumentyifakty* ['Soft Power'. The best way to promote language is the dialogue between science and culture. *Arguments and Facts*]. Available at www.aif.EN/society/education/ myagkaya_sila_luchshiy_sposob_prodvizheniya_yazyka_-_dialog_nauki_i_kultury.

Bovt, G. (2013) Myagkayasilarusskogoslova, Rossijskijsovet po mezhdunarodnymdelam [Soft power of the Russian word. *Russian Foreign Affairs Council*]. Available at http:// russiancouncil.ru/analytics-and-comments/analytics/myagkaya-sila-russkogo-slova/

Budaev, A. V. (2015) Myagkayasilavovneshnejpolitikerossiiistokiosobennostiperspektivygosud arstvennoeupravlenie, Ehlektronnyjvestnikvypusk ['Soft power' in the foreign policy of Russia: origins, features, prospects. *Public administration.* E-Bulletin] 48: 189–205. Available at http://ejournal.spa.msu.ru/uploads/vestnik/2015/vipusk__48._fevral_2015_g._/ pravovie_i_polititcheskie_aspekti_upravlenija/budaev.pdf.

Filatova, I. and Davidson, A. (2013) *The Hidden Thread: Russia and South Africa in the Soviet Era.* Johannesburg: Jonathan Ball.

Gerasimova, V. A. (2018) Instrumentyiresursy'myagkojsily'Rossiinaprostranstve UNS, *Postsovetskieissledovaniya* [Tools and resources of 'soft power' of Russia in the CIS]. *Post-Soviet Studies,* 1(6): 574–575.

Hilger, A. (2017) Communism, decolonization and the Third World, pp. 317–340 in N. Naimark; S. Pons, and S. Quinn-Judge (eds.) *The Cambridge History of Communism.* Cambridge: Cambridge University Press.

Karasin, G. B. (2010) Interv'yu stats-sekretarya — zamestitelyaMinistrainostrannyh del Rossii G.B. Karasinazhurnalu'Svobodnayamysl'. The interview of the State Secretary — Russia's Deputy Foreign Minister G. B. Karasin with the magazine. 'Free Thought' 12. Available at www.mid.ru/bdomp/brp_4.nsf/6a5f93a96aa86373c3256f6d00540599/ 25c601b45628acd4c3257824002b6fe4

Karpov, M. V. (2013) Sovremennaya Rossiya v pole myagkojsilyKitayanekotoryeaspektyte oriiipraktikivzaimodejstviya. *Strany SNG iBaltii v globalnojpolitikeKitaya* [The modern Russia in the area of 'soft power' of China. *The UIS and the Baltic States in global politics of China*] pp. 22–38. Moscow: Russian Institute for Strategic Studies.

Katsakioris, C. (2010) Soviet lessons for Arab modernization: Soviet educational aid towards Arab countries after 1956. *Journal of Modern European History,* 8(1): 85–105.

Kiseleva, Y. (2015) Russia's soft power discourse: Identity, status and the attraction of power. *Politics,* 35(3–4): 316–29.

KoncepciyaVneshnejPolitikiRossijskojFederacii (2008) [Foreign Policy Concept of the Russian Federation] Available at www.kremlin.ru/acts/news/785

Korsakov, D. (2016) ElenKuraginairebyata: Pochemu v anglijskoj «Vojnei mire» P'eri Andrej takpomolodeli? *Komsomol'skayapravda* [Ellen Kuragina and fellows: Why in the English version of 'War and Peace' Pierre and Andrew are so young? *Komsomolskaya Pravda*], May 11. Available at www.spb.kp.ru/daily/26489.4/3358461/

Kulturologia, R. F. (2013) Pyat'russkihpisatelej, stavshih Nobelevskimilaureatami [Five Russian writers who became Nobel laureates] Available at https://kulturologia.ru/blogs/ 101213/19473/

Lankina, T. and Niemczyk, K. (2015) Russia's Foreign Policy and Soft Power, pp. 97–113 in D. Cadier and M. Light (eds.) *Russia's Foreign Policy. Ideas, Domestic Politics and External Relations.* Basingstoke: Palgrave Macmillan.

Lavrov, S.V. (2008) Interv'yuMinistrainostrannyh del RossiiS.V.Lavrova po tematikeotnoshenij s zarubezhnymirusskoyazychnymiobshchinami, opublikovannoe v «Rossijskojgazete» 30 oktyabrya 2008, Mezhdunarodnyeotnosheniyagoda. [The Foreign Minister Sergey Lavrov's interview on relations with foreign Russian-speaking communities, *Rossiyskaya Gazeta*], October 30. Available at www.mid.ru/bdomp/nsdgpch.nsf/bab3c4309e31451 cc325710e004812c0/432569ee00

Lenta.ru (2005) V Rossiisozdanpropagandistskijtelekanaldlyainostrancev [Russia has created a propaganda channel for foreigners], June 7. Available at www.lenta.ru/news/2005/06/ 07/channel/

Leontiev, V. P. (2012) SocialnyesetiVKontakte Facebook idrugie [*Social networks: VKontakte, Facebook and others*], p. 14. Moscow: OLMA Media Group.

Li, Yan (2019) *China's Soviet Dream.* New York: Routledge.

Moskovskienovosi (2012) Rossiya imenyayushchijsyamir. Stat'yaVladimiraPutina v Moskovskihnovostyah [Russia and the changing world. Vladimir Putin's article in *Moscow News*], February 27. Available at www.mn.ru/politics/78738

Novosti iskusstva (2014) 50 samyhdorogihnynezhivushchihrossijskihhudozhnikov [50 most expensive living Russian artists, *Art News*], February 27. Available at www. theartnewspaper.ru/posts/527/

Nye, J. (2004) *Soft Power: The Means to Success in World Politics.* New York: PublicAffairs.

Nye, J. (2013) What China and Russia Don't Get About Soft Power. *Foreign Policy.* April 29. Available at http://foreignpolicy.com/2013/04/29/what-china-and-russia-dont-get-about-soft-power/.

Obuchenie (2018) *Obuchenie inostrannyh grazhdan v vysshih uchebnyh zavedeniyah rossijskoj federacii, Statisticheskij sbornik* [Training of foreign citizens in higher educational institutions of the Russian Federation. Statistical compendium] 15(9). Moscow: Sociocentre.

Ozerova, M. (2013) Russkijyazyk v bede: 'myagkojsile' ne hvataetdeneg. *Moskovskijkomsomolec* [The Russian language in trouble: 'soft power' lacks money. MK.RU], April 10. Available at www.mk.ru/politics/2013/04/10/839555-russkiy-yazyik-v-bede-myagkoy-sile-ne-hvataet-deneg.html

Polyakova, A. (2014) Strange bedfellows: Putin and Europe's far right. *World Affairs*, 177(3): 36–41.

PoslaniePrezidentaFederal'nomuSobraniyu (2013) [Message from the President to the Federal Assembly], October 12. Available at www.kremlin.ru/acts/bank/38057

Putin, V. (2015) Nashazadacha – sdelat' russkuyuliteraturu, russkijyazykmoshchnymfaktorom idejnogovliyaniyaRossii v mire [Our purpose is to make Russian literature and Russian language the powerful factors of ideological influence of Russia in the world]. Available at http://file-rf.ru/context/3036.

Rolland, R. (1954) ZHizn'Tolstogo.Gosudarstvennoeizdatel'stvohudozhestvennojliteratury [*Tolstoy's Life*]. Moscow: State Publishing House of Fiction.

Russian.china.org.cn (2017) Kitajskiestudentyzanimayuttrete mesto po kolichestv usrediinostrancev v vuzahRossii [Chinese students take third place in the number of foreigners in Russian universities] Available at http://russian.china.org.cn/exclusive/txt/2017-08/20/content_41442011.htm

Russkiy Mir Foundation (2015) *Grants.* Moscow: Russkiy Mir Foundation. Available at https://russkiymir.ru/en/grants/

Russian.rt (2016) Kononenko, M. Na myagkoj storone sily [On the soft side of power]. *RT Russian*, June 16. Available at https://russian.rt.com/opinion/307901-na-myagkoi-storone-sily

Russian.rt (2018) Маргарита Симоньян назвала главную цель RT [Margarita Simonyan names the main goal of RT]. *RT Russian*, January 17. Available at https://russian.rt.com/world/news/471158-margarita-simonyan-cel-rt

Sherr, J. (2013) *Hard Diplomacy and Soft Coercion.* Washington: Brookings Institution Press.

Sheregi, F. E., Dmitriev, N. M. and Arefiev, A. L. (2003) Rossiya namirovomrynkeobrazova tel'nyhuslug, *Demoskop* [Russia in the world market of educational services. *Demoscope*, 97–98.] Available at www.demoscope.ru/weekly/2003/097/analit03.php.

Torkunov, A. V. (2012) Obrazovaniekak'myagkayasila'vovnejshnejpolitikeRossii, *Vestnik MGIMO-Universiteta* [Education as the 'soft power' in the foreign policy of Russia. *Bulletin of MGIMO University*] 4: 85–93.

Tupitsyna, I. N. and Neymatova, B. A. (2008) Sociokulturnayamissiyatelekanala Russia Today, UchenyezapiskiRossijskogogosudarstvennogosocialnogouniversiteta [Social and Cultural Mission of Russia Today TV Channel. *Scholarly notes of Russian State Social University*] 2: 87.

UNESCO (1972) *Statistical Yearbook*, pp. 458–460. Paris: UNESCO.

UNESCO (1993) *World Educational Report, Training of specialists for foreign countries in Russia,* p. 29. Paris: UNESCO.

UNESCO (1999) *UNESCO Statistical Yearbook.* Paris: UNESCO.

Wishon, J. (2013) Soviet globalization: Indo-Soviet public diplomacy and cold war cultural spheres. *Global Studies Journal*, 5(2): 103–114.

11

INDIA

Culture as soft power

Daya Kishan Thussu

Since 2013 India has been the world's third largest economy after China and the United States (on the basis of purchasing-power parity) and in overall GDP terms it was fifth largest, surpassing Britain in 2019 (IMF, 2019). In parallel with this economic power, India's soft power is on the rise. With the revolution in media production and distribution, as well as in mobile and online communications, India's cultural products and concepts now reach all corners of the globe. India's public-diplomacy strategy under the Hindu-nationalist Bharatiya Janata Party government of Prime Minister Narendra Modi elected in 2014, has been to emphasize India's intellectual, religious and cultural wealth using the country's considerable media and creative industries and the global Indian diaspora, as reflected in a 2017 documentary, *India Boundless – A Place in the Heart of the World*, produced for the Public Diplomacy Division of India's Ministry of External Affairs (India Boundless, 2017).

In his 2004 book *Soft Power: The Means to Success in World Politics*, Joseph Nye suggests that soft power is an integral part of foreign policy, especially for states seeking to 'incorporate the soft dimensions into their strategies for wielding power' (Nye, 2004: 1). Its role in foreign policy is important precisely because 'in behavioural terms, simply put, soft power is attractive power' (ibid.: 6), pursued in order to influence the behaviour of other states. Acknowledging Nye's definition of soft power, developed primarily in relation to the US, this chapter will suggest that India's global presence and influence – artistic, spiritual and intellectual – are rooted in its civilizational power. Its soft power assets, including mass media, diaspora, religion, culture and popular cinema, help to create awareness and appreciation of India globally (Tharoor, 2008, 2012; Thussu, 2013; Kugiel, 2017).

This chapter examines the role of culture in promoting India's soft power, with a special focus on links with key BRICS partners, especially China. The chapter discusses this within an historical perspective, particularly through Buddhism as, arguably, the most important and enduring idea to have emanated from Indic civilization and of particular significance in relation to China. Another important dimension of India's international presence is its large and widespread English-speaking diaspora, increasingly viewed by the Indian government and corporations as a vital source of soft power. The chapter will go on to examine government efforts to promote Indian culture and contrast that with the success of the commercial and highly popular film industry, which has a global audience, thanks to the digitalization of commerce and media. India has the world's second largest Internet population and its creative and cultural industries have the potential to circulate across various digital domains, resulting in globalized production, distribution and consumption practices.

Finally, the chapter will examine India's global image as the world's largest democracy, a particular distinction among the BRICS countries. India has retained and arguably strengthened democracy in a multi-lingual, multi-racial and multi-religious society, a model now under threat in many Western democracies. Although India's secular structures – both social and cultural – and pluralist ethos are being undermined by the current majoritarian government, the chapter argues that the still greater challenge for India's soft power is its failure to eliminate poverty among so many of its citizens – India is home to the world's largest number of people living in extreme poverty.

The rise in India's global economic status has coincided with the relative economic decline of the West, creating the opportunity for an emerging economic power, such as India, to participate in global governance structures hitherto dominated by the US-led Western alliance (Narlikar, 2017; Karnard, 2018). Given its history as the only major democracy that did not blindly follow the West during the Cold War years but pursued a non-aligned foreign policy, India has the potential now to take up a more significant leadership role globally. Despite growing economic and strategic relations with Washington, it maintains close ties with other major and emerging powers, most notably with its BRICS partners. In addition, India's presence at the Group of 77 developing nations and at the G-20 leading economies of the world has been effective in articulating a Southern perspective on global affairs.

Historicizing soft power

How much 'attractive power' does India possess? Although as a nation state India is just over 70 years old, as a distinctive civilization it has a much older history. Dating back more than 5,000 years, Indic civilization is one of the most ancient and continuous cultural formations in the world, with wide-ranging influences in areas from religion and philosophy, arts and sciences, language and literature, trade and travel (Thussu, 2013). As the origin of four of the world's major religions – Hinduism, Buddhism, Jainism and Sikhism – and as the place where many faiths have coexisted for millennia, India offers a unique and syncretized religious discourse. Buddhism was founded in India and remains the most enduring and powerful idea associated with India today and connects Indian culture with countries across Asia. In addition, both Christianity and Islam have long associations with India. Some of the earliest Christian communities were established in India: St. Thomas is supposed to be buried in Chennai in southern India, and one of the world's oldest mosques is located in Kerala, where Jewish communities have also lived for millennia.

The dissemination of Hindu and Buddhist ideas across Asia was substantial: it is no coincidence that the official airline of Indonesia, the world's largest Muslim country, is named *Garuda*, the Sanskrit name for the eagle on which the Hindu God Vishnu rides. The Indian contribution to Islamic thought (and via that to European intellectual culture) in mathematics, astronomy and other physical and metaphysical sciences is widely recognized, though India's cultural influence in historical terms was directed not towards the West but to Asia. The dispersion of ideas associated with Hinduism and Buddhism across east and southeast Asia from the third century BC onwards created a strong cultural and communication dimension to the millennia-old relationship between India and the rest of Asia (Mookerjee, 1947; Sen, 2005). Buddhism was at the heart of this interaction, with the widest dissemination of the ideas emanating from India (Sen, 2003 and 2017). Narratives of the Buddha's life and teachings are still a cultural referent in much of Asia, while traces of Indic languages, religious rituals, cuisine, dance and other art forms survive in parts of southeast Asia, notably in Thailand, Cambodia and Indonesia – evident from monumental temple complexes, notably Angkor Wat in Cambodia and Borobudur and Prambanan in Indonesia (Sen, 2005; Thussu, 2013).

Buddhism was also a central link between India and China, indicating a very long historical association between the two great civilizational powers of Asia (Xinru, 1988; Sen, 2005; Sen 2003 and 2017). Centres of higher education such as Nalanda, an international Buddhist university based in India between the fifth and twelfth centuries, existed for 500 years before universities were established in Europe (and has been recently revived as part of a pan-Asian project linking China and India, as well as some other Asian nations). The interest in Buddhist thought and texts in China led to great Chinese scholars such as Xuan Zang (602–664) visiting Nalanda to exchange ideas on law, philosophy and politics and translating hundreds of manuscripts from Sanskrit to Mandarin. Indian scholars and religious leaders also visited China on a regular basis and these intellectual exchanges continued for centuries. Over a period of time, the 'Sinification' of Buddhism took place, manifested in the mixing of Chinese and Indic beliefs and the development of Chinese Buddhist texts and commentaries (Sen, 2017). Even today Buddhism remains a powerful link between the two civilizations.

In modern times the cultural link between the two nations was symbolized by poet-philosopher Rabindranath Tagore – the first non-Western writer to win the Nobel Prize for Literature in 1913 – whose visit to China in 1924, in the words of a leading Chinese scholar, led to 'a wide-ranging Sino-Indian civilizational dialogue, and a very significant landmark in the annals of Sino-Indian cultural intercourse' (Liming, 2011: 15). On his return to India, Tagore set up the *Cheena Bhavana* (China House) at his university, *Visva-Bharati* – the first place in India to teach Chinese language, literature and history (Chung *et al.*, 2011). Tagore remains one of the most respected foreign poets in China even today. Such cultural interactions have a strong soft-power dimension to them and should be considered in any Sino-Indian dialogue. As one commentator has noted, the connections between India and China must be 'placed within the context of Asian and world history, and the relationship in contemporary times analyzed with reference to global interdependence' (Sen, 2017: 4).

In Russia too, Indic ideas evoked interest: Gerasim Lebede, who spent 12 years in India between 1785 and 1797, became the father of Indology in Russia. Sanskrit was taught in Moscow University from the 1840s and a Sanskrit Chair was founded in 1855 at St. Petersburg University. The Russian Academy of Sciences also established a Chair of Oriental Linguistic Studies (Chelyshev and Litman, 1985). Adding to this legacy is India's long and continuing encounter with European modernity and its contribution to a distinctive worldview, epitomized by Mahatma Gandhi, the apostle of non-violence and tolerance, whose thoughts influenced such leaders as Martin Luther King and Nelson Mandela, prompting scholars to speak of a 'pax-Gandhiana' (Parel, 2016).

Faith-based diplomacy

Emphasizing the millennium-old cultural and communication links with other Asian nations, the Indian government has propounded the idea of '*sanskriti evam sabhyata*' (culture and civilization) as a core principle for promoting India's image globally. One indication of such an approach is that a pro-government think-tank, the India Foundation organized its first soft power conference with an emphasis on India's past glories (India Foundation, 2018). Invoking India's past, which the Modi government has been keen to emphasize, makes sense in an age in which cultural revivalism is occurring across the globe. Modi's 'faith-based' diplomacy promoting Buddhism is particularly pronounced: it is not without symbolic significance that the first foreign visit Modi made after being elected Prime Minister in 2014 was to Buddhist Bhutan. Since then, in his official visits to Asian nations such as Nepal, Japan, China, Mongolia and South Korea, he has repeatedly invoked Buddhism. Although less than 1 per cent of the Indian population are Buddhists, Modi's government declared *Buddha Purnima* (Buddha's birthday) an official holiday to be celebrated each year (Mazumdar, 2018). With its focus on peace and non-violence, Buddhism is seen as a useful soft-power tool for India, which has traditionally projected itself as a peace-loving nation (despite being a nuclear power, the world's largest importer of arms and having the third largest armed forces in the world).

The rebuilding and revival of Nalanda University as a pan-Asian project, funded by other Asian countries, in addition to India, including China, Japan, South Korea, Thailand and Singapore, was also influenced by soft power considerations. However, the university has yet to take off properly in India, due to the absence of proper infrastructure, academic apathy and financial constraints (although courses started in 2014). Meanwhile, in 2017, China launched the Nanhai Buddhism Academy in Hainan province as a global Buddhist university in partnership with Buddhist centres in Sri Lanka, Nepal, Thailand and Cambodia. The cultural links which such educational connections could provide might also be used to promote faith-based tourism, as India is home to some of the best-known Buddhist sites – Mahabodhi Temple Complex in Bodh Gaya (the place where Buddha is supposed to have attained enlightenment), Nalanda – both UNESCO World Heritage sites – and Sarnath (where he gave his first sermon).

Yoga and ayurveda as soft power

A related aspect of Modi's religion-based diplomacy is the promotion of yoga and ayurveda as part of soft-power projection, in which his government has been very active. Soon after taking office, the Modi government engaged in intense lobbying within the United Nations General Assembly, gaining the support of 175 member states for the resolution proposing an international day of yoga. Since 2015, International Yoga Day is celebrated by the UN on June 21. Today yoga is practised around the world and in 2018 even the conservative and deeply Islamist Saudi Arabia recognized yoga as a sport. Drawing on an ancient Hindu spiritual tradition to promote an Indian 'alternative' lifestyle fits in well with a Hindu nationalist leader who is himself a devoted yoga enthusiast and a very public practitioner (Mazumdar, 2018; Gautam and Droogan, 2018). Another key part of India's spiritual soft power project is promotion of ayurveda – the knowledge (Sanskrit: *veda*) needed for longevity (*ayus*) – the classical system of Indian medicine. The earliest surviving ayurveda texts date from the second century AD: the *Caraka Samhita* (Caraka's Compendium) attributed to the renowned physician and medical theorist Caraka, and the *Susruta Samhita* (Susruta's Compendium), composed in the fourth century AD (Wujastyk, 2003).

That such traditional knowledge should be protected and promoted has been on the agenda of the Indian government since 1995 when a department for the Indian System of Medicine and Homeopathy was created, renamed in 2003 as the Department of Ayurveda, Yoga and Naturopathy, Unani, Siddha and Homoeopathy (AYUSH). Soon after assuming office in 2014, Modi's government elevated the Department into a Ministry to 'ensure the optimal development and propagation of AYUSH systems of healthcare'. The Ministry's Central Council for Research in Ayurvedic Sciences, the apex body is tasked with 'coordinating, formulating, developing and promoting research in ayurveda on scientific lines', as the Ministry website states. The Indian healthcare industry is aligning with the government vision to globalize this traditional healing method and the global ayurveda market is expected to grow to $10 billion by 2022, according to a recent industry report by the Confederation of Indian Industry (CII) (CII/PwC, 2018). As the Chair of the CII's ayurveda core group noted, promoting Indian expertise could bring in foreign exchange and has 'soft diplomacy' benefits, introducing foreigners to Indian traditions (quoted in Doshi, 2018). According to one commentator, 'the Modi government has raised the bar on the relationship between India's soft power potential and its foreign policy. For the first time, the Indian state is beginning to make systematic use of the rich cultural and human resources that have previously developed quite independently of its policies' (Martin, 2015).

Diasporic soft power

A key dimension of India's growing global soft-power profile is its extended and increasingly visible diaspora, scattered around the globe and estimated at over 28 million (according to figures from India's Ministry for External Affairs), who have excelled in many spheres of life and enriched the cultural, economic and intellectual experience of countries such as the US and Britain (Kapur, 2010; Thussu, 2013; Chakravorty, Kapur and Singh, 2017; also see essays in Hegde and Sahoo, 2017). This is especially so in the United States, where an estimated 4.6 million people of Indian origin live, a large number of whom are high-profile professionals and business tycoons (Kapur, 2010; Chakravorty, Kapur and Singh, 2017).

The most articulate and effective manifestation of this soft-power attribute is the growing presence of members of the Indian diaspora in influential positions in Ivy League universities, international media and multilateral organizations, as well as transnational corporations. In 2019, two of the world's top digital corporations were led by Indians who studied for their first university degrees in India: Satya Nadella, the CEO of Microsoft and Sundar Pichai, Chief Executive of Google. Nitin Nohria became the tenth Dean of the Harvard Business School in 2010 – the first Asian to be elevated to such a position, while the Nobel Laureate, Sir Venkatraman Ramakrishnan was elected the President of Britain's Royal Society in 2015. Harvard University Professor, Gita Gopinath was appointed in 2018 as Director of Research of the International Monetary Fund.

In US politics too, the Indian presence is growing: Nikki Haley, President Donald Trump's former UN ambassador is of Indian origin, as is Bobby Jindal, the former Governor of Louisiana. In 2020, in the UK government three key ministries were held by people of Indian origin: Rishi Sunak as Chancellor of the Exchequer, Priti Patel as Home Secretary and Alok Sharma, Secretary of State for Business, Energy and Industrial Strategy. Many Indians have also reached top positions in international media organizations: prominent examples include Bobby Ghosh, who had the distinction of being the first non-American to be chosen as editor of *Time International* and Fareed Zakaria, editor-at-large of *Time* and a leading CNN commentator and *Washington Post* columnist, while Ravi Agrawal was appointed the managing editor of *Foreign Policy*.

In a globalized and interconnected world, diasporas can be a vital strategic instrument and channel of communication to further foreign policy goals, depending on their economic and political influence within the centres of global power (Kapur, 2010; Rana, 2013). Such 'soft power resources' have become an important component in foreign policy priorities for Modi. He has underlined the need to further strengthen the linkages between India and its diaspora, as indicated in his various stage-managed 'town-hall' events in the US and the UK, full of razzmatazz, notably the 2014 mega show in New York's Madison Square Garden as well as the 2015 rally at London's Wembley Stadium, and most recently, the 'Howdy Modi' event in Houston with US President Trump in September 2019 (Yee, 2014; Addley, 2015; Paul, 2019). These carefully choreographed shows were very well attended and received wide media coverage. Such strategies are being deployed by India's government, in collaboration with increasingly globalizing Indian industries, to project India as an investment-friendly, pro-market democracy. Indian corporations, too, are keen to engage with the diasporic elites to further their own interests. One commentator described these as 'baby steps to develop a cohesive, strategic and institutionalized approach to the use of soft power' (Lahiri, 2017: 40).

As India's international profile has grown in recent decades, members of its diaspora are reconnecting with the homeland. Although Modi has prioritized engagement with the diaspora, he is benefitting from steps taken by his predecessors, especially Prime Minister Atal Behari Vajpayee, who headed the pro-business BJP-led coalition government in 1998. Vajpayee created the annual celebration *Pravasi Bharatiya Diwas* (Non-Resident Indian Day) on 9 January, symbolically chosen to mark the return of Mahatma Gandhi to India from South Africa in 1914 to lead the Indian nationalist movement. The phrase '*Vishwa Bharati*' (Global Indian) was also coined during Vajpayee's rule, when in 2004 a dedicated Ministry of Overseas Indian Affairs was set up. Though Modi's government has demoted it as a division within the Ministry of External Affairs (MEA), it did establish a *Pravasi Bharatiya Kendra* (NRI Centre) in India's capital in 2016 to provide an official 'home' for diasporic Indians, for conferences, events and conversations.

Cultural diplomacy has been a distinct element of the Modi government's global outreach. The Public Diplomacy Division within the MEA is involved in organizing soft-power related events abroad in collaboration with the Indian Council for Cultural Relations (ICCR), the government agency responsible for India's soft power projection that regularly organizes 'Festivals of India' around the world. One notable example was the India@UK 2017, celebrated to mark the 70th anniversary of India's independence – a public-private partnership promoting Indian arts and music, as well as India's creative and cultural industries, including a London version of the Jaipur Literary Festival (the world's largest literary festival in operation since 2006 and growing every year in terms of attendance and scope) in the British capital.

In addition, ICCR also promotes India's intellectual traditions. In 2019, the ICCR funded 69 Chairs of Indian Studies in universities around the world, as well as offering more than 3,400 scholarships for students to study in Indian universities. It also operates cultural centres globally, the most prominent being the Nehru Centre in London, which, since its establishment in 1992, has emerged 'as the premier institution engaged in India's cultural interface with UK', as its website states. Such government-run cultural centres – 36 in 2019 – also exist in other BRICS countries: the *Centro Cultural da Índia* in Sao Paulo, Brazil; the Jawaharlal Nehru Cultural Centre in Moscow; the Swami Vivekananda Cultural Centre in Beijing, and the Indian Cultural Centre in Johannesburg and Durban. Three other major centres are planned in Tel Aviv, Paris and Washington but the Parliamentary Committee on

Foreign Affairs noted in 2019 that the ICCR, whose job was 'to use soft power diplomacy', was slow in implementing government decisions. It concluded that there had been 'no progress during the last three years' and recommended that the centres should be 'equipped with credible human resources along with judicious allocation of funds' (Government of India, 2019: 50).

The soft power of Bollywood

The official 'Festivals of India' and cultural centres abroad that focus on India's traditional cultures have had limited success as they are perceived, accurately, as government-sponsored initiatives targeting a global elite. Much more effective in soft power terms is India's privately-owned and -run popular film industry – Bollywood – the world's largest film industry in terms of the number of films produced (Gehlawat, 2015). Indian movies are watched and enjoyed in large parts of the world, from the Middle East and North Africa to Central and Southeast Asia, although the largest overseas audience for them is the south Asian diaspora (Gera Roy, 2012; Schaefer and Karan, 2013; Swaminathan, 2017; Athique, 2019, among others).

In the context of the BRICS nations, apart from Brazil, Indian films have had a long-established relationship with Russia, China and South Africa, the latter through the diasporic connection. During the Cold War years, when Hollywood films were not easily available in the Soviet Union or China, Indian films were imported to provide the melodramatic escapism not offered by the often drab and dull state-propaganda films. Indian actor Raj Kapoor was extremely popular in the Soviet Union and his 1954 film *Awara* (Vagabond) was the most successful Indian film in the country and helped cement the Indo-Soviet relationship for decades afterwards. Kapoor's films were popular in Communist China as well and other Indian films were regularly imported for their socialist or progressive and often feel-good storylines. With the opening-up of the Chinese cinema market to Hollywood in the 1990s, Indian film imports declined substantially. However, in recent years, some Indian films have done very well in the Chinese market.

Since formally receiving the status of an industry by the Indian government in 2000, authorizing banks to provide loans to filmmakers and insurers to insure film financiers, the Indian film industry has become a source of export revenue, as well as an instrument for promoting India's soft power (Thussu, 2013; Swaminathan, 2017). This has also helped encourage foreign investors to engage with the Indian entertainment industry, resulting in growing investment from the telecom, software and media sectors. The ensuing corporatization and the synergies this created made it possible for Bollywood content to be available on multiple platforms – satellite, cable, online, mobile- and contribute to the creation of a globalized production, distribution and consumption system (Punathambekar, 2013). As a result, Indian film exports have grown steadily over the past two decades and industry estimates suggest that by 2018 the entertainment and media sector in India was worth $19 billion and was expected to increase as its markets further globalized (KPMG, 2019).

China is an important market for films and the successful performance of Indian films has the potential to contribute significantly in smoothing the relationship between the two BRICS partners. Appealing to Chinese audiences, Chinese actress Zhu Zhu was cast as the leading lady in the 2017 Bollywood film *Tubelight*, set against the backdrop of the 1962 India-China border war. This appeal has not gone unnoticed by Hollywood giants, who have expanded their involvement in India and set up joint ventures with Indian companies to enter the Indian market and indeed the global market for Indian cinema.

One notable example is Disney's 2016 Bollywood production *Dangal* starring Aamir Khan, which made $217 million in the international market, with China accounting for $178.3 million of this figure, making it the most successful Indian film internationally. The film was released in China in 2017 dubbed into Mandarin as *Shuajiao Baba* (Let's Wrestle, Dad!) and generated about five times its India earnings (Yau, 2018). Aamir Khan has a huge fan following among the Chinese youth – who call him *Mishu*, 'Uncle Aamir' in Chinese: on Sina-Weibo, Khan's official account had more than 1.2 million followers. As Table 11.1 demonstrates, Indian films are being watched by Chinese audiences, although very few Indian films are annually released in China because of the import quota system. Beyond box office figures, millions more watch the films through social media forums and there are many Bollywood-oriented social media groups on Chinese websites such as Douban and Baidu BBS (Bi, 2019).

Bollywood is also increasingly being watched not in theatres but on laptops and other mobile digital devices, with both Amazon Prime and Netflix having special rates for Indian films for the global audience. Yet the industry's growth continues to be limited by various factors, including a poor communication

TABLE 11.1 Bollywood in China

Film	Year of release	Box office revenue, in million yuan
Dangal	2017	1,300
Secret Superstar	2018	747
Andhadhun	2019	324
Bajrangi Bhaijaan	2018	283
Hindi Medium	2018	208
PK	2015	118
Mom	2019	111
Toilet-A Love Story	2018	94
Dhoom 3	2014	20
3 Idiots	2011	14

Source: Compiled from industry and media sources.

infrastructure as well as piracy, which accounts for a substantial annual loss of revenue (KPMG, 2019).

Communicating India

Unlike the entertainment industry, Indian news and current affairs continue to be largely domestically oriented and therefore absent in the global news arena. As a result, the capacity to communicate India's cultural attributes to a globalized audience is largely underdeveloped. Of the major countries with ambitions for a global role, India is the only one whose national broadcaster (*Doordarshan*) is not available in the major capitals of the world. Unlike non-English speaking countries such as China (CGTN), Russia (RT), Qatar (Al Jazeera English), Iran (Press TV) and Turkey (TRT-News), whose English-language 24/7 news networks are widely distributed around the world, the Indian viewpoint is notably missing in the global news sphere, at a time when news media are a key instrument of public diplomacy.

While India's English-language private news networks, such as NDTV 24x7, CNN-News 18, India Today TV, Republic TV, Times Now and WION (World is One News) are available globally, they have rarely ventured out of their diasporic constituencies. These networks do not appear to be interested in catering for an international news market. Instead, the international dimension of the commercial news channels functions primarily to reach the global diasporic Indian audience, who are perhaps more interested in coverage of India itself than in international affairs. For a nation with a developed model of journalism and one of the world's largest English-language news markets, it is ironic that Indian journalism is losing interest in the wider world at a time when Indian industry is increasingly globalizing and international engagement with India is growing across the globe. Although an external service of *Doordarshan*, DD World, was launched in 1995 – now called DD India – it has not made any impact either on diasporic audiences or among a more general international viewership. As a report about global *Doordarshan* has noted, 'Foreign policy is important and the world wants to know what the Indian government has to say on a wide range of issues. So far, India's foreign policy and its communication have been reticent' (Lakshman, 2014: 5).

Digital diplomacy

Despite Prime Minister Modi's penchant for managing media messages and his reputation as a formidable communicator, his government has done little to address the shortcomings in India's external communication strategy. Where television has failed, will the Internet succeed in communicating India's soft power? India's Ministry of External Affairs was one of the early adopters of social media platforms to connect with diasporic communities. Though MEA's twitter account @IndianDiplomacy was set up in 2010, since Modi took over in 2014 the Ministry has been using social media more effectively, promoting a positive cultural narrative for 'Brand India'. The MEA India Facebook page, created in 2012, is also widely followed in diplomatic and diasporic circles. It also maintains two You Tube channels (MEA India and Indian Diplomacy) and has accounts on various platforms, including Instagram, Soundcloud, Flickr, LinkedIn, as well as a Google+ channel. Such digital diplomacy has been spurred on by Modi's own considerable social media presence (Tandon, 2016). However, the deployment of diasporic and digital diplomatic resources do not alone make a country attractive on the world stage; these assets need to be translated into influencing the behaviour of other states and stakeholders, requiring a concerted effort by policy makers (Mukherjee, 2014).

The democratic dimension of India's soft power

One dimension of soft power that perhaps deserves greater emphasis, and so far has been generally overlooked is India's achievement in remaining 'the world's largest democracy'. India has an electorate of 900 million (larger than the combined number of voters in the US, Russia and Europe) and more than 100 registered political parties. This largely successful experience of democracy is unprecedented outside the 'democratic West'. India's democratic record is demonstrated by the election of Modi, the son of a *chaiwala* (tea seller) to the highest office in the land in 2014 and again in 2019 with a much wider margin, who is never shy of publicly extolling his very humble background. Such social mobility is coupled with a secular and federal political infrastructure that has been in place for seven decades and encompasses different ethnic, religious and linguistic interest groups.

India has proved wrong the dire predictions of many commentators at the time of independence from Britain in 1947 that a country mired in poverty, ignorance and illiteracy could not sustain a democratic system and would descend into autocratic dictatorship (Sen, 2005). The scale and scope of the Indian electoral process, which is more highly developed than some in Europe or the US (electronic voting machines were introduced in India as far back as 1982, years before any major Western democracy), offers opportunities for other developing countries to learn from the Indian experience, from understanding voter behaviour among a largely poor electorate to the importance of an independent and effective Election Commission. Beyond the electoral aspects of democracy, India also demonstrates that a unified nation state can function as a socially diverse, culturally plural, multilingual and multi-faith country. Such heterogeneity may be India's major strength in a globalized world, where the capacity to deal with diversity is likely to grow in importance (Thussu, 2013). However, the polity in India is being challenged by growing majoritarian nationalism as well as criminalization and commercialization of politics, features which undermine efforts to promote its global image (Vaishnav, 2017).

How effective is India's soft power?

Unlike China or Russia, India's soft power initiatives are not centrally managed by the government (Sinha-Palit, 2017). Indeed, the government takes a backseat, while India's creative and cultural industry, its religions and spirituality, as well as its active diaspora and commercial corporations help promote Indian interests abroad, a phenomenon likely to accelerate in a networked world. However, the intangible nature of soft power makes it hard, if not impossible, to measure. To increase India's soft power, especially among other developing nations, would require India's policymakers to seriously address the daily deprivation that millions of its citizens suffer. Images of India tend to highlight violence, inequality and the abuse of women, minorities and other disadvantaged sections of society.

Despite its impressive economic performance in the past two decades, India is still home to more poor people than the whole of Sub-Saharan Africa (Kohli, 2012; Drèze and Sen, 2013). On virtually every international index, India remains low in the ranking of nations: according to the UN-defined Human Development Index, India fared worst among its BRICS compatriots, ranking in 2018 at 129 out of total of 189 countries for which data was analysed (Human Development Report, 2019). Although in the past two decades the number of those in extreme poverty in democratic India has been significantly reduced by 300 million, its record pales in comparison with China, a one-party authoritarian state, which has been able to raise 700 million of its citizens out of extreme poverty. The exponents of India's soft power must consider why India's example of a multicultural democracy has not been generally appreciated by other developing countries, many of which view with admiration if not awe the Chinese model of development as worth emulating. India continues to be seen outside India as a nation of extreme poverty, social inequalities and communal strife. Yet India is a major donor to the least developed countries and, since 1964, the Indian Technical and Cooperation Programme has been a 'visible symbol of India's role and contribution to South-South cooperation' and one of the 'major pillars of India's soft power diplomacy' (Government of India, 2019: 245).

The Modi government's reluctance to engage more fully with India's 200 million Muslims – the world's largest minority – is driven by a populist Hindu nationalism. Its emphasis in promoting India's Buddhist and Hindu legacy is in striking contrast with its silence on the positive aspects of India's Islamic legacy: had British imperialism not divided India in 1947, it would have been the world's largest Muslim country in terms of population. The Islamic legacy – in terms of music, cuisine, language, arts and architecture – is intertwined in the cultural fabric of contemporary India (Ahmed, 2019). To exclude it from the national cultural narrative is likely to undermine India's soft power efforts, especially among the 50 Muslim-majority nations in the world with which India has deep cultural and commercial ties. In addition, a large proportion of Indian Muslims are poor and marginalized, especially in terms of gender discrimination. If India has to evolve into a developed country, it cannot afford to ignore, let alone antagonize, its largest minority. Modi's public diplomacy could focus instead on projecting India as home to a tolerant version of Islam, contributing to a 'dialogue' rather than 'clash' of civilizations.

Apart from ideological reasons, prompted by this majoritarian mindset, efforts to promote India's soft power are also hampered by the rather limited resource base of its diplomatic infrastructure: the country has fewer than 1,000 diplomats serving in 169 missions and consulates across the globe: in comparison the figure for China is 7,500. As one commentator has rightly observed, 'India's assets are countered by its considerable liabilities' (Kugiel, 2017: 157). One result of such an under-resourced diplomatic service is that India has thus far not succeeded in its long-standing demand for a permanent seat on the UN Security Council or a more recent request to the membership in the Nuclear Suppliers Group.

One way to deal with this structural problem is to encourage the commercial sector to participate in the policy arena, a pattern well-established in the US. Modi's outreach to private think tanks to project an Indian perspective on global affairs has been generally successful. The most significant manifestation of this public-private partnership is the annual Raisina Dialogue, which marked its fifth anniversary in 2020. Organized by the Ministry of External Affairs in collaboration with the Observer Research Foundation (ORF), India's leading think tank based in New Delhi, this has emerged as a major international event where an Indian perspective on global issues is discussed and debated. The ORF is also a crucial organization in terms of India's BRICS diplomacy, providing policy input and hosting events about BRICS-related issues. Other such collaborations include organizing events and conferences with the Gateway of India Dialogue, conducted with the Mumbai-based think-tank, Gateway House: Indian Council on Global Relations.

Although India has traditionally followed a non-aligned foreign policy, eschewing Cold War bloc politics, under Modi's leadership there has been an unmistakable shift towards the US, partly justified by the growing military, economic and cultural ties that bind the world's largest and its richest democracies (Narlikar, 2017). The bilateral trade between the two nations is worth over \$120 billion annually and the strong and vocal Indian diaspora makes the relationship multi-faceted. Modi's government has cooperated with the US in such areas as defence and intelligence sharing and in checking Chinese advances in South Asia and the Indian Ocean. Nevertheless, India is also keen to emphasize the multi-polarity of world power relationships. It has been suggested that 'India has not sacrificed one dimension of power for another but is in the midst of building up a comprehensive smart power strategy' (Kugiel, 2017: 57).

Beyond majoritarian considerations, Modi and his mandarins should recognize that India's soft power will only be effective internationally when the country is able to substantially reduce, if not eliminate, the pervasive and persistent poverty in which a majority of its citizens live. If this could be achieved within a multi-cultural and multi-lingual democracy, then India would indeed offer a new development model and, together with a more effective public diplomacy, its status as a major civilizational and economic power would receive due recognition around the world. Until this happens, as one commentator notes: 'India remains in a transitory phase where its hard power is yet to become preponderant even regionally to the point where it can meaningfully project its soft power in order to create a political environment conducive to its international goals' (Mukherjee, 2014: 55). Within the context of the BRICS group, India could deploy its considerable cultural power to follow the Buddhist idea of the *Madhya Marg* (the middle path), becoming a link between its BRICS partners China and Russia, and the Western world.

References

Addley, Esther (2015) Narendra Modi greeted by cheers and chants at Wembley reception. *The Guardian*, 13 November.

Ahmed, Hilal (2019) *Siyasi Muslims – A Story of Political Islams in India*. New Delhi:Viking.

Athique, Adrian (2019) Soft power, culture and modernity: responses to Bollywood films in Thailand and the Philippines. *International Communication Gazette*. 81(5): 470–489.

Bi, Mengying (2019) Bollywood films' popularity in China opening door for cultural exchange. *Global Times*, October 14, Available at www.globaltimes.cn/content/1166842.shtml

Chakravorty, Sanjoy, Kapur, Devesh and Singh, Nirvikar (2017) *The Other One Percent: Indians in America*. New York: Oxford University Press.

Chelyshev,Yevgeni and Litman, Alexei (1985) *Tradition of Great Friendship*. Moscow: Raduga Publishers.

Chung, Tan, Dev, Amiya, Bangwei, Wang and Liming, Wei (eds.) (2011) *Tagore and China*. New Delhi: Sage.

CII/PwC (2018) *Ayurveda 2.0: On the Cusp of Change*. New Delhi: The Confederation of Indian Industry and PricewaterhouseCoopers.

Doshi,Vidhi (2018) How ghee, turmeric and aloe vera became India's new instruments of soft power. *Washington Post*, January 29.

Drèze, Jean and Sen, Amartya (2013) *An Uncertain Glory: India and its Contradictions*. Princeton: Princeton University Press.

Gautam, Aavriti and Droogan, Julian (2018) Yoga soft power: how flexible is the posture? *The Journal of International Communication*, 24(1): 18–36.

Gehlawat, Ajay (2015) *Twenty-First Century Bollywood*. New York: Routledge.

Gera Roy, Anjali (ed.) (2012) *The Magic of Bollywood: At Home and Abroad*. New Delhi: Sage.

Government of India (2019) *Report of the Standing Committee on External Affairs (2018–19)*. New Delhi: Lok Sabha Secretariat, December.

Hegde, Radha and Sahoo, Ajaya (eds.) (2017) *Routledge Handbook of the Indian Diaspora*. New York: Routledge.

Human Development Report (2019) *Human Development Report 2019: Beyond Income, Beyond Averages, Beyond Today: Inequalities in Human Development in the 21st Century*. New York: United Nations Development Programme.

India Boundless (2017) *India Boundless – A Place in the Heart of the World*. New Delhi: Public Diplomacy Division, Ministry of External Affairs, produced by Wide Angle Films. August 15, Available at www.youtube.com/watch?v=hj60g06VQCk

India Foundation (2018) Focus: Soft power. *India Foundation Journal*, 7(2): 2–34. New Delhi: India Foundation.

IMF (2019) *World Economic Outlook*, April. Washington: International Monetary Fund.

Kapur, Davesh (2010) *Diaspora, Development, and Democracy: The Domestic Impact of International Migration from India*. Princeton: Princeton University Press.

Karnad, Bharat (2018) *Staggering Forward: Narendra Modi and India's Global Ambition*. New Delhi: Penguin.

Kohli, Atul (2012) *Poverty Amid Plenty in the New India.* Cambridge: Cambridge University Press.

KPMG Report (2019) *India's Digital Future: Mass of Niches- KPMG in India's Media and Entertainment Report 2019.* Mumbai: KPMG India, August.

Kugiel, Patryk (2017) *India's Soft Power: Foreign Policy Strategy.* London: Routledge.

Lahiri, Swaroopa (2017) Soft power – a major tool in Modi's foreign policy kit. *Journal of South Asian Studies,* 5(1): 39–47.

Lakshman, Nandini (2014) *Doordarshan Diplomacy.* Mumbai: Gateway House-Indian Council on Global Relations, Report No. 11, September.

Liming, Wei (2011) Historical significance of Tagore's 1924 China visit, pp. 13–43 in T. Chang, A. Dev, W. Bangwei and W. Liming (eds.) *Tagore and China.* New Delhi: Sage.

Martin, Peter (2015) Yoga diplomacy: Narendra Modi's soft power strategy. *Foreign Affairs.* January 25. Available at www.foreignaffairs.com/articles/india/2015-01-25/yoga-diplomacy

Mazumdar, Arijit (2018) India's soft power diplomacy under the Modi administration: Buddhism, diaspora and yoga. *Asian Affairs,* 49(3): 468–491.

Mookerji, Radha Kumud (1947) *Ancient Indian Education (Brahminical and Buddhist).* London: Macmillan.

Mukherjee, Rohan (2014) The false promise of India's soft power. *Geopolitics, History, and International Relations,* 6(1): 46–62.

Narlikar, Amrita (2017) India's role in global governance: a Modi-fication? *International Affairs,* 93(1): 93–111.

Nye, Joseph (2004) *Soft Power: The Means to Success in World Politics.* New York: Public Affairs.

Parel, Anthony (2016) *Pax Gandhiana: The Political Philosophy of Mahatma Gandhi.* New York: Oxford University Press.

Paul, Sonia (2019) 'Howdy, Modi!' was a display of Indian Americans' political power. *The Atlantic,* September 23.

Punathambekar, Aswin (2013) *From Bombay to Bollywood: The Making of a Global Media Industry.* New York: New York University Press.

Rana, Kishan (2013) Diaspora diplomacy and public diplomacy, pp. 70–84 in R. Zaharna, A. Arsenault and A. Fisher (eds.) *Relational, Networked and Collaborative Approaches to Public Diplomacy: The Connective Mindshift.* New York: Routledge.

Schaefer, David and Karan, Kavita (eds.) (2013) *Bollywood and Globalization: The Global Power of Popular Hindi Cinema.* London: Routledge.

Sen, Amartya (2005) *The Argumentative Indian.* London: Penguin.

Sen, Tansen (2003) *Buddhism, Diplomacy, and Trade: The Realignment of Sino-Indian Relations, 600–1400.* Honolulu: Association for Asian Studies and University of Hawai`i Press.

Sen, Tansen (2017) *India, China, and the World: A Connected History.* Lanham: Rowman and Littlefield.

Sinha-Palit, Parama (2017) *Analyzing China's Soft Power Strategy and Comparative Indian Initiatives.* New Delhi: Sage.

Swaminathan, Roopa (2017) *Bollywood Boom: India's Rise as a Soft Power.* New Delhi: Penguin.

Tandon, Aakriti (2016) Transforming the unbound elephant to the lovable Asian hulk: why is Modi leveraging India's soft power? *The Round Table: The Commonwealth Journal of International Affairs,* 105(1): 57–65.

Tharoor, Shashi (2008) India as a soft power. *India International Centre Quarterly,* 35(1): 32–45.

Tharoor, Shashi (2012) *Pax Indica: India and the World of the Twenty-first Century.* New Delhi: Penguin.

Thussu, Daya Kishan (2013) *Communicating India's Soft Power: Buddha to Bollywood*. New York: Palgrave-Macmillan.

Vaishnav, Milan (2017) *When Crime Pays: Money and Muscle in Indian Politics*. New Haven: Yale University Press.

Wujastyk, Dominik (2003) *The Roots of Ayurveda: Selections from Sanskrit Medical Writings*, translated with an Introduction and Notes by D. Wujastyk. London: Penguin.

Xinru, Liu (1988) *Ancient India and Ancient China: Trade and Religious Exchanges, AD 1–600*. New Delhi: Oxford University Press.

Yau, Elaine (2018) How Bollywood hit the mark in China. *South China Morning Post*, December 11.

Yee, Vivian (2014) At Madison Square Garden, chants, cheers and roars for Modi. *The New York Times*, September 29.

12

CHINA'S CULTURAL POWER RECONNECTS WITH THE WORLD

Ying Zhu and Michael Keane

China's so-called 'going global' strategy has evolved over the past two decades, from dispatching state-sanctioned messages via official domestic media organizations towards what is now a diverse multi-platform strategy, which makes use of commercial digital platforms. One key part of the 'going global' strategy is taking Chinese enterprise, investment and technology to the world, including the Asia-Pacific, Africa and, notably, to countries participating in the Belt and Road Initiative (BRI), China's outward-bound blueprint. A second part is a cultural strategy: to connect overseas audiences of non-Chinese origin in these countries to China's tradition and history. Residing among the overseas audiences are many persons of Chinese heritage. Thanks to the ubiquity of online platforms, the Chinese diaspora can be 'reconnected' with the homeland.

In this chapter, we look at the role played by digital media platforms to connect and, in many cases, reconnect audiences to the latest narrative of China's rise. We examine examples of Chinese media content that offer a new narrative of China, while challenging its effectiveness. The China that the Chinese diaspora now sees from the newly burnished online images is a prosperous modern nation with global cultural and economic ambition, under the control of a relatively stable one-party state. We contrast the success of China's outward-bound media industries in the global diaspora to its attempts to gain a strong cultural positioning in new territories.

The rise to power of Xi Jinping as paramount leader of the People's Republic of China (PRC) in 2012 came somewhat unexpectedly for many in the international community. Xi was one of several candidates positioned to run for the nation's top job, following the end of the Hu Jintao stewardship. That Xi was annointed should not come as a total surprise in hindsight, given his Communist Party blue blood lineage. His father was a leading general in the People's Liberation Army during the Communist Revolution. Xi's own cultivation of a cohort of followers while climbing the party ladder also helped his cause.

Following his appointment, Xi wasted little time creating and embellishing the profile of a charismatic and strong leader, which in part entailed the downgrading of the successes of his two immediate predecessors and linking his status with Mao Zedong (1949–1976). In fact, Xi's standing was elevated above that of Deng Xiaoping in political campaigns commemorating the 40th anniversary of reform and opening up. Though he initiated China's 'reform and opening-up' policy in the late 1970s, Deng is conspicuously absent from campaigns promoting Xi's thoughts: in effect, Deng's more liberal model for China is at odds with the current regime. Deng's achievements, notably with respect to depoliticizing everyday life, institutionalizing political succession, shunning leadership personality cults and setting an active but non-confrontational external stance, have all been reversed by Xi.

The chapter begins with a brief discussion of elements of power. While typologies of power, including hard, soft and smart power, contribute to public diplomacy (Nye, 2011), international relations, image management and public relations (see Kurlanitz, 2007; Creemers 2015; d'Hooghe, 2015; Hartig, 2016), an evaluation of this literature is beyond the scope of this chapter. Our focus in this chapter is on communications media and for this reason we discuss cultural soft power and, recognizing that cultural dissemination and consumption happens mostly online, we draw attention to 'digital power'.

In the first section, the chapter considers consumption of Chinese narrative content. Using the reception of Chinese cinema as a case in point, we argue that Chinese films are mostly playing to the already converted, to domestic audiences and those in the diaspora with access to online platforms. We look at the qualified success of two Chinese blockbusters, one a co-production, *The Great Wall* (directed by Zhang Yimou, 2016), and the other a propaganda-laden action movie, *Wolf Warrior 2* (directed by Jing Wu, 2017). The discussion also examines the uptake of Chinese television in the Asia-Pacific, a region where there are large Chinese-speaking audiences.

The chapter then turns to the question of digital power, how it changes the image of China globally and how digital platforms allow China to rapidly disseminate narrative content. The final section looks at where Chinese culture might venture next, asking if Eurasia, now increasingly mentioned within Chinese media and policy discourses under the auspices of the BRI, might constitute a new frontier.

Power and glory: the great rejuvenation

While Chinese culture is going to the world, thanks largely to the money being poured into the cause by the Chinese government, its reception is muted in the 'liberal' West. Despite the efforts of China's propagandists to garner positive coverage in overseas media, to promote what the state now calls Chinese 'discourse power' and, in doing so, to extend the idea that China is a harmonious open society, Chinese film and television industries have not 'gone global'. In fact, Chinese media content has achieved limited success in most international markets due mainly to perceptions that its narratives are tainted by its authoritarian political system and diminished by the spectre of censorship. China thus encounters what has been called a 'cultural trade deficit' (Keane, 2007) in areas that are conspicuous to mostly younger audiences, namely the content industries. In other words, the attraction of foreign media in China is greater than the consumption of Chinese media outside China. Rectifying this imbalance remains a problem.

Before engaging with the fate of the content industries, however, let us briefly consider a 'new world order', one in which China plays a leading role. There has been no shortage of opinion on this topic, with the Singaporean ex-diplomat Kishore Mahbubani a prominent critic of Western hubris (Mahbubani, 2018). Certainly, with Donald Trump's retreat from a rules-based world order enshrined in neoliberalism, the US's global role – and its global presence – is undergoing revision. Meanwhile, in the sphere of power and influence, China has stepped up to the plate. Power – and changing perceptions of national power – is the currency of today's world, and as we will show, this theme is reflected in big-budget blockbusters.

Xi Jinping's presence as a powerful leader is enhanced by China's massive economic growth since the nation opened its doors to foreign investment in 1978. China joined the World Trade Organization (WTO) in 2001, then the world's largest trade cartel. While China was always a large landmass, it has also become a 'big nation' (*daguo*), part of the global community. China accepted the condition of market opening for the trade-off of greater access to foreign technologies and know-how. During Hu Jintao's tenure as leader (2002–2012), national rejuvenation, a theme initially articulated during the economic reform era, moved centre stage among Beijing's policy elites. China's 'peaceful rise' was unveiled in the early 2000s as a counterpoint to Western colonialism and hegemony.

Already the concept of 'great power' had produced a range of scholarly treatises (Kennedy, 1987; Layne, 1993; Iriye, 1995). In the sixteenth and seventeenth centuries, European 'great powers' colonized the New World and propagated ideas, many of them about Christianity, in the global South and then in East Asia. In 2004, a major CCTV documentary was commissioned, the 'rise of the great powers' (Zhu, 2012). Lessons could be learnt from history and China would now advance, showing the world the wonders of its great civilization, albeit without imposing a religious tradition. In the rhetoric emanating from Beijing, China would advance a 'community of shared destiny' (*renlei mingyun gongtongti*).

Most prominent of all power slogans emanating from Beijing, however, is the 'great rejuvenation' (*weida fuxing*), coincidentally the name of a book authored by Xi Jinping, which is readily available for foreigners, translated into English on Amazon. com. More than just a 'big nation' China intends to be a strong nation (*qiangguo*) (Zheng, 2005). Xi's think tanks have opted for 'cultural empowerment' (*wenhua qiangguo*). The cultural empowerment discourse contains a number of elements, which will become evident in this chapter. The most relevant theme for our discussion, however, pertains to 'going out' (*zou chuqu*), specifically the internationalization of China's culture and ideas. In the words of Xi Jinping, China needs to 'tell its story well' (Bandurski, 2017). In the sphere of journalism, China's message is going out; it is reaching the eyes and ears of audiences in places where China has provided substantial economic aid, and where governments are reluctant to criticize China. The question remains as to how engaged these audiences are, how they view China's influence, and how they might respond to a 'community of shared destiny'.

China has an unprecedented presence globally: China-made products abound and Chinese tourists can be observed in increasing numbers all over the world. Despite its economic presence and its considerable political clout in the United Nations, expert opinion is divided as to the reality of China's global power. Susan Shirk (2008) has called China a 'fragile superpower'; David Shambaugh opts for 'partial power' (Shambaugh, 2013). Writing about China's rise to power, Jae Ho Chung (2015) notes three positions: the Confident School (China's rise is irreversible); the Pessimist School (China's rise is likely to falter); and the Not yet/Uncertain School (too early to say). Many agree on the inter-dependence between hard power, which arises from military and economic power, and soft power.

Soft power becomes cultural power

Many accounts have appropriated 'soft power' to depict China's political development and overseas expansion over the past decade (Kurlantzick, 2007; Yan and Xu, 2008; Li, 2009; Sun, 2010; Barr, 2011; Zhao, 2013). The genesis of the concept references Joseph Nye, the American political scientist, who coined the term in 1990 (Nye, 1990). Nye said that the soft power of a country rests on three resources: a country's culture, its political values and its foreign policies. Soft power has become an oft-cited indicator of cultural influence in Asia (McCray, 2002; Ding, 2008; Chua, 2012; Jin, 2016; Chitty *et al.*, 2017). What distinguishes China's soft power from global discourses is the emphasis placed on culture. At the 17th National Congress of the CCP in October 2007, then-President Hu Jintao said that '[c]ulture has become an increasingly important source of national cohesion and creativity …'. In 2011, a year before handing over to Xi Jinping, he reiterated, 'in international terms, where competition and comprehensive national power is a notable characteristic, the positions and function of culture are even more prominent, so that when major great powers have a prominent strategy of advancing cultural soft power so as to strengthen national core competitive power' (Hu, 2011). Significantly, in this address the turn to cultural empowerment was evident.

Of course, China's media has received a share of scholarly coverage under the rubric of soft power. Accounts are mostly in the field of public diplomacy, following the lead of Nye's work and are largely confined to journalism and public broadcasting (Sun, 2010; Zhang, 2011; Thussu *et al.*, 2018). With few exceptions, accounts of China's media going out follow Nye's 'resource' model of soft power, essentially a model of transmission, one that largely fails to adequately account for actual engagement, i.e. consumption. In most accounts, one hears about the government charm offensives, the increase in overseas channels and subscribers, and the number of online hits of Chinese language websites. However, a lack of robust and verifiable data exists in relation to consumption.

Culture is and always has been a key area of concern in China. Efforts to shore up China's reputation as a culturally influential nation have led to little success and thus there has been a great deal of consternation in government circles over the past two decades. China's cultural trade deficit became evident following ascension to the WTO, leading to animated debates about cultural security (*wenhua anquan*). Arguably, China has no urgent need to win over global audiences from a profit standpoint as the PRC domestic market is big enough. The issue is more about the ability to tell its stories on its own terms abroad; in other words, to correct what China sees as negative stereotypes of Chinese people and Chinese culture. Cultural empires need effective public diplomacy to buttress and sustain their appeal.

As Japanese and South Korean content built its presence in China in the 1990s and 2000s, initially via animation and later via television drama, film, fashion and games, Chinese think tankers went searching for a solution. It was concluded that these small powers were tapping into modern forms of culture, while carefully mining traditional sources. China needed a strategy that signified its cultural superiority by elevating its own tradition. The result was 'cultural empowerment' (*wenhua qiangguo*), a theme that fitted neatly with Chinese nascent dreams of national rejuvenation, which rests upon confidence in the nation's cultural heritage. China's cultural appeal was thus central to its global competitive strategy.

Under Xi Jinping, China's self-annointed story teller (Bandurski, 2017), 'cultural self-confidence' (*wenhua zixin*) has become a key idea. It has featured heavily in reports published in the Chinese Academy of the Social Sciences' 'Blue Books'. A 2017 Chinese Communist Party think-tank text, entitled *The Chinese Logic of the Construction of Cultural Power*, notes how Xi Jinping 'utilized a series of new values, new ideology, new judgements, to further respond to the question confronting the Chinese people at this point in history: why and how to construct a socialist strong cultural power …' (Shen, 2017). While Party intellectuals churn out the rhetoric and allies of China extol the virtues of a 'civilizational state' (Jacques, 2009), the task of making Chinese culture relevant to the world falls to screenwriters, directors and the producers of narrative content.

The strong nation: narrative forms of cultural power

Film is an obvious candidate for branding a nation and exemplifying a nation's power, and Hollywood has long played a role in showcasing US political and cultural power abroad (Zhu, 2017). China, too, has enlisted its film industry into doing its power bidding overseas. Yet the result has not been particularly encouraging. Leaving aside the occasional critical hit by a few leading filmmakers in the art film and festival circuit, reception outside China is underwhelming.

Zhang Yimou's much vaunted co-production *The Great Wall*, which some thought might garner an Academy Award nomination, received moderate ratings of 6/10 on IMDB, and even less, 35 per cent, on the Rotten Tomatoes site. The rating on Douban, the Chinese online rating site, was a disappointing 5.4/10 (Qin, 2016). Following its opening week, *The Hollywood Reporter* found lessons for

Sino-American productions: in particular 'the difficulties of finding stories that meld Eastern and Western characters and the challenges of blending crews, which in Wall's case meant hiring 100 interpreters and solving conflicts that allegedly took place among some below-the-line workers' (McClintock, 2017). The film grossed only $34.8 million in North America. In South Korea, the box-office takings were less than $4 million.[1]

As Coonan *et al.* (2017) noted in their *China File* discussion, *The Great Wall* is a Sino-Hollywood co-production run amok. Spectacularly made with the director's trademark of scale, order, colour, light and rhythm, the film suffers from anaemic character and story development. Burdened with a Chinese nationalist fantasy that displays Chinese military might and pageantry at its most excessive, the film leaves little room for sophisticated characters and human drama. Dwarfed by the gigantic Great Wall, the gunpowder-crazed European mercenaries appear dumbfounded by the enormity of China and Chinese culture. They are, in time, taught a moral lesson by the righteous Chinese female commander on fighting for trust and honour instead of gunpowder. The hackneyed narrative fits the myth of Western barbarians being tamed and enlightened by Chinese civilization. It is as if the entire Western canon of medieval adventures did not exist. The film is a reminder that big budgets, star power and excessive visual effects do not magically translate into compelling stories, Hollywood or Chinese. The film did little for Chinese soft power but it did make money, grossing $334 million worldwide against its $150 million production budget.

Then came the mega blockbuster *Wolf Warrior 2*, featuring a renowned kung-fu master. While breaking domestic box-office records for Chinese cinema, it bombed in South Korea, although this rejection may have been partly a result of political disputes associated with the crisis of 2016–2017 generated by the deployment of US THAAD (Terminal High Altitude Area Defense) missiles to South Korea, despite strong opposition from Beijing. It also failed dismally to engage foreign critics, thanks to an implausible narrative that sees the Chinese hero, Leng Feng beat up the bad guys, while rescuing both African locals and Chinese nationals. He even uses his smartphone (Chinese technological superiority) to record terrorist atrocities and transmit location details to the Chinese navy, which then launches a precision-guided missile, which seems more like a parody of the Rambo franchises to foreign viewers: wrote film critic Roger Ebert, '*Wolf Warrior 2* is for anyone who wishes more modern action movies were like bad *Rambo* rip-offs, only minus Stallone's charms, and amplified by Michael Bay-levels of soul-dead military/gun fetishism'.[2]

Television provides another useful benchmark for audio-visual exports. Zhu (2012) details the international ambitions of China's national television broadcaster, China Central Television (CCTV). Its recent incarnation China Global Television Network (CGTN), reaches out to the world in English (as well as in other major international languages: Spanish, French, Russian and Arabic), and CCTV channels are accessible in international hotel chains. Many Chinese tourists use these hotels and it is no doubt reassuring to see familiar voices on the screen together with the echoes of national propaganda. However, despite the tie-ins with hotel chains, the influence of Chinese television among foreign audiences is not increasing. Li Huailiang (2016), an expert on China's foreign cultural trade, points out that uniformity in content and over-concentration in certain markets in Asia such as Singapore, Hong Kong and Taiwan are two big issues for growth potential, as most growth has occurred in these places, where TV drama sales have constituted the bulk of the market.

Chinese television has been most successful in Asia, capitalizing on an interest in historical re-enactments. State data on official sales of Chinese television programmes from 2008 to 2016 clearly show the challenges of breaking into non-Asian markets. The Taiwanese market, where Mandarin is spoken, remains the strongest performer, while there has been growth in Japan and South Korea. But European, African and US markets have not shown growth: between 2008 and 2016, sales of TV programmes (all genres) to Europe remained low, as was the case in US and African markets. In 2008, sales of TV programmes in Europe were \$2.53 million, in the US \$1.64 million and in Africa \$0.41 million. In 2016, the numbers were \$2.90, \$2.03 and \$0.36 million, respectively.[3]

The Asian content-streaming site, Viki, which is headquartered in San Francisco, offers a limited buffet of Chinese content; elsewhere content is accessible with digital subscription services using set-top boxes (modems). When Netflix entered in an association with iQIYI in 2015 and reformatted the successful serial *Empresses in the Palace* for their international audiences, the response was underwhelming. The problem was twofold; first, most Chinese-speaking audiences had already seen the original 76-episode version; second, the reformatted version (six 90-minute episodes) left out a lot of the story, perhaps to make it more palatable for Western audiences. While the complexity of the story and its allusions to contemporary society were attractive to Chinese mainlanders and people with significant Chinese cultural literacy, such subtleties were lost in translation and in the process of reformatting for Netflix consumption. Adding to cultural dissonance is the omnipresent reality of propaganda.

What is evident in these examples, however, is that Chinese content plays well to Chinese-language audiences and there are large numbers of these scattered globally. Digital platforms have made access and reception easier. For many people who left China when television and movies were lacklustre in content and characterized by excessive government propaganda, recent productions, including reality television formats, show China in a different light. The modernization of Chinese film and television, therefore, has led many overseas Chinese to reconnect to the nation (Keane, 2016). In this regard, digital platforms represent a new mode of Chinese cultural power.

The strong nation: digital cultural power rising

Significantly, the rhetoric of cultural empowerment following Xi Jinping's rise to the Party presidency marked a period in which China rapidly upgraded its online network capabilities, leading to the launch of the Internet+ development blueprint in 2015 and the inclusion of the digital creative industries in the 13th Five Year Plan.[4] The government's active encouragement of the digital economy, notably via the slogan 'mass entrepreneurship, mass innovation' (*dazhong chuangye, wanzhong chuangxin*) signalled to the world that China is a connected nation, both domestically and internationally.

Chinese people's take-up of digital affordances and low-cost production technologies have led to an unprecedented abundance of media content, both domestic and imported (Keane, 2016). In addition, there is a belief that new distribution channels will take Chinese-made content to a wider audience of admirers, not just those in the Asian region or the faithful in the diaspora. In this sense, the older model of soft power, in which Confucius Institutes, CCTV channels and overseas delegations were designated national cultural flagbearers fades somewhat; the digital distribution model is contingent on the power of platforms, which allow instantaneous sharing and frequent downloading of content. Digital power engages Chinese speakers and persons of Chinese ethnic origin around the globe; they are connected to the motherland, the home nation, by digital resources.

Notwithstanding its limited global appeal in the global Internet ecosystem, China has more people online than any other nation. In 2018, China had more than one billion Internet users and, according to industry accounts, this figure is projected to grow to 1.14 billion by 2022.[5] In this sense the term 'digital power' becomes relevant. Online distribution has transformed the media industry in China largely thanks to improvements in video compression technologies and the state-supported provision of fast broadband, making personal viewing – and sharing – of content on mobile phones, computer terminals and tablets a viable and popular option. The Internet has been a game changer, not only for traditional (state-owned) media industries but for commercial media companies, consumers and regulators. In effect, the technological capacity to express and compress words, images and sound in digital form has transformed the costs of making and transmitting culture, the kinds of skill-sets that are valued in the market, the relationship between professionals and amateurs, as well as the formats and genres that (online) consumers now anticipate.

While the Western hemisphere is dominated by Facebook, Amazon, Netflix and Google (FANG), China and Chinese speakers are connected by BAT. The B of BAT is Baidu: its most popular content platform is iQIYI, an entertainment distribution platform that was acquired in 2013. Like its US competitor Netflix, iQIYI provides users with direct portals to all its video programmes available on the Internet. iQIYI's video search 'brain' utilizes algorithms, arguably providing its audience with the most accurate recommendations. Youku Tudou, now owned by Alibaba (the 'A'), represents a combination of professionally generated content, user-generated content and self-made content. After acquisition of its majority shareholding by the Alibaba group in 2012, Youku Tudou was able to integrate enormous online resources to a single platform, and set up the biggest video search engine – Souku, while having China's largest e-commerce company as its parent company. The final member of BAT is Tencent, which is developing what it calls a pan-entertainment ecosystem. Judging from its scale in overseas collaborative partnerships with HBO, Time Warner and Paramount, it is establishing a super-media platform that will place it at the top of the pyramid.

However, a recent report on domestic consumption of media content in China attests to little or limited international 'connection'. In a *New York Times* article entitled 'A Generation Grows Up in China Without Google, Facebook or Twitter', Wen Shengjian, a 14-year-old boy in China told the reporter that he knew the names of Google, Facebook, Twitter and Instagram but had no use for them (Yuan, 2018). An 18-year-old young man from a southern Chinese city of Liuzhou is a fan of basketball, hip-hop music and Hollywood superhero movies and plans to study chemistry in Canada but has never heard of Google or Twitter. China's 'blockade' in the past decade of Google, Facebook, Twitter, Instagram, the *New York Times*, to name a few, has led to a generation of Chinese growing up unconcerned about being connected virtually to a world outside of what is permissible by the party's censorship apparatus. Beijing's Internet regulator, the Cyber Administration of China, shut down or revoked the licences of more than 3,000 websites it deemed inappropriate for Chinese users. Complacency and aversion to politics might be at work here but being exposed to only homegrown apps and online services has led to a generation of youth who appears 'uninterested in knowing what has been censored online, allowing Beijing to build an alternative value system that competes with Western liberal democracy' (ibid.).

Beyond the kingdom known as BAT are new contenders, most notably Bytedance, which relies on AI technologies (algorithms) to learn individual preferences for targeted recommendation of news and other content, as well as targeted ads and offers; it also uses AI to help content creators and curators to craft viral videos. Founded in 2012, the company launched Douyin in 2016 and its international version, TikTok in the following year. In 2020, TikTok exploded in a global scale. The irony is that most international users are unaware that this playful video sharing app is owned by a Chinese company, which restricts content topics for people in the PRC, while allowing its international version to flirt with licentious and even litigious content (Li, 2019). Within China, Douyin has been contributing to the great rejuvenation by encouraging its users to generate 'positive energy' (*zheng nengliang*), while exuding 'transcendental Chinese patriotism' (Du, 2014: 5; also see Xu *et al.*, 2020).

Though Chinese apps have 'gone viral' abroad, Chinese cultural and entertainment content remains domestically bound, with little traction beyond China. The draconian Chinese government policy that compulsively vets content and reduces content to a mere echo chamber for Party directives remains one of the major obstacles towards making Chinese content appealing globally. Nevertheless, numerous reports are conducted in China each year about why China's cultural power is not as potent as Hollywood's. The blame is usually laid on a misunderstanding by audiences and producers alike; in other words, foreigners don't understand China and are unable to appreciate its culture; and Chinese producers don't understand foreigners' tastes. The elephant in the room left unaddressed is government censorship.

Cultural power and the 'Digital Silk Road'

The chapter so far has considered problems facing China's media and cultural industries as they attempt to break into global markets. In the past, success in Western markets has been much sought after. While Ang Lee has tasted success in Hollywood, an academy award for a 'Chinese film' would be a great soft power achievement for Beijing. *The Great Wall* was touted as a contender; yet the prize now seems so far away. Southeast Asian markets like Singapore, Thailand and Indonesia are likewise hard to conquer, thanks to the popularity there of South Korean and Japanese media.

The solution, however, may be closer to home. Digital platforms, while having a global reach, are creating opportunities in Africa and Central Asia. Chinese media penetration in Africa has been the subject of a number of recent studies and reports (Marsh, 2018; Lim and Bergin, 2018; Xiang, 2018), although no clear or compelling evidence is available to show a deep yearning across Africa for Chinese narrative content. Vivien Marsh (2018) has looked at the challenges of CGTN English language news services in Africa and the concept of promoting 'constructive journalism'. China's intervention endeavours to show a more positive light on African development, reflecting a Chinese traditional model of governance known as '*tianxia*' – all under heaven. Similarly, the expansion of CGTN into Africa disseminates stories approved by Beijing that resonate with the image of a benevolent China.

Established in 2016, CGTN is free in many parts of Africa thanks to a distribution deal with *StarTimes*, a Chinese digital media provider with strong links to the state (Lim and Bergin, 2018). In May 2017, a news report published in both the *People's Daily* and the English language *China Daily* quoted the CEO of StarTimes, Zhang Junqi, who was addressing an audience in Beijing attending the 7th Africa Digital Television Seminar. Zhang spoke of African people's love of Chinese television dramas. The same news report even quoted a local Tanzanian villager who said 'that without the help of Chinese enterprises, he and his fellow villagers couldn't afford to watch all the programmes they enjoy' (*China Daily*, 2017). The report noted that *StarTimes* had accrued ten million subscribers in Africa since 2007. While a significant number, it's somewhat difficult to equate availability of content with engagement. The same credibility problem bedevils the *China Daily*, between 200,000 and 900,000 copies of this mouthpiece of the CCP are distributed globally (Hartig, 2018).

When one considers nations situated on China's periphery, there is potential to build audiences. China's ambitious development project, the BRI, was unveiled in 2013 in Kazakhstan by Xi Jinping. The BRI aims to connect Asia, Europe and Africa along five routes. The Silk Road Economic Belt focuses on linking China to Europe through Central Asia and Russia, connecting China with the Middle East through Central Asia, and bringing together China and Southeast Asia, South Asia and the Indian Ocean. The twenty-first century Maritime Silk Road, meanwhile, focuses on using Chinese coastal ports to link China with Europe through the South China Sea and Indian Ocean, and connect China with the South Pacific

Ocean through the South China Sea. The BRI now embraces nearly 100 countries; many of these nation-states are located in central Asia. While ideas travelled along the Silk Road for centuries, broadband now connects people. Digital devices offer ways to consume film, television, and online media. Chinese companies, including Huawei and ZTE, Xiaomi, Alibaba and Tencent are moving westwards, providing the connections that are needed. The so-called Digital Silk Roads thus provides China with a way to extend its influence.

In March 2018, Alibaba sponsored an 11-day training programme in Hangzhou for 37 young entrepreneurs from seven BRI countries (Malaysia, Thailand, Indonesia, Pakistan, Cambodia, the Philippines and Vietnam) on e-commerce, technological and business innovations (Bai, 2018). Similar efforts were taken by another Chinese tech giant, Huawei, in November 2017, when it sponsored the First Central Asian Innovation Day in Astana, Kazakhstan, announcing the theme 'Explore the New Digital Silk Road'. The conjecture is that if more people in this region use communication platforms or services that are owned, controlled, serviced, or invested in by Chinese companies, China's cultural power can be extended. The region is strategic and culture is therefore a strategic force. A large film and television production centre has been established in the new city of Horgos, situated in China's Xinjiang Uighur autonomous region, close to the border of Kazakhstan and thousands of production companies have set up business there.

China's ambitions in the BRI are strategic and economic. However, as noted by Marsh in the case of Africa, once again we see the traditional concept of 'all under heaven' (*tianxia*) embodied in the extension of cultural power. Xi Jinping has called for the 'construction' of a 'community of shared destiny' (*renleimingyungongtongti*) in the region. What this entails is unclear and there are risks in imposing a secular Chinese model of social governance in a region where religions and cultures have collided for centuries. Ostensibly packaged as a form of cosmopolitanism for our age, the 'community of shared future' is reflected in films like *Wolf Warrior 2*, where Chinese heroes save African brothers and sisters, and television dramas such as *Legends of the Silk Roads* (2015), where Uighurs and Han Chinese interact peacefully. The propagation of Chinese content is therefore intended to espouse Chinese values of standing up against the imperial powers, helping others in developed countries and 'nationalities' living harmoniously. Is China succeeding in its public relation's campaign? In examining the CCP's attempts to improve China's image around the world since Xi Jinping came to power in 2012, a new volume, *Soft Power with Chinese Characteristics: China's Campaign for Hearts and Minds* (Edney, Rosen and Zhu, 2020) paints a picture of a Chinese leadership that is often struggling to convert material resources into genuine international affections.

Notes

1 www.the-numbers.com/movie/Great-Wall-The/South-Korea#tab=summary
2 www.rogerebert.com/reviews/wolf-warrior-2-2017
3 www.stats.gov.cn/tjsj/ndsj/2017/indexch.htm; (Keane, 2015:70–71)

4 For China's Five Year Plan see http://en.ndrc.gov.cn/newsrelease/201612/P02016120
 7645765233498.pdf
5 www.statista.com/statistics/278417/number-of-Internet-users-in-china/

References

Bai, Yunyi (2018) tianmaoshuangshiyituidongdongnanyashehuikejibiange [Tmall Double 11 promote social-technological evolution in Southeast Asia]. *Global Times*, 14 November.

Bandurski, David (2017) The fable of the master storyteller. *Media Beat*. The China Media Project. Available at http://chinamediaproject.org/2017/09/29/the-fable-of-the-master-storyteller/

Barr, Michael (2011) *Who's Afraid of China: The Challenge of Chinese Soft Power*. London: Zed Books.

China Daily (2017) Chinese TV series become a hit in Africa. *China Daily*, 28 May. Available at www.chinadaily.com.cn/travel/2017-05/28/content_29536377.htm

Chitty, Naren, Li, Ji, Rawnsley, Gary and Hayden, Craig (eds.) (2017) *The Routledge Handbook of Soft Power*. London: Routledge.

Chua, Beng-Huat (2012) *Structure, Audience and Soft Power in East Asian Pop Culture*. Hong Kong: HKU Press.

Chung, Jae Ho (ed.) (2015) *Assessing China's Power*. London: Palgrave Macmillan.

Coonan, Clifford, Zhu, Ying, Rosen, Stanley and Landreth, Jonathan (2017) Is the search for a China-Hollywood blockbuster doomed? *Foreign Policy*, February 24.

Creemers, Rogier (2015) Never the twain shall meet? Rethinking China's public diplomacy policy. *Chinese Journal of Communication*, 8(3): 306–322.

d'Hooghe, Ingrid (2015) *China's Public Diplomacy*. Leiden: Brill.

Ding, Sheng (2008) *The Dragon's Hidden Wings: How China Rises with its Soft Power*. Lanham: Lexington Books.

Du, Shanshan (2014) Social media and the transformation of 'Chinese nationalism': 'Igniting positive energy' in China since the 2012 London Olympics. *Anthropology Today*, 30(1): 5–8.

Edney, Kingsley, Rosen, Stanley and Zhu, Ying (eds.) (2020) *Soft Power with Chinese Characteristics: China's Campaign for Hearts and Minds*. London: Routledge.

Hartig, Falk (2016) *Chinese Public Diplomacy: The Rise of the Confucius Institute*. New York: Routledge.

Hartig, Falk (2018) *China Daily*-Beijing's global voice, pp. 122–140 in D. K. Thussu, H. De Burgh and A. Shi (eds.) *China's Media Go Global*. London: Routledge.

Hu, Jintao (2011) jianding buyi xzou zhongguo tese shehui zhuyi wenhua fazhan daolu, nulijianshe shehui zhuyi wenhua qiangguo [The path of cultural development of socialism with Chinese characteristics must go with making efforts to make China a strong socialist nation] qiushililun wang, October 18. Available at www.qstheory.cn/zywz/201201/t20120101_133218.htm.

Iriye, Akiri (1995) Japan's drive to great power status, pp. 268–329 in M. Jensen (ed.) *The Emergence of Meiji Japan*. Cambridge: Cambridge University Press.

Jacques, Martin (2009) *When China Rules the World: The Rise of the Middle Kingdom and the End of the Western World*. London: Penguin.

Jin, Dal Yong (2016) *New Korean Wave: Transnational Cultural Power in the Age of Social Media*. Urbana: University of Illinois Press.

Keane, Michael (2007) *Created in China: The Great New Leap Forward*. London: Routledge.

Keane, Michael (2015) *The Chinese Television Industry*. London: Palgrave.

Keane, Michael (2016) Disconnecting, connecting, reconnecting: How Chinese television got out of the box. *International Journal of Communication*, 10: 5426–5443.

Kennedy, Paul (1987) *The Rise and Fall of the Great Powers*. New York: Random House.

Kurlantzick, Joseph (2007) *Charm Offensive: How China's Soft Power is Transforming the World*. New Haven: Yale University Press.

Layne, Christopher (1993) Why new great powers rise. *International Security*, 17(4): 5–51.

Li, Minjiang (2009) *Soft Power: China's Emerging Strategy in International Politics*. Lanham MD: Rowman and Littlefield.

Li, Huailiang (2016) Chinese culture 'going out': an overview of government policies and an analysis of challenges and opportunities for international collaboration, pp. 129–143 in M. Keane (ed.) *The Handbook of Cultural and Creative Industries in China*. Cheltenham: Edward Elgar.

Li, Luzhou (2019) *Zoning China: Online Video, Popular Culture and the State*. Cambridge: MIT Press.

Lim, Louisa and Bergin, Julia (2018) Inside China's global propaganda plan. *The Guardian*, 7 December.

Mahbubani, Kishore (2018) *Has the West Lost It?: A Provocation*. London: Penguin.

McClintock, Pamela (2017) Matt Damon's 'The Great Wall' to lose $75 million: future of US-Sino co-productions in doubt. *The Hollywood Reporter*, 3 February. Available at www. hollywoodreporter.com/news/what-great-walls-box-office-flop-will-cost-studios-981602

McGray, Douglas (2002) Japan's Gross National Cool. *Foreign Policy*, May-June: 44–54.

Marsh, Vivien (2018) Tiangao or tianxia: the ambiguities of CCTV English language news for Africa, pp. 103–121 in D. K. Thussu, H. De Burgh and A. Shi (eds.) *China's Media Go Global*. London: Routledge.

Nye, Joseph (1990) *Bound to Lead: The Changing Nature of American Power*. New York: Basic Books.

Nye, Joseph (2011) Smart power. *The Huffington Post*, 25 May.

Qin, Amy (2016) The Great Wall: what filmgoers and critics are saying. *New York Times*, 16 December.

Shambaugh, David (2013) *China Goes Global: The Partial Power*. New York: Oxford University Press.

Shen, Zhuanghai (2017) *The Chinese Logic of the Construction of Cultural Power* (wenhuaqiangguojianshe de Zhongguoluoji). Beijing: Peoples' Publishing House.

Shirk, Susan (2008) *China: Fragile Superpower*. Oxford: Oxford University Press.

Sun, Wanning (2010) Mission impossible? Soft power, communication capacity, and the globalization of Chinese media. *International Journal of Communication*, 4: 54–72.

Thussu, Daya Kishan, de Burgh, Hugo and Shi, Anbin (eds.) (2018) *China's Media Go Global*. London: Routledge.

Wang, Kaihao (2018) Survey shows Chinese movies gain ground in North America. *China Daily*, 15 May.

Xiang, Yu (2018) China in Africa: refiguring centre-periphery media dynamics, pp. 213–229 in D. K. Thussu, H. De Burgh and A. Shi (eds.) *China's Media Go Global*. London: Routledge.

Xu, Chen, Kaye, D. B. V. and Zeng, Jing (2020) #*PositiveEnergy*Douyin: constructing 'playful patriotism' in a Chinese short-video application. *Chinese Journal of Communication*, DOI: 10.1080/17544750.2020.1761848

Yan, Xuetong and Xu, Jin (2008) zhongmeiruanshilibijiao [The comparison of the US and China's soft power and its implications for China] *Shijiejingjiyuzhengzhi (World Economics and Politics)* 7: 21–27.

Yuan, Li (2018) A generation grows up in China without Google, Facebook or Twitter. *New York Times*, August 6. Available at www.nytimes.com/2018/08/06/technology/china-generation-blocked-internet.html

Zhang, Xiaoling (2011) China's international broadcasting: a case study of CCTV International, pp. 37–71 in J. Wang (ed.) *Soft Power in China: Public Diplomacy through Communication*. New York: Palgrave.

Zhao, Yuezhi (2013) China's quest for 'soft power': imperatives, impediments and irreconcilable tensions? *Javnost – The Public*, 2 (4): 17–29.

Zheng, Bijian (2005) China's peaceful rise to great power status. *Foreign Affairs* 84(5): 18–24.

Zhu, Ying (2012) *Two Billion Eyes: The Story of China Central Television*. New York: The New Press.

Zhu, Ying (2017) Film as soft power and hard currency: The Sino-Hollywood courtship. *The Online Journal of the China Policy Institute*, July 5. Available at https://cpianalysis.org/2017/07/05/film-as-soft-power-and-hard-currency-the-sino-hollywood-courtship/

13

CONTENDING SOFT POWERS

South African media on the African continent

Herman Wasserman and Musawenkosi Ndlovu

The prospects for South African transnational media becoming one of the contending soft powers in the African continent are evaluated in this chapter. Prompting the decision to evaluate these prospects are the following interrelated factors, which so far have hardly been studied together in international communication. First, South African transnational media, once considered an African sub-regional superpower (Teer-Tomaselli, Wasserman and de Beer, 2007) and bent on northward expansion into the rest of the African continent (Ndlovu, 2003), are showing signs of stagnation. Second, while South African regional media are stagnating, there has been renewed and intensifying competition between Asian and Western media in Africa since 2000, which appears to be undermining the role of South African transnational media. Third, in various African countries, domestic/national and commercial-oriented media enterprises are growing. This growth further diminishes the space for South African transnational media to develop as a soft power in the continent. In this context, we then evaluate if there are still prospects for them to be a contending soft power in the African continent.

The evaluation of South Africa's transnational media is contextualized within a detailed history of the relationship between South Africa and the 'rest' of the African continent. The rationale for this approach is as follows. The South African media industry's soft power, in and of itself, and as one component of the several South African micro soft powers, configures and is (re)configured by the sum totality of macro soft power that is brand South Africa in Africa. The South African transnational media cannot, as such, be evaluated and discussed in isolation of what South Africa represents in the continent, however polysemic its reception could be. In presenting the South Africa-Africa relationship as a conceptual framework for appreciating South African transnational media soft power, certain key aspects – historical-political, economic, cultural and person-to-person – are paid special attention in this chapter because of their explanatory value. After these aspects are examined, the chapter considers whether South African media can still contribute to the country's soft power on the continent, in the light of the ongoing transformation of Africa's media sphere by a range of other players as mentioned above.

Soft power in Africa

The notion of 'soft power' was coined by the American political scientist Joseph Nye (1990) to describe the way in which a country like the US could achieve its strategic objectives by enhancing its attractiveness rather than using hard threats and sanctions. In recent years, the term has received something of a revival in global media studies in the context of the media's role in shifting geopolitical relations, in particular China's 'going out' strategy in international relations. China's push into the African continent, in particular, has been characterized by a concomitant expansion of its activities in the media sphere, which has frequently been viewed as a form of 'soft power' (see e.g. Li and Rønning, 2013; Zhao, 2013; Wasserman, 2016). Similarly, the media can act as a vehicle for soft power to be exercised on a regional, intra-African basis. The South African media's role in such regional relationships is a noteworthy example.

As much as South African media are integral to the country's overall soft power on the African continent, they come across as inconsistent and disjointed. After the collapse of Africa2Africa and SABC Africa channels, except for Channel Africa, there is no clear pre-planned soft power strategy by South African media in the continent (see below). The media then, if they intend to be a serious contender among other emerging, as well as historically entrenched soft powers on the African continent, would have to re-examine themselves and increase their efforts. Various interrelated factors may even directly hamper their Africa-oriented transnational advances and contribute to the further weakening of their contribution to the country's broader soft power on the continent:

- First, the historically, largely negative political relationship between South Africa's governing elite and its counterparts in many other African countries.
- Second, strongly related to the first, the largely negative perception of South Africa's private and public institutions on the continent.
- Third, South African citizens' negative and often xenophobic attitudes towards fellow Africans from outside their own country.
- Last, the contemporary transformation of the African region's media sphere itself.

Regarding the first factor, that of the poor relationship between South Africa's governing elite and their continental counterparts, the legacy of South African colonial and apartheid governments still, to a considerable degree, mediate the perception and reception of even post-apartheid governments on the continent (Adebajo, 2017: 36). While South African 'soft power' is evident at the societal level, some African elites 'actively resist the pull of South Africa-based ideas' (Alden and Soko, 2005: 367). Although South Africa has made great strides in improving its image on the continent since it became a democracy in 1994, its foreign policy and military involvement on the continent in the post-apartheid years have often detracted from the soft-power boost the country received during Nelson Mandela's presidency, 1994–1999 (Louw-Vaudran, 2016: 10). As far as its corporate elites are concerned, South African companies' aggressive expansion on the continent in the post-apartheid era has often earned itself the criticism of being a 'sub-imperialist' or regional hegemon in sub-Saharan Africa (Louw-Vaudran, 2016: 11).

If soft power is a non-military instrument a country deploys to attain its intended influence, South Africa's influence on the African continent has historically been limited. In short, South Africa's political and economic elite have usually been viewed with great suspicion on the African continent, even when making soft-power overtures in the post-1994 democratic era (Barber, 2005: 1083). There is concern in some parts of the continent that South Africa continues to use its historical institutional strengths to dominate the continent, especially regional forums such as the Southern African Development Community. In his book which compares Nigeria and South Africa, *The Eagle and Springbok*, the Nigerian scholar Adekeye Adebajo argues that 'hegemony may be insufficient to describe the preponderance of power that South Africa enjoys over its neighbours', adding that '… Batswana, Swazis, Basotho, and Namibians certainly have many reasons to complain that they are closer to South Africa, and too far from God' (Adebajo, 2017: 37).

Recognizing this suspicion and how the South African political elite had engaged with the African continent in the past, Maite Nkoana-Mashabane, South Africa's Minister of International Relations, once remarked that 'the approach of this leadership would be to work with partners … so that it does not become a South African thing; so, it does not become us talking down to neighbours and African brothers and sisters. That's what Africans hate, they do not want to be told, or talked down to … that reminds them of our colonial past' (in Monare, 2009: 11).

In the colonial era, white, minority-ruled South Africa was seen on the continent as an extension or a conduit of Western imperialism, with an attitude of superiority towards black Africa. Cecil Rhodes, the British-born imperialist, who dreamt of building a railway from the Cape to Cairo 'described Africa north of the Limpopo as South Africa's "natural hinterland" and "attempted to establish a Southern African federation built around South Africa"' (Adebajo, 2017: 29, 34). Subsequent Afrikaner leaders such as Jan Smuts, D. F. Malan and J. G. Strijdom, although vilifying Rhodes for his association with British imperialism, viewed South Africa not only as an extension of the West in Africa, but also as a civilizing and enlightening force in the continent. While Malan spoke of 'preserving Africa for white Christian civilisation' (Nolutshungu, 1975: 298), Hendrik Verwoerd believed that South Africa would determine the continent's foreign policy (Barber and Barratt, 1990: 2) and further 'claimed that whites had brought civilisation, economic development, and political order to Africa' (Adebajo, 2017: 35).

It could therefore be argued that, in the colonial and apartheid eras, South Africa attempted to use a kind of soft power – one rooted in Eurocentric notions of 'civilisation' and 'progress' – to solidify its dominance, backed up by Western states, who used it as their proxy on the continent. The colonial and apartheid governments did also avail themselves of brute hard military power, but this was backed up by the 'soft power' of a particular, racialized interpretation of Christian values and enlightenment (Davenport and Saunders, 2000). This colonialist form of soft power and regional diplomacy, however, started faltering from the 1960s onwards, when the winds of change were sweeping through the continent. The postcolonial period that brought independence to African states saw the diminishing influence of Western powers, who nevertheless continued leveraging their power through their proxies during the Cold War.

Importantly, while in the 1960s Western powers were receding in Africa, the Portuguese authoritarian regime was still intent on continuing its control over African colonies, Mozambique and Angola (Bender and Yoder, 1974). The Portuguese regime from which these colonies were trying to free themselves was, like the apartheid state, anti-communist and anti-socialist. The presence of a Portuguese government that could crush communism and anti-colonialism in the African region, where South Africa was trying to exert its influence, was good for Pretoria. These political conditions were about to change.

When António de Oliveira Salazar, the strong-man Prime Minister of Portugal, suffered a stroke in 1968 and had to be replaced by a 'reformist' Marcelo Caetano, the Portuguese *Estado Novo* regime became weaker. The regime, like South Africa, was increasingly facing international isolation, albeit for different reasons: unpopular wars in Mozambique and Angola, where the US and the Soviet Union both wanted to extend their ideological influence. The Portuguese regime, already poor by European standards, was also facing stronger domestic opposition, as the wars in the African colonies were further bankrupting the country. A huge chunk of the country's budget was going to colonial administration and military budgets to crush insurgencies in the colonies. Ceatano was overthrown in 1974 in Lisbon by a military coup organized by left-wing Portuguese military officers, a hugely symbolic political action which 'had a profound impact on the course of events in Portugal's five hundred year old African empire' (Bender and Yoder, 1974: 23).

With these two neighbouring states free from colonial control, the space for apartheid South Africa's diplomacy in the region shrank even further. When Pretoria's closest neighbour, Zimbabwe, also gained its independence a few years later in 1980, four years after Angola and Mozambique, this left apartheid South Africa isolated in the region. It now had to rely on its proxy forces in the Southern African region for support: the MNR (*Resistencia Nacional Moçambicana*) in Mozambique, UNITA (*União Nacional para a Independência Total de Angola*) in Angola, the Lesotho Liberation Army, the Zambian Mushala group and various Zimbabwean dissident groups (Evans, 1984:3). These groups had little, if any, ideological similarities with

Pretoria. They were only useful because they were fighting, for different ideological reasons, 'the Front-Line States', made up of five newly independent countries in Southern Africa – Angola, Botswana, Mozambique, Tanzania and Zambia, which South Africa had sought to destabilize since 1978 (Metz, 1986: 492).

South Africa and its own 'colony', South West Africa (now Namibia) remained the only two countries under white administration in the African region. The strong sense of pan-Africanism that underpinned the African independence movement created a bond between the newly independent states and brought further pressure to bear on apartheid South Africa's soft-power attempts in the region. Many of the newly independent post-colonial states in the region were supported by the Soviet Union and its allies, and were inspired by Marxism – the antithesis of Pretoria's capitalism, so that apartheid South African diplomacy had little space to manoeuvre in the region and its soft power was restricted. In response to this, the apartheid government's Foreign Minister, Pik Botha called for an 'anti-Marxist' Constellation of Southern African States (CONSAS), a regional security and economic bloc (Evans, 1984: 2).

In a spectacular rebuke of South Africa, the Frontline States countered this attempt by issuing the Arusha Declaration, calling for 'the creation of the SADCC (Southern African Development Co-ordination Conference) to promote economic liberation and the development of a regional communications strategy in order to reduce economic dependence on Pretoria' (Evans, 1984). When Zimbabwe, which had been eyed by Pretoria to be part of CONSAS as part of a divide-and-rule strategy because of its then economic strength and geopolitical strategic location, gained its independence in 1980 and joined the SADCC, Pretoria's CONSAS attempt collapsed. Parallel to the victory for the frontline states by establishing the SADCC, was the further rise in the African National Congress' confidence in the possibility of a victory in South Africa. Its insurgency, through its military wing *Umkhonto we Sizwe*, escalated. Several incidents attributed to MK, such as the bombing of the South African fuel company Sasol's plant on 31 May 1981, then South Africa's Republic Day, led Pretoria to pair its diplomacy/soft power, including using the external service of the state broadcaster South African Broadcasting Corporation (SABC) for propaganda purposes in the region (see below) with ferocious hard, military power. It gave it a name: *Swaardmag* (power of the word).

> The new military technocrats in the SSC [State Security Council] preached a regional strategic policy based on armed power in order to reverse the groundswell of Pan-Africanism and ANC insurgency. … [they] rapidly instituted a new counter-revolutionary warfare strategy of destabilization … The aims were, and remain, simple: smash the stability of the Front-line States and blunt the development of SADCC while simultaneously striking at the ANC and its host nations.
>
> *(Evans, 1984:4)*

Given this historical legacy, democratic South Africa is still tainted by the colonial brush by sheer virtue of its continued economic and, to a lesser extent, political power and influence on the continent. As Louw-Vaudran points out:

> In many ways, South Africa today acts like a continental superpower because of its role in peacekeeping missions and its strong economic influence. But it has also been accused of behaving much like the formal colonial powers. It is sometimes seen as being neo-colonialist by bullying other countries into taking certain decisions in multilateral institutions like the AU (African Union) … Business people are also described as neo-colonialist when they set up shop in African countries with huge marketing campaigns, clearly branded as South African, with little regard for local sensitivities.
>
> *(2016: 11)*

After South Africa's negotiated settlement, with the new Government of National Unity in place in 1994 and Mandela as its head, South Africa went on a charm offensive in Africa. The new democratic government concentrated much of its soft power attempts on the continent, but there was 'an element of self-doubt about its approach, as well as suspicion from other African states' (Barber, 2005: 1083). At the core of a Mandela-headed, ANC-led new government's foreign policy was 'the pursuit of human rights-broadly interpreted to cover economic, social and environmental as well as political rights' (Barber, 2005: 1079). With human right abuses in several African countries rife, the ANC's soft power strategy backfired and isolated Mandela diplomatically in some instances. One major example, noted by several scholars (Barber, 2005; Adebajo, 2017), is worth mentioning as it speaks to the difficulties of the country's soft power on the continent today.

When the Mandela government took office in 1994, Nigeria was ruled by a human rights-abusing dictator, General Sani Abacha. A special military tribunal under Abacha's regime had found leaders of the Ogoni people, including Ken Saro-Wiwa, guilty of plotting a coup and attacking chiefs. The tribunal ordered their execution. The protest campaign of the Ogoni people, in fact, had been organized against the continued environmental degradation of the Ogoniland by petroleum companies and Nigerian government's complicity.

The possible execution of the 'Ogoni nine' angered Mandela who had a human rights-oriented approach to foreign policy. He sent his deputy Thabo Mbeki, who had spent time in Nigeria during his exile years, and Archbishop Desmond Tutu, who, as a human rights advocate and chair of the country's Truth and Reconciliation Commission, became one of the prominent faces of democratic South Africa's brand of soft power. Mandela sincerely believed, in November 1995, at his first Commonwealth Conference, in Auckland, New Zealand, that the 'Ogoni Nine' would receive clemency from Abacha. He, instead, woke up to the news that they had been brutally hanged. He was embarrassed and betrayed. While the South African newspaper *Mail and Guardian* blamed Pretoria and Mandela for the 'blunder' and unpreparedness for the tragedy, Saro-Wiwa's friend and Nigerian-born writer and academic, Kole Omotoso, defended Mandela and pointed to the new government's inexperience in foreign affairs in Africa (*Mail and Guardian*, 1995).

Mandela felt humiliated by Abacha and campaigned for the expulsion of Nigeria from the Commonwealth, and won, and recalled South Africa's High Commissioner to Nigeria. In December 1995, he called on the Southern African Development Community to take collective action against Nigeria. When he failed to get the support from SADC leaders – some accusing him of breaking African unity – he realized the limits of South African soft power on the continent. Nigerians described Mandela's attitude as 'horrific and terrible' and spoke of South Africa as 'a white state with a black head' (Barber, 2005: 1084).

Despite South African diplomatic and soft power successes in some parts in Africa, this insulting view of Mandela was not limited to Nigeria. During the anti-apartheid struggles, and before 1994, there were some prominent African leaders who were frustrated by the ANC's multiracial approach and by what they perceived to be ANC's patience with white South Africans and the reluctance of *Umkhonto Wesizwe* to go to apartheid South African and fight. The Pan-Africanist Congress, whose ideology the apartheid government wanted to defeat, was more popular among leaders of other African states. Mandela himself once wrote: 'There are many who say they (the Pan-Africanist Congress) may be naïve but they are the only organisation in South Africa that is in step with the rest of Africa' (Kotch, 2013: 1).

Thabo Mbeki, who took over as President of South Africa from Mandela in 1999 was formerly the deputy president responsible for foreign affairs and, as the government representative who had pleaded with Nigeria for the clemency of the Ogoni Nine, had been humiliated. This experience was to shape his policy of 'quiet diplomacy' towards Zimbabwe, a policy derided as ineffective in South Africa. Mbeki did not want South Africa and the ANC government to be perceived as being not in 'step with the rest of Africa', and therefore did not risk a more robust diplomatic engagement with Zimbabwean President Robert Mugabe that could have alienated African leaders. Mbeki introduced the philosophy of 'the African Renaissance' and introduced a plan to improve Africa's economy, the New Partnership for Africa's Development. He warned fellow South Africans in 1996, in parliament, not to embarrass themselves by exaggerating their strength in the continent (Adebajo, 2017: 20).

His successor, Jacob Zuma was less interested in African affairs and during his presidency (2009–2017) South African foreign policy seemed to be focused on BRICS and SADC to have a strong soft power influence within Africa itself (Bendile, 2018: 1). Zuma's presidency, riddled with allegations of corruption and misuse of power, largely accounted for the decline of South Africa's soft power on the continent. As Louw-Vaudran (2016) points out, the admiration that the ANC government received during the Mandela years and the historical sympathy that the ANC gained as a liberation movement, has since dissipated. Zuma does not have the same stature internationally as his predecessors and during his term in office South Africa has also started to act in an increasingly bullish way on the continent.

Instead of leading by example, South Africa struggles to garner soft power and is often seen as acting in a neo-colonialist and self-interested way. It is a declining superpower, both in terms of hard and soft power (ibid.: 209).

Zuma's successor, Cyril Ramaphosa was welcomed as heralding a 'new dawn' in the country. It still remains to be seen how his presidency will impact on South Africa's 'soft power' and foreign policy strategies on the continent. One of the first things that Ramaphosa's new Minister of International Relations and Co-operation, Lindiwe Sisulu did, was to appoint a panel of international relations experts to review South Africa's foreign policy. Sisulu told Parliament that in the memory of Mandela, the country had:

> a responsibility to regain that stature that he left for us … That stature that allowed us to punch above our weight and succeed … We'll regain that stature and put all our efforts into making sure that we make the world a better place for all […] in a new dispensation of the fifth administration … a New Dawn … a period of renewal, of change, of adherence to good governance and responsiveness to our people.
>
> *(Bendile, 2018: 1)*

It is this philosophy that speaks to the context within which South Africa's soft power on the continent is being pursued. The new administration seems to have signalled its intention to return to the forms of foreign policy engagement the country practised during the Mandela and Mbeki eras. It is no accident that Sisulu's panel is headed by Aziz Pahad, the long-time deputy foreign minister under both Mandela and Mbeki.

From BRIC to BRICS

A notable new set of international relations that is bound to continue to shape South African foreign policy is its membership of the BRICS group of emerging nations. If the country is to pair its human rights-oriented approach to foreign policy with a greater emphasis on economic diplomacy in Africa, it might bring it in subtle confrontation with its BRICS partner China. China, who has been engaging in a strong push into Africa in recent years, backed up by its own media initiatives as a form of soft power (Zhao, 2013; Wasserman, 2016), has often been criticized for its lack of concern for press freedom, human rights and labour rights (Hairong and Sautman, 2009; French, 2014).

Moving away from such political concerns, the South African diplomatic strategy is foregrounding economic diplomacy (Bendile, 2018: 1). There is a long history of South African business activities outside the country's borders. The country has closer economic ties with the West than with any other region in Africa. The European Union is South Africa's biggest regional trade partner, while in terms of country-to-country trade, China is biggest trading partner. A review panel was established by the Minister of International Relations and Co-operation to recommend how South Africa may want to create a space for economic growth in the rest of Africa. However, this focus might bring further complications, given criticism of South African businesses on the continent as having a neo-colonialist approach (Louw–Vaudran, 2016: 11).

South African businesses grew alongside colonization of the continent, and are therefore often viewed as having benefitted from exploitative cheap labour systems and extraction of profit back to South Africa. The financing and regulatory mechanisms in South Africa have allowed the country's companies to expand into the rest of the continent, particularly in the southern African region. When international trade sanctions imposed on South Africa during apartheid started to be removed in the 1990s, South African capitalism moved northwards with speed, being perceived by many as taking a mercantilist approach in Africa (Alden and Soko, 2005), which is not good for South Africa's soft power. South Africa controls about 60 per cent of the sub-regional economy and many fear that institutions such as the SADC could be used as instruments by a black-led government to fulfil the historical aims of South African white leaders and big businesses of incorporating neighbouring vassals into a South African-dominated 'constellation' of states (Adebajo, 2017: 36).

A further factor that has contributed to the decline of South Africa's soft power on the continent has been the xenophobic attitudes displayed by South Africans against their fellow Africans. Within South Africa, these attitudes have often manifested in outbreaks of severe violence meted out against other African nationals residing in South Africa. These xenophobic attacks were widely condemned inside the country and received much media coverage, although such coverage often focused on the eruption of violent events themselves rather than in-depth coverage of the underlying issues or advance warnings of tensions (Wasserman, Bosch and Chuma, 2018).

These attacks have also contributed to the erosion of South Africa's image on the continent. As Louw–Vaudrian (2016: 22) explains, many African states actively supported the anti-apartheid struggle and provided refuge to activists exiled from apartheid South Africa. They find it disappointing that post-apartheid South Africa displays such xenophobic attitudes and does not do more to reciprocate for the support it received during the years of liberation struggle. It is against the above historical background of perceptions of South Africa as an extension of Western colonialism, the brief optimism about South Africa's moral leadership on the continent in the immediate post-apartheid years and the subsequent erosion of South Africa's soft power as a result of its perceived role as regional economic and political hegemon, that the media's potential role as purveyor of South African soft power on the continent has to be evaluated.

Media as soft power

South African media's presence in most parts of the African continent goes as far back as colonial times (Ziegler and Asante, 1992). South African print media were visible in many parts of the continent, and since they were often linked to colonial mining interests, they were perceived to be an extension of Western and South African imperialism. When Zimbabwe gained its independence, the first thing it did was to launch an agency that was to prepare the buying out of South African media in the country (ibid.).

The South African radio services became available in neighbouring countries in 1966, with Radio RSA (The Voice of South Africa) created as the international broadcasting service of the South African Broadcasting Corporation (SABC) – lasting until 1992, the end of the apartheid era. The service was renamed Channel Africa. Radio stations that were not SABC's external service were also available in South Africa's neighbouring countries of Botswana, Namibia (directly controlled by South Africa) and Swaziland. In line with the apartheid government's strategy of countering activities of the ANC and other movements in the frontline states, SABC radio services were extended in the neighbouring countries for propaganda purposes. Later, SABC TV became a more powerful propaganda tool for the apartheid regime and its signals could be picked up in neighbouring countries. This too gave South Africa a bad name in the continent.

In the early 1990s, South Africa's commercial broadcasting started growing in the sub-Saharan region of Africa. In 1986, South Africa launched its first private subscription television service, MNet, which later expanded into African broadcast markets. M-Net began as an individual pay-TV channel and it has, however, over the years undergone immense growth, including the launch of its international service into Africa in 1992. The growth into Africa via terrestrial rebroadcast began in Namibia in 1992, with countries such as Botswana, Ghana, Nigeria and Egypt following (CMNALL-E301, 1999). M-Net is said to have more than 1.23 million subscribers in 41 countries across the continent. The main M-Net channel focuses on films and sport, but also offers general entertainment programmes (CMNALL-E301, 1999; South African Yearbook 2001/2). In 1995 M-Net launched the world's first digital direct-to-home subscriber (DTH) satellite service called DStv, which carried over 30 video channels and 40 audio programmes to the whole of Africa (Jensen, 1999: 183), prompting critics to see it as an extension of South African sub imperialism (Kandjii, 2001).

SABC's Channel Africa (formerly Radio RSA) radio station funded by the Ministry of International Relations and Co-operation, and launched in the early 1990s is perhaps the only well-planned media-centric means of South African soft power in Africa. Its mission is clear: 'to support South Africa's Foreign Policy' and contribute to the 'development of Africa, support peace, democracy and good governance through the production and broadcast of innovative, dynamic and stimulating news, current affairs and informal knowledge building content in English and other major African languages' (Channel Africa, 2018: 1). Apart from broadcasting in English, French and Portuguese, the channel also provides radio programmes in such African languages as Chinyanja, Silozi and Kiswahili.

Continuing with its advance into Africa, in 1998, the SABC, in conjunction with Multichoice Company, launched its two Africa-orientated pay channels: SABC

Africa and Africa2Africa, on the DStv bouquet (Paterson, 1998). These channels aimed to differentiate themselves from other South African and foreign channels broadcasting into African media space. Both Africa2Africa and SABC Africa intended to be leading content providers in Africa, producing entertainment either for Africa, about Africa or by Africa and bring African news to Africa, from Africa. Not only did these channels rise during Mbeki's presidency, they also shared his philosophy of pan-Africanism and an African renaissance (Ndlovu, 2011).

However, the efforts by South African commercial media to expand their footprint on the continent – and, concomitantly, act as a vehicle for South African 'soft power' – seem uncoordinated and accidental. Its strategy seems much more haphazard than that of its BRICS counterpart, China, which has embarked on a concerted effort to penetrate the continent with its media. South Africa's former colonizer, Britain, has also been more successful at crafting a strategy for media presence across the continent. Each of South Africa's media houses that advances northwards into the rest of Africa does very much so on its own (unless it provides a platform from which the other can piggyback). South African media's northward 'trek' is normally in search of new media audiences for its products and services other than in pursuit of some predetermined South African-centric ideology. It is therefore questionable whether this media expansion will serve the country's soft power objectives, or, through its dominant position on the commercial landscape, create perceptions of a regional hegemon that might in fact hinder such efforts.

The decline of South Africa as regional media power?

While the competition between the established Western and rapidly expanding Chinese media into the African media and cultural space is intensifying, the African regional media is either slowly retreating into the nation-state territory or showing signs of fragility. The main casualty has been pan-African news journalism, which has never fully developed. This has wide implications for the representation of Africa in the global public sphere.

As noted earlier, African regional media have been dominated by South Africa, a regional media power (Teer-Tomaselli, Wasserman and de Beer, 2007), with Multichoice (Africa) being the most prominent. While Multichoice is still the dominant pay-TV content supplier on the continent, it is considering withdrawing from the continent and selling off its Multichoice Africa arm (Moneyweb, 2017: 1). This decision as such is not problematic if it were to allow new African-based entrants to offer Africa-wide news and entertainment; but, as shall be shown below, it is the global media organizations that are most likely to take up this space given the economic fragility and dependence of African pay-tv content suppliers. Multichoice Africa, however, is not the latest to withdraw.

Through its Africa2Africa and SABC Africa channels, the state broadcaster SABC had in the past engaged in a regionalization and trans-nationalization project. Conceptualized within the African Renaissance philosophy and underpinned by the imperative to de-colonize the African informational sphere process, the channels were SABC's most ambitious and unambiguous project aimed at counteracting Western media 'imperialism' and negative framing of the continent. However, the two channels disintegrated, in part, because of poor financial planning and organizational weaknesses within the SABC (Ndlovu, 2011).

In recent years, the SABC – whose slogan is 'Africa's News Leader' – has revisited its ambition of being a regional news supplier. It (re)launched a 24-hour news channel – SABC NEWS International – in 2013 on the satellite channel DStv Africa, an example of a well-established broadcaster's determination to advance into the African media and cultural space. The SABC, however, does not have the resources to execute this ambition, as its financial woes continue to increase. The other South African company that had aimed to capitalize on SABC's difficulties on the one hand and Multichoice's continued success on the other, is Sabido, owners of e.tv. To augment its Africa focus, e.tv launched e.tv Africa in 2010 and its syndicated broadcasts were provided on a free-to-air, predominantly terrestrial basis in Kenya, Namibia, Zimbabwe, Nigeria, Ghana, Tanzania, Uganda, Rwanda, Guinea, Burundi and the Central African Republic and Botswana. The company's e.News Channel Africa (ENCA) projected itself not as another South African news channel, but a carrier of African news and current affairs (Ndlovu, 2011). Its signature magazine programme 'Africa 360' and the programme's slogan 'see Africa like you have seen it before' was testimony to this point. The channel was available in Africa on DStv, as well as on the Sky digital satellite platform in Britain. However, its economic sustainability has been a constant worry. It is not only the South African broadcast media organizations that are in regional decline. Print media with regional ambitions are floundering too. The *African Independent* weekly newspaper, launched in 2015 for Africa-wide audiences, was being repackaged and folded into a glossy magazine in 2017, while the *Sunday Times* withdrew its *Sunday Times Africa* edition. *The Mail and Guardian Africa* is a spent force too.

Conclusion

South African transnational media can still be used as instruments of the country's soft power in the African continent, if this is necessary. It would be a difficult journey ahead, however. South African transnational media faces the following problems in relation to advancing its attractiveness in the continent. The first problem relates to the association of South African media industry with other South African commercial enterprises that are trying to dominate the continent in this era of late capitalism and globalization. The South African transnational media, even the domestic public-service broadcaster, when advancing northward to other African countries, adopts a commercial stance, leveraging on its long-established infrastructure and brand names in the continent. This makes it to be perceived as part and parcel of the economic hegemony trying to dominate the continent. This will need to be managed.

The second problem is the shrinking space for South African soft power where South African media would have hoped to grow. The space is shrinking in four dimensions: first, there is growth of Asian media in the African continent, particularly the unprecedented expansion of the financially well-resourced and ideologically-focused Chinese global media. This crowds out and decentralizes South African transnational media that is already financially wobbly and ideologically confused. Second, the space is being shrunk by the ideological reaction of Western news media to this Chinese (news) media growth in the African continent (Ndlovu, 2018). Chinese media's resolute expansion into African media/cultural space has undoubtedly caused, among other factors, Western global media in Africa to re-evaluate their strategic position in the continent. The BBC World Service, for example and having had its funding cut by the British government in 2013, had its funding increased in 2015. Subsequent to this funding increase, mainly meant for expansion in Africa, the BBC World Service, in September 2017, launched three news websites for Ethiopia and Eritrea, in three languages: AfaanOromoo, Amharic and Tigrinya (BBC.com, 2018).

Third, there is also further growth of the already well-established Western media in Africa and there is growing competition between/amongst media of the West themselves for African audiences. Whereas, for example, CNN and BBC used to be very visible in Africa, there is now growing visibility of MSNBC (US), Bloomberg Africa (US), CNBC Africa (US), France 24, DW (Germany), RTP (Portugal), Fox News (US) and Euronews (Europe). Fourth, there is a rise of new, cheaper (some African-owned) satellite providers in various regions of the continent. These providers will make it possible for African audiences to access news and information from beyond their national broadcasters and widen their range of choice and exposure to global media. These providers include, among others, the Zuku/Wananchi Group, a cable network that is currently available only in Nairobi and Mombasa. This platform supports broadband, pay-TV and telephony services through a single cable into customers' homes and claims to provide the fastest Internet speed in East Africa. Zuku's Satellite TV services – beaming mostly US-based entertainment channels – are currently available in Kenya, Uganda, Tanzania, Malawi and Zambia (Zuku, 2018). Another such player is Zap, a digital satellite television provider mainly for Portuguese-speaking countries in sub-Saharan Africa. Launched in Angola in 2010, Zap offers 150 channels, featuring TV series, films, music, children's programmes, news, sports and documentaries (Zap, 2018).

The third problem is that the South African economy, from which South African media draw most of their revenues, is doing very badly. The continent-wide ambitions of South African transnational media are therefore restricted. For example, not only is South African Multichoice/DStv losing premium subscribers to Netflix, it is also battling the Chinese-owned and other African-owned, cheaper satellite providers in the continent. The SABC, once full of ambition to expand to the whole of the continent, is broke. E.tv, too, is not in strong financial position.

Notwithstanding the above, it would be premature to conclude here that South African media can no longer be or be used as instruments of soft power in the continent. South African media, taken as whole, still have a lot of clout. On the news content front, for example, ENCA and SABC International 24-hour news channels are available in most packages that DStv offers to various audiences in Africa. Perhaps the only other African 24-hour channel that is transnational and Africa orientated is the Nigerian TVC. It is carried by Chinese-owned Starsat. South African news channels have a space to grow in the continent should they have objectives to and should their financial fortunes change for better. On the entertainment front, DStv has continued to be one of the foremost platforms for pan-African entertainment. DStv has become the place for watching African movies and music. It is one of the foremost platforms for watching African football as well. Multichoice is still in the number one strong position in the continent as satellite provider, followed by the Chinese Starsat and the French Vivendi.

Lastly, the survival of South African transnational media's soft power rests in collaborations with national/local media industries of various African countries. These partnerships will need to be at various levels: co-media ownerships, pro-gramme exchanges, staffing/human resources, skills exchange, etc. Against the context presented above and for as long as what South African media do in the continent is not seen as just a South African project, there is space for South African transnational media to exert and expand their soft power.

References

Adebajo, A. (2017) *The Eagle and Springbok: Essays on Nigeria and South Africa*. Auckland Park: Fanele/Jacana.

Alden, C. and Soko, M. (2005) South Africa's economic relations with Africa: hegemony and its discontents. *Journal of Modern African Studies*, 43(3): 367–392.

Barber, J. and Barratt, J. (1990) *South Africa's Foreign Policy: The Search for Status and Security*. Cambridge: Cambridge University Press.

Barber, J. (2005) The New South Africa's foreign policy: principles and practice. *International Affairs*, 81(5): 1079–1096.

Bender, G. J. and Yoder, P. S. (1974) Whites in Angola on the eve of independence: the politics of numbers. *Africa Today*, 21(4): 23–37.

Bendile, D. (2018) New panel to reboot South Africa renaissance status. Available at: https://mg.co.za/article/2018-05-11-00-new-panel-to-reboot-sas-african-renaissance-status.

Channel Africa (2018) Channel Africa: about us. Available at: www.channelafrica.co.za/sabc/home/channelafrica/aboutus.

CMNALL-E/301 (1999) Department of Communication. Unisa: Pretoria.

Davenport, R. and Saunders, C. (2000) *South Africa: A Modern History*. London: Macmillan.

Evans, M. (1984) The front-line states, South Africa and Southern African security: military prospects and perspectives. *Zambezia*, 5(XII).

French, H. W. (2014) *China's Second Continent*. New York: Alfred A Knopf.

Hairong, Y. and Sautman, B. (2013) The beginning of a world empire? Contesting the discourse of Chinese copper mining in Zambia. *Modern China*, 39(2): 131–164.

Jensen, M. (1999) Sub-Saharan Africa, pp. 180–196 in *World Communication and Information Report 1999*. Paris: UNESCO.

Kandjii, K. (2001) The role of the SABC in reclaiming the 'public sphere' for Africa media. Paper read at the Freedom of Expression Institute workshop on the Corporatisation of the SABC. Unpublished.

Kotch, N. (2013) Mandela's African odyssey. Available at www.news24.com/Archives/City-Press/Mandelas-African-Odyssey-20150429-2

Li, S. and Rønning, H. (2013) Half-orchestrated, half freestyle: soft power and reporting Africa in China. *Ecquid Novi: African Journalism Studies*, 34(3): 102–124.

Louw-Vaudran, L. (2016) *South Africa in Africa: Superpower or Neo-colonialist?* Cape Town: Tafelberg.

Mail and Guardian (1995) Crisis in Nigeria. *Mail and Guardian*, 17 November.

Metz, S. (1986) The Mozambique National Resistance and South African foreign policy. *African Affairs*, 85(341): 491–507.

Moneyweb (2017) Naspers said to consider sale of Multichoice Africa. Moneyweb.co.za. Available at: www.moneyweb.co.za/news/companies-and-deals/naspers-said-to-consider-sale-of-multichoice-africa/#to-comments

Monare, M. (2009) Africa will top the foreign policy to-do list. *Sunday Independent*, 17 May, p. 11.

Ndlovu, M. (2003) The South African Broadcasting Corporation's Expansion into Africa: South African media imperialism? *Communicatio*, 29 (1&2): 297–311.

Ndlovu, M. (2011) The meaning of South African media's expansion into the rest of the African continent. Available at: https://periodicos.ufsc.br/index.php/desterro/article/view/21549

Ndlovu, M. (2018) Prospects of African regional news media. Paper presented at the International Communication Association conference, Prague, Czech Republic, 24–28 May.

Nolutshungu, S. C. (1975) *South Africa in Africa: A Study of Ideology and Foreign Policy*. Manchester: Manchester University Press.

Nye, J. (1990) *Bound to Lead: The Changing Nature of American Power*. New York: Basic Books.

Paterson, C.A. (1998) Reform or re-colonisation? The overhaul of African television. *African Review of Political Economy*, 78(25): 571–583.

Sisulu, L. (2018) Speech by L. N. Sisulu, Minister of International Relations and Cooperation on the occasion of the Budget Vote of The Ministry of International Relations and Cooperation, 15 May, Parliament. Available at www.dirco.gov.za/docs/speeches/2018/sisu0515a.htm

Teer-Tomaselli, R., Wasserman, H. and De Beer, A. S. (2007) South Africa as a regional media power, pp. 153–164 in D. K. Thussu (ed.) *Media on the Move: Global Flow and Contra-flow*. London: Routledge.

Wasserman, H. (2016) China's 'soft power' and its influence on editorial agendas in South Africa. *Chinese Journal of Communication*, 9(1): 8–20.

Wasserman, H., Bosch, T. and Chuma, W. (2018) Communication from above and below: media, protest and democracy. *Politikon*, 45(3): 368–386.

Ziegler, D. and Asante, M. K. (1992) *Thunder and Silence: The Mass Media in Africa*. Trenton, NJ: Africa World Press.

Zhao, Y. (2013) China's quest for 'soft power': imperatives, impediments and irreconcilable tensions? *Javnost – The Public*, 20(4):17–30.

PART IV

BRICS and changing communication practices

14
BRICS JOURNALISM AS A NEW TERRITORY FOR LOCALIZING JOURNALISM STUDIES

Jyotika Ramaprasad and Svetlana Pasti

This chapter takes a second look at some of the findings of an empirical study of BRICS journalists, reported earlier in two collaborative publications (Pasti and Ramaprasad, 2015, 2018), using the ethical and epistemological analytic techniques of the BRICS perspective as proposed by Albuquerque and Lycarião (2018). Thus, respectively, we refrain from making normative comparisons within and outside BRICS, and we do not use country evaluations of BRICS made by non-academic, Western agents. The purpose is to situate interpretations locally, within the historical legacies and current dynamics of journalism, including its imported influences, in these countries. We selected journalists' beliefs about professionalism, functions of journalism and roles of journalists as variables to reconsider in this light because they comprise the essence of news. We also included social media use because they provide a new venue through which journalists practise their profession and deliver functions and roles, and is thus a new avenue to journalistic freedom.

Historically, the 'journalisms' of BRICS countries have all been sites of liberation movements, either against colonial Western powers (Brazil, India, China and South Africa) or tsarist autocracy (Russia). Today, the journalisms of BRICS are located in the relatively new conditions of their communist, post-communist, post-colonialist and post-apartheid societies, which are part of the global economy and have experienced the global trends of digitalization and liberalism. Contemporary BRICS journalists combine, to different extents, their domestic understandings of journalism, including emancipatory activities for marginalized populations, with ideas and practices from other parts of the world. This mix of local perspectives and global trends has given each country its own character, within which its journalism and journalists are situated.

Localizing journalism studies

In our empirical study, we did not consider the BRICS countries as sites of raw data to be analyzed through the prism of Western theory (Willems, 2014). First, we started from the vantage point of these countries, using in-depth semi-structured interviews that allowed journalists to voice their beliefs and provide researchers with nuanced and organic viewpoints that a standardized questionnaire, employed within a positivist framework and seeking a high level of generalization and universalizing theories, cannot. Second, to accomplish this large study in a localized manner, we adopted a *committee approach*, 'in which an interdisciplinary and multicultural team of individuals who have expert knowledge on the cultures, languages and research field in question jointly develop the research tools' (Hanitzsch, 2008: 101). As part of this approach, researchers from BRICS collected and provided interpretations of the data. And third, in this chapter, we conduct a place-based interpretation of the data rather than compare it against any normative understandings of journalism and its practices that might imply a hierarchy of countries in terms of their moral positions in the profession. Thus, we do not compare one BRICS country with another or one or more of the BRICS countries with Western countries and its normative assessments. Together, these three research strategies constitute our 'localization' approach.

Due to the genesis of communication and journalism studies in the West and other factors, such as the primacy of English as the language of research and larger opportunities for funded research in the West, journalism studies research has been dominated by Western scholars and is unmistakably influenced by the Western canon in terms of theoretical approaches, analytic methods and interpretive models (Josephi, 2005). Western societies, particularly the United States, support private ownership and task journalism with keeping the public informed and journalists with staying sources of power, especially the government, so that journalism and journalists may fulfil what it considers their primary function, that of sustaining democracy.

Journalism in the service of democracy and, in the US, journalists as adversaries to government, both ensconced in a private ownership system: these then have been the hegemonic normative underpinnings of considerable research in journalism, from which vantage point global journalism practice and journalists' beliefs and values have been, more or less, judged (Josephi, 2005; Nerone, 2013). When other forms of journalism and its practice, and their differing relationship with society, are identified in research results or in critical essays, they are generally considered deviations and receive considerable resistance from Western scholars, practitioners and commentators.

This Western bias impoverishes journalism studies research, depriving it of a fuller understanding of journalists' beliefs, views and practice, both within and outside the Western sphere. In a more general application beyond simply journalism studies, but in a more specific reference to the European region, Miike (2010) discusses the problems of Eurocentrism. According to him, Eurocentrism uses cultural origin to favour certain experiences; it essentializes all experience to the European one. It thus 'totalizes', adding up everything to the European perspective, and 'trivializes', diminishing all else (Miike, 2010: 3). Today, this increasing recognition and acknowledgement of Western bias has led scholars to call for 'de-Westernizing' or 'internationalizing' media studies (see, for example, Banda *et al.*, 2007; Breit, Obijiofor and Fitzgerald, 2013; Korkonosenko, 2015; Mano, 2009; Thussu, 2009, 2013).

From the point of view of avoiding any type of 'centrism', be it Eurocentrism (Miike, 2010), Asiacentricity (Miike, 2010) or Afrocentricity (Asante, 2007), BRICS represents an ideal constellation, uniting different regional cultural centers (Europe, Asia, Latin America and Africa), and thus eliminating a centre of domination. Thus, the very fact of conducting a study of BRICS journalists by researchers from the BRICS countries may be considered a joint act against normative frameworks. Further, and more specifically, we question the normativity of Western ideas about journalism, through our analysis of journalists' beliefs about the qualities of a professional journalist, the functions of journalism and the roles of a journalist and their social media use.

Sample

To implement data collection, two provincial and two major cities from each country in the BRICS coalition were selected: In Brazil, Brasilia, Rio de Janeiro, Vitoria, Juiz de Fora; in Russia, Moscow, St. Petersburg, Yekaterinburg, Petrozavodsk; in India, New Delhi, Hyderabad, Kolkata, Pune; in China, Beijing, Shanghai, Guangzhou, Wuhan, and, in South Africa, Johannesburg, Cape Town, Durban and Port Elizabeth. The study included both traditional media (print, radio and television) and, at the time, the rising online news media. To accommodate local conditions, where purely online news outlets were small in number or non-existent, news portals and online versions of traditional news media were included; this was the case for India and South Africa.

Parameters that were common across the countries were as follows: journalists were selected from a spectrum of media types (television, radio and so on), of media ownership (private, mixed and state, i.e., government owns more than 50 per cent of direct or indirect assets, as applicable), and of influence (quality, i.e., influential in public life, and popular, i.e., having a large audience). Here, too, local considerations were important: for example, while the Brazilian team defined quality news vehicles as those having the highest impact on the political agenda, the South African team defined them as community media.

Altogether, with a few exceptions, 24 news outlets were selected from each capital city and 12 from each provincial city, with two journalists from each major/provincial city outlet. The final sample included 729 journalists from the five BRICS countries as follows: 487 capital and 242 provincial city journalists, and 484 offline and 245 online journalists. The in-depth interviews began in December 2012 and were completed by the end of January 2015.

In the in-depth interviews, journalists were asked to narrate the three main qualities of journalistic professionalism, the functions of journalism as an institution, and the roles of journalists who have their own agency. These variables provide us with an opportunity to highlight the localizing approach we adopt in this chapter. They comprise the essence of journalism and thus are often the target for normative reductionism and evaluation. Journalists were also asked to address their social media use given its relative newness at the time of the study and the opportunities it provides journalists to gather and deliver news even in restricted contexts, and thus allows for new freedoms.

The BRICS perspective as an exercise in localizing

For a localization perspective to work, it is important to consider epistemologies. Kivikuru (2009) mentions an example of an epistemological shift, influenced by Western narratives about journalism, which took place over time in communication research in Africa, a shift from development to democracy as a primary value. In the face of such narratives, some important strategies to consider in journalism studies research include using place-based epistemologies of journalism that are derived inductively from the local context in the interpretation of findings (Wasserman and de Beer, 2009).

In an exercise relevant to our adoption of a localizing approach in discussing findings, Albuquerque and Lycarião (2018) explored the potential of BRICS to provide an alternative to the Western normative perspective adopted often in international media studies. They suggested that BRICS is a 'performative category', i.e., a heterogeneous group of countries, diverse in their historical, political, economic and cultural conditions, but united 'by a common struggle for recognition' in a US-centered neoliberal world order that is characterized by Western hegemony. BRICS embodies the idea of a future where the global order is not unipolar, i.e., one that is not dominated by any one country or an alliance of countries (de Coning, 2016). For Albuquerque and Lycarião, this 'collective project' or 'common agenda' translates into a 'BRICS perspective' (2018: 2878), one that explores the impact of the unipolar world order on academic research and, in doing so, offers an analytic strategy comprising ethical, epistemological and methodological aspects. Such an analysis makes manifest the premises of mainstream international media studies research and provides an alternative interpretive mode, which in our view echoes in some aspects the localizing model we have adopted.

From the ethical viewpoint, the BRICS struggle is 'against similar ways of thinking and acting that establish and sustain status difference and economic and political inequality' (Downey, 2008: 70). Essentially, this viewpoint, which finds value in the diversity of the BRICS countries, calls for a multipolar approach in international media studies rather than using normative comparison with a unipolar ideological order. Thus, according to the ethical aspect of the BRICS perspective, it is imperative to avoid an interpretive strategy that places countries in a hierarchy that considers some countries as 'less' than others. In essence, no one country should be held up as the virtuous model.

The epistemological aspect of this analytic strategy positions itself in opposition to the approach in much international media studies research that uses the premises and data mostly from non-academic agents, such as Freedom House, whose roots often lie in neoliberalism. It 'emphasizes the political biases lying behind the data presented by these agents' (Albuquerque and Lycarião, 2018: 2884). The strategy's methodological angle 'considers the countries under analysis from a relational perspective and explores other units of analysis existing [at the] supranational and … infranational [levels]' (ibid.: 2882). In a relational approach, countries are not analyzed in isolation 'as existing apart from other societies', and the analysis explores the countries' relationship with supranational and infra-national units in terms of power asymmetry and thus influence of the more powerful on those in the periphery (ibid.: 2883). Supra-national institutions are mostly Western transnational sites that are often neoliberal in their orientation and, due to their power advantage, are able to influence research agendas. Infra-national institutions are within-country elite groups that perpetuate in-country colonization of sub-elite groups.

The methodological approach has some degree of overlap with the ethical and epistemological approaches in that, first, it refers to the moral hierarchy of virtuous and not, which is created in country-comparative media research when the analysis adopts methodological nationalism, i.e., treats a country as a homogeneous unit to be normatively compared with other units, and, second, suggests researchers pay attention to asymmetrical power relations that allow non-academic Western organizations to influence research agendas.

Implementing localized interpretation

This chapter uses Albuquerque and Lycarião's (2018) ethical and epistemological analytical facets for localizing reflection on some results of the BRICS journalism study. It is able to engage with its methodological analytic approach only insofar as it overlaps with the ethical and epistemological facets; analyzing results from the supra- and infra-power relations perspective is outside the scope of this chapter.

To implement the ethical aspect, we deconstruct the existing stereotype of non-Western countries as lagging behind the West, by training our reflection out of Western normativity. From the epistemological point of view, we generate new knowledge based on empirical evidence from our study rather than use non-academic, Western organizations as the only arbiters of authoritative knowledge. We describe the new opportunities for journalistic freedom in BRICS that are emerging in the era of social media, rather than rely on the 'ready-made knowledge' of the freedom rankings created by Freedom House (FH), whose measurements are influenced by Western ideas of freedom and are not free from bias (Steiner, 2016; Fonte and Gonzalez, 2018). According to Albuquerque and Lycarião (2018: 2882), 'Possibly, no other agent has been as influential in [objectifying a Western-centered moral order] as FH, whose Free Press Index has been ubiquitously employed as having a self-evident value, despite evidence about its methodological flaws (Becker, 2003), political bias (Gianonne, 2010), and institutional ties with the US government (Tsygankov and Parker, 2014)'.

Social media in news making

Other than South Africa, the BRICS countries today have all become world leaders in terms of the number of Internet users (Worldatlas, 2018). When we conducted interviews with journalists in 2012–2015, the number of Internet users in the BRICS countries was much smaller, but these four countries were still among the top ten Internet users. China occupied the first position, India the third place, Brazil the fifth and Russia the sixth place (Internet Live Stats, 2014).

An analysis of news-making practices reported by BRICS journalists confirms that social media has become a new tool in the everyday work of these journalists. The commonalities and differences among the countries were as follows: in Brazil, India and South Africa journalists relied solely on global social media, i.e., US technical inventions with economic and political domination in the Internet market, whereas in China and Russia journalists used both global media and domestic media (WeChat, Weibo, VKontakte), which also became global later.

A majority of journalists in Brazil and South Africa shared a preference for the three global social media giants: Facebook, Twitter and Instagram. In both Brazil and South Africa, the most convenient way to access social media and consume and share information was mobile phones (Wasserman *et al.*, 2018: 52). In Brazil, almost all respondents (97 per cent) had their own social media profiles (Paiva, Guerra and Custodio, 2015: 20). The majority of journalists in Brazil assessed social media positively as a new tool at work but some also noted 'the danger of false information' and 'the need for surveillance of information supplied by the user'. Some wished 'for stronger regulation to meet the challenges of the virtual world' (Wasserman *et al.*, 2018: 57). In South Africa, almost all the journalists regularly used such social media as Facebook and Twitter in their work. At the same time, some online journalists were concerned that Twitter was a threat to their positions because it enabled 'people to remain abreast of the news without having to consume formal, online media' (ibid.: 59).

Access to the Internet in India was also mostly mobile driven; newsrooms had unlimited access to the Internet and journalists had smartphones. In the words of two Indian journalists respectively: 'It is a changed world; reporters are filing stories from their phones' and 'it is a new age wherein stories are already being done at one tenth of the cost with the help of mobile phones' (Vemula *et al.*, 2018: 163).

India was the only country whose journalists used WhatsApp as one of their main tools to gather news and immediately transmit it to the news desk or to publish it on their media site. Journalists appreciated the integration of social media with news media because it facilitated gathering information and communicating with sources, and also promoting their media outlets and themselves in the public sphere of the Internet (ibid.). In Hyderabad, an online journalist suggested the term 'explanatory journalism' to describe journalism that emerges from such integration of social media with news media:

> We can embed tweets about what someone is saying. So now the whole idea of calling someone, going to a person, and getting his quote is not necessary; you can just embed the person's tweet or hyperlink to older stories related to the person, which makes it all the more credible. For example, get the Prime Minister himself and put his quote. You can take his tweet and embed it to your story. All these possibilities are there where news becomes more accessible, and the idea that we have of explanatory journalism can happen smoothly.
>
> *(ibid.: 165)*

Both India and China had the largest number of young journalists (age 18–29) in the BRICS group. In India, 52 per cent of journalists in traditional media and 63 per cent in online media were between 18 and 29 years old. In China, these percentages were 69 and 71 per cent respectively. Both countries also had a high post-2000 generation workforce. In China, '95 per cent in both traditional and online news media' and in India '80 per cent in traditional news media and 93 per cent in online news' were from this generation (Pasti and Ramaprasad, 2016: 21). These journalists grew up with new technology and thus could easily introduce it into their work; in fact, due to this technology, journalism became a very attractive and easy occupation for them. One Indian journalist observed how quick and easy it was for young journalists to do their job: 'The other day I was covering an event and I saw this guy recording everything that the speaker was saying and it was automatically converted into a Word file, and there was nothing much for him to do except maybe editing' (Vemula *et al.*, 2018: 166). In Beijing, a reporter at a radio station said that new media were a symbol of the future orientation of the media industry: 'New media integrate various forms such as texts, pictures, audio, and video, so it is able to grow comprehensively to attract audiences' (Ramaprasad *et al.*, 2018: 36).

In contrast to journalists in Brazil, India and South Africa, a majority of journalists in Russia used both global (Facebook, Twitter, Instagram and LinkedIn) and domestic social media (VKontakte and Livejournal). Some Russian journalists, both in the capitals and the provinces, made diversified use of different social media. In Yekaterinburg, the respondents noted: 'VKontakte for personal communication, Facebook for work'. A similar explanation was given by a St. Petersburg journalist:

> Initially, the idea of any social networks was ... people [communicating] among themselves; [thus] a person must have one account to communicate with friends .... [and for journalists] to publish events from [their] life and profession – another account ... Let's say you don't call [by phone] to take a comment, but take it through Facebook.
>
> *[by asking your information source for a comment]*

Facebook only came to Russia in 2008, when the domestic social network Vkontakte, initiated in 2006, had already begun to win an audience. According to Konradova, Vkontakte became popular among young users because of its multimedia content, while Facebook turned out be 'more politicized and functioned as a platform for liberal and democratic opposition', which was mainly concentrated in large cities in Russia (Konradova, 2020: 67–68).

The use of social media in Russia for journalistic work also differed by type of city (metropolis and province) and its specific urban environment. For example, in Petrozavodsk, a small city far removed from Moscow, journalists preferred VKontakte, which had both audiences as well as sources for journalists. In St. Petersburg, most online journalists used VKontakte, Facebook and Twitter, and half of the traditional media journalists used VKontakte, and some used Twitter and Facebook.

Unlike some South African journalists, who considered social media as competition, Russian journalists did not believe that social media could compete with traditional media or online news media. They argued that social media were used mostly for communication, not for producing journalism. For example, a Russian journalist said that social media 'could serve as a source of information exchange and for exchange of some links'; i.e., only as a tool in a journalists' work. Another spoke more specifically: 'I take it as a news feed, where I can find the links, but no more, because these media certainly do not replace traditional ones' (Wasserman *et al.*, 2018: 58).

Similar to Russian journalists, journalists in China also used both global (Facebook, Twitter, Instagram and LinkedIn) and domestic (WeChat, Weibo, QQ, Renren and Douban) social media, but they considered domestic social media more important. It must be noted that Chinese journalists mentioned nine popular social media altogether. This was two to three times more than the number of social media that journalists mentioned in other BRICS countries. In essence, Chinese journalists are well informed from various sources. This finding characterizes a Chinese journalist as curious and dynamic in searching for information, likely out of necessity, but still an indication of resourcefulness in finding independent sources of information (those international social media officially blocked by the government) to supplement the information from the domestic social media that are controlled by the government.

Indicating how Chinese journalists used the banned global social media in their work, Simons *et al.* write:

> [the] authorities are clearly content to turn a blind eye to media practices that breach the rules but are recognized, in other respects, as serving markets and facilitating business activity. Many international news sites and social media platforms are blocked in China. However, four interviewees had it as an explicit part of their work duties to 'leap over' the Great Firewall of China to gather international news. These reporters used VPNs as part of

their job descriptions ….These kinds of jobs existed across both Party outlets and quasi-private media enterprises. Even those journalists who did not have access to international news in their job description routinely used VPNs. The Great Firewall of China was for them and, they assumed, most of their educated audience, an inconvenience rather than an effective restriction on the free flow of information.

(Simons et al., 2017: 233–234)

From an epistemological perspective, this finding from interviews with Chinese journalists gives us pause with regard to the evaluation of the freedom of journalists in China by Freedom House, which ranks China as a non-free country in terms of freedom of the Internet (Freedom House, 2019). As mentioned above, Freedom House is not a neutral arbiter in assessing the freedom of the press in the world and its role in international media research is to strengthen the centrist position of the West. Its critics tirelessly draw attention to its neoliberal political bias (Giannone, 2010; Sapiezynska and Lagos, 2016; Steiner, 2016; Fonte and Gonzalez, 2018) and methodological flaws (Bollen, 1986; Becker, 2003; Coppedge *et al.*, 2011).

Freedom House assesses Internet freedom using the following three criteria: obstacles to access, restrictions on content and violations of user rights. It is clear that authoritarian rule in China will affect the level of political rights, and the civil and journalistic freedoms in the country, but these measures do not allow for the opportunities that are opening up in China due to new conditions for China's integration into the world market and international communication, i.e., the digitalization and globalization of Western and Chinese social media. Freedom House considers the official ban on Facebook and Twitter in China as an obstacle to access, but it does not assess how this ban actually works in practice, and in the process indirectly provides a picture that underestimates the use of social media for journalistic work by Chinese journalists. It is common knowledge that virtual private networks (VPNs) make it possible to bypass the firewall and get access to Google, Facebook, Twitter and other sources in China, though this has become more difficult in recent years.

In today's digital world without borders, Chinese journalists are globalizing through these informal practices of using global social media platforms (Facebook, Twitter, YouTube, Instagram, etc.), which provide room for alternative opinions. These journalists look for alternative ways to create a space of autonomy and make professional choices about sources of information and the nature of their use in the context of their own situation with regard to their relations with government. In other words, how journalists work in the non-Western context has its own dynamics of formal and informal practices. We may surmise that by regularly using these global social media as alternative sources of information and communication, Chinese journalists gradually legitimize them as the norm in their professional practice. Our analysis counters the stereotype of Chinese journalists as being completely unfree and totally controlled in their journalistic work.

Core qualities of a professional

To analyze journalists' beliefs about professionalism, we examined journalists' perceptions of (1) the three core qualities of a professional, (2) the key functions that journalism as an institution should fulfil and (3) the key roles that journalists who have their own agency should perform (see Table 14.1). The answers from journalists about functions and roles did not differ much but they are presented separately in the text below to highlight the few differences in how they see institutional functions versus journalists' roles.

The BRICS journalists showed similarities in their understanding of the key qualities of a professional but differed in the hierarchy of these qualities. For journalists of Brazil and India, the moral qualities of honesty and sincerity were the most important in defining a professional journalist. For them, these qualities lead to an understanding of a journalist as a trustworthy person. Such prioritization

TABLE 14.1 Three core qualities of professional journalists

Country	Cities: Metro (2) Provincial (2)	Quality 1	Quality 2	Quality 3
Brazil	Brasilia/ Rio de Janeiro	Honest, sincere/ independent, not prejudiced, not corrupt/ good writing and technical skills	Competent, knowledge of subject/ethical in general and in profession/ multitasker	Courageous, stubborn Ethical
	Juiz de Fora/ Vitoria	Honest, sincere/ competent/ knowledge of subjects	Good writing skills	
Russia	Moscow/ St. Petersburg Yekaterinburg/ Petrozavodsk	Skills in gathering, analyzing, writing, and using technology/ experience in profession/ generally erudite and scholarly	Ethical/ objective and honest/ competent in subject	Communicative managerial skills
		Skills in gathering, analyzing, writing, and using technology/ generally erudite and scholarly	Honest and sincere/ ethical	Competent in subject

TABLE 14.1 Cont.

Country	Cities: Metro (2) Provincial (2)	Quality 1	Quality 2	Quality 3
India	New Delhi/ Hyderabad	Honest and sincere/ unbiased, ethical	Independent/ good writer/ educated	Competent, knowledge of subject
	Kolkata/Pune	Truthful/honest/ balanced/ unbiased/ethical	Hardworking/ dedicated/ committed/ impartial/ empathetic/ sensitive	News- orientation/ integrity
China	Beijing/ Shanghai	Good writer/ objective/ curious	Ethical in general and in profession	Competent, knowledgeable about subject/ independent
	Guangzhou/ Wuhan	Competent, knowledge of subject/ability to judge news values/ social interaction ability/interview skills	Ethical in general and in profession	Independent/ good writer/ generally erudite and scholarly/ courageous/ gritty/rational
South Africa	Johannesburg/ Cape Town Durban/ Port Elizabeth	Independent Independent	Unbiased Unbiased	Not corrupt Not corrupt

of the moral qualities of honesty and sincerity among journalists in Brazil and India is perhaps due to the cultural-historical tradition of development journalism that included reducing inequalities and making the lives of ordinary people better; enabling social change is among the professional expectations from these journalists.

In Brazil, professional journalism has been democratized through the strong tradition of alternative journalism in the form of community media, which are non-profit institutions with 'the widespread participation of ordinary people in production, decision-making, and management ... designed to meet the interests of local communities – especially social, ethnic, sexual, or religious minorities' (Bosch, Paiva and Malerba, 2018: 196). In India, working towards social change is part of the ethos of journalism, encoded in various journalistic codes of ethics.[1] Indian journalists indicated that all qualities apart from honesty can be learned and developed in everyday practice, but the existential choice between honesty and dishonesty is one that everybody makes alone, and it is exactly this inner choice that shapes a person's ethical values. Thus, Indian journalists considered technical skills, competence and knowledge of the subject and even independence as secondary.

For journalists of South Africa, the primary quality of the professional was independence, followed closely by being unbiased and uncorrupt in that order. This priority for independence in the value hierarchy of professionalism can be explained in the context of the relatively recent post-apartheid media freedoms, wherein the memory of the past is still acute in society and the profession, and where 'local journalists safeguard their professional independence' and believe 'that there should never be a time when government can control access to either the Internet or political and entertainment content' (Ndlovu, 2015: 124).

The journalists of China and Russia were similar in how they defined their priorities. At the top were the professional values of technical mastery, competence, erudition and knowledge of the subject. It appears then that these journalists' understanding of the profession leaned towards the rational and administrative rather than the emotional. The moral qualities of honesty and sincerity, and being ethical in general and in the profession, were second for them to professional and technical skills. This hierarchy may be related to the structure of the field or the lingering effects of this structure, i.e., the status of journalism in society, one that is subordinated to political power and works on the whole as an appendage of the state machine at the four structural levels of media systems established since the Communist time: national, regional, city and local media. Freidson (1988) provided a similar assessment at least for Soviet professionals who, he indicated, did not have economic freedom or freedom from state ideology, but did have authority over technical expertise.

In all BRICS countries, except Russia, journalists included independence as a key quality of a professional. In today's Russia, many journalists both agree with and acquiesce to the notion that the media serve either party/state interests or commercial interests and sometimes even serve state interests in private media, in the conditions of the post-Soviet quasi-media market and gradually tightening state control over the media, the Internet and civil society. For example, the Foreign Agent Law that came into force in 2012 resulted in the closure of many non-governmental organizations and required them to refuse foreign funding under threat of closure. Since 2017, this law has also become applicable to the media. In the opinion of the Chairman of the Glasnost Defense Foundation, Alexei Simonov, 'Today, Russian media are formed by two opposite vectors: on the one hand – a sense of their own dignity and on the other hand – money. [Media] where dignity wins [are decreasing]'. Simonov believed that only 10 to 15 per cent of the media have refused to resort to servility. For example, in Moscow this group included only *Novaya Gazeta, radio EkhoMoskvy, Vedomosti* and *Kommersant* (A. Simonov, personal communication, 19 October 2017).

Key functions of journalism

In response to our question on the three key functions that journalism should fulfil, BRICS journalists indicated providing information as the most important function but with different nuances. Brazilian journalists spoke about 'informing with objectivity', and Indian journalists about 'provide right [accurate] information', phrasing that implied the moral quality of being honest. In Russia, China and South Africa, however, journalists did not add an evaluatory phrase, while Indian journalists did not limit the main function of journalism to a single function. For them, it also included enabling communication between people and institutions, providing cognitive fodder for people, educating, regulating for societal order, engaging in activism in the vein of empowering people and working on social justice. That is, for them journalism is something more than just production of news, it is seen 'as a resource to drive development' (Ramaprasad *et al.*, 2018: 27). For this reason, perhaps, Indian journalists did not prioritize the commercial functions of journalism. Indian journalists were also an exception in the BRICS group in that they did not mention 'entertainment' as one of the three key functions of journalism. While not as all-encompassing as in India's case, the service orientation was present among journalists from the other countries as evident in their (and Indian journalists') mention of the function of enlightening and educating the public.

Investigative journalism, akin to watchdog journalism, seeking to keep politics and business accountable to society, was not very popular among BRICS journalists. Only in the metropolitan cities of Brazil and the metro cities and provinces of South Africa did journalists consider investigative journalism as one of the key functions of journalism. Indian journalists did not mention this function at all. Both communist China and post-communist Russia do not have a deep tradition of and conditions for investigative journalism as it is understood in the West: 'to discover information of public interest that somebody is trying to hide'.[2] Investigative journalism may be permitted by the authorities for certain liberal publications in certain cities, for example, in Moscow or in Guangzhou.

Key roles of journalists

Journalists' perceptions about their key roles were not too dissimilar to their beliefs about the functions of journalism. Thus, BRICS journalists were unanimous in indicating that disseminating information was the journalist's main role, with nuanced differences. Brazilian journalists used the phrase 'report objectively', whereas Russian, Chinese and South African journalists stayed with 'provide news', and 'inform the public'. In India, journalists put 'educate and enlighten', 'protect people and society' and 'work towards social justice, to be watchdog' on an equal footing with the role of informer, in that they considered all of these as main roles.

In South Africa, a key role was to 'empower community', in Brazil, it was to 'provide service to society', and in Russia and India, it was 'to help people' and to 'engage in activism'. In Russia, journalists saw themselves as 'teachers', 'enlighteners', 'moderators' and 'providers of communication between society and power'. The state-owned media journalists of China and Russia were similar in their perception of journalists as intermediaries between the government and society, a perception emanating from the service status of the journalism profession in the social structure of these societies, wherein state media journalists are trustees of the authorities. These journalists receive information from government agencies to inform society, but they also inform the government about the needs and aspirations of the people. In the interpretations of Chinese journalists, their role is to be 'a bridge between the government and the public', but also to be a 'supervisor', a 'public opinion guider', a 'social order maintainer', a 'social observer and rational thinker', a 'social progress promoter' and an 'opinion expresser'.

Conclusions

Our aspiration in this chapter was to gain new insights in the understanding of the evolution of BRICS journalism as a profession and practice by problematizing BRICS journalism as a new territory for localizing journalism studies. The chapter took the approach of understanding BRICS journalists' beliefs about aspects of their work from a distributed perspective rather than from a reductionist viewpoint, providing details and interpretations at the local level and avoiding normative comparisons and the use of Western measures of freedom. Specifically, our localization perspective drew considerably from Albuquerque and Lycarião's (2018) analytical frames, the ethical, epistemological and methodological, of which we adopted the first two.

From an ethical angle, one that links the BRICS perspective to the struggle for recognition in a world dominated by ways of thinking and action that posit status difference, we presented evidence of BRICS journalists' Internet and social media use as being diverse, serving journalists within their particular time and space in each country, without inferences of better and worse. BRICS journalists have successfully globalized and adapted to the era of social media; social media are their new work tool in news-making, and are used for their work-related and personal communication, as well as for various other purposes depending on their situation.

Journalists' use of social media was heterogeneous, with both cross- and within-country differences. In particular, the differences in use of global versus domestic social media among BRICS countries seem to be somehow politically conditioned, separating those countries with an experience of communism – China and Russia – from those without – Brazil, India and South Africa. Possibly, this difference speaks to the political will of China and Russia to have a certain sovereignty over the global Internet, including their domestic social media as part of their national Internet sovereignty.

Using the ethical point of view in our analysis of journalistic perceptions of professionalism, we hold none of the variety of models we found as a norm. In Russia and China, technical expertise/competence was an important characteristic; in Brazil and India, the understanding of professionalism was driven by moral requirements to be honest and sincere. In South Africa, journalists prioritized qualities such as independence, lack of bias and lack of corruption.

These priorities of professional qualities reflect specific professional cultures formed in specific historical contexts and contemporary circumstances. As indicated earlier, the journalisms of these countries have all been sites of liberation movements against either colonial Western powers (Brazil, India, China and South Africa) or tsarist autocracy (Russia) but, at the same time, have absorbed some of the ideas prevailing in their society, as well as some ideas exported from Western countries. If some journalists espoused professional orientations similar to those of Western journalists, it is not evidence that these journalists and their countries are better than the other BRICS journalists.

From an ethical perspective, our findings on the functions of journalism and the roles of journalists are also presented without any normative comparisons that would place certain BRICS countries as superior to others. The palette of these local models from information disseminator, educator, enlightener, critical thinker and watchdog to public opinion guider, social progress promoter, intermediator between society and power and engaged activist includes both those that are close to Western models of journalism and those that are distant. This diversity indicates a wealth of professional cultures that amalgate the historical and the contemporary, the local and the global.

In our epistemological analysis, we acknowledge the diversity of views about the use of social media, and we particularly consider the use of social media by journalists in China and note how Freedom House's assessment of Internet freedom there does not take into account actual practice. Freedom House's approach stems both from the method itself and from the neoliberal political bias of this NGO funded by the US government, with many of its prominent officials, at a personal level, having close ties with the US national security apparatus (Tsygankov and Parker, 2014). In sum, the patterns of liberalism are not able to discern the emerging spaces and dynamics of freedom in a communist society. Chinese journalists reported regular use of global social media in their work despite the formal ban on them. While in China, formal controls are in place, everyday practice is often based on the complex interplay of formal and informal rules, and skillful strategies to try and maintain professional autonomy in the conditions of political control (Jian and Liu, 2018).

The epistemological analysis of what professionalism means to BRICS journalists indicates the diversity and richness of professional models of journalism deeply rooted in their history of domestic traditions but also Western influences idiosyncratically translated into their own cultural context, models that have at different times responded to the challenges of time and circumstance in their societies. To understand the different professional cultures of journalists in the BRICS countries, we should remember the history of their journalism and their society.

Historically, in the communist countries, Russia and China, journalism was conceived as the political function of the party and formed as the mouthpiece of the government for building a new communist classless society idealized as a kingdom of equality and justice for everybody. Journalism was supposed to work as a well-functioning mechanism of the party and state machinery to help build this classless society of equal opportunities for people. That is, technical mastery of the occupation was important for journalists while the communist party and the state took care of ideology. This understanding, one of the features of the professional culture of journalists formed in communist times when journalism was only a state service, remains today and legitimizes journalists' wish to perform the roles of being an intermediary between government and society and of promoting social order. Lenin's 1901 political testament for media, 'a newspaper is not only collective propagandist and a collective agitator, it is also a collective organizer', remains in force (Lenin, 1901). In China, the party/state tradition of being a mouthpiece for the communist party and the people (Pan and Lu, 2003) is alive today in the professional mindset of Chinese journalists (Ramaprasad *et al.*, 2018).

In former colonial countries, journalism faced a struggle for independence from colonizers who long imposed their own media agenda, disregarding the interests and rights of the local population. Journalism was part of the struggle for justice and liberation from the oppression of the colonialists. Moral strength was on the side of the oppressed; they maintained the truth and they won. This historical and genetic memory of the power of truth and justice lives in the current generations of journalists and influences their values and choices in work. Thus, for Brazilian and Indian journalists, professionalism was understood and reflected as a moral ethos that helps to fulfill the mission of goodness and justice that is beyond just a role or function. In South Africa, it is the recent history of apartheid that is one explanation for the journalists' ranking of independence as the primary quality of the professional, followed closely by lack of bias and corruption; these would be most relevant for journalism's participation in the current challenges of democratization in the country.

Our epistemological analysis of functions and roles is similar to the analysis of professionalism in that these too are rooted in the historical and cultural knowledge systems of each country. The BRICS journalists were similar in their feelings of proximity to people and their desire to help people to understand the world and to get a picture of the day, but in some countries they also provided help to those who had specific complaints about an injustice at work or poor service provided by a company, and responded to requests for help from citizens in difficult life situations.

Journalists differed by country in their relationship with the authorities, accepting roles from watchdog and critic to functioning as a bridge between the government and the public. These self-perceptions of journalistic roles are based on ideals, practices and traditions of journalism in the respective countries. Some of the roles identified by BRICS journalists are similar to the values incorporated in development journalism. In the West, this journalism is considered to be a journalism of 'as you [the government] say', but for many in the developing world, it references the idea of journalism in the service of social justice issues. While neoliberalism has entered the media markets of BRICS, these journalists do not rate highly the commercial function of media – entertainment.

As a final exercise, we asked BRICS journalists to identify the three most important socio-political changes that their country needed to enable journalism to perform its functions. BRICS journalists were more or less in solidarity in their answers. They said that their country needed 'more democracy' and more 'media and economic independence' (see Table 14.2).

BRICS countries also differed in their answers, indicating the specific current problems in each country, solving which would also help to strengthen democratic development and protect journalism. For example, journalists in Brazil spoke about the need 'to end corruption and oligopoly', while journalists in Russia, India and China saw the need 'to increase political competition' in their countries. In China, journalists also wanted changes that would 'protect the rights of journalists'; in India,

TABLE 14.2 The three most important socio-political changes journalists believe are needed for journalism to perform its functions

Country	Cities: Metro (2) Provincial (2)	Change 1	Change 2	Change 3
Brazil	Brasilia/ Rio de Janeiro	Ensure media and economic independence	Reform legislation	End corruption and oligopoly
	Juiz de Fora/ Vitoria	Ensure media and economic independence	Require diploma	Foster appreciation of professionals
Russia	Moscow/ St. Petersburg	Have more democracy/ ensure media and economic independence	Have socialist/ liberal values	Have developed and civilized society with culture of mutual respect/ increase political competition/ compliance with the laws/have openness among authorities
	Yekaterinburg/ Petrozavodsk	Have more democracy	Nothing to change/ensure media and economic independence	Ensure media and economic independence

(continued)

TABLE 14.2 Cont.

Country	Cities: Metro (2) Provincial (2)	Change 1	Change 2	Change 3
India	New Delhi/ Hyderabad	Ensure media and economic independence	Have more democracy	Increase political competition
	Kolkata/Pune	Keep politicians/ government from interfering with news/ have people support media on issues that will assist them in solving problems with government	Increase literacy rate	Create access to government/ make information available
China	Beijing/ Shanghai	Relax media regulation	Strengthen legislation	Protect rights of journalists
	Guangzhou/ Wuhan	Have more democracy	Ensure media and economic independence	Increase political competition
South Africa	Johannesburg/ Cape Town	Ensure media and economic independence	Have more democracy	
	Durban/Port Elizabeth	Ensure media and economic independence	Have more democracy	

changes that would 'provide access to the government', and in Russia, changes that would create 'openness of the authorities'. Only in India, journalists noted that 'the literacy rate in the country should be increased' and that 'people should support the media in issues that will assist (journalists) to solve issues with the government'.

On a final note, in the world of media today, digitization and the advent of social media have made the dichotomy of 'center-periphery' less and less relevant in its traditional understanding of physical proximity to and distance from a centre of power, because distance and borders are disappearing in this digital world. Further, according to Xiang (2017), the changes in global leadership are creating a horizontal rather than vertical configuration of power so that, instead of centre-periphery, we now have centre-semi-periphery-periphery, in which China occupies a semi-peripheral position. The 56th Munich Security Conference introduced a new term, 'Westlessness', to describe current trends in the world and the role of the West in a new era of great-power competition (Munich Security Report, 2020). International journalism studies would do well to stay away from normative comparisons, irrespective of which country or region takes the centre position if 'Westlessness' indeed occurs.

Notes

1 http://presscouncil.nic.in/Content/62_1_PrinciplesEthics.aspx; www.unesco.org/new/fileadmin/MULTIMEDIA/HQ/CI/4.%20India%20AINEC%20code%20of%20ethics.pdf.
2 https://dictionary.cambridge.org/dictionary/english/investigative-journalism.

References

Albuquerque, A. and Lycarião, D. (2018) Winds of change? BRICS as a perspective in international media research. *International Journal of Communication*, 12: 2873–2892.

Asante, M. K. (2007) *An Afrocentric Manifesto: Toward an African Renaissance*. Malden, MA: Polity.

Banda, F., Beukes-Amiss, C. M., Bosch, T., Mano, W., McLean, P. and Steenveld, L. (2007) Contextualizing journalism education and training in Southern Africa. *Ecquid Novi: African Journalism Studies*, 28(1–2): 156–175.

Becker, J. (2003) Keeping track of press freedom. *European Journal of Communication*, 18(1): 107–112.

Bollen, K. A. (1986) Political rights and political liberties in nations: an evaluation of human rights measures, 1950 to 1984. *Human Rights Quarterly*, 8(4): 567–591.

Breit, R., Obijiofor, L. and Fitzgerald, R. (2013) Internationalization as de-Westernization of the curriculum: The case of journalism at an Australian university. *Journal of Studies in International Education*, 17(2): 119–135.

Bosch, T., Paiva, R. and Malerba, J. P. (2018) Community radio for the right to communicate: Brazil and South Africa, pp. 196–209 in S. Pasti and J. Ramaprasad (eds.) *Contemporary BRICS Journalism: Non-Western Media in Transition*. London: Routledge.

Coppedge, M., Gerring, J., Altman, D., Bernhard, M., Fish, S., Hicken, A., Kroenig, M., Lindberg, S., McMann, K., Paxton, P., Semetko, H., Skaaning, S., Staton, J. and Teorell, J. (2011) Conceptualizing and measuring democracy: A new approach. *Perspectives on Politics*, 9(2): 247–267.

de Coning, C. (2016) BRICS and coexistence, pp. 25–48 in C. de Coning, T. Mandrup and L. Odgaard (eds.) *The BRICS and Coexistence: An Alternative Vision of the Global Order*. London: Routledge.

Downey, J. (2008) Recognition and the renewal of ideology critique, pp. 59–74 in D. Hesmondhalgh and J. Toynbee (eds.) *The Media and Social Theory*. London: Routledge.

Fonte, J. and Gonzalez, M. (2018) Freedom house turns partisan. *National Review*, February 15.

Freedom House (2019) *Freedom on the Net. China*. Available at https://freedomhouse.org/country/china/freedom-net/2019

Freidson, E. (1988) *Profession of Medicine: A Study of the Sociology of Applied Knowledge*. Chicago: University of Chicago Press.

Giannone, D. (2010) Political and ideological aspects in the measurement of democracy: The Freedom House case. *Democratization*, 17(1): 68–97.

Hanitzsch, T. (2008) Comparing journalism across cultural boundaries: state of the art, strategies, problems, and solutions, pp. 93–105 in M. Löffelholz and D. H. Weaver (eds.) *Global Journalism Research: Theories, Methods, Findings, Future*. Oxford: Blackwell.

Internet Live Stats. (2014) Internet Live Stats. July 1, Available at www.InternetLive Stats.com

Jian, G. and Liu, T. (2018) Journalist social media practice in China: A review and synthesis. *Journalism*, 19(9–10): 1452–1470.

Josephi, B. (2005) Journalism in the global age: Between normative and empirical. *Gazette*, 67(6): 575–590.

Konradova, N. (2020) The rise of Runet and the main stages of its history, pp. 39–61 in S. Davydov (ed.) *Internet in Russia – A Study of the Runet and its impact on social life*. Berlin: Springer.

Kivikuru, U. (2009) From an echo of the West to a voice of its own? Sub-Saharan African research under the loophole. *Nordicom Review*, 30: 187–195.

Korkonosenko, S. G. (2015) Global de-Westernization trend in media studies and Russian journalism theory. *Central European Journal of Communication*, 8(2): 175–186.

Lenin, V. I. (1901) Where to begin? pp. 13–24, *Lenin Collected Works*. Vol. 5. Moscow: Foreign Language Publishing House.

Mano, W. (2009) Re-conceptualizing media studies in Africa, pp. 277–293 in D. K. Thussu (ed.) *Internationalizing Media Studies*. London: Routledge.

Miike, Y. (2010) An anatomy of Eurocentrism in communication scholarship: The role of Asiacentricity in de-westernizing theory and research. *China Media Report Overseas*, 6(2): 1–13.

Munich Security Report 2020 (2020) *Munich Security Report 2020*. Munich, Available at https://securityconference.org/assets/user_upload/MunichSecurityReport2020.pdf

Ndlovu, M. W. (2015) What is the state of South Africa journalism? *African Journalism Studies*, 3(36): 114–138.

Nerone, J. (2013) The historical roots of the normative model of journalism. *Journalism*, 14(4): 446–458.

Paiva, R., Guerra, M. and Custodio, L. (2015) Professional, social and regulatory characteristics of journalism in online and traditional media in Brazil. *African Journalism Studies*, 3(36): 8–32.

Pan, Z. and Lu, E. (2003) Localizing professionalism: discourse practices in China's media reforms, pp. 215–236 in C. C. Lee (ed.) *Chinese Media, Global Contexts*. London: Routledge.

Pasti, S. and Ramaprasad, J. (eds.) (2018) *Contemporary BRICS Journalism: Non-Western Media in Transition*. London: Routledge.

Pasti, S. and Ramaprasad, J. (2016) Digitalization and journalists in the BRICS countries. *Brazilian Journalism Research*, 12(1): 12–33.

Pasti, S. and Ramaprasad, J. (eds.) (2015) The BRICS journalist: profession and practice in the age of digital media. Special issue *African Journalism Studies*, 3(36): 1–138.

Ramaprasad, J., Pasti, S., Paulino, F.O., Zhou, R. and Ndlovu, M. (2018) Professionalism: continuities and change, pp. 23–48 in S. Pasti and J. Ramaprasad (eds.) *Contemporary BRICS Journalism: Non-Western Media in Transition*. London: Routledge.

Sapiezynska, E. and Lagos, C. (2016) Media freedom indexes in democracies: A critical perspective through the cases of Poland and Chile. *International Journal of Communication*, 10: 549–570.

Simons, M., Nolan, D. and Wright, S. (2017) 'We are not North Korea': Propaganda and professionalism in the People's Republic of China. *Media, Culture & Society*, 39(2): 219–237.

Steiner, N. D. (2016) Comparing Freedom House democracy scores to alternative indices and testing for political bias: are US allies rated as more democratic by Freedom House? *Journal of Comparative Policy Analysis: Research and Practice*, 18(4): 329–349.

Thussu, D. K. (ed.) (2009) *Internationalizing Media Studies.* London: Routledge.

Thussu, D. K. (2013) De-Americanizing media studies and the rise of 'Chindia'. *Javnost-The Public*, 20(4): 31–44.

Tsygankov, A. P. and Parker, D. (2014) The securitization of democracy: Freedom House ratings of Russia. *European Security*, 24 (1): 77–100.

Vemula, R.K., Guerra, M., Paschoalino, C. and Moura, L. S. (2018) Technological manifestations in the newsroom: India and Brazil, pp. 159–172 in S. Pasti and J. Ramaprasad (eds.) *Contemporary BRICS Journalism: Non-Western Media in Transition.* London: Routledge.

Wasserman, H. and de Beer, A. S. (2009) Towards de-Westernizing journalism studies, pp. 448–458 in K. Wahl-Jorgensen and T. Hanitzsch (eds.) *The Handbook of Journalism Studies.* London: Routledge.

Wasserman, H., Ramaprasad, J., Sodré, M., Anikina, M., Vemula, R. K. and Xu, Y. (2018) Newsmaking: navigating digital territory, pp. 49–71 in S. Pasti and J. Ramaprasad (eds.) *Contemporary BRICS Journalism: Non-Western Media in Transition.* London: Routledge.

Willems, W. (2014) Beyond normative de-Westernization: Examining media culture from the vantage point of the global South. *The Global South*, 8(1): 7–23.

Worldatlas (2018) List of countries by internet users. Available at www.worldatlas.com/articles/the-20-countries-with-the-most-internet-users.html https://raec.ru/activity/analytics/

Xiang, Y. (2017) China in Africa: refiguring centre-periphery media dynamics, pp. 213–229 in D. K. Thussu, H. de-Burg and A. Shi (eds.) *China's Media Go Global.* London: Routledge.

15

NEOLIBERAL CAPITALISM AND BRICS ON SCREEN

Tatu Laukkanen and Iiris Ruoho

This chapter examines screen entertainment in Brazil, Russia, India and China after their economic liberalization. It takes under scrutiny some characteristic phenomena in order to start developing analytical tools to approach the BRICS formation (including South Africa) through popular culture in a totalizing and comparative manner. We call this approach, ´BRICS as method´ – an interpretive framework for thinking through the heterogeneous, multi-platform entity of entertainment of the BRICS countries, none of which are monolithic entities themselves. As the contributors of *Mapping BRICS Media* (Nordenstreng and Thussu, 2015) have shown, each country in the group has a variety of different media institutions and corporations, both private and public, even if some entities in the polities are hegemonic (like *Globo* in Brazil). Also, of course, the huge sphere of screen entertainment in all the countries already encompasses narratives and messages of great variety in their aesthetics and politics. As with other countries, in BRICS nations too, global media culture, in conjunction with economic liberalization, has transformed the role of the media in entertainment.

This chapter concentrates mainly on popular TV dramas and films. China and Russia are fore-grounded but the analysis extends to the BRICS quintet in many respects. The chapter largely leaves out the review of South Africa, however the analytical tools developed here can be used in the analysis of South African media and other 'emerging economies' outside of the BRICS grouping. Our analysis not only concerns popular television and film productions in a time of vertical integration of international and domestic media conglomerates but also sheds light on the trans-medial and hybrid qualities of BRICS media systems, in which content and technology spills on and influences, in reciprocal fashion, new and old media platforms. Still the main thrust of the chapter is that current media content not only traverses different platforms and aesthetics, but also reflects social and cultural changes felt more strongly in the unevenly developed BRICS. 'BRICS as method' scans for these conflicts with particular care, as the method, like the BRICS association itself, is first and foremost about political economy.

The first part of the chapter is devoted to the analysis of the popular Chinese TV drama *Cell Phone* (*Shouji*, 2010). The aim of the analysis is to show how a hugely popular series of screen entertainment is symptomatic of ongoing social and cultural change in the most powerful BRICS country. It serves as an example of a non-Western TV drama that highlights the contradictions raised by the growing economy for society and culture. The domestic television drama, like our key example here, is a genre with a rich tradition in the United States where it originated from, however *Cell Phone* deals with themes particularly topical in the BRICS countries. The chapter shows that TV drama production, such as *Cell Phone*, is an example of screen entertainment that problematizes and offers a multi-aspect take on an unevenly developed economy, which has had a recent encounter with neoliberal capitalism and its accompanying deterritorialization of old norms and culture.

The second part of the chapter focuses on the appropriation of another media form, the blockbuster film and how it is manifested on BRICS screens. Here the chapter specifically looks at what we call the 'nationalist blockbuster', particularly popular in China and Russia. The negotiation of these genres and forms of television and film are selected for analysis not only because of their huge impact and popularity, but also in order to start to answer the question posed by Daya Thussu and Kaarle Nordenstreng in the first volume of the BRICS media anthology: that is whether the impressive growth of media in the BRICS countries and their greater visibility across the globe signal an end to globalization as Westernization, and does this expansion 'provide an antidote to Western-dominated media frames?' (2015: 1). This chapter provides a conflicting answer of yes and no, since the idea of the nationalist (domestic) blockbuster (global) has an inherent contradiction.

Rather than being mere imitation of classic Western televisual and cinematic forms, we argue that often BRICS media producers use TV drama to negotiate and react to the ethical dilemmas of capitalist deterritorialization and neoliberal policy in a fashion particular to the emerging economies of the BRICS countries. Both the genres of serial TV drama and the blockbuster film have been massively popular throughout the BRICs in recent decades and are valuable texts with which to comparatively analyze representations of politico-economic change in a time of neoliberal policy implementation, as well as the representation of different subjectivities and ideas of community and the nation. Seeing the BRICS as a cultural bloc and introducing the concept of 'BRICS as method' to the study of media, we argue that these genres and forms have been appropriated in the BRICS to articulate the recent cultural changes in these countries and are not merely a manifestation of their insertion into the circulation of global televisual and cinematic flows. We show that the themes and politics of these narratives are tied to the BRICS' position in the world system and they are reactions to neoliberalist policy, often implemented under duress.

Negotiating cultural norms and values: contemporary Chinese TV drama

Today, of all the television genres, the series drama boasts the highest ratings across China. Indeed, Chinese TV dramas have always been the dominant genre in the TV market since its inception in the post-Mao era. Between 6pm and midnight, Chinese TV dramas capture the attention of up to 80 per cent of the nationwide audience. The Internet has also become the most important platform for many drama series in China. Most of the advertising revenue now comes from TV ads that are placed around these dramas. Television dramas not only entertain audiences but also provide topics for discussion. The first massively popular soap opera, *Yearnings* (*Kewang*), aired in 1990, was influential in the re-imagination of the national identity and culture after the Cultural Revolution (Lu, 2000; Keane, 2001; Rofel, 2007).

Numerous researchers highlight the important role of the Chinese television drama as a social and cultural interpreter. Janice Hua Xu argues that television is a symbol of modernity in China: 'television ushers in a new cultural order that challenges long-standing habits and ideologies. Compared with the print media, which is censored more meticulously, television is more representative of an open global culture' (Xu, 2008: 153).

Against the backdrop of a variety of international studies, it is possible to state that Chinese TV drama consists of multiple social, cultural and historical voices. This is also true of the *Cell Phone* series, which, among other things, depicts the lives of media professionals, journalists and media consumers. The drama negotiates the ways in which people are thought to have been affected and influenced by media and consumer culture. In this process, *Cell Phone*'s storytelling evinces the gazes of both the documentary and drama (Caughie, 2000: 37–38). The polyphonic nature of the Chinese television drama aligns with the evolution of the Brazilian telenovelas, which used to be mainly narratives of the elites in big cities but now have stories about the new middle class, such as *Avenida Brazil* (2012). This series was sold to over 150 countries and remains the most successful telenovela produced by Globo's studios.

When discussing China's screen entertainment, however, one should keep in mind that the state arm in charge of media censorship, SAPPRFT (State Administration of Press, Publication, Radio, Film and Television) which in 2018 was made defunct with its operations moved elsewhere, has been a powerful institution. Now under the Xi administration it has taken a conservative step back to socialist and patriotic values in media policy. The government decrees that entertainment needs to be patriotic, emanating the right values of harmony and progress, and domestically produced, even though the situation on the ground is often different. SAPPRFT recently ordered a reduction in the airing of foreign TV formats, like *The Voice of China*, which was hugely popular.

The policies of SAPPRFT were, however, selectively instrumentalized and Chinese screen entertainment is often highly ambivalent. The creators of *Cell Phone*[1] brought both artistic ambition and social critique to the project (e.g. Song,

2010: 422). Indeed, *Cell Phone* is a public arena for various, but still limited, social groups expressing their feelings in the post-reform era of China. On the other hand, the TV drama is generating a broad public discussion including the issues of a globalizing world, consumerism and cultural transformations. Despite censorship, television can offer multiple ways of reading and experiencing reality (Keane, 2001; Ng, 2014). Therefore, partly because of state control and censorship rules, television drama can – paradoxically – be an ambiguous and polyphonic piece of work.

SAPPRFT has stated that 'only domestically invented TV programmes in the Chinese cultural tradition can properly convey the "Chinese Dream", core socialist values, patriotism and Chinese traditions' (Brzeski, 2016). As Joseph Straubhaar has noted, international format TV shows, such as Shine Group's *Master Chef*, which has aired in all the BRICS countries, are often a hybrid production, with locals doing the below-the-line work of producing the actual show. Brazil and India have created a few formats for license, but the BRICS still lag behind in this category (Straubhaar, 2015). China's initiative of reining in foreign formats is in line with the intention of becoming an intellectual property right and above-the-line producer instead of a manufacturer, which reflects its strategic aims for a resurgent China in the global economy in general.

As a variety of scholars has argued, a strong union of economics and politics (Hu, 2007; Zhao, 2008; Sparks, 2010) has shaped the post-reform era in China. For this reason, Chinese media culture is a combination of a vibrant market economy and a highly authoritarian political system, exemplified by SAPPRFT. Many areas of the media industry are open to private capital and even public television stations and film studios need to generate a profit. Jason McGrath has noted that entertainment took centre stage due to the new market conditions that the Chinese film industry had to negotiate in the 1990s: 'The expectation that government owned studios turn a profit, combined with the sudden domination of the domestic box office by newly permitted Hollywood imports, meant that domestic film makers would have to emphasize turning out an entertaining product as never before in the People's Republic' (McGrath, 2012: 90). McGrath wrote this in his study of the *hesuipian* phenomenon, 'New Year's celebration' films, the particularly Chinese genre in which the director of the feature film version of *Cell Phone*, Feng Xiaogang established himself as one the most commercially successful mainland Chinese filmmakers.

State media, such as China Central Television (CCTV), are forced to compete for advertising revenue and viewers. This dual system also affects the professional role of Chinese journalists. However, there is no single orientation among journalists. The binary characterization of tabloid-style entertaining versus Party-sanctioned propagandistic journalism is too simplistic to reflect the day-to-day reality of Chinese media professionals (Hassid, 2011). Not only journalists but also Chinese artists and intellectuals have experienced rapid changes in their traditional roles. Especially after the 1980s, their social role transformed from cultural heroes to experts, scholars, professionals and entertainers. This change of the social role and representation of the intellectual is not unlike that of post-socialist Russia nor even of post-Nehruvian socialist India, but in China the change has occurred in a shorter time span and with more intensity. Chinese intellectuals have responded to these changes using various tactics and, while some of them have adapted to these changes, many have not (Wang, 1998: 10). *Cell Phone's* fictional characters belong to both academia and media and work at a public television station feeling the pressures of the market. The series depicts how the professional elite seeks to protect their privileged positions and adjust to new conditions. Emergent celebrity culture is also depicted: in *Cell Phone* younger rural characters seek to gain status via media by becoming celebrities (via reality TV shows, micro-blogs, etc.).

This transformation of subjectivity in the post-Mao era is facilitated in the remaking of public spaces and stories, such as television shows, through which people discover themselves (Rofel, 2007: 3–4). Following Foucault, Rofel sees consumerism and consumption (particularly of entertainment and media) as a key technology of the self, different commodities becoming the building blocks of the new Chinese subjectivity defined by a selective cosmopolitanism. This subjectivity is forged as cosmopolitan; however, this worldliness is selective as it is facilitated by global capitalism, consumerism and the entertainment provided by domestic and global media that are often hard to tell apart. A similar operation can be seen in the BRICS in general: the rise of the new middle classes, often forging their identity through consumption, is synchronous with the rise of BRICS countries.

With this process often comes historical amnesia, particularly of the political radicalism of Mao's time – an erasure of both past and imaginable futures – a quality attributed, of course, to postmodern culture in general (see for example Jameson, 1990). Aligning with Rofel's study of the younger generation of the Chinese, Pavan Varma (2007) argues that a new exclusive cosmopolitanism has risen in post-socialist India, in which consumerism largely forms the identity of the middle classes that actively take part in an amnesia of past value systems like Nehruvian socialism or Gandhian ideals. Similar studies abound of post-Soviet Russia (see Kivinen, 2015). *Cell Phone,* however, in its polyphonic form does not participate in this historical memory loss as it recognizes and problematizes the position of the shift in the status of the intellectual. In the sense it registers both residual (the Confucian/Maoist intellectual) and emerging trends (social media celebrity) in culture.

Cell Phone articulates the work and lives of the media elite and young migrants from the countryside, and, through the different characters reflecting the diversity of national topography, age, social class and gender, it provides an insight into Chinese society in flux. The show deals with a variety of issues topical in emerging economies, such as urbanization and the changing relationship between the centre and periphery, the globalization of culture and the introduction of new media and communications technologies. These issues and the accompanying deterritorialization of traditional culture are also often seen in popular film productions but the 36-part series offers a wider range of issues about the changes associated with economic liberalization, including feminism, migration and immigration, consumerism and marketization, the porousness of the private and the public and the reassessment of subjectivity itself.

Cell Phone is an adaptation of Liu Zhenyan's book that was also the basis of a popular film. Like the original film, the adaptation for television of *Cell Phone* was very popular, but it was not consumed mainly on traditional TV but more on the Internet, such as the Chinese website Sohu. These connections of cinema, TV and the Internet are another dimension of BRICS popular culture that demonstrate global trend of utilizing various media platforms for the same content. A variety of media platforms is not only affecting the means of distribution: the aesthetics traditionally associated with television, film or digital platform narration are also transcending traditional boundaries and becoming intertwined.

In entertainment, the aesthetics and forms, as well as the content itself have been inspired by telecommunication and digital technology. For example, the films of Ram Gopal Varma and Anurag Kashyap from India or José Padilha from Brazil, some of the critically acclaimed and commercially successful directors of their respective countries, are known for their televisual aesthetic, and their films foreground new digital communications technologies that are central to the narrative. The interflow of media technologies and the mediatization of society, as well as the narratives they give rise to are of course not exclusive to the BRICS nations, but the prevalence of these themes and aesthetics show that BRICS entertainment and media are well into and exhibit a globalized postmodern form in which the medium itself is an important part of the *mise-en-scéne* and narrative. In addition, it can be said that this new aesthetic and content is felt with greater impact in the BRICS countries, which have experienced these technological leaps too quickly and at huge scale. For example, the ubiquitous cell phones and television in Varma's films would have been inconceivable in the 1980s when landlines were scarce and the state-run *Doordarshan* the only TV broadcaster. *Cell Phone*, both the film and series, is a good example of the above-mentioned inter-BRICS trend.

The case of *Cell Phone*

Both the film and TV series *Cell Phone* exemplify a trend in screen entertainment throughout the BRICS that exhibit great anxiety over new communications technologies. Television and the mobile phone, and increasingly the Internet, are portrayed in BRICS films not only in a positive manner but also as presenting threats and anxieties (Laukkanen, 2017: 730–733). New technologies in these representations do not connect people, rather they are a source of mistakes, worry and conflict, as the films *Company* (2002) and *On a Wednesday* (2008) from India or *Elite Squad 2* (2010) from Brazil, demonstrate, to mention a few. In China, even Fifth Generation directors like Chen Kaige, have taken on the challenges of new technologies. His *Caught in the Web* (the Chinese title meaning *Flesh Search*, 2012) is based on a real-life event in which a Beijing resident was shamed on-line after a cell-phone video recorded on a bus with her behaving rudely spread on the Internet.

The *Cell Phone* TV series focuses on changes and transformations in the television and other media industries in post-reform China. Set in Beijing and Henan province, with a range of storylines and scenes, *Cell Phone* illustrates the rise of media as a social, cultural and historical force in the stories of its characters – a process that reflects, inter alia, the concept of mediatization (see Adolf, 2011: 358–360). Typical of this process is that relationships between people become increasingly mediated and that the media affect both society and culture through many practices and vice versa, and social and cultural transformations in turn affect media and its logic. The series draws attention to media competition, fan and celebrity culture, journalistic ethics and the influence of social media, especially on the youth.

At the centre of *Cell Phone* are the two male protagonists presenting their seemingly oppressive relationship with the media profession, including their experience of 'phone slavery', and the control of their wives. The narrative often revolves around the male protagonists' efforts to negotiate their social and intellectual roles and territories. In her analysis of male images in contemporary television drama in China, Geng Song argues that the representations of masculinity are becoming increasingly hybrid and that the male imagery, a product of social change, is tied to new formations of power (Song, 2010: 426). This challenges the idea of hegemonic masculinity. However, hybrid masculinity 'unites various and diverse practices in order to construct the best possible strategy for the reproduction of patriarchy' (Demetriou, 2001: 337; Song, 2010: 405). In *Cell Phone*, the male bond between the two leading protagonists and the strain it is put under is used to question the current, market-oriented media culture that pushes the traditional media elite far away from the ideals of high culture and responsible journalism and sometimes towards different forms of cynicism (see Zhong, 2010: 91–93).

This criticism can be understood from the perspectives of tradition and history: Confucian philosophy has traditionally directed high expectations towards the educated classes who are firmly established at the upper echelons of a hierarchical social order, whereas Maoism, instead, has promoted the media's role as a unique bridge between those who are elected to power and the ordinary people, the Party being the vanguard of the proletariat. Although the Confucian stance obviously points to a bygone China (even though many argue that Confucian traditions suiting the needs of the ruling elite are being resuscitated) such didactic, hierarchical and informational characteristics have been associated with the preliberalization media in all the BRICS nations in one way or another.

The deterritorialization of culture, accompanied by other developments, such as women and sexual minorities demanding their rights, threatens conservative cultural values and patriarchy as described above in *Cell Phone*. This renegotiation of the man's role, not only of the intellectual but also particularly the blue-collar male often depicted in crisis, is evident on BRICS screens. For example, Andrei Zvygiantsev's high-profile film *Leviathan* serves as a good example of a drama about the plight of the common man in Russia, whereas the nationalist blockbusters produced in Russia and their heroic figures could be seen as conservative reactions to the changing expectations of masculinity.

Both the *Cell Phone* novel and film place great emphasis on the charm of the 'the other woman' or 'the third partner'. In Chinese audio-visual culture, these figures have also become symptomatic of male desire and discontent as noted by Zhong (2007). The game between wives and their cheating husbands is also familiar to the Chinese audience. The series uses this contest as a metaphor for consumer society. Consumption is tied especially to femininity and the trade between wives and husbands. By showing wives spending money at shopping centres while their husbands compensate for their misconduct by offering them expensive lunches and gifts, the drama echoes the message of the 2004 megahit TV series *Chinese-Style Divorce*. This successful show, according to Xiao, demonstrated how commodities have become the tokens of love, which transforms interpersonal democracy based on egalitarian communication into a 'democracy of consumption' offering an illusionary equality through open access to the privilege of commodity consumption (Xiao, 2010: 748). This 'engineering of souls for the market' (Keane, 2001) makes it difficult to distinguish a market-oriented emotional subject from a rational bourgeois subject and political pragmatism in *Cell Phone*.

In *Cell Phone*, conflicts over sponsorship and corruption arise, which opens up a window of opportunity to leading character Fei Mo to have his own TV show, an offer he initially refuses. After the talk show, 'Tell It Like It Is', hosted by Fei ends, he starts his own show, which is reminiscent of CCTV's real, well-known *Lecture Room* (see Zhu, 2012: 153–168), consisting of public lectures on Chinese history and culture. Fei Mo is asked by the TV station to turn academic discussions of aesthetics into something entertaining and approachable for the television audience. He agrees to this and changes his lectures into stories about the four ancient beauties of China – the legends of four women distinguished for their appearance.

This kind of educational entertainment, to some extent, is regarded as degrading among academics; some scholars are accused of 'dumbing down' the knowledge from their field to cater to the 'vulgar taste' of the public and Fei Mo faces this dilemma. However, as the star of his own programme, Fei Mo no longer feels that he is wasting his knowledge and intelligence. This is his pragmatic tactic to adjust to the new situation: he is simultaneously a man of the house and a man of the market. These sort of new hybrid men – good householders and cosmopolitan business people – are a new breed of character on BRICS screens, a good example being the cosmopolitan yet conservative NRI (non-resident Indian) characters of Hindi cinema family dramas, popular since the 1990s.

Nevertheless, an antipathy towards a strong market ideology can be seen in *Cell Phone* (Ahmed, 2010: 34–37). The media professionals, such as channel managers, who have adopted a business-oriented stance, exemplified by their jargon espousing Western-style managerial concepts and tabloid-style journalism, represent their own kind of alien group in the drama. However, while the media elite/intellectuals like Fei Mo are shown struggling to maintain their position in the rapidly commercializing media world under profit-extracting managers, the same changes may appear as possibilities for individualization among people who have so far had relatively little control over their own lives.

The drama highlights youth as inspired by the possibilities of the Internet: members of the digitally native generation yearning to achieve something more than their parents did. In the case of *Cell Phone*, this means dreaming of becoming a microblogger or even a TV celebrity. Exemplary here is the case of the girl from Henan province, Niu Canyun, whose slightly naïve character is based on the 'Sister Lotus' case from the mid-2000s. A hotly debated figure on Chinese-language websites and an international phenomenon, Sister Lotus (pseudonym) came from a small town in provincial China, was turned down in university admissions but was able to become a celebrity by posting pictures of herself on the web. Sister Lotus was a harbinger to the rise of the *diaosi*, a now widespread phenomenon of the digital generation in which a common person net-streams her life to millions of followers who are also their sponsors, a sort of reality TV 2.0.

In contrast to middle-class city dwellers, the Internet, mobile phones and television certainly seem to offer the rural working class the opportunity to gain status and income, as well as new experiences and chances to explore and express their individuality. *Cell Phone* addresses this possibility, only suggestively, through the character of young Niu. Her successful blogging could be seen as offering empowerment; however, in the context of the story, it may also suggest the detrimental influence of popular culture. Yet the drama also makes it possible to interpret that the people are not mere victims. For example, blogging seems to provide young people with the chance to gain attention and a sense of belonging, for example, to certain value systems to which they aspire (Yuval-Davis, 2006: 199). At the same time, the drama portrays media as a fantasy machine representing the promise of a better life, especially for the rural working class and youth, who are looking to improve their living conditions. In the context of *Cell Phone*, people living in the countryside direct a good deal of positive affective energy towards the media in a socialist market economy and post-Maoist culture.

An antidote to Hollywood: nationalist blockbusters

The BRICS countries are keen to assert their power in the world, but at the same time contribute to the ideological erosion of the era of liberalization. This can be seen in the production of what can be called nationalist blockbusters, particularly from China and Russia, which are hugely popular domestically but negligibly in the international market. If Hollywood blockbusters often produce a narrative of US hegemony throughout the world in which they are consumed, the nationalist blockbusters produce regional counter-narratives to these US productions, while often mimicking Hollywood product in the blockbuster form. A survey of these nationalist blockbusters shows that war films – unlike their Hollywood big brothers that have a message of US-led universalism, foregrounding liberty and independence – build community, often through suffering and sacrifice, and display a clearly nationalist message, often steeped in gendered history. In terms of geopolitics and the politics of challenging West-centric history, the nationalist war film – what could also be called the sub-imperial blockbuster – could be seen as a cinematic push for geopolitical multi-polarity or even as an sub-imperial stance, an ambition, it could be argued, shared at least by China and Russia.

The regional nature of the nationalist blockbuster has to be understood through the film market. Both domestic and Hollywood blockbusters circulate in most BRICS markets; however, domestic productions circulate and accrue capital minimally if at all in the US and the rest of the world. This is part of a greater system, in which the emerging BRICS markets, with their growing middle classes, are highly sought after by global media operators. China, now the world's biggest box office, is being penetrated by and referenced or perhaps better put, interpellated in several Hollywood blockbusters. For example, the 2016 Disney animation *Zootopia*, about a society of animals that was hugely popular in China, had versions in which some characters were tailored for specific markets; a newscaster figure was a panda in the version released in China and a jaguar in the Brazilian one. Under the pressure of such competition, local BRICS producers feel a need to turn to national and communitarian narratives to ensure commercial success.

The domestic production of nationalist blockbusters serves to counter Hollywood product at the box office and, if some patriotism is injected, so much the better in the eyes of the administration that supports the projects. *Wolf Warrior 2* (2017), the highest grossing film in mainland China until then, is about a former PLA-special forces soldier who performs Rambo-like heroics against mercenaries in Africa, an entertaining take on China's geopolitical interests. Nationalist blockbusters are good business: *Stalingrad* (2013), a CGI-dominated take on the 1942 battle, was Russia's greatest box-office success for years. In 2019, *T-34*, another nationalist blockbuster set in World War II, surpassed it. True to blockbuster form, *Stalingrad* had a huge budget by Russian standards, costing about $30 million. It had all the features of the typical blockbuster: a special-effects driven film, in classic narrative film style, incorporating various genres such as action and romance, done with a large budget. The battle of Stalingrad, the main event of the 'Great Patriotic War', received the epic treatment demanded by its status in the Russian historical imagination, being the first Russian film to be shot and exhibited in IMAX 3-D.

Collaboration with Hollywood and inter-BRICS investment is happening between the BRICS countries. Indian and Chinese investors back Hollywood films and studios and Bollywood and Greater Chinese stars appear in Hollywood films and vice-versa. The Indian film industry collaborates with the other above-mentioned film industries, in recent years particularly with the Chinese, this collaboration going much further than the tradition of popular Hindi films being shot in foreign locations. These BRICS co-productions go towards meeting the wishes of cultural policy makers, who have outlined collaboration between the countries in the media industries in general at the 2015 BRICS Media summit in Beijing and the film industry at the 2016 BRICS film festival in India. Here again it should be remembered that these top-down initiatives or recommendations have been preceded by many intra-BRICS films, often by independent filmmakers.

State cultural institutions wield great power over the industry in the BRICS countries, where film production is still heavily subsidized or dependent on the state, as in Russia and China, who have clear strategies for the production of blockbusters. *The Guardian* reported in 2002 on the initiative of the Russian government, just a few years after Russia's economy started to grow after the 1990s, to grant 1.5 billion roubles over two years to film production, with the condition that preference would be given to films of a patriotic and historical nature, along with children's cinema (Walsh, 2002). Since 2002, this blockbuster project of the Russian state has gained momentum. The follower of Goskino (which was placed under the Ministry of Culture in 2000), the Kino Fund, initiated in 2009, is bound by its rules to finance blockbuster films. Since 2010, the fund has made grants from its $100 million budget to finance the highest grossing domestic films, which are usually hagiographies of famous Russians and narratives with a positive light on the country. Most of the financing for *Stalingrad* came through government institutions and state-backed companies, the Kino Fund contributing $13 million.

In terms of production values, nationalist blockbusters (*da pian*, 'big films') top the finance charts in China as well. *Flowers of War* (2011), depicting the battle of Nanjing in 1937 and the ensuing Japanese atrocities, was the most expensive Chinese production at its time, with its $94 million budget only topped by Zhang Yimou's *The Great Wall* (2017). If the Hollywood blockbuster aims at a global audience, the Chinese nationalist blockbuster is mainly meant for the consumption of the country's nationals, be they domestic or diasporic. Though if they can fill seats outside of their respective nation, the money and soft power are welcome and formal, narrative and other strategies, such as hiring international stars, attest to the producer's intention to cross over internationally.

The Great Wall is a good example of how BRICS film producers go through great pains to get international exposure. The film tried to present itself as entertaining, spectacular and as politically bland as possible. Starring Hollywood A-lister Matt Damon, the film was set in a bygone (depoliticized) historical era and, in block-buster fashion, its narrative offered a platform for a bundle of action sequences set in a romanticized, even touristy Chinese setting. Action film is a highly exportable form, as East Asians have shown time and again, yet the film failed outside China, while, domestically, like *Flowers of War*, it was a great success.

Even though nationalist blockbusters are some of the greatest successes in the countries' film histories, it should be kept in mind that they are by no means a sure bet in the domestic market either. The largest budget ever for a Russian film, $55 million, was spent on Nikita Mikhalkov's spectacular flop *Burnt by the Sun 2* (2010), another blockbuster style film about World War II. *The Founding of the Army* (2017) by Hong Kong director Andrew Lau was a disappointment at the box-office in China, even though endorsed by the authorities. This film about the People's Liberation Army was the third part of a state-supported epic blockbuster 'founding trilogy', preceded by *The Founding of a Republic* and *Birth of a Party* (hagiographic narratives of Mao and the CCP), both of which did well at the box office.

For a long time, the Chinese administration has endorsed so-called *zhuxuanlu* or 'main melody', films buttressing the administration and its values, but progressively films have become entertainment-oriented. Like capitalism and authoritative government, market-oriented entertainment and nationalism also intertwine in Chinese films. In post-Soviet Russia, the return to nationalist narratives is a particularly notable development, as civic and other collectivist grand narratives were scorned for a long time after the fall of the USSR, as Seth Graham (2008) has noted. No doubt decades of globalization and the growth of the Russian economy has created the window of opportunity for the nationalist blockbuster, the same going for China and, as some scholars suggest, India.

The fact that a significant number of blockbuster films in Russia and China are nationalist is understandable, even without the obvious influence of state funding and other forms of support. Filmmaking is a particularly capital-intensive operation and when reaching up to the blockbuster standard, even more so. It comes as no surprise then that producers hedge their bets by making films on events or themes that are of interest and marketable to a national audience. The aesthetics, distribution and marketing, and ancillary strategies of the Hollywood blockbuster are imitated all over the world, especially in Brazil, Russia, India and China, which now have the necessary market conditions. These countries have large domestic markets and, in the case of China and India, big diasporic audiences as well; the ability to mobilize capital; state-backed film financing organizations (such as the Kino Fund in Russia); the technology, and the political desire, or even need, to produce blockbusters after a period of cultural deterritorialization and economic liberalization. In the BRICS countries this sort of film-making also obviously aligns with the country's internal and external narrative of being on the rise ('India Shining', 'Chinese Dream', etc.) and making their own mark on global economics and politics, and Western-centric global historical narratives, challenging selective Hollywood cinematic historicism, for example the way World War II is presented in global blockbusters such as *Dunkirk* (2017).

While in Russia the unstable 1990s saw the collapse of the film industry, the boom of the following decade under Vladimir Putin gave rise to new players in the film and television industries that crossed boundaries. Producers like Aleksander Rodniatskii became important figures (Strukov, 2015). Rodniatskii produced Bondarchuk's *Stalingrad* (2013), but also art-house fare like *Elena* (2011) and the controversial *Leviathan* (2014) by Andrei Zvyagintsev. This role in both the spheres of the nationalist blockbuster and art-house film, as well as different platforms such as film and television, is emblematic of the necessary flexibility of the BRICS filmmakers or media operators. The torn intellectuals working at the television station in *Cell Phone*, discussed in the previous section, are a fictional representation of this.

The film industries in Brazil and South Africa, like that in Russia, have been fighting a losing battle against Hollywood for most of the recent decades. The film industry in Brazil in the early 1990s also collapsed when state financing was cut due to the neoliberal policies of President Collor de Mello. Also, as in Russia, the

Brazilian film industry has been able to recover, with a combination of government and business interests. Brazilian companies now get tax breaks for financing culture, including cinema, and a parade of corporate logos adorn Brazilian films before the opening credits start rolling. With the rise of these industries, Brazilian filmmakers, like their Chinese and Russian counterparts, have become more aware of the spectator as consumer.

In Brazil the new *Cinema Novo* (New Cinema), a Latin American movement, is more entertainment-oriented than the original Brazilian *Cinema Novo* that was politically radical but deemed by many critics as elitist. The 'new Latin American' films such as *City of God* (Meirelles, 2002) are in turn criticized for being commercial and reformist. Brazilian critics (e.g. Bentes, 2003: 124) argue that the new Brazilian cinema utilizes a 'cosmetics of hunger', as they go cinematically slumming – the concept a pun on the radical 'aesthetics of hunger' of Glauber Rocha (1939–1981) and *Cinema Novo*. The opposite argument comes from the critics who defend these films, emphasizing that, while commercial, they still foreground social problems and, unlike the more *auteur* and politically oriented films of earlier decades, are popular.

Cinema Novo directors of the 1960s and 1970s tried to cover revolutionary themes and vast political and philosophical questions, often with the use of allegory, setting their frequently formally adventurous films in the impoverished countryside and (later in the movement) in the disenfranchised parts of cities. Contemporary Brazilian cinema is more occupied with 'realist accounts' of Brazil's social problems, often situated in the megacities and their favelas. There has been a change from an elite/utopian intellectual outlook to a genre – (often crime-) oriented commercial/popular sociological one. As noted, Brazilian cinema has been commercially and critically successful and has been able to cross over to global audiences with films such as *City of God*, *Central Station* (1998) and the *Elite Squad* films.

As already discussed, the imitation of successful formulas and use of cross-border talent is not a Hollywood monopoly. *Stalingrad* featured internationally known German star Thomas Kretchmann and its music was composed by noted Hollywood composer Angelo Badalamenti. In China, the use of Hong Kong film talent in many recent mainland Chinese productions is an attempt to tap into Hong Kong cinema's global reach. The Kung Fu craze of the early 1970s, followed by the successes of the 'gun fu' films of John Woo and *wuxia* epics like Ang Lee's *Crouching Tiger, Hidden Dragon* act as an inspiration and a formula to be followed. This list of crossover successes includes the films of Jackie Chan, who has done work in Hollywood, such as the *Rush Hour* series, as well as intra-BRICS productions such as the Sino-Indian *Kung Fu Yoga* (2017). As many Hong Kongers, Chan now works in the lucrative mainland China industry, another example of how martial arts is an important soft power vehicle for China. This is demonstrated by another China Hollywood collaboration, the remake of the *Karate Kid* (2010), understandably marketed in China with another name *Kung Fu Dream*.

Scholars have argued that a paradoxical conservative Hindu nationalist ideology that is neoliberally oriented is inculcated in post-liberalization popular Hindi cinema. Films that exhibit this trend, such as the trendsetter megahit *Dilwale Dulhania Le Jayenge (Brave Heart Will Take Away the Bride)* (1995) that was followed by many later emulations by directors such as Karan Johar, feature affluent cosmopolitan yet staunchly 'Hindustani gentlemen'. These dual characters are often NRIs that, unlike earlier representations are in the era of economic liberalization seen in a positive light, just as the romantic films moved away from stories featuring class conflict to strictly affluent surroundings. Even though these are not the sort of historical war and action films, such as the ones from China and Russia, these films in their homogenizing fabrication of the nation, family values, patriarchy and Hinduism could be seen to be the nationalist blockbusters of India.

Here one must note that India also has its share of war films that fit the contradictory qualifications of the nationalist blockbusters, such as the films of J. P. Dutta, produced after economic liberalization and the rise of the Hindu nationalist Bharatiya Janata Party. Some war films from India such as *Border* (1997) and *L.O.C Kargil* (2003) represent the politics of the post-liberalization era, before which such depictions or even the naming of the enemy as Pakistani would have been avoided, and correlate with the patriotic Chinese and Russian blockbusters. A recent example of the Indian variant of the nationalist blockbuster is *Kesari* (2019) about the 1887 battle of Saragarhi in which a small Sikh detachment serving in the British army defended and died protecting a fort in Afghanistan against a superior Afghan force.

Conclusion

Taking the BRICS as an interpretive framework or method, we have explored how popular TV dramas and blockbuster films can be seen as reflecting themes arising from the economic and geopolitical positions of the BRICS countries, as a result of liberalization and the globalization of media and culture over recent decades. In the screen entertainment analyzed in this chapter, the list of these themes is long: the changing role of the intellectual, the rural/urban divide with the impoverishment of the countryside and internal migration, as well as the ethical problems and new forms of subjectivity and community that consumerism and technological development give rise to. The Chinese TV drama *Cell Phone* brings out these contradictions. While the media elite struggles to maintain its position in the rapidly commercializing media world, the same changes may offer the potential for individualization among, for example, young rural women, who have relatively little control over their own lives. The drama highlights youth, who are increasingly inspired by the Internet and can imagine achieving something more than their parents did. In the case of *Cell Phone*, this means dreaming of becoming a micro-blogger or a TV celebrity fitting to the rampant celebrity culture that has arisen in recent decades.

While the TV drama creates tension from the dilemmas arising out of the emerging economies and foregrounds the deterritorialization that goes with the unleashing of global capitalism, the nationalist blockbuster is an example of popular entertainment that offers both entertainment and an idea of community, as an example of reterritorialization. The nationalist blockbusters from Russia, China and India often replicate cinematically the 'shared dysphoria' that produces what the researchers call 'identity fusion', a visceral sense of oneness, achieved through communal pain. For example, in *Stalingrad* (where all the main characters die for the motherland), the idea of Russia as a great power is seen to relate to a populace that has seen an economic resurgence since 2000 (now diminished), but on the other hand has not had an ideology to match the post-1990s material gains. In other words, the new middle class needs an idea to supplement consumption that they aggressively embraced; the nationalist blockbusters are a part and parcel of capitalism with *Gemeinschaft* (community).

The BRICS countries have had to negotiate their entertainment productions to meet and articulate the needs of the changed economy of an unequal, neoliberal and in some cases of the BRICS, an authoritarian corporate state, open to the world market. One of the consequences of this is the use of the Hollywood blockbuster style filmmaking that offers some form of ideology in the vacuum of a post-socialist polity – nationalism wrapped in spectacle. The commodification of nationalism in the nationalist blockbuster should also be understood and studied in relation to its consumption: multiplex cinema theatres, often part of shopping malls, have mushroomed in the BRICS countries in the last two decades. These private homogenized global spaces of exclusive inclusivity also contribute to the class stratification of the BRICS countries. Even though the explosion of the multiplex and its cultural consequences have been studied, for example in India (Athique and Hill, 2010; Pendakur, 2012) and Russia (Norris, 2012), using BRICS as an interpretive framework could yield an understanding of the phenomenon as an emerging market game changer in many ways.

Some of the emerging economies could be seen as sub-altern formations, which produce a 'sub-imperial' cinema as their national blockbusters circulate domestically and regionally in a US-dominated global market. This chapter agrees with the scholars who argue that global screen entertainment is still West-centric, particularly in cinema though less in television, but it can be said that such domination is gradually diminishing with the rise of BRICS entertainment as discussed above. As the cases of the Chinese TV drama and the nationalist blockbusters demonstrate, the nationalist blockbusters are clear displays of domestic successes, but the 'authenticity' or homegrown status of the product may be hybridized given the growing collaborations with or through forms appropriated from US-dominated global media. The struggle over the BRICS markets is huge, the future uncertain. In light of, for example, the co-competition in the field of entertainment and screen interflows described in this chapter, a productive way to analyze the BRICS media is precisely to not see it in Manichean dichotomy with Western media. Rather it should be viewed as an assemblage of residual and emerging as well as hybrid product with changing competition between the entities involved that include interests both private and public, independent media makers and capitalists, whose positions are often intermingled. A Cold War-like binary, therefore, would be misleading, especially in the field of screen entertainment.

The BRICS have to be understood not only as a politico-economic category but also as a cultural category. This chapter starts bringing together the BRICS as a cultural bloc in the field of entertainment and screen studies, but this does not mean that the approaches taken here would not be useful in other emerging nations. We do not wish to discard old concepts used to study media in the twentieth century – such as national, post-socialist, socialist, Third World, modern, postmodern and global media – because they are all still useful and components of all of them are to be found in the BRICS context. However, these categories are inadequate for explaining the phenomena of screen entertainment, be it film or television in the contemporary world system that has seen the formation of the BRICS grouping. Many of the above concepts are useful and our aim here is not to debunk them: there is a need for a large conceptual arsenal in order to understand the complexity of what is screened in the world today and concomitantly unthink the West-centric theoretical register. The concept of the BRICS and the BRICS as method is now the most useful way to understand the entertainment produced and consumed in the bloc of states categorized as 'emerging economies'. BRICS as method, with new vocabularies and concepts such as the nationalist blockbuster or BRICS cinema, enables a better understanding of the increasingly complex media systems in a new configuration of geopolitics and changing global economy.

Note

1 *Cell Phone* is directed by Yan Shen and Lei Wang; screenplay by Fang-jin Song; produced by Jun Wang and Xiao Zhang.

References

Adolf, M. (2011) Clarifying Mediatization: Sorting through a current debate. *Empedocles: European Journal for the Philosophy of Communication*, 3(2): 153–175.

Ahmed, S. (2010) Happy Objects, pp. 29–51 in M. Gregg and G. J. Seigworth (eds.) *The Affect Theory Reader*. Durham: Duke University Press.

Athique, A. and Hill, D. (2010) *The Multiplex in India*. New York: Routledge.

Bai, R. and Song, G. (eds.) (2014) *Chinese Television in the Twenty-First Century: Entertaining the Nation*. London: Routledge.

Bentes, I. (2003) The *sertão* and the *favela* in Contemporary Brazilian Film, pp. 121–137 in L. Nagib (ed.) *Brazilian Cinema*. London: I. B. Tauris.

Brzeski, P. (2016) China Cracks Down on International Formats. *Hollywood Reporter*, June 20. Available at www.hollywoodreporter.com/news/china-cracks-down-international-formats-904345

Caughie, J. (2000) *Television Drama: Realism, Modernism, British Culture*. Oxford: Oxford University Press.

Demetriou, D. (2001) Connell's Concept of Hegemonic Masculinity: A critique. *Theory and Society*, 30: 337–361.

Graham, S. (2008) Taking Stock of our Stocktaking, *Kinokultura*, Available at www.kinokultura.com/2008/21-graham.shtml

Hassid, J. (2011) Four Models of the Fourth Estate: A typology of contemporary Chinese journalists. *The China Quarterly*, 208: 813–832.

Hu, Z. (2007) The Chinese model of and paradigm of media studies. *Global Media and Communication*, 3(3): 335–339.

Jameson, F. (1990) *Postmodernism, or, The Cultural Logic of Late Capitalism*. Durham: Duke University Press.

Keane, M. (2001) Television Drama in China: Engineering souls for the market, pp. 176–202 in R. King and T. Craig (eds.) *Global Goes Local: Popular Culture in Asia*. Vancouver: University of British Columbia Press.

Kivinen, M. (2015) Onko Venäjän Keskiluokka Vastavoima, pp. 133–145 in M. Kivinen and L. Vähäkyla (eds.) *Venäjän Palatseissa ja Kaduilla*. Helsinki: University of Helsinki Press.

Laukkanen, T. (2017) *Contemporary BRIC Cinema and the Politics of Change*, PhD dissertation, Hong Kong. Hong Kong University.

Lee, H. and Cho, Y. (2012) Introduction: Colonial modernity and beyond in East Asian contexts. *Cultural Studies*, 26(5): 601–616.

Lu, S. H. (2000) Soap opera in China: The transnational politics of visuality, sexuality, and masculinity. *Cinema Journal*, 40(1): 25–47.

McGrath, J. (2012) Meta-cinema for the Masses. *Modern Chinese Literature and Culture*, 17(2): 90–132.

Ng, H. W. (2014) Rethinking Censorship in China: The case of *Snail House*, pp. 87–103 in R. Bai and G. Song (eds.) *Chinese Television in the Twenty-First Century: Entertaining the Nation*. London: Routledge.

Nordenstreng, K. and Thussu, D. K. (eds.) (2015) *Mapping BRICS Media*. London: Routledge.

Norris, S. (2012) *Blockbuster History in the New Russia, Movies, Memory and Patriotism*. Bloomington: Indiana University Press.

Pendakur, M. (2012) Digital Pleasure Palaces: Bollywood seduces the global Indian at the multiplex. *Jump Cut*, No. 54. Available at www.ejumpcut.org/archive/jc54.2012/PendakurIndiaMultiplex/text.html

Rofel, L. (2007) *Desiring China. Experiments in Neoliberalism, Sexuality, and Public Culture*. Durham: Duke University Press.

Shackleton, L. (2018) China Box Office Grows by $2Bn. To reach $8.6Bn, in 2018. *Screen Daily*, January 2. Available at www.screendaily.com/news/china-box-office-grows-by-2bn-to-reach-86bn-in-2017/5125239.article

Song, G. (2010) Chinese Masculinities Revisited: Male images in contemporary television drama serials. *Modern China*, 36(4): 404–434.

Sparks, C. (2010) China's media in comparative perspective. *International Journal of Communication*, 4: 552–566.

Straubhaar, J. (2015) The BRICS as emerging cultural and media powers, pp. 87–103 in K. Nordenstreng and D. K. Thussu (eds.) *Mapping BRICS Media*. London: Routledge.

Strukov, V. (2015) *Contemporary Russian Cinema, Symbols of a New Era*. Edinburgh: Edinburgh University Press.

Varma, P. K. (2007) *The Great Indian Middle Class*. New Delhi: Penguin.

Walsh, N. P. (2002) Russian Cinema Holds Out for a New Type of Hero. *The Guardian*, September 28.

Wang, H. (1998) Contemporary Chinese thought and the question of modernity. *Social Text*, 55: 9–44.

Xiao, H. F. (2010) Love is a capacity: The narrative of gendered self-development in Chinese-style divorce. *Journal of Contemporary China*, 66(19): 735–753.

Xu, J. H. (2008) Family Saga Serial Dramas and reinterpretation of cultural tradition, pp. 33–46 in Y. Zhu, M. Keane and R. Bai (eds.) *TV Drama in China*. Hong Kong: Hong Kong University Press.

Yu, H. (2009) Mediation Journalism in Chinese Television. Double-time narrations of SARS, pp. 129–149 in Y. Zhu and C. Berry (eds.) *TV China*. Bloomington: Indiana University Press.

Yuval-Davis, N. (2006) Belonging and the politics of belonging. *Patterns of Prejudice*, 40(3): 197–214.

Zhao, Y. (2008) *Communication in China. Political Economy, Power, and Conflict*. London: Rowman and Littlefield.

Zhao, Y. (2012) Your Show's been cut: The politics of intellectual publicity in China's brave new media world. *Javnost*, 19(2): 101–118.

Zhong, X. (2007) Mr. Zhao and off the screen. Male desire and its discontent, pp. 295–315 in Z. Zhang (ed.) *The Urban Generation. Chinese Cinema and Society at the Turn of Twenty-first Century*. Durham: Duke University Press.

Zhong, X. (2010) *Mainstream Cultural Refocused: Television Drama, Society, and the Production of Meaning in Reform-Era China*. Honolulu: University of Hawaii´i Press.

Zhu, Y. (2012) *Two Billion Eyes: The Story of China Central Television*. New York: The New Press.

Zhu, Y., Keane, M. and Bai, R. (2008) Introduction, pp. 1–17 in Y. Zhu, M. Keane and R. Bai (eds.) *TV Drama in China*. Hong Kong: Hong Kong University Press.

16

BRICS DE-AMERICANIZING THE INTERNET?

Daya Kishan Thussu

This chapter argues that, while the Internet continues to be dominated by the West, in particular the US, in terms of its infrastructure, economics and governance, this domination is increasingly being challenged by the BRICS countries, notably China, Russia and India. China already has the world's largest Internet population, followed by India, primarily driven by mobile communications. As in the rest of the world, Russia, Brazil and South Africa, too, have witnessed a major expansion of online communication. With the world becoming increasingly mobile, networked and digitized, the question arises whether BRICS communication flows will help to pluralize and democratize information and communication agendas and create a new global communication order, leading to a de-Americanization of the Internet. The BRICS nations are playing a crucial role in this process, given their growing presence and assertiveness related to global cyber-issues, despite some strong divergences within the group. The chapter discusses the process of de-Americanization within five domains: infrastructure, commerce, regulation, weaponization and surveillance of cyber space, and the developmental dimensions of the Internet. In all five domains, the contributions of the BRICS nations are delineated, especially in relation to the dominant agenda setters for the Internet, namely the US and the digital corporations based there.

The infrastructure of the BRICS Internet

The BRICS nations in recent years have strengthened their digital infrastructure for the Internet, a key element contributing to the global digital supremacy of the US, the originator of the Internet (Aouragh and Chakravartty, 2016). From outer space to undersea cables, US-based companies continue to dominate Internet hardware. The growing privatization of global digital infrastructure by mainly US-based 'space barons' (Davenport, 2018) has contributed, for example, to the growth of the satellite industry: of the nearly 2,000 active satellites orbiting the Earth in 2019, the US accounted for 849, compared with China at 284, Russia with 152 and India at 57. Similarly, the exponential increase in fibre-optic submarine cables, through which 99 per cent of international data is transmitted, also has a strong US imprint on it, a fact which is resented by countries such as Russia and China (Starosielski, 2015). Major digital corporations – notably Microsoft, Google, Facebook and Amazon – are investing in undersea cables: in 2018 they owned or leased more than 50 per cent of the undersea bandwidth (Satariano, 2019). As the volume and value of global data surges, the storage and processing of digital data becomes a crucial component of infrastructure. Out of 4,422 co-location data centres, 80 per cent were located in developed countries, with the US alone accounting for about 40 per cent of the total (UNCTAD, 2019). Russia, for example, has pointed out that of the 13 root servers essential to the functioning of the global Internet, 10 are located in the US and the other three are 'on the territory of US allies' (Japan, the Netherlands and Sweden) (Nocetti, 2015: 121).

US infrastructure projects have strong governmental backing, including the US Global Positioning System (GPS), a vital element of the satellite communications infrastructure and a key part of the US government's National Strategy for Space. However, some BRICS nations have supplemented if not replaced US domination of the hardware of digital communication. Russia, India and China have developed their own satellite navigation systems (GLONASS, NAVIC and BeiDou, respectively). China has ambitions to create a global system to rival the GPS, especially as the digital dimension of the Belt and Road Initiative (BRI) is concerned with constructing 'a China-centred digital Silk Road that ties neighbouring countries more closely to China through submarine, terrestrial, and satellite links' (Shen, 2018: 2692). The country's Hongyun satellite project, started in 2016, aims to build a space-based communications network to provide broadband Internet connectivity to users around the world, especially in developing countries. India has also established itself as a key player in the budget satellite business: in 2014, it launched *Chandrayaan*, a probe into orbit around Mars, on a cost of merely $76 million (see essays in Pillai and Prasad, 2017).

The BRICS nations have had limited success, however, in intra-BRICS infrastructure exchanges and cooperation (with the exception of the long-established Indo-Russian collaboration in space technology). The 2012 plan to create a 34,000 km 'BRICS undersea cable' network, which would have linked Fortaleza in Brazil, Cape Town in South Africa, Chennai in southern India, Shantou in China and Vladivostok in Russia, did not get beyond the planning stages (Zhao, 2015). If it had been built, it would have been a symbolic act of de-Americanizing the infrastructure of the Internet. The project demonstrated intra-BRICS tensions, which have increased especially in relation to BRI, despite its official discourse of achieving a 'common destiny' for humankind. A report by a leading defence-related think tank in India noted: 'BRI's overall expanse in general, and its growing control over the digital and space domain in particular, allows Beijing to bend this common destiny

towards satisfying its own geopolitical, geo-economic and geostrategic ambitions'
(Lele and Roy, 2019: 56).

China is ahead of almost every other nation in terms of infrastructure for 5G
technology, giving it mastery of its own industrial future and that of countries using
its mobile services for the new Internet of Things (IoT) (DeNardis, 2020). With the
world's largest smartphone market and Internet population, 5G mobile network
investments in China are projected to reach $405 billion by 2030. Privately-owned
Huawei, the world's largest telecoms equipment supplier, with an estimated 40 per
cent global market share, is pushing for global 5G projects in 170 countries. China
is also ahead of most countries in the field of Artificial Intelligence (AI): *A Next
Generation Artificial Intelligence Development Plan* released in 2017, envisages China
becoming 'world-leading' in certain AI fields by 2025 and evolving into the 'primary' centre for AI innovation by 2030.

To achieve this ambition, the Chinese government is working with its leading
private corporations, the so-called BAT – Baidu (China's biggest search engine),
Alibaba (Chinese equivalent of Amazon) and Tencent (the country's biggest social
media platform) – to create its AI 'national team' (Jing and Dai, 2017). Digital
entrepreneurs such as Kai-Fu Lee already speak of China as an 'AI Superpower'
(Lee, 2018). Unlike China, India's approach to AI is not so commercial, viewing
it not only as a means for economic growth but also for social inclusion. In
2018, the country's premier government think tank, the National Institution for
Transforming India (NITI Aayog) published a discussion paper outlining India's
national AI strategy – #AIforAll – which speaks of developing India to serve as 'a
garage or tinkering lab to develop new AI technologies for other developing countries'. It urges AI initiatives to evolve 'scalable solutions for emerging economies
…' #AIforAll means 'technology leadership in AI for achieving the greater good'
(NITI Aayog, 2018: 5).

Commerce: the changing contours of the Internet economy

These developments in digital infrastructure have enabled the rapid expansion of
global digital trade, defined as 'digitally enabled transactions in goods and services,
whether digitally or physically delivered' (OECD, 2019: 136). In 2017, global digital
advertising spend (at $200 billion) overtook TV advertising for the first-time. The
economic geography of the digital economy, notes UNCTAD's *Digital Economy
Report 2019*, 'does not display a traditional North-South divide'. Instead, it is consistently being led by the US and China, which 'account for 90 per cent of the
market capitalization value of the world's 70 largest digital platforms' (UNCTAD,
2019: xvi).

Seven 'super platforms' – Microsoft, Apple, Amazon, Google, Facebook, Tencent
and Alibaba, the report notes, 'account for two thirds of the total market value'
(ibid.). Digital platforms are increasingly important in the world economy: in 2017,
the combined value of platform companies with a market capitalization of more
than $100 billion was estimated at more than $7 trillion. Google had 90 per cent of

the market for Internet searches; Facebook accounted for two thirds of the global social media market and was the top social media platform in more than 90 per cent of the world's economies. Amazon boasts almost 40 per cent share of the world's online retail activity and its Amazon Web Services accounts for a similar share of the global cloud infrastructure services market (UNCTAD, 2019: xvii).

Such commercial success was achieved by strong support from various US administrations from the mid-1990s, the period when the Internet began to be privatized and globalized. The US has an inbuilt advantage – the Internet was conceived, constructed and communicated to the world from the US and the companies based there, a reality which has remained almost constant as digital economies have expanded in scope and scale (Lee and Jin, 2018; Moore and Tambini, 2018). The 1997 report, *A Framework for Global Electronic Commerce*, published during the Clinton Presidency, called for the private sector to take the lead in the development of the Internet, adding: 'governments must adopt a non-regulatory, market-oriented approach to electronic commerce' (US Government, 1997). In 2006, the Bush administration established the Global Internet Freedom Task Force with its main aim to 'maximize freedom of expression and the free flow of information and ideas' (US Government, 2006). Subsequent US administrations have deepened and enlarged the market logic of cyberspace (US Government, 2018). Given this, it is not surprising that as, in rest of the world, US-based digital corporations and platforms dominate cyberspace within the BRICS countries. With the exception of China, all other BRICS nations are integrated and dependent on US corporations, though Russia demonstrates some autonomy in this field – see Tables 16.1 and 16.2.

In Russian cyberspace, despite the popularity and availability of US-based digital platforms, Russian companies continue to hold sway. Vkontakte (Vk.com), a home-grown social media network; Yandex (the search engine) and Mail.ru (with 100 million users across its social-media, messaging, email and online-gaming properties) are widely used in Russia and by the Russian-speaking global diaspora. The Russian-language Runet is the predominant Internet provider, while the contribution of the Internet economy to the Russian economy was estimated in 2018 at $62.2 billion (Davydov, 2020: v). In the other three BRICS nations, despite their growing domestic markets, the dependence on US-based global digital companies

TABLE 16.1 Most accessed websites in BRICS countries (excluding China)

Brazil	*Russia*	*India*	*South Africa*
Google.com.br	YouTube.com	Google.com	Google.com
Google.com	Yandex.com	Google.co.in	YouTube.com
YouTube.com	Vk.com	YouTube.com	Google.co.za
Facebook.com	Google.ru	Amazon.in	Facebook.com
Globo.com	Mail.ru	Facebook.com	Yahoo.com

Source: Adapted from Government of Brazil, 2019, data December 2018–June 2019.

TABLE 16.2 Popular apps in BRICS countries (excluding China)

	Brazil	*India*	*Russia*	*South Africa*
Search engines	Google	Google	Google Yandex Rambler	Google
Video streaming	YouTube	YouTube	YouTube	YouTube Netflix
Social media	Facebook Instagram Snapchat Twitter	Facebook	Vkontakte	WhatsApp Facebook Twitter
Messaging	WhatsApp Telegram Skype	WhatsApp	Telegram	WhatsApp

Source: Adapted from Government of Brazil, 2019.

is evident. In Brazil, 91 per cent of mobile Internet users in 2018 were on WhatsApp and 86 per cent on Facebook (Government of Brazil, 2019).

India: the world's largest 'open' Internet

With more than 600 million users, India is home to the world's largest 'open' Internet (since the Chinese one, the world's largest, is not open). India is the second largest market for smartphones in the world after China and high-speed broadband penetration was at 53 per cent in 2019 (KPMG Report, 2019). According to a McKinsey report, Indians now download more apps – 12.3 billion in 2018 – than citizens of any other country except China, while the average Indian social media user spends 17 hours on the platforms each week, more than social media users in China and the US (McKinsey Global Institute, 2019). The highest number of registered users of both Facebook and WhatsApp are in India: 350 million and 400 million respectively. Unlike China, India has a huge demographic dividend: 70 per cent of Indians are below the age of 35, increasingly digitally savvy, upwardly mobile and globalized and this youth population is highly active on the Internet (Jeffrey and Doron, 2013; Agrawal, 2018; Arora, 2019).

YouTube, which has the world's largest audience in India, provides an option to consumers, introduced in 2016, to find content in their own language: 95 per cent of India's video consumption is in Indian languages, not in English. There are over 230 million regional language users online, compared to 175 million English users (KPMG Report, 2019). With 245 million people each month watching online videos, the Indian audience is impacting on the global entertainment business. In 2019, for a very brief period in February, Swedish video blogger PewDiePie, who has 80 million followers on YouTube, was replaced by the Hindi music channel

T-Series as the most subscribed channel on YouTube, according to the *Financial Times* (Poonam, 2019).

Such digital success stories have been made possible by a concerted effort by the Indian government and private corporations to digitize the world's largest democracy. India's Jio Platform, part of Reliance, the country's leading conglomerate, with interests in energy, retail, e-commerce and media (owning India's biggest television news network TV-18) has transformed digital life for most Indians. In the first three years since its launch in 2016, Jio's cheap mobile Internet services, including free calls and affordable data, had won it 400 million users, helping to open up India's largely untapped digital markets (Mukherjee, 2019).

Cyber-capitalism with Chinese characteristics

Unlike India and rest of the world, Chinese Internet platforms are all Chinese (Hong, 2017a; CNNIC, 2019). Much of the international literature on the Internet in China is focused on issues surrounding censorship and control. Relatively little attention has been given to its thriving and globalizing electronic economy – what I have termed elsewhere as 'cyber-capitalism with Chinese characteristics' (Thussu, 2018: 26). One fundamental reason why a Chinese Internet exists and in fact is booming, is that it was able to create, protect and develop its own digital properties by restricting the entry of global giants such as Google, which exited China in 2010 (Sheehan, 2018). Today, Chinese digital companies are increasingly globalizing: a notable example is TikTok, the short video app from Chinese company Byte Dance, which has grown explosively since its 2016 launch, with 800 million monthly active users – 300 million of them outside China. In 2019, TikTok became the most downloaded app on the iOS App Store.

The Alibaba group owns multiple online market places including Taobao, a consumer-to-consumer platform with more than 600 million active monthly users, many outside China in Southeast Asia, Turkey, Europe and India. Baidu runs China's largest search-engine, owning multiple content, advertising and app services, and Tencent Games is the world's largest video game company. In 2018, Chinese companies raised $6.75 billion in the US IPO market, with companies in the telecommunications, media and technology industry accounting for about 70 per cent of total IPOs. These included the video streaming platform, Iqiyi ($2.25 billion); the online group discounter, Pinduoduo ($1.63 billion); the streaming app provided by Tencent, QQ Music ($1.07 billion); the *anime* video streaming platform, Bilibili ($483 million) and the livestreaming gaming platform, Huya ($180 million) (Sheehan, 2018; *China Internet Report 2019*).

According to the *China Internet Report 2019*, published annually by the Hong Kong-based, Alibaba-owned newspaper, *South China Morning Post*, Tencent topped the Chinese cyber giants with a market value of $418 billion, followed by Alibaba at $416 billion. To put these figures in context, in 2019 the top five global Internet corporations (in terms of market capitalization) were all US-based conglomerates: Microsoft ($1 trillion), Amazon ($888 million), Apple

($875 million), Alphabet ($741 million) and Facebook ($495 million). These companies do not merely operate in a national space but are integrated in global flows of capital: Alibaba, for instance, received investment from US-based Goldman Sachs and the Japanese Soft Bank (which also invested in Toutiao, NetEase and Didi). Other major Western investments included Walmart in JD.com and Google in Baidu. Investment is also flowing the other way: in 2018, Baidu, Alibaba and Tencent invested in 280 companies of which 42 were overseas investments (*China Internet Report*, 2019).

China's sophisticated digital payment system, built on digital wallets and QR codes, is ahead of many Western nations. Ali-Pay (part of Alibaba, in operation since 2011 and now called Ant Financial) accounts for 60 per cent of the Chinese e-commerce market and WeChat Pay (introduced in 2013 and owned by Tencent) had more than one billion monthly users in 2019. These two digital payment services are increasingly being used outside China and are seen as being highly suitable for adoption by countries with less-developed banking industries (World Bank, 2018a).

Although still in its early stages, Intra-BRICS digital commerce is also growing, arguably the, initial signs of a process of de-Americanizing cyber trade. In 2019, China's investment in India exceeded $8 billion, including Alibaba's in Paytm, India's best-known digital payment system, while Tencent invested in India's first billion-dollar gaming company, Dream11 (Gateway House, 2020). TikTok had as many as 200 million users in India in 2019 (in contrast to Instagram's 80 million). In 2018, Alibaba set up a joint venture with the Russian mobile operator Megafon and Mail.ru to create the AliExpress Russia e-commerce website (*Economist*, 2019). South Africa's media conglomerate Naspers has investments in Tencent and Mail.ru, as well as in the Indian online travel company, Make My Trip and Brazil's mobile marketplace, Movile (Teer-Tomaselli, Tomaselli and Dludla, 2019).

Regulation: BRICS and cyber sovereignty

Governance and regulation of cyberspace remain a crucial component of contemporary international relations and a hotly contested terrain, especially since new issues about cyber security and digital property rights have gained salience in a networked, globalized and mobile electronic marketplace (Brousseau, Marzouki and Méadel, 2012; Negroponte and Palmisano, 2013). Over the past decade, two competing views have emerged: the 'sovereigntist', in which national governments take the major decisions about governance and regulation – vocally championed by China and Russia – and the US-led, market-oriented, privatized network model promoting a 'multi-stakeholders' approach (Mueller, 2010; Ebert and Maurer, 2013; DeNardis, 2014), reflecting, as an OECD report notes, the 'Internet's own DNA: open, distributed, borderless, multi-stakeholder and global' (OECD, 2019: 152). The US position has consistently been anchored in the principles of what Goldsmith has labelled 'commercial non-regulation' and 'anti-censorship' (Goldsmith, 2018). While the 'multi-stakeholder model' has strong supporters among three, West-leaning BRICS nations – South Africa, India and Brazil – Russia and China have argued for a UN-approved and managed governance structure with the International Telecommunication Union (ITU) undertaking a primary role in defining and implementing governance.

Such moves are stoutly resisted by the US. In 2013, Eric Schmidt, the then Executive Chairman of Google and Jared Cohen, Director of Google Ideas, predicted that the Internet would 'fracture and fragment', leading to its 'Balkanization', with 'co-existing and sometimes overlapping but in important ways, separate national systems' (Schmidt and Cohen, 2013: 85). The BRICS nations, especially China and Russia, have been instrumental in contributing to this 'fragmentation', which to them is not 'Balkanization' but an attempt to reclaim their cyber sovereignty, 'to align the Internet with their jurisdictional boundaries' (Mueller, 2017: 3). According to Mueller, the fragmentation debate is 'really a power struggle over the future of national sovereignty in the digital world. It's not just about the Internet. It's about geopolitics, national power, and the future of global governance' (ibid.).

China and Russia have serious concerns that US control of the Internet compromises their sovereignty and security. Both countries exercise extensive and deeply embedded control and censorship regimes. The so-called 'Great Firewall of China' – an effective information filtering mechanism – is claimed by many journalistic accounts to be 'the world's biggest and most sophisticated system of Internet censorship' (Griffiths, 2019), a view supported by recent research (Yang, 2016; Roberts, 2018). In Russia, government control over Internet intermediaries and service providers is strong, as attested by Western narratives, journalistic (Soldatov and Borogan, 2015) and academic (Oates, 2013; Nocetti, 2015; for a different perspective also see essays in Davydov, 2020).

In democracies such as India there is also concern about losing control over its cyberspace. In 2011, India proposed a new UN Committee for Internet Related Policies, taking a sovereigntist approach but the effort was not successful. At the UN-sponsored ITU World Conference on International Telecommunication held in Dubai in 2012, Russia and China introduced a proposal for equal rights among nation states 'to manage the Internet', which was rejected by the US and its Western and other allies, forcing it subsequently to be withdrawn and the ITU to adopt a non-binding resolution. 'A truly global platform is being undermined by a collection of narrow national Internets', is how a task force report from the US Council on Foreign Relations described the proposal (Negroponte and Palmisano, 2013: 4). Of the 144 members of the ITU, 89 nations signed the resolution, while 55, including the US, either chose not to sign or abstained. Among the BRICS nations, Russia, China, Brazil and South Africa voted for, while India voted against – demonstrating once again a divergence on Internet-related issues.

Under the left-leaning government of President Dilma Rousseff, NETmundial – a 'global multi-stakeholder meeting on the future of Internet governance' – was held in Sao Paulo in Brazil in 2014, which, while reaffirming the multi-stakeholder model, also demanded that governance structures 'must respect, protect and promote cultural and linguistic diversity in all its forms' (Drake and Price, 2014). The disunity of BRICS was visible here too: Russia and India did not vote in favour of the proposal.

Also in 2014, with the disclosures by Edward Snowden of the extensive surveillance programme and worldwide mobile phone tracking by the US National Security Agency (Greenwald, 2014; *Washington Post*, 2014), security and privacy issues came to the fore on Internet governance debates and the BRICS countries were the most vocal in their demand to protect their cyberspace. Russian President Vladimir Putin demanded that Russian Internet firms move their servers to Russia and the Kremlin launched a group of 'cyber guards' to search for 'prohibited content'. In 2019, the Russian Duma approved a law on 'digital sovereignty', which tried to 'separate Russia's Internet from the global one' (*Economist*, 2019: 43). In the same year, Russia was instrumental in passing a resolution at the UN General Assembly for a cybercrime treaty, framed around national sovereignty, which would allow greater control of online content by governments, anathema to the West, champions of a 'free and open' Internet.

Unlike its other BRICS partners, China's Internet is an example of cyber sovereignty in practice, with the 'party-state' – a strong advocate of de-Americanizing the Internet – controlling both the infrastructure and software of Sino-cyberspace. In a 2018 essay written soon after taking over as chief of the Cyberspace Administration of China, Zhuang Rongwen outlined his country's plan to 'exert full control over the information flowing over China's portion of the Internet', adding that 'whoever masters the Internet holds the initiative of the era, and whoever does not take the Internet seriously will be cast aside by the times' (cited in Creemers, Triolo and Webster, 2018). Utterances such as these have led to reactions from Western governments, Internet corporations and think tanks. The 2018 US National Cyber Strategy document is explicit in its strategy, urging that the US government 'will continue to work with like-minded countries, industry, civil society, and other stakeholders to advance human rights and Internet freedom globally and to counter authoritarian efforts to censor and influence Internet development' (US Government, 2018: 25).

Demanding data localization

One area of particular concern to governments, as well as of great commercial interest to US-based digital corporations, is the control and exploitation of data. The BRICS nations – especially its two populous Asian members – are home to the world's largest potential sources of data to be mined. Data has been transformed into a valuable global commodity and a transnational currency of the digital age; 'a new economic resource for creating and capturing value', according to UNCTAD's *Digital Economy Report,* which adds that 'control over data is strategically important to be able to transform them into digital intelligence' (UNCTAD, 2019: xvii).

The growth in mining, trading and manipulation of data in the data-driven economy has provided extraordinary power to largely US-based digital giants, who deal with an enormous amount of private data and public information (US

Government, 2016; Mayer-Schoenberger and Ramge, 2018). Data control by digital platforms – what Jin has labelled 'platform imperialism' (Jin, 2015: 11) and the potential for 'digital colonization' (Couldry and Mejías, 2019) have raised widespread concerns among BRICS governments. As an UNCTAD report notes, global Internet Protocol traffic, 'a proxy for data flows', has grown exponentially in the past two decades. In 1992, global Internet networks carried approximately 100 gigabytes (GB) of traffic *per day*. By 2017, such traffic had surged to more than 46,600 GB *per second*, and was projected to reach 150,700 GB *per second* by 2022 (UNCTAD, 2019: 9, emphasis added).

It is not surprising then that the US government and corporations have been aggressively promoting data liberalization and strongly resisting attempts at data localization, which is seen by the US as a threat to 'a free and open global Internet'. A 2013 task force report by the US Council on Foreign Relations recommended that all future trade agreements between the US and its trading partners contain 'a goal of fostering the free flow of information and data across national borders while protecting intellectual property and individual privacy' (Negroponte and Palmisano, 2013: x). The National Cyber Strategy of the US also maintains that its key objective is to 'promote the free flow of data across borders' (US Government, 2018: 15).

According to the *Digital Trade Restrictiveness Index* produced by the Brussels-based European Centre for International Political Economy, China, Russia and India were the three countries with the 'most restrictive policy environment for digital trade' (Ferracane, Lee-Makiyama and van der Marel, 2018: 8). In 2015, Russia implemented a new law that demanded companies store data about Russian citizens on Russian territory. According to the law, foreign companies which operate within Russian cyberspace have to notify the national Internet watchdog, *Roskomnadzor* about their data location. In 2019, the Russian search engine Yandex set up a 'public interest fund' that could provide the Russian government power over key governance decisions to ensure that Russian data remains within the country.

As discussed above, China has always had control over its data, so localization issues there have a different trajectory and are more concerned with what happens when Chinese Internet providers access and trade in data in other countries, such as data harvested from global consumers of apps like TikTok. In India, Chinese-owned and operated smartphones – Huawei, Xiaomi, Oppo and Vivo – account for 70 per cent of the market (the world's second biggest). Given that China already leads the world in such areas as AI and digital mobile payments, and is exporting its model globally through the BRI, it will also resist attempts at data localization.

Despite being the second-largest economy in the continent after Nigeria, debates on data localization and sovereignty in South Africa have been relatively limited, with the government approving its National Cyber Security Policy Framework only in 2012. Though more active on Internet governance-related issues as mentioned above, Brazil, too, was late to the issue of data localization: the Data Protection Law (*Lei Geral de Proteção de Dados*), which regulates the collection and treatment of personal data, was approved in 2018 and modified a year later by the Brazilian

Congress, creating the National Data Protection Authority (*Autoridade Nacional de Proteção de dados*).

The Indian position towards data localization is compounded by the fact that, as the country runs a large proportion of the global business-process-outsourcing (BPO) market through its globally connected outsourcing companies, including Infosys, Tata Consultancy Services, Wipro and Cognizant, much of their work is dependent on US clients and their international data. Although India has largely supported the US multi-stakeholder approach to Internet regulation and the US giants – Facebook, Google and Amazon and their affiliates – continue to shape the Indian cyberspace, in the past decade Indian Internet companies have begun to demand localization of Indian data, a move supported by the nationalist government of Prime Minister Narendra Modi, which is setting up national data-sharing regimes and infrastructure.

In 2018, India demanded that international tech and payment firms such as Mastercard, Visa and American Express store Indian data locally, reflecting the need to maintain India's technological sovereignty. A panel headed by the co-founder of Infosys, Kris Gopalakrishnan, working on the government's cloud-computing policy, recommended that data generated in India should also be stored within the country, to ensure that 'data generated from India can be utilized for the benefit of Indian citizens, governments, and private players'. While agreeing that 'the flow of data across borders is essential for a free and fair digital economy', the report warned that 'India's national interests may require local storage and processing of personal data' (Srikrishna Report, 2018: 10). India wants, conceptually at least, to be the one to articulate a global South perspective on data localization. Distinguishing itself from the three main approaches to data localization represented by the US (no restrictions), the European Union (qualified restrictions) and China (strong restrictions), the report suggests that India could forge a 'fourth path', 'not only relevant to India, but to all countries in the global South looking to establish or alter their data protection laws in light of rapid developments in the digital economy' (ibid.: 13).

Indian policy makers are looking to Chinese success in creating indigenous digital corporations that are now increasingly going global. Aruna Sundararajan, India's Secretary of Telecommunications told the *New York Times*, 'we don't want to build walls, but at the same time, we explicitly recognize and appreciate that data is a strategic asset' (quoted in Goel, 2018). India's draft e-commerce policy, released in 2019, speaks of 'India's data for India's development', adding 'data are the new oil therefore, just like oil, or any other natural resource, it is important to protect data' (Government of India, 2019). Invoking Mahatma Gandhi's movement against British colonization, Reliance Industries Chairman Mukesh Ambani told a high-profile conference in 2019 that India needed a new movement against 'data colonization … [as] data is the new wealth' (quoted in Langa, 2019). Such nationalistic rhetoric has a pragmatic side to it, as Reliance Jio is the biggest player in the country's cyberspace, having invested heavily in digital infrastructure to promote its suite of apps (Mukherjee, 2019). Nevertheless, data localization has become a focus of attention to counterbalance US hegemony of the Internet and the BRICS countries, particularly, Russia, China and India, can provide an alternative discourse on data sovereignty that could be a model for the majority world to use the resources of Internet for economic development.

Weaponization of information and digital warfare

The increasing use of online platforms for disinformation campaigns by governments, corporations and other interest groups, carried out by individuals or bots using algorithms, has created the threat of what has been termed as 'computational propaganda' (Woolley and Howard, 2018). As elsewhere, such weaponization of information is in evidence within BRICS democracies, for example, WhatsApp being 'weaponised as social media' during the election of far-right presidential candidate Jair Bolsonaro in Brazil in 2018 (Evangelista and Bruno, 2019) or anti-Muslim hate in Indian cyberspace (Mirchandani, 2018).

Russia and China are singled out by Western governments as indulging in the 'weaponization' of information. It could, however, be argued that the use of information as a weapon is as old as communication itself and in modern times the US has excelled in this arena. Countries such as Russia and China are concerned about the close relationship between the US government and Internet corporations based in that country. Putin went so far as to label the Internet as 'a CIA project' (*Economist*, 2019). Countries with closed information systems are also concerned that the US could use its Internet dominance to foster regime change (Klimburg, 2017). They have good reason to believe this: George W. Bush's 2003 *National Strategy to Secure Cyberspace* and the Obama administration's 2009 *Cyberspace Policy Review* established a US Cyber Command to integrate US cyber operations, including offensive military cyber operations abroad (US Government, 2003 and 2009).

This has grown more strident under the Trump administration, as the *National Cyber Strategy*, issued in 2018 by the Department of Defense, speaks of 'defend forward' by thwarting cyber threats 'before they reach their targets' and disrupting 'malicious cyber activity at its source'. Among its goals are punishing what it called 'malicious actors', such as Russia and China, countries (along with Iran and North Korea) that use 'cyber tools to undermine our economy and democracy, steal our intellectual property, and sow discord in our democratic processes' (US Government, 2018: 2–3). Such policy discourses are also reflected in academic literature emanating from the US (for example, Carlin and Graff, 2018).

Kremlin dezinformatsiya

In Western discourses on information warfare, Russia gets even more attention than China. Reports about Russia's 'Internet Research Agency' sometimes labelled as a 'troll farm', promoting pro-Kremlin propaganda online, have captured global attention (Chen, 2015). The alleged Russian cyber-attack on Ukraine in 2015 was one early example of Russian online aggression against an adversary (Greenberg,

2019). The most controversial case of the weaponization of cyber information, including social media, is the alleged Russian interference in the 2016 US presidential elections (Singer and Brooking, 2018; Hall Jamieson, 2018). However, a US study of the US-based twitter accounts of American citizens found scant evidence on the effect of disinformation targeted at Western public opinion except that it mostly caters to right-wing audiences (Hjorth and Adler-Nissen, 2019).

With its motto of 'question more' the Russian international news network RT (formerly Russia Today), which claims to be the most watched 24/7 news channel on YouTube, is considered by many as a major vehicle for disinformation. Its output has been creating ripples in Western media and policy circles, an indication of what has elsewhere been called the 'RT effect', particularly visible within the US and Western Europe (Thussu, 2019: 216). An 8,700-word investigation in the *New York Times* framed the global operations of RT and other Russian overseas media as part of 'hybrid' warfare undertaken against the West and its liberal world order (Rutenberg, 2017). A study of RT's YouTube programming found that the channel's targeting of strategic groups outside the West, including Arabic-speakers, was less successful than among English and Spanish audiences (Orttung and Nelson, 2019).

A European Parliament panel report was explicit about what it called 'Russian influence campaigns', suggesting that they 'have disseminated disinformation, undermined the public discourse with bots, inflated controversial viewpoints at the fringes of the political spectrum, and hacked political actors across the globe' (European Parliament, 2019: 26). The European Union has set up a portal – EUvsDisinfo – to collate and to analyse disinformation cases. In the US, the think tank, Atlantic Council runs a 'Digital Forensic Research Lab' to monitor and manage disinformation, with support from civil society groups especially the tech-savvy 'digital Sherlocks', as its 2019 report calls them, 'skilled at identifying disinformation' and 'skilled at identifying coordinated disinformation activity driven by inauthentic accounts, often in real time' (Polyakova and Fried, 2019: 3).

China and cyber espionage

Online spying is part of the weaponization of the Internet and here China receives the most opprobrium in the US-led Western media. Espionage has technical, political, psychological and legal dimensions in a rapidly changing strategic landscape (Lin and Zegart, 2019). Even before the Snowden revelations and the advent of what Zuboff has called 'surveillance capitalism' (Zuboff, 2019), the NSA led an extensive international surveillance operation called Echelon. Through a combination of spy satellites and digital surveillance devices, Echelon intercepted and eavesdropped on international electronic communication – phones, e-mail, radio signals, airline and maritime frequencies.

Satellite intelligence from commercial companies such as Space Imaging, co-owned by Google Earth, hugely benefit from the highly lucrative global satellite imaging market. In 2010, Google won an exclusive $27 million contract to provide

US intelligence with 'geospatial visualization services' (Levine, 2017). As cyberspace has emerged as the new frontier for geopolitics, governments have become entrepreneurial in their sponsorship, deployment and exploitation of hackers – 'cyber proxies' and 'mercenaries' – to project or protect their national interests (Maurer, 2018).

China's growing assertion in reshaping the cyber domain and its preparations for what it calls 'war under conditions of informatization' (Cheng, 2016: 2) is another example of moves to de-Americanize the Internet. Reports of Chinese spies hacking into US government computer systems to procure intellectual property from industrial manufacturers and military contractors, allegedly sponsored by the Chinese government, have been circulating in US media and academic literature (Singer and Friedman, 2014; Wolff, 2018). 'Perhaps the most damaging channel for stealing US intellectual property is cyberespionage', said a report, *Chinese Influence Activities in the United States*, published by the Hoover Institution. 'Cyberespionage is both a means for pilfering US science and technology, as well as a method of intelligence collection for potential attacks against the American military, government, and commercial technical systems' (Hoover Institution, 2018: 125).

A 2018 cover story in *Bloomberg Businessweek* alleged that Chinese agents had inserted surveillance microchips into servers used by leading corporations, including Apple and Amazon (Robertson and Riley, 2018). In the same year, the US Justice Department charged two Chinese nationals with 'Global Computer Intrusion Campaigns', targeting intellectual property and confidential business information. Of particular interest to Western observers are the activities of Huawei, against whom charges of surveillance and spying are routinely made: in 2010, the NSA secretly broke into Huawei's headquarters in an operation code-named 'Shotgiant' to spy on its 5G technology. 'Americans were trying to do to Huawei the exact thing they are now worried Huawei will do to the United States', reported the *New York Times*, wryly (Sanger *et al.*, 2019).

Digital connectivity for development: lessons from BRICS

Beyond commerce and surveillance, one area where de-Americanizing the Internet is perhaps most likely to emerge is in the field of developmental communication, where the BRICS nations could demonstrate a significant impact. Four of the five members are considered to be 'developing' countries, with the exception of Russia, which appears in the top 50 highly developed countries (at number 49) of the Human Development Index, according to the 2019 UN Human Development Report. The other four rank at 79 (Brazil), 85 (China), 113 (South Africa) and 129 (India), out of the 189 countries for which data was analysed (Human Development Report, 2019).

As mentioned above, investment in digital infrastructure is seen as a crucial component for development in the BRICS countries. The Brazilian government's *Plano Nacional de Banda Larga* (National Broadband Plan), announced nearly a decade ago to meet the country's growing Internet needs, has extended the fibre-optic network to the interior regions and installed submarine cables. In 2017 a public consultation for a new national connectivity plan, *Internet para Todos* (Internet for All) was introduced (Mari, 2018). By 2019, more than 67 per cent of households had access to the Internet. In South Africa, Internet penetration has reached nearly 60 per cent, partly as a result of the government's 'SA Connect' programme, in operation since 2013, aiming to provide affordable broadband access to public institutions, while the 2016 National Integrated ICT Policy White Paper aims to transform the country into 'an inclusive and innovative digital and knowledge society'.

It is in China and India, though, that the impact of the Internet on development has been most profound. The growing use of mobile phones and digital platforms, made possible as a result of government and private initiatives on public Wifi, has expanded digital communication with a developmental dimension. This has helped millions of farmers and micro-entrepreneurs to improve their health, education and livelihoods. In 2015, India launched its 'Digital India' programme, supported by $75 billion from public and private investment in a phased manner. China's mobile finance systems have become successful models and are being replicated in several developing countries where China has become deeply entrenched in the communication sector (Murphy and Carmody, 2015). Its ambitious project of building a 'digital Silk Road', with fibre-optic cables, mobile networks, satellite relay stations and data centres, has a strong developmental dimension (Hong, 2017b). The total amount of ICT aid to Africa between 2000 to 2014 amounted to just over 3 per cent of Chinese aid to the continent – $7.13 billion out of $288 billion – 'the ICTs could work as conduits for Chinese Internet-based industries' – both hardware and software (Wang, Bar and Hong, 2020: 1505).

Less discussed internationally but an equally important developmental project is India's *Aadhaar* (Sanskrit for 'foundation') – the world's biggest biometric identification system run by the Unique Identification Authority of India (UIAI) – which provides a unique identification number to 1.3 billion citizens to ensure that they receive entitlements under various welfare schemes in a transparent manner. Nandan Nilekani, a former Head of Infosys, who was the founding Chair of the UIAI notes that, 'instead of seeking to exert tighter control over the Internet within its borders, the country has created open digital platforms from scratch and tailored them to the Indian context. And instead of leaving them in the hands of a few private technology companies, the Indian government has built these systems as public goods' (Nilekani, 2018: 21).

In 2012, the government launched the ambitious National Optical Fibre Network project (since renamed *BharatNet*), the world's largest rural broadband project, to connect the country's 250,000 *gram-panchayats* (village councils) with high-speed Internet 'to deliver government services online' (NITI Aayog, 2018: 89). The share of Indians with a digital financial account 'has more than doubled since 2011, to 80 per cent, thanks in large part to the more than 332 million people who opened mobile phone-based accounts under the government's *Jan-Dhan Yojana*, mass financial-inclusion programme' (McKinsey Global Institute, 2019: 1). These

'Internet-driven changes, especially for India's poor', writes Agrawal, 'will reshape not only India, but, eventually, the global order' (Agrawal, 2018: 8).

Such examples of Internet-driven, poverty-reduction programmes raise interesting questions about the efficacy and relevance of a largely Western-centred developmental discourse. As Unwin has argued, not only have the largely Western ICTs increased inequality in the pursuit of development, they have turned ICT4D on its head: 'Instead of "ICTs for Development" (ICT4D) we have become increasingly and surreptitiously enmeshed in a world of "Development for ICTs" (D4ICT) where governments, the private sector, and civil society are all tending to use the idea of "development" to promote their own ICT interests' (Unwin, 2017: 9).

Scholars originally from the BRICS nations have challenged Western-oriented and -originated discourses of development communication. The Nobel Laureate, Amartya Sen's notion of 'development as freedom' has had a profound impact on developmental thinking (Sen, 1999). More recent work has critiqued the political economy of development communication for focusing on the symptoms of underdevelopment articulated by Western-dominated international agencies and project-based initiatives, rather than investigating the causes of poverty and the agency of social movements and community communication (Dutta, 2011; Thomas, 2019).

Within Chinese intellectual space, there is growing recognition of the need for 'South-South Development Cooperation from China and other emerging market economies', which, it is argued, 'is more likely to bring "quick wins" in poverty reduction and inclusive, sustainable growth' (Lin and Wang, 2017: 6). China's record of considerably reducing, if not eliminating, poverty is extraordinary: within the last three decades China has raised more than 700 million of its people out of poverty. Arguments for 'democratization in development thinking', are becoming vocal, 'several different paradigms could coexist, and developing countries could select from the menu, based on their own developmental needs', ibid.: 14).

UNCTAD counsels that 'special attention needs to be given to ways that can enable more countries to take advantage of the data-driven digital economy, as producers, innovators and exporters' (UNCTAD, 2019). This has also been recommended by the World Bank (see World Bank, 2016 and 2018b) as well as a 2019 UN report, which acknowledges that 'digital dividends coexist with digital divides' and proposes 'digital cooperation' to 'create a platform for sharing digital public goods, engaging talent and pooling data sets, in a manner that respects privacy, in areas related to attaining the Sustainable Development Goals' (UN, 2019: 8). If such global 'digital cooperation' is to be achieved, BRICS nations could have a key role to perform, especially in relation to eliminating poverty.

BRICS de-Americanizing the Internet?

The Internet was American – it emerged from the United States and has its roots in Cold War military history (Levine, 2017). Its gradual privatization and commercialization led to the construction of a digital global village and the world's largest marketplace connected via instantaneous communication across time zones and continents. However, the Internet is growing up and away from its parent. In the mid-1990s, 60 per cent of the consumers who used the Internet were based in the US: by 2019 that number had shrunk to a single digit at 7 per cent, while large-population nations, such as China and India, are remaking the Internet into a multi-lingual and multicultural forum for a more pluralistic and democratic cyber-space (Arora, 2019).

Although the differences between the Indian and the Chinese Internets are striking in terms of infrastructure, regimes of censorship, development of digital capitalism and regulatory and global governance, they share certain similarities: a huge population base, a culture of copying and adapting technology and a certain strategic autonomy in the realm of policy. These Asian giants represent 'alternative models of digital capitalism', from *jugaad* (innovative hacks) practices in India, to *shanzhai* (copying) in China (Braybrooke and Jordan, 2017). 'These two trends of proliferating digitalization and digital production', notes a recent study, 'form the twin pillars of newly emerging digital economies' (Graham, 2019: 3).

As has been argued elsewhere, India and China, with a combined population of 2.8 billion, have the potential, together with their BRICS partners, to engineer a new world information and communication order, one no longer determined and run by the US. Unlike its predecessor – the 1970s NWICO demanded by the 'Third World', rooted in Cold War logic and articulated largely by politicians – NWICO 2.0 for the digital age will be shaped by the increasingly globalizing populations of the BRICS nations (Thussu, 2015).

The new order of online communication is likely to lead eventually to a de-Americanization of the Internet, a process that arguably is taking shape without a conscious or deliberate policy. Given the demographic and cultural logic of the scale and scope of forthcoming changes, an Internet beyond the West offer exciting opportunities for a 'post-American', more diverse world. It is worth remembering that, in countries such as Brazil, China and India, a large proportion of people are yet to go online, while in the Western world the saturation point was passed a decade ago. India alone will add another 700 million netizens to its total in the next five years, with its own version of a global conversation. Adam Segal of the US Council on Foreign Relations predicts that China is on the way to become a 'cyber-superpower', noting that 'the Internet has long been an American project. Yet today the United States has ceded leadership in cyberspace to China' (Segal, 2018: 10). 'Whatever Washington does', he predicts, 'the future of cyberspace will be much less American and much more Chinese' (ibid.: 18). However, as this discussion of the five dimensions of Internet developments in BRICS (infrastructure, commerce, regulation, 'weaponization' and development) has shown, the future of the Internet may be messier than this neat binary, with the other BRICS nations (Russia, India, Brazil and South Africa) and major current and emerging global actors – the EU, Turkey, Japan, Iran, Egypt, Nigeria, South Korea and Indonesia – providing multiple levels of digital discourse in a multilingual and de-centred Internet.

References

Agrawal, Ravi (2018) *India Connected: How the Smartphone is Transforming the World's Largest Democracy*. New York: Oxford University Press.

Aouragh, Miriyam and Chakravartty, Paula (2016) Infrastructures of empire: towards a critical geopolitics of media and information studies. *Media, Culture & Society*, 38(4): 559–575.

Arora, Payal (2019) *The Next Billion Users: Digital Life Beyond the West*. Cambridge, MA: Harvard University Press.

Braybrooke, Kaitlyn and Jordan, Timothy (2017) Genealogy, culture and techno-myth: Decolonizing Western information technologies, from open source to the maker movement. *Digital Culture and Society*, 3 (1): 25–46.

Brousseau, Eric; Marzouki, Meryem and Méadel, Cécile (eds.) (2012) *Governance, Regulation, and Powers on the Internet*. Cambridge: Cambridge University Press.

Carlin, John and Graff, Garrett (2018) *Dawn of the Code War: America's Battle Against Russia, China, and the Rising Global Cyber Threat*. New York: PublicAffairs.

Chen, Adrian (2015) The Agency, *The New York Times*, June 2.

Cheng, Dean (2016) *Cyber Dragon: Inside China's Information Warfare and Cyber Operations*. Santa Barbara, CA: Praeger.

China Internet Report (2019) *China Internet Report 2019*. Hong Kong: *South China Morning Post*. Available at www.scmp.com/china-Internet-report.

CNNIC (2019) *Statistical Report on Internet Development in China*. Beijing: China Internet Network Information Center (CNNIC), August. Available at https://cnnic.com.cn/IDR/ReportDownloads/201911/P020191112539794960687.pdf

Couldry, Nick and Mejías, Ulises (2019) *The Costs of Connection: How Data is Colonizing Human Life and Appropriating it for Capitalism*. Los Angeles: Stanford University Press.

Creemers, Rogier, Triolo, Paul and Webster, Graham (2018) China's new top Internet official lays out agenda for Party control online, *DigiChina*, September 24. Available at www.newamerica.org/cybersecurity-initiative/digichina/blog/translation-chinas-new-top-Internetofficial-lays-out-agenda-for-party-control-online/.

DeNardis, Laura (2014) *The Global War for Internet Governance*. New Haven: Yale University Press.

DeNardis, Laura (2020) *The Internet in Everything: Freedom and Security in a World with No Off Switch*. New Haven: Yale University Press.

Davenport, Christian (2018) *The Space Barons: Elon Musk, Jeff Bezos and the Quest to Colonize the Cosmos*. New York: PublicAffairs.

Davydov, Sergey (ed.) (2020) *Internet in Russia: A Study of the Runet and its Impact on Social Life*. Berlin: Springer.

Drake, William and Price, Monroe (eds.) (2014) *Beyond NetMundial: The Roadmap for Institutional Improvements to the Global Internet Governance Ecosystem*. August. Available at www.global.asc.upenn.edu/app/uploads/2014/08/BeyondNETmundial_FINAL.pdf.

Dutta, Mohan (2011) *Communicating Social Change: Structure, Culture and Agency*. New York: Routledge.

Ebert, Hannes and Maurer, Tim (2013) Contested cyberspace and rising powers. *Third World Quarterly*, 34(6): 1054–1074.

Economist (2019) Putin tries to build an internyet. *Economist*, March 9: 43–44.

European Parliament (2019) *Polarisation and the use of technology in political campaigns and communication*. Panel for the Future of Science and Technology. Brussels: European Parliamentary Research Service. March.

Evangelista, Rafael and Bruno, Fernanda (2019) WhatsApp and political instability in Brazil: Targeted messages and political radicalisation. *Internet Policy Review*, 8(4): 1–23.

Ferracane, Martina, Lee-Makiyama, Hosuk and van der Marel, Erik (2018) *Digital Trade Restrictiveness Index*. Brussels: European Center for International Political Economy, May.

Gateway House (2020) *Chinese Investments in India*. Mumbai: Gateway House-Indian Council on Global Relations, February. Available at www.gatewayhouse.in/wp-content/uploads/2020/03/Chinese-Investments-in-India-Report_2020_Final.pdf

Goel, Vindu (2018) India pushes back against tech 'colonization' by Internet giants, *The New York Times*, August 31. Available at www.nytimes.com/2018/08/31/technology/india-technology-american-giants.html

Goldsmith, Jack (2018) *The Failure of Internet Freedom: Probing the demise of a non-regulation, anti-censorship, global Internet agenda*. June 13, Knight First Amendment Institute, Columbia University. Available at https://knightcolumbia.org/content/failure-Internet-freedom

Government of Brazil (2019) *BRICS in the Digital Economy: Competition Policy in Practice*. 1st report by the Competition Authorities Working Group on Digital Economy. Brasilia. Available at www.cade.gov.br/acesso-a-informacao/publicacoes-institucionais/brics_report.pdf

Government of India (2019) *Draft National Policy Framework on Electronic Commerce in India*. New Delhi: Ministry of Commerce and Industry, 23 February. Available at https://dipp.gov.in/sites/default/files/DraftNational_ecommerce_Policy_23February2019.pdf

Graham, Mark (2019) Changing connectivity and digital economies at global margins, pp. 1–18, in M. Graham (ed.) (2019) *Digital Economies at Global Margins*. Cambridge, MA: MIT Press.

Greenberg, Andy (2019) *Sandworm: A New Era of Cyberwar and the Hunt for the Kremlin's Most Dangerous Hackers*. New York: Random House.

Greenwald, Glenn (2014) *No Place to Hide: Edward Snowden, the NSA, and the US Surveillance State*. New York: Metropolitan.

Griffiths, James (2019) *The Great Firewall of China: How to Build and Control an Alternative Version of the Internet*. London: Zed.

Hall Jamieson, Kathleen (2018) *Cyberwar – How Russian Hackers and Trolls Helped Elect a President*. New York: Oxford University Press.

Hjorth, Frederik and Adler-Nissen, Rebecca (2019) Ideological asymmetry in the reach of pro-Russian digital disinformation to United States audiences. *Journal of Communication*, 69: 168–192.

Hong, Yu (2017a) *Networking China: The Digital Transformation of the Chinese Economy*. Chicago: University of Illinois Press.

Hong, Yu (2017b) Pivot to Internet Plus: Molding China's Digital Economy for Economic Restructuring? *International Journal of Communication*, 11: 1486–1506.

Hoover Institution (2018) *Chinese Influence and American Interest: Report of the Working Group on Chinese Influence Activities in the United States*. Los Angeles: Hoover Institution Press at Stanford University.

Human Development Report (2019) *Human Development Report 2019: Beyond Income, Beyond Averages, Beyond Today: Inequalities in Human Development in the 21st Century*. New York: United Nations Development Programme.

Jeffrey, Robin and Doron, Assa (2013) *The Great Indian Phone Book: How the Cheap Cell Phone Changes Business, Politics, and Daily Life*. London: Hurst.

Jin, Dal Yong (2015) *Digital Platforms, Imperialism and Political Culture*. New York: Routledge.

Jing, Meng and Dai, Sarah (2017) China recruits Baidu, Alibaba and Tencent to AI 'national team'. *South China Morning Post*, November 21.

Klimburg, Alexander (2017) *The Darkening Web: The War for Cyberspace*. London: Penguin.

KPMG Report (2019) *India's Digital Future: Mass of Niches- KPMG in India's Media and Entertainment Report 2019*. Mumbai: KPMG India, August.

Langa, Mahesh (2019) Mukesh Ambani urges Modi to take steps against data colonization by global corporations. *The Hindu*, January 18. Available at www.thehindu.com/news/national/mukesh-ambani-urges-modi-to-take-steps-against-data-colonisation/article26025076.ece

Lee, Kai-Fu (2018) *AI Superpowers: China, Silicon Valley, and the New World Order*. New York: Houghton Mifflin Harcourt.

Lee, Micky and Jin, Dal Yong (2018) *Understanding the Business of Global Media in the Digital Age*. London: Routledge.

Lele, Ajey and Roy, Kritika (2019) *Analysing China's Digital and Space Belt and Road Initiative*. IDSA Occasional Paper No. 55. New Delhi: Institute for Defence Studies and Analyses, November.

Levine, Yasha (2017) *Surveillance Valley: The Secret Military History of the Internet*. New York: Public Affairs.

Lin, Herbert and Zegart, Amy (2019) *Bytes, Bombs, and Spies: The Strategic Dimensions of Offensive Cyber Operations*. Washington: Brookings Institution Press.

Lin, Justin and Wang, Yan (2017) *Going Beyond Aid: Development Cooperation for Structural Transformation*. Cambridge: Cambridge University Press.

Mari, Angelica (2018) 'Internet for All' plan advances in Brasil. ZDNet, February 8, Available at https://zd.net/2IFz6Na.

Maurer, Tim (2018) *Cyber Mercenaries: The State, Hackers, and Power*. Cambridge: Cambridge University Press.

Mayer-Schönberger, Viktor and Ramge, Thomas (2018) *Reinventing Capitalism in the Age of Big Data*. London: John Murray.

McKinsey Global Institute (2017) *Digital China: Powering the Economy to Global Competitiveness*. New York: McKinsey Global Institute.

McKinsey Global Institute (2019) *Digital India: Technology to Transform a Connected Nation*. New York: McKinsey Global Institute, March.

Mirchandani, Maya (2018) *Digital Hatred, Real Violence: Majoritarian Radicalisation and Social Media in India*. New Delhi: Observer Research Foundation, July 29.

Moore, Martin and Tambini, Damien (eds.) (2018) *Digital Dominance: The Power of Google, Amazon, Facebook, and Apple*. Oxford: Oxford University Press.

Mueller, Milton (2010) *Networks and States: The Global Politics of Internet Governance*. Cambridge, MA: MIT Press.

Mueller, Milton (2017) *Will the Internet Fragment? Sovereignty, Globalization and Cyberspace*. Cambridge: Polity

Mukherjee, Rahul (2019) Jio sparks Disruption 2.0: infrastructural imaginaries and platform ecosystems in 'Digital India'. *Media, Culture & Society*, 41(2): 175–195.

Murphy, James and Carmody, Pádraig (2015) *Africa's Information Revolution: Technical Regimes and Production Networks in South Africa and Tanzania*. Oxford: John Wiley.

Negroponte, John and Palmisano, Samuel (2013) *Defending an Open, Global, Secure, and Resilient Internet*. Washington: Council on Foreign Relations, Independent Task Force Report. Available at https://cdn.cfr.org/sites/default/files/pdf/2013/06/TFR70_cyber_policy.pdf.pdf

Nilekani, Nandan (2018) Data to the people: India's inclusive Internet. *Foreign Affairs*, 97(5): 19–26.

NITI Aayog (2018) *Strategy for New India@75*. New Delhi: NITI Aayog, November.

Nocetti, Julien (2015) Contest and conquest: Russia and global Internet governance. *International Affairs*, 91(1): 111–130.

Oates, Sarah (2013) *Revolution Stalled: The Political Limits of the Internet in the Post-Soviet Sphere*. New York: Oxford University Press.

OECD (2019) *Going Digital: Shaping Policies, Improving Lives*. Paris: Organization for Economic Cooperation and Development.

Orttung, Robert and Nelson, Elizabeth (2019) Russia Today's strategy and effectiveness on YouTube. *Post-Soviet Affairs*, 35(2): 77–92.

Pillai, Rajeswari and Prasad, Rajagopalan Narayan (eds.) (2017) *Space India 2.0: Commerce, Policy, Security and Governance Perspectives*. New Delhi: Observer Research Foundation.

Polyakova, Alina and Fried, Daniel (2019) *Democratic Defense Against Disinformation 2.0.* Washington: Atlantic Council, June.

Poonam, Snigdha (2019) How India conquered YouTube. *The Financial Times*, March 14.

Roberts, Margaret (2018) *Censored: Distraction and Diversion Inside China's Great Firewall*. Princeton: Princeton University Press.

Robertson, Jordan and Riley, Michael (2018) The big hack: How China used a tiny chip to infiltrate U.S. companies. *Bloomberg Businessweek*, October 4.

Rutenberg, Jim (2017) RT, Sputnik and Russia's new theory of war. *The New York Times*, September 13.

Sanger, David, Barnes, Julian, Zhong, Raymond and Santora, Marc (2019) America pushes allies to fight Huawei in new arms race with China. *The New York Times*, January 26. Available at www.nytimes.com/2019/01/26/us/politics/huawei-china-us-5g-technology.html

Satariano, Adam (2019) How the Internet travels across the oceans. *The New York Times*, March 10.

Schmidt, Eric and Cohen, Jared (2013) *The New Digital Age: Reshaping the Future of People, Nations and Business*. London: John Murray.

Segal, Adam (2018) When China rules the web: Technology in service of the state. *Foreign Affairs*, 97(5): 10–18.

Sen, Amartya (1999) *Development as Freedom*. Oxford: Oxford University Press.

Sheehan, Matt (2018) How Google took on China – and lost. *MIT Technology Review*, December 19.

Shen, Hong (2018) Building a digital silk road? Situating the Internet in China's Belt and Road Initiative. *International Journal of Communication*, 12: 2683–2701.

Singer, Peter and Brooking, Emerson (2018) *LikeWar: The Weaponization of Social Media*. New York: Houghton Mifflin Harcourt.

Singer, Peter and Friedman, Allan (2014) *Cybersecurity and Cyberwar: What Everyone Needs to Know*. New York: Oxford University Press.

Soldatov, Andrei and Borogan, Irina (2015) *Inside the Red Web: The Struggle Between Russia's Digital Dictators and the New Online Revolutionaries*. New York: Public Affairs.

Srikrishna Report (2018) *A Free and Fair Digital Economy: Protecting Privacy, Empowering Indians*. New Delhi: Committee of Experts under the Chairmanship of Justice B. N. Srikrishna. Available at http://meity.gov.in/writereaddata/files/Data_Protection_Committee_Report.pdf

Starosielski, Nicole (2015) *The Undersea Network*. Durham: Duke University Press.

Teer-Tomaselli, Ruth, Tomaselli, Keyan and Dludla, Mpumelelo (2019) Peripheral capital goes global: Naspers, globalisation and global media contraflow. *Media, Culture & Society*, 41(8): 1142–1159.

Thomas, Pradip (2019) *Communication for Social Change: Context, Social Movements and the Digital*. New Delhi: Sage.

Thussu, Daya Kishan (2015) Digital BRICS: Building a NWICO 2.0? pp. 242–263 in K. Nordenstreng and D. K. Thussu (eds.) *Mapping BRICS Media*. London: Routledge.

Thussu, Daya Kishan (2018) Globalization of Chinese media: The global context, pp. 17–33, in D. K. Thussu, H. de-Burgh and A. Shi (eds.) *China's Media Go Global*. London: Routledge.

Thussu, Daya Kishan (2019) *International Communication: Continuity and Change*. Third edition. New York: Bloomsbury Academic.

UNCTAD (2019) *Digital Economy Report 2019-Value Creation and Capture: Implications for Developing Countries*. Geneva: United Nations Conference on Trade and Development, September.

United Nations (2019) *The Age of Digital Interdependence: Report of the UN Secretary-General's High-level Panel on Digital Cooperation*. New York: United Nations, June.

Unwin, Tim (2017) *Reclaiming ICT4D*. Oxford: Oxford University Press.

US Government (1997) *A Framework for Global Electronic Commerce*. Washington: The White House, July.

US Government (2003) *National Strategy to Secure Cyberspace*. Washington: White House. February. Available at www.uscert.gov/sites/default/files/publications/cyberspace_strategy.pdf

US Government (2006) *Global Internet Freedom Task Force*. Washington: Secretary of State. Available at https://2001–2009.state.gov/g/rls/rm/78142.htm

US Government (2009) *Cyberspace Policy Review: Assuring a Trusted and Resilient Information and Communications Infrastructure*. Washington: White House, Available at https://fas.org/irp/eprint/cyber-review.pdf

US Government (2016) *Measuring the Value of Cross-border Data Flows*. Washington: Department of Commerce. Available at: www.ntia.doc.gov/files/ntia/publications/measuring_cross_border_data_flows.pdf.

US Government (2018) *National Cyber Strategy of the United States of America*, Washington: White House. September. Available at www.whitehouse.gov/wp-content/uploads/2018/09/National-Cyber-Strategy.pdf

Wang, Rong, Bar, François and Hong, Yu (2020) ICT aid flows from China to African countries: A communication network perspective. *International Journal of Communication*, 14: 1498–1523.

Washington Post (2014) *NSA Secrets: Government Spying in the Internet Age*. Washington Post E-book, published in partnership with Diversion Books.

Wolff, Josephine (2018) *You'll See This Message When it is Too Late: The Legal and Economic Aftermath of Cybersecurity Breaches*. Cambridge, MA: MIT Press.

Woolley, Samuel and Howard, Philip (eds.) (2018) *Computational Propaganda: Political Parties, Politicians, and Political Manipulation on Social Media*. Oxford: Oxford University Press.

World Bank (2016) *Digital Dividends- The World Development Report 2016*. Washington: World Bank.

World Bank (2018a) *Toward Universal Financial Inclusion in China: Models, Challenges, and Global Lessons*. Washington: The World Bank/The People's Bank of China, February.

World Bank (2018b) *Information and Communications for Development 2018: Data-Driven Development*. Washington: World Bank.

Yang, Guobin (2016) *The Red Guard Generation and Political Activism in China*. New York: Columbia University Press.

Zhao, Youzhi (2015) The BRICS formation in reshaping global communication: possibilities and challenges, pp. 66–86 in K. Nordenstreng and D. K. Thussu (eds.) *Mapping BRICS Media*. London: Routledge.

Zuboff, Shoshana (2019) *The Age of Surveillance Capitalism*. New York: Profile Books.

INDEX

Taylor & Francis eBooks

www.taylorfrancis.com

A single destination for eBooks from Taylor & Francis with increased functionality and an improved user experience to meet the needs of our customers.

90,000+ eBooks of award-winning academic content in Humanities, Social Science, Science, Technology, Engineering, and Medical written by a global network of editors and authors.

TAYLOR & FRANCIS EBOOKS OFFERS:

A streamlined experience for our library customers

A single point of discovery for all of our eBook content

Improved search and discovery of content at both book and chapter level

REQUEST A FREE TRIAL
support@taylorfrancis.com